THE GREAT MAYA DROUGHTS

WATER, LIFE, AND DEATH

RICHARDSON BENEDICT GILL

UNIVERSITY OF NEW MEXICO PRESS

ALBUQUERQUE

2000

13   12   11   10   09   2   3   4   5   6

ISBN-13: 978-0-8263-2774-1

Library of Congress Cataloging-in-Publication Data

Gill, Richardson Benedict.
    The great Maya droughts : water, life, and death / Richardson Benedict Gill.
— 1st ed.
        p. cm.
Includes bibliographical references and index.
        ISBN 0-8263-2194-1 (cl)   ISBN 0-8263-2774-5 (p)
    1. Mayas—History. 2. Droughts—Central America. 3. Droughts—Mexico.
I. Title.
        F1435.G49 2000
        972.81'016—dc21   00-008555

This work is dedicated to my mother

Josephine Gill Hudson

whose belief in me, encouragement, support, and love
caused me to believe I should write it
and without whom I could not have accomplished it.

K'in tun yaabil

the hieroglyph for drought

(Ciudad Real 1984:249; Kelley 1976:174, 206–207)

TABLE OF CONTENTS

13. SUMMARY AND DISCUSSION 363

LIST OF FIGURES

7. THERMOHALINE CIRCULATION 173

8. VOLCANOES AND CLIMATE 191

9.   GEOLOGY, HYDROLOGY, AND WATER 247

10.   PALAEOCLIMATOLOGY 273

LIST OF TABLES

ACKNOWLEDGEMENTS

I am sincerely grateful to my stepfather, Edward J. Hudson, for the effort he has expended on this book, reading, editing, commenting, and discussing over the years of its development. I am especially grateful for the loyalty, generosity, and support he demonstrated in dealing with the trials of the world which presented themselves during the preparation of this work.

Dr. Richard E. W. Adams has been my mentor in archaeology and has consistently encouraged me to pursue my interests in the Maya Collapse. He has read and critiqued many versions of the manuscript leading to this book and helped me to think through many situations of conflicting evidence. I admire and respect the standards of scholarship he insists on. Most importantly, however, I appreciate his friendship.

I must extend a special note of gratitude to Dr. Joel Gunn who read and constructively criticized the manuscript of this book, writing long, detailed critiques. He insisted that I do an enormous amount of additional research and work—that I really had hoped to dodge. He helped me focus on the important aspects of my theory, and the result, this book, is so much better because of him and his efforts on its behalf.

I appreciate the enthusiasm of Dr. Durwood Ball at the University of New Mexico Press for publishing this book. It has been a pleasure to work with Barbara Guth, Nancy Ford, Liz Varnedoe, and Susan Hughes during the editing of the manuscript and the production of the book.

Dr. Richard Newbold Adams has pioneered the incorporation of concepts of self-organization and dissipative structures in anthropology. I am most appreciative of his insight, his suggestions, and his help.

Dr. Fred Valdez Jr., Dr. Tom Hester, Dr. Norman Wagner, and Dr. Brian Goodman have provided very valuable constructive criticism which has improved the quality of this work. Drs. Haraldur Sigurdsson, Stefan Hastenrath, Ilya Prigogine, Peter Allen, and Carole Crumley have been invaluable sources of technical information and suggestions in volcanology, meteorology and climatology, self-organization, and heterarchies. I appreciate the statistical assistance of Dr. Nandini Kannan in analyzing data.

Mr. James R. Brooks, my first boss, former Senior Vice President and Chief of Internal Control at Gill Savings, spent weeks reviewing the numbers used in the preparation of the theories and supporting graphs presented in this book and checking the bibliographic references. He taught me the value of an audit in business decades ago, and he has demonstrated the value of an audit in developing the scientific concepts in this work. I appreciate his friendship and support. Josephine Veliz, my secretary at Gill Savings and afterwards, has checked and rechecked the bibliographic references for accuracy.

Sister Patrice Nugent provided a very poignant translation of a passage by Cassiodorus Senator from sixth century Latin.

Drs. Floyd Lounsbury, Gordon Willey, E. Wyllys Andrews V, David Freidel, Mike Baillie, Justine Shaw, Robert Tilling, Jason Curtis, Reid Bryson, Diane Smith, Servando de la Cruz Reyna, Gabriel Dengo, Rubin Meyer, Minze Stuiver, Ignacio Galindo, Charles Lincoln, Munro Edmonson, Victoria Bricker, Wilbert Thomas, Rufus Getzen, Silvia Gonzalez, Mark Brenner, and Ruth Krochok, and Messrs. Jack Eaton, David Johnstone, and Jeff Witter have helped enormously with articles, data, analyses, and discussions of many aspects of my hypothesis.

The Usumacinta Group at the Guatemalan Instituto Nacional de Electrificación (INDE), the staffs of the Instituto Nacional de Sismología, Vulcanología, Meteorología e Hidrología in Guatemala, at the National Center for Atmospheric Research in Boulder, and the National Climatic Data Center in Asheville have been very generous with their time and data. Ing. Guillermo Enrique Ortega Gil, Met. José G. Rosales Huerta and the staff of the Observatorio Meteorológico in Tacubaya, DF, and the staff of the Archivo General de la Nación in Mexico City were most hospitable and helpful during my research in their archives.

One cannot write a book of this kind without relying repeatedly on libraries and the help of librarians. At The University of Texas at San Antonio, I am particularly grateful to Dr. Michael Kelley, Judy Lankford, and Susan McCray; at Trinity University, Richard Meyer, and Craig Likness; and at The University of Texas at Austin, Dennis Trombatore, JoAnne Hawkins, Suzanne K. McAnna, and Warren Wilson-Reiner.

I appreciate the efforts of Mr. Raymond Steves and the staff of Kinko's on Broadway in San Antonio for their cooperation, help, and understanding of deadlines and Cuqui Mazal and the staff at Starbucks at The Quarry for their hospitality and for providing an environment where a substantial part of the editing of this book could be accomplished.

Cesarea Manzanares, Josephine Veliz, and Cleofas Zapata have held my personal life and my household together while I devoted myself to my work. I am grateful for the cooking, cleaning, mailing, copying, fetching, faxing, filing, driving, and so much more which they have so enthusiastically done.

John Poindexter allowed me to set up shop in the towers of the restored adobe forts on his Cibolo Creek Ranch in West Texas, where a substantial part of this manuscript was written. His hospitality, his generosity, and his friendship are much appreciated.

Edward F. Kelley has never tired of hearing daily reports of the progress of my studies and my writing and has always found a way to encourage me when I needed it. One could not ask for a better friend.

I cherish the bright, cheerful sunshine in my life, my daughter, Genevieve Dorn Gill, who always thought it was very normal for her father to be writing a book.

Finally, I especially appreciate beyond measure the support, encouragement, friendship, loyalty, partnership, and love of Virginia Alicia Pittman-Waller, MD, who makes an enormous difference in my life every day.

1. CLIMATE AND CATASTROPHE

Millions of people died, and until now, no one knew why. The devastation is almost impossible for us today to understand. One by one and by the millions, the people died of starvation and thirst. They died in their beds, in the plazas, in the streets, and on the roads. Their corpses, for the most part, lay unburied and were eaten by the vultures and varmints who entered the houses to eat the bodies of people who didn't die in the open.

There was nothing they could do. There was nowhere they could go. Their whole world, as they knew it, was in the throes of a burning, searing, brutal drought. Their fields and woods were paper dry and on fire. The smell of smoke was everywhere. There was nothing to eat. Their water reservoirs were depleted, and there was nothing to drink.

Some tried to move, but there was no place to go. If they found respite for a few years from death, it soon caught up to them in their new location.

Entire cities and states disappeared. Those small areas where meager populations survived, only barely survived. In the emptied, desolate cities, surviving squatters moved into palaces and temples and tried to eke out an existence in the emptiness, only to be driven out or killed by recurring drought.

Bad drought is mean, ugly, and cruel. It is not just a statistical meteorological anomaly or a sociological abstraction. Men, women, and children suffer in horrible ways. A thousand years ago, people suffered and died in isolation, by themselves, with no one to come to their aid.

Bad drought is relentless and inexorable. There is nothing anyone can do. Nothing works. It just goes on and on and gets worse and worse until everyone is dead, no life is left, and the cities are empty and still.

The mystery of the Maya Collapse has proven to be a strong magnet which has attracted many inquiring and creative minds over the last one hundred fifty years, as it has attracted you and me. In a previous work, I catalogued over eighty-eight proposed theories, explanations, or hypotheses, and, as of 1999, my list exceeded one hundred. Almost all of the explanations I have gathered are thoughtful, sincere attempts to shine light on the darkness of the Maya Collapse.

Many of the expositions, however, suffer from a major flaw. They state a proposition and jump straight to a conclusion without explaining the intervening steps that lead from one to the other. They fail to explain the mechanics of how their theory leads to the disappearance of millions of people.

Archaeology is not an experimental science in which we can test our hypotheses in laboratory environments. We are left to make sense of an imperfect archaeological record which consists mainly of holes and gaps with sparse fragments of evidence in between. The best we can do is to marshall many weak lines of evidence which converge on a solution to our puzzle because none by itself can be considered proof positive.

You have already read what happened to the Maya. In the pages that follow I will mobilize a number of arguments which will lead us to the conclusion that the Maya died of famine and thirst, and I will show, step by step, how a civilization can disintegrate when it is assaulted by drought and how a drought can occur in the Maya Lowlands.

The story of famine and death is not pretty, but we will learn a lot along the way about how human beings relate to the physical world in which we live.

INTRODUCTION

Human beings, hunter-gatherers, first moved to the Maya Lowlands around 8000 BC. Farmers arrived around 2000 BC. Agriculture flourished, surpluses grew, and, along with them, the complexity and richness of Maya culture. The size of the populations soared until between four million and fourteen million people were living in the Maya Lowlands around AD 800, according to varying estimates. Then it all ended. Most lowland Maya cities were deserted between AD 800 and 900. Those few that survived were seriously depopulated. In the end, at the time of Spanish contact, and even until recent decades, much of the area that during the Classic period was once the most fertile and productive and the most intensely settled lay overgrown by jungle and deserted.

The ultimate focus of Maya archaeology in the Lowlands must be to answer the question: Why? Millions of people disappeared, and until now, there has not been a convincing explanation of what happened. It has not been, however, for a lack of suggestions. In over one hundred theories, explanations, and hypotheses for the collapse of Classic Maya civilization I

have gathered, the authors proposed a myriad of different possible explanations, most of which attribute the Collapse to causes internal to the civilization, and almost all attribute the Collapse to the effect of human
actions. Thus, the Maya disappeared as a result of administrative deficiencies, or declining agricultural productivity due to poor agricultural practices, or war, or a precarious system of social organization which could not
cope with the population levels achieved at the end, and so on. In short,
the Collapse was their own fault (Gill 1994:169–207).

In this book, we will examine a totally different point of view: the Collapse occurred as a result of external natural circumstances that the Maya
neither controlled nor caused. They were the victims, not the perpetrators.
The timing of the Collapse was coincidental with whatever was occurring
within Maya society at the time. The Classic Maya died as a result of a series of devastating droughts which occurred during the ninth and tenth
centuries, depriving them not only of food, but even more critically, of
water.

In 1988, when I first publicly proposed the idea that the Maya were the
victims of a drought, at a Society for American Archaeology annual meeting in Phoenix, there was no direct evidence that such a drought had occurred. Recently, as we will see, David Hodell, Jason Curtis, and Mark
Brenner, researchers from the University of Florida, have provided unambiguous evidence of a severe 200-year drought between AD 800 and 1000,
the most serious during the 7,000-year time span of the lake sediment core.
Studies performed at other locations have corroborated the evidence for a
Terminal Classic drought in the Maya Lowlands.

Yet the idea that external events, like a dramatic climate change, could
drive the collapse of a civilization meets considerable resistance among
many archaeologists. Most social scientists have a tendency to view the
changes which occur in societies solely in terms of the society itself. But
human societies live in a physical world, and human beings are totally unable to control many of its major characteristics. We are totally powerless
in the face of the large-scale dislocations and devastation wrought by
earthquakes, floods, avalanches, hurricanes, eruptions, and droughts. An
impressive example of the overwhelming force of nature is the Snowball
Earth hypothesis. If it is correct, about 750 to 500 million years ago, during
the Neoproterozoic, the Earth alternated between being one huge snowball, frozen solid from pole to pole, with the oceans frozen as far as the
equator, and having extreme greenhouse conditions far hotter than now,
driven by volcanically produced carbon dioxide levels 350 times greater
than those of today. Such wild extremes emphasize our own meager, feeble, nonexistent abilities to dissuade Mother Nature when her course is
set. In more recent times, ice ages and interglacials have effected drastic,
though less dramatic, alterations in the physical environment and, on a
shorter time scale, so have short-term climatic changes like devastating

droughts and little ice ages over which we have no control (Hoffman et al 1998:1342).

The debate over internal processes and external shocks, over long-term uniform processes and catastrophic upheavals, is not restricted to archaeology alone. In other historical disciplines where time plays a central role, like geology, evolutionary biology, history, and demography, researchers have similarly tried to sort out the role of internal processes and external events. Archaeological theory has not developed in a vacuum. It owes much of its theoretical foundation to the intellectual milieu in which archaeologists live. It will help us understand the debate in archaeology if we examine the milieu in which our theories have developed. The history of the debate in geology has anticipated and informed the formulation of many of the important principles of archaeology and other time dependent disciplines. It bears a closer look.

EARLY BIBLICAL CATASTROPHISM

In 1654, Archbishop James Ussher, an Irish scholar and the Archbishop of Armagh, calculated the age of the Earth from the chronology of events in the Bible. According to him, it was created on October 26th, 4004 BC. The date was subsequently printed in many Bibles. That didn't leave much time for the major features of the continents to have been created, so early geologists resorted to catastrophes to explain the rise of mountains and the cutting of valleys (Albritton 1989:6; Hallam 1983:82).

The Reverend Thomas Burnet was a prominent Anglican clergyman who became the private chaplain of King William III. Between 1680 and 1690, he published the four books of *Telluris Theoria Sacra* or *The Sacred Theory of the Earth*, first in Latin, later in English. He started from the point of view that the Bible must be true and tried to design a physics of natural causes that would explain the presumed truth of the Biblical account of the Earth's history. Burnet conceived of the original Earth as a perfect sphere. Then came Noah's flood which he said left the cracked crust of the Earth "a broken and confused heap of bodies." The biblical story of Noah and the flood is well known, of course, being a later version with slightly differing details of the Sumerian flood tale which dates from as early as 3400 BC—and may itself have earlier origins. In the Sumerian version, the flood lasted six days. In the centuries of retelling leading to the Hebrew version, as we know, the flood had grown to forty days. Burnet's approach was typical of the geological methodology of the seventeenth century, which had to resort to catastrophic explanations in order to squeeze the Earth's history into a few thousand years (Albritton 1989:1–2; Burnet quoted in Gould 1987:22, 26–28).

STRATIGRAPHY

The first insight into the principles of stratigraphy were published by Nicolaus Steno in 1669. He laid down a fundamental tenet of modern geology and archaeology: in a sequence of sedimentary strata as originally deposited, any stratum is younger than the one upon which it rests and is older than the one resting upon it. "Therefore at the time the lowest stratum was being formed, none of the upper strata existed." Stratigraphy, of course, is very important in modern archaeological fieldwork. Further, he postulated that all strata, whether horizontal, vertical, or inclined today, were parallel to the horizon at the time of their deposition. For the first time, then, Steno proposed that many of the rocks of the continents were formed by natural, ongoing processes rather than by divine creation or catastrophes. His ideas were still constrained, however, by the biblical chronology which required these natural processes to march in quicktime (Steno quoted in Albritton 1989:11–12).

HUTTON'S DEEP TIME

It fell to a reluctant author, a Scottish theorist who is considered by some to be the father of modern geology, to take the next major step. James Hutton, a graduate of the University of Edinburgh, was awarded an MD from the University of Leiden, but decided to become a farmer in the Southern Uplands of Scotland and to invest his profits in business enterprises. After fourteen years of farming and successful investing, he had achieved a degree of financial stability, and he chose to return to Edinburgh where he quickly moved into intellectual circles. Although his ideas had already crystallized in his mind at around age thirty-two, it was not until after the establishment of the Royal Society in Edinburgh that he finally felt compelled to publish his theory in 1788—at the age of sixty-two (Albritton 1989:27).

Hutton was the first to peer into the abyss of time. He saw that the processes which have resulted in the formation of the Earth's features were slow acting and required enormous amounts of time to effect their results. Erosion of the land by running water, by which "our plains are formed from the ruins of the mountains," required an immense span of time. "Time which measures every thing in our idea, and is often deficient to our schemes, is to nature endless and as nothing" (Hutton first quoted in Albritton 1989:26, 29 and then in Gould 1987:64).

UNIFORMITARIANISM

By 1830, geology was freed from the shackles of biblical time. Hutton's understanding of time had widespread support, and the biblical chronology was no longer widely accepted. Between 1830 and 1833, Charles Lyell, a lawyer by training and trade, published his three volume *Principles of Ge-*

ology. It was undoubtedly the most influential geological treatise to appear in the nineteenth century. In it, he proposed his view of geological uniformity, which has come to be known by the unfortunate term, uniformitarianism (first applied to his ideas by a reviewer, William Whewell, in 1832). Geology, for the next hundred fifty years, was dominated by Lyell's principles. Since his ideas have had such a major impact on the development not only of geology, but of other time dependent disciplines like evolutionary biology and are today discussed by archaeologists, it is worthwhile taking the time to look at them in more detail (Albritton 1989:45; Gould 1987:105).

Lyell's original concept of uniformity rests on the following distinct meanings:

1. *The uniformity of law*: natural laws are constant in space and time.
2. *The uniformity of process*: if a past process can be rendered as the result of a process now acting, do not invent an extinct or unknown cause as its explanation.
3. *The uniformity of rate, or gradualism*: the pace of change is usually slow, steady, and gradual; phenomena of large scale, from mountain ranges to grand canyons, are built by the accumulation, step by countless step, of insensible changes added up through vast times to great effect.
4. *The uniformity of state, or nonprogressionism*: originally proposed but subsequently abandoned, it postulated that change is not only stately and evenly distributed throughout space and time, but that the history of our Earth follows no vector of progress in any inexorable direction. Our planet always looked and behaved just about as it does now. Change is continuous, but leads nowhere. In the end, though, Lyell had to abandon the uniformity of state when he embraced Charles Darwin's theory of evolution, which does encompass a progression of forms (Gould 1987:119–123; Huggett 1990:105–106).

Lyell caricatured and derided the proposals of the catastrophists, as they came to be called. In the telling and retelling since, their positions became even more distorted. Catastrophists were seen as biblically motivated miracle mongers, actively preventing the establishment of geology as a science. The belief in catastrophe, of course, does not necessarily imply a young Earth or any religious beliefs at all (Gould 1987:112).

The concept of uniformity, or uniformitarianism, has had a major impact on other fields of science. In particular, it underlies Darwin's principle of gradualism in evolution. As he put it, "If we look to long enough intervals of time, geology plainly declares that species have all changed; and they have changed in the manner required by the theory, for they have changed slowly and in a graduated manner" (Darwin 1859:233).

Although recent archaeological theories and philosophy have not been strictly uniformitarian in nature, their development has been informed by the gradualistic, internal spirit of Lyell's uniformity and Darwin's gradualism. According to archaeological theorist and historian

Bruce Trigger, "Archaeologists must also invoke uniformitarian principles in order to use an understanding of modern geological and biological processes to infer how such processes have helped to shape the archaeological record." Archaeologist Lewis Binford, in fact, advanced the proposal that "we must make uniformitarian assumptions if we are to gain any understanding of the past." In a uniformitarian spirit, the New Archeology, processual thinking, system analysis, and other recent trends have focused on internal, ongoing processes, to the virtual exclusion of catastrophic, external perturbations (Lewis Binford 1981:27; Trigger 1989b:19).

Neocatastrophism

The most prominent catastrophist of Lyell's time was Georges Cuvier, a man who Stephen Jay Gould has called "the finest intellect in the nineteenth century." He is credited with establishing comparative anatomy and vertebrate palaeontology as disciplines. He was also an empiricist who believed in the literal interpretation of geological phenomena. He saw that, read literally, the geologic record is primarily a tale of abrupt transitions, at least locally. Strata change abruptly, not gradually, as can be seen in figure 1. Marine rock lies above terrestrial rock with no gradation from one to another. One can see this phenomenon especially clearly in a painted desert where rocks of different colors alternate sharply with one another. Faunal transitions as well are almost always abrupt, both from species to species and from biota to biota. The catastrophists tended to accept as reality what they saw: abrupt transitions of sediments and fossils, indicating rapid changes of environments, climates, and faunas. Despite the physical evidence, however, the uniformitarians carried the day and dominated geological thinking for a century and a half (Albritton 1989:36; Gould 1987:113, 133).

It was generally regarded that uniformitarianism and catastrophism were mutually exclusive concepts. Geologic catastrophism, therefore, was relegated to the status of a failed hypothesis. Hypotheses invoking truly catastrophic events, even relatively tame ones, were frowned upon. As Gould has remarked:

> Lyell's gradualism has acted as a set of blinders, channelling hypotheses in one direction among a wide range of plausible alternatives....Again and again in the history of geology after Lyell, we note reasonable hypotheses of catastrophic change, rejected out of hand by a false logic that brands them unscientific in principle. (Gould 1987:176)

Although some archaeologists, like Gordon Childe, were willing to accept the evidence of natural catastrophes, anticatastrophist thinking has strongly influenced archaeology in recent decades where catastrophist hy-

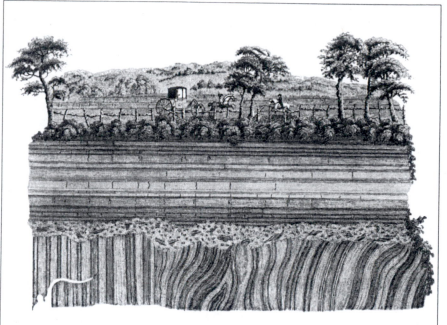

HUTTON'S UNCONFORMITY

Figure 1. John Clerk of Eldin's celebrated engraving of James Hutton's unconformity at Jedburgh, Scotland, first published in Hutton's 1795 essay, *Theory of the Earth*. Younger horizontal strata overlay older strata which had been tilted vertically and eroded. The deep time depicted in this illustration represents a turning point in human knowledge and in the understanding of time (Gould 1987:60).

potheses have been derided as unicausal or monocausal. As processual thinking gained ground, multicausal theories came to be the favored solutions. As Bruce Trigger has described the New Archeology or processual archaeology, "The basic claim was that as a result of ecological constraints, societies did not develop differently in the presence of external stimuli from how they would have developed in their absence. It was also assumed that cultural patterns contained much random variation which provided them with the resources to cope with changing ecosystemic relations" (Childe 1956:138; Trigger 1989b:23).

Theories which proposed a single, driving process were labeled prime mover theories and dismissed out of hand just as catastrophist theories in geology were. Joseph Tainter, for example, in his book, *The Collapse of Complex Societies*, summed up the anticatastrophist point of view in archaeology in the following terms:

As obvious and favored as catastrophe theories are, they are among the weakest explanations of collapse. The fundamental problem is that complex societies routinely withstand catastrophes without collapsing. Thus, catastrophe arguments present an incomplete causal chain: the basic assumption, rarely explicated, must be that the catastrophes in question somehow exceeded the abilities of the societies to absorb and recover from disaster....

As a matter of practicality, though, catastrophe explanations are too simple to accommodate the complexities of human societies and the collapse process. Human societies encounter catastrophes all the time. They are an expectable aspect of life, and are routinely provided for through social, managerial, and economic arrangements. It is doubtful if any large society has ever succumbed to a single event catastrophe. (Tainter 1988:53)

In geology, it was left to J. Harlen Bretz to try to breathe life into the moribund concept of catastrophism. In 1923, he advanced the hypothesis that about 12,000 to 15,000 years ago, during the most recent glaciation, a great flood of water suddenly swept across the states of Montana, Idaho, Oregon, and Washington, through the Cascade Mountains to the Pacific, stripping off the surface sediments and giving the area its name, Channeled Scablands. The flood cut deep gorges in the basalt, the largest of which is the Grand Coulee, with walls up to 275 m (900 ft) high. There was a series of great waterfalls up to 105 m (350 ft) high and 5 km (3 mi) wide, many times the size of Niagara Falls. The flow of water in this flood was approximately ten times the combined flow of all the rivers of the world today. Lake Missoula was a large ice-dammed lake lying roughly in today's Idaho and Montana, the size of Lakes Ontario and Erie combined. The dam was located near Sandpoint, Idaho. When the ice dam was breached, an almost unimaginable quantity of water was released over the course of just a few days. The resulting flood scoured the landscape and gorged the coulees (Ager 1993:19, 22; Pendick 1999:4B).

Bretz's theory was bolstered in 1940 when US Geological Survey geologist James Pardee found ripples on an ancient lakebed like the ones that form on streambeds today—but Pardee's ripples were 15 m (50 ft) high and hundreds of meters long. Only a staggering amount of water could have formed them (Pendick 1999:4B).

Although it was earlier accepted by many geologists, it took a period of nearly fifty years for Bretz's hypothesis to finally break through the brick wall of uniformitarianism and gain formal acceptance. Bretz was awarded the Penrose Medal of the Geological Society of America in 1979, at age ninety-six, and the USGS accepted the Bretz hypothesis in 1982—forty-nine years after it was proposed (Ager 1993:19, 22).

Modern thought, by the way, has suggested that it was not just a simple breaking of the ice dam, but rather a glacial outburst flood or *jvkuhlaups*, a process in which water began flowing beneath the dam when the hydrostatic pressure got high enough, at a lake level depth of around 600m (2,000ft). The flow of water under the dam began as a trickle which carved out a larger and larger tunnel, until it eventually undermined the dam and it collapsed altogether. It may also have happened more than once (Ager 1993:19, 22; Pendick 1999:4B).

Similar catastrophic floods have since been identified in other parts of the world, as we'll see when we talk about Lake Agassiz in chapter 7, and even on other planets, like Mars. When a previously unrecognized phenomenon gains acceptance, it is suddenly recognized everywhere, as happened with glaciations, turbidity currents, storm deposits, and other catastrophic phenomena. Besides huge floods, today, cataclysmic volcanic eruptions, extraterrestrial impacts, and near impacts are all widely accepted. Catastrophism has finally gained respectability in modern geological theory. Modern catastrophists, or neocatastrophists, share with Georges Cuvier the view that the rock record attests to mass extinctions and the occurrence of rare, widespread events of immense magnitude during the course of Earth's history, but these events are no longer seen as foreordained (Ager 1993:22; Albritton1989:17; Huggett 1990:4).

EVOLUTIONARY BIOLOGY

In evolutionary biology, as we have seen, Lyell's principles of uniformity underlaid Darwin's belief in gradualism, which dominated evolutionary theory for over one hundred years. It was Niles Eldredge and Stephen Jay Gould who finally proposed that gradualism fails as an explanation for the evolution of all species. They offered instead their theory of punctuated equilibria. They postulated that the history of species is one of long periods of stasis broken, or punctuated, by periods of very rapid change. According to their view, new species do not evolve gradually, they proliferate rapidly following the isolation of a founder population and subsequent speciation, as might happen following sudden mass extinctions. As they put it, "The history of evolution is not one of stately unfolding, but a story of homeostatic equilibria, disturbed only 'rarely' (i.e., rather often in the fullness of time) by rapid and episodic speciation" (Eldredge and Gould 1972:83–84).

Catastrophism, then, has come to play a major role in evolutionary thinking. In 1980, for example, the father and son team of Nobel laureate physicist Luis Alvarez and his geologist son Walter Alvarez, together with Frank Asaro and Helen Michel, proposed the radical idea that the end of the Cretaceous era and the demise of the dinosaurs were due to the impact on Earth of an extraterrestrial bolide, either an asteroid or a comet. This catastrophe, of course, set the stage for the subsequent rise of the mammals. The importance of their concept to our story is that the drastic changes in geology and evolutionary biology that it describes were caused by a true external shock. Floods may be considered internal to the Earth's system, but a bolide from outer space is clearly external. As a result, external shocks are now being seen throughout geology and evolutionary biology. We will look at the role of climate in the evolution of *Homo sapiens* later in this chapter (Alvarez et al 1980).

A GEOLOGICAL SYNTHESIS

In geology, what has emerged from the theoretical battles of the nineteenth and twentieth centuries is a synthesis of uniformitarianism and catastrophism which is best described by the rock strata themselves: long periods of uniformitarian stability in which the strata are built up, coupled with abrupt catastrophic shifts which result in sudden changes in rock types as can be seen so clearly in figure 1. The two are not antithetical hypotheses but rather complementary processes, and as we will see in the next chapter, this alternation is a phenomenon seen in organizational systems throughout nature. The internal process of uniformitarianism is regularly interrupted by a catastrophic perturbation, quite possibly, but not always, external. It is no longer a matter of either/or but rather of the two working together throughout geologic history.

In chapter 3, we will develop a similar synthesis for archaeology. In fact, many organisms, physical, biological, and social, go through periods of processual stability and evolving change but then suddenly undergo a wrenching catastrophe, which drastically changes the course of an organism's or a society's evolution or brings it to an end or to a rebirth in a new form. It is certainly possible that such change is due to internal processes, but it is also possible that such change is due to external shocks.

CLIMATE AND HISTORY

In this book, of course, we aren't primarily interested in catastrophic floods, we are much more interested in climate, and we aren't really interested in rocks, but in people. Let's look, then, at two of archaeology's closest relatives, history and demography, fields in which time and human beings play very fundamental roles, as they do in archaeology.

Rather than retracing the intellectual debate of external events versus internal processes in history and demography, let's look specifically at the role of climate, which is generally considered an external event and has also been a hotly debated topic.

Historians have not been of one mind concerning the impact of climate on history. The early attempts to relate climate to history were marred by the poor meteorological and palaeoclimatological record. Some early writers unfortunately made use of compilations which were unreliable. In addition, meteorology itself, how weather worked around the world, was poorly understood. In trying to tie climate to archaeology, archaeological chronologies had not been worked out, so poor climatology was being related to poor archaeology. Many early attempts seem to have been based more on faith and hope than anything else—but the process had to start somewhere.

Early attempts to tie climate and history, initiated by historian Ellsworth Huntington, have been labelled "climatic determinism" by historians and are included in "environmental determinism" by archaeologists. Some detractors have accused such historians and archaeologists of trying to maintain that the whole course of human history is determined by climate and environment. Of course, no one took such a radical position. What climatic determinists have argued, however, is that climatic factors are among the more important influences on the development of civilizations. As historical meteorologist Hubert Lamb put it, "Climatic history must be central to our understanding of human history" (Lamb quoted in Ingram, Wigley, and Farmer 1981:18).

Among some historians, however, there has been considerable skepticism. In 1967 agricultural historian Emmanuel Le Roy Ladurie wrote: "Underlying all such theories is the lazy but highly contestable postulate that climate exercises a determining influence on history." He believed that the necessary quantitative evidence had not been produced to demonstrate any connection between climate and history (Le Roy Ladurie 1967:24).

The study of the interactions between climate and history embraces a number of different aspects like climate reconstruction, the identification and measurement of the impact of climate on past societies, the adaptation of societies to climatic stress, and human perceptions of climate and climatic change. Most historians were ready to accept a role for climate but were looking for a way to measure its influence. Subsequent research in this area has provided a mass of quantitative meteorological, demographic, economic, and historical data relating to the interaction between climate and history, economics, and demography. By 1990, even Le Roy Ladurie accepted that some rigorous scholars had, finally, begun to present studies indicating a relationship between climate and agricultural markets (Ingram, Farmer, and Wigley 1981:3; Le Roy Ladurie 1990:69; de Vries 1981:44).

Others had been more willing to accept a role for climate in human affairs. Such eminent historians as Will and Ariel Durant wrote in 1968, "Climate no longer controls us as severely as Montesquieu and Buckle supposed, but it limits us....Let rain become too rare and civilization disappears under sand, as in Central Asia; let it fall too vigorously, and civilization will be choked with jungle, as in Central America" (Durant and Durant 1968:15).

No less a legendary historian than Fernand Braudel sought answers in climate with regard to the global economic expansion and the increase in population in the eighteenth century. He asked:

Why did these phenomena occur at the same time throughout the world when space had always been available? The simultaneity is the problem. The international economy, effective but still so fragile, cannot assume sole responsibility for such a general and powerful movement. It too is as much consequence as cause.

One can only imagine one single general answer to this almost complete coincidence: changes in climate. Today they are no longer dismissed by academics as a joke. (Braudel 1973:19)

Braudel has hit upon a critical point in the study of the ninth-century collapse in the Maya Lowlands: it was similarly simultaneous, extending across a thousand kilometers (hundreds of miles) and covering many independent polities. Any solution to the mystery of the Maya Collapse must address the issue of simultaneity.

In 1946, in fact, Maya archaeologist Tatiana Proskouriakoff recognized the dynamic of simultaneity, though not necessarily of climate, at work in the Maya Collapse. She wrote, "Though it is conceivable that the disappearance of the population may have been a gradual process, the catastrophically sudden extinction of the arts can be explained only in the terms of some widespread and unforeseen disaster that afflicted most Maya cities soon after A.D. 800" (Proskouriakoff 1946: third page of introduction, no page number).

Even now, not all historians are willing to accept a role for climate in human history, but among the growing numbers who do, their position was well summarized by T. K. Rabb:

In general, it is stability, and thus predictability, that allows effective societies to develop and take root. The single worst consequence of a climatic regime is a demand for constant change and adaptation. At such times, the negative impact on human history, forcing withdrawals from settlements, trade routes, and occupations, has been unmistakable. (Rabb 1983: 637)

CLIMATE AND DEMOGRAPHY

Some of the most dramatic work tying climate to the fate of human beings has been done by demographers. Studies performed in Sweden, England as a whole, and London, for example, determined that a decrease in winter temperature is significantly correlated with an increase in mortality—independent of the harvest. The same studies in England and London found that cooler summers tend to reduce mortality. Furthermore, it seems that colder than average winters in Sweden reduce human fertility, and in England cooler winters and warmer summers also reduce fertility. These results are further corroborated by studies in Sweden and Croatia showing decreases in mortality associated with abundant harvests. Other studies have been carried out in Sweden, France, and Croatia demonstrating similar relationships between weather and the increase or decrease in human populations. In recent decades, the quantitative evidence linking climate and the fate of human beings that Le Roy Ladurie insisted on seeing has been produced. Demographer Patrick Galloway, therefore, can now speak of "the striking synchrony in the long-term movements of temperature, agricultural yield, and population series across space and time. The results of this analysis suggest that an important driving force behind the long-term fluctuations in population may be long-term variations in climate and their effects on carrying capacity and vital rates" (Galloway 1986:11, 20–21).

Enough evidence has now been developed that Berkeley economist and demographer Ronald Lee could conclude that, in historical Europe, "Typically, a 1°C [1.8°F] warming would depress prices by about 10 percent through an unknown increase in output and thereby indirectly raise population growth rates by about 0.1 percent per year. So analysis of short-run variations suggests that climate did indeed affect human populations in the past, in roughly equal measure indirectly through agricultural productivity and directly through vital rates." He also found that a 1°C warming of winter temperature would reduce annual mortality by about 2 percent and a 1°C cooling of summer would reduce annual mortality by about 4 percent. In short, then, Lee found that mortality in England was increased by cold temperatures in winter and hot temperatures in summer, and fertility was decreased by the same conditions, a very clear and direct tie between climate and the fate of human populations (Ingram, Farmer, and Wigley 1981:28; Lee 1981:398; 1987:456).

> Speaking roughly and speculatively, I do find some evidence from England, and Europe as a whole, that long-run warming affected productivity similarly, but more weakly than in the short run. Direct effects on population growth rate likewise appear similar and undiminished relative to the short run. Taking these results at face value, temperatures that were 1°C warmer, and perhaps less variable, would raise carrying capacity by 5 percent or so in northwest Europe and thereby raise the equilibrium population equally. But the direct effects on vital rates would lead to continued population growth even after the 5 percent increase had been attained; in the final equilibrium, population would be 10 or 15 percent larger than before, and real wages substantially lower. The initial effect of mild weather was beneficial, but the longer run impact may have been impoverishing, by raising population growth rates independently of incomes and therefore requiring a greater degree of economic hardship to reestablish demographic stationarity. Such possibilities make the historical

study of the role of climate more difficult, but also more important. (Lee 1987:457)

Of course, we don't have specific demographic data from the ninth
century Maya Lowlands to demonstrate that there was a relationship between the weather and the fate of Classic populations. We do know from
Colonial historical records that periods of drought inflicted severe mortality on the Maya, and it would stretch the imagination to believe that such
clear correlations in Colonial times would not be in effect in ancient Maya
times as well. We can reasonably assume that the Classic Maya were directly affected by relatively small changes in climatic conditions which resulted in relatively small changes in population, just as Europeans have
been. If so, it is not an unreasonable step to take to ask whether catastrophic changes in climate, like a devastating drought, would have had catastrophic effects on the population.

LONG-TERM ECOTONE SHIFTS

If climate can have such a specific effect on populations, can it have a
more widespread effect on culture and history?

Archaeologist Carole Crumley carried out a fascinating study of the
relationship between climate and culture in northwestern Europe in which
she identified the three major climatic regimes seen in figure 2: oceanic,
continental, and Mediterranean. Each regime brings different weather patterns over Europe, and the movement of the boundaries back and forth is
primarily due to the shifting locations of the jet stream (Crumley
1994b:190).

The major climatic regimes are closely, although not perfectly, aligned
with the major biotic provinces of Europe. The boundaries between those
biotic provinces and climatic regimes are known as ecotones, and they separate not only vegetational provinces, but cultural regions as well. The ecotones represent a zone of transition between adjacent ecological systems
and generally mark abrupt changes. According to Crumley, the position of
today's ecotone separating Mediterranean and continental climatic regimes in Europe can be clearly seen at the southern edge of the Massif Central, where the vegetation changes in less than a meter (yard) from
Mediterranean to temperate flora. In the Rhône-Saône corridor, the shift in
roof tiles and culinary practices gives Crumley the strong sensory impression of moving from southern to central Europe. The ecotone's past position, width, and permanence can be derived through palynology,
palaeoethnobotany, and other palaeoclimatological studies. Crumley has
shown that the European ecotones can migrate over substantial distances,
as shown in figure 3. Over the past two millennia, in fact, the ecotone dividing the Mediterranean and continental climatic regimes has migrated
north and south from 36°N along the North African coast to 48°N along

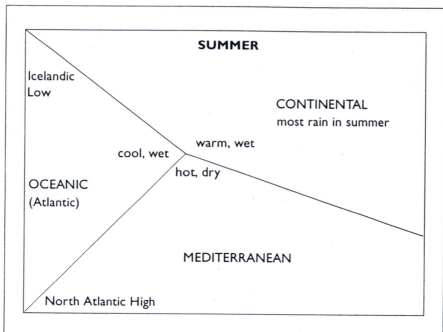

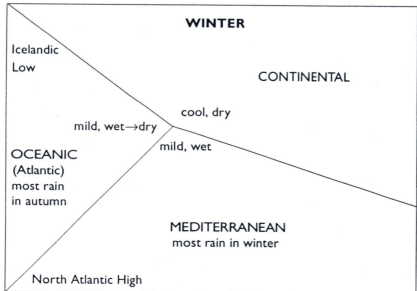

EUROPEAN CLIMATIC REGIMES AND ECOTONES

Figure 2. The dominant climatic regimes of Europe. The boundaries between regimes, known as ecotones, *lines*, can range over 1,000 km (600 mi) (adapted from Crumley 1994b:191).

the North Sea and Baltic Sea coast of northwestern Europe—a distance of 8° of latitude, approximately 880 km (500 mi) (Crumley 1994b:197; di Castri and Hansen1992:6).

As Crumley has reconstructed Europe's climatic history, from about 1200 to 500 BC, it was in the grip of a long cold period with particularly severe winters. The ecotone dividing continental from Mediterranean climatic regimes was located far to the south in North Africa. It was a period of substantial climatic variability as the region was alternately dominated by oceanic and continental regimes. In response, Celtic culture evolved practices to maximize agricultural production under alternating oceanic and continental conditions and to minimize the risk associated with climatic variability (Crumley 1994b:193).

By 300 BC, the ecotone had moved far to the north, perhaps, Crumley suspects, as far north as northern Burgundy, where it stayed until around AD 300, a period known as the Roman Climatic Optimum. The shift brought a Mediterranean climate to most of western Europe, with warm dry summers and wet winters. The Roman pattern of settlement and land use was markedly different from the Celtic pattern because it was designed for a Mediterranean climate. The Roman agricultural strategy emphasized extensive production of a few crops, supported large urban populations, and was well suited to a semiarid climatic regime. What it lacked, however, was the flexibility of the multispecies agriculture and pastoralism of the Celts, a system much more suited to periods of uncertain climate (Crumley 1994b:193–199).

Between AD 500 and 900, the ecotone once again retreated far to the south, far enough, in fact, that the Nile had ice on it in 829. It once again lay roughly along the North African coast (Crumley 1994b:196).

What follows is the fascinating part of Crumley's work. During the first millennium BC, Celtic peoples occupied the northern half of the range of the Mediterranean-continental ecotone. South of the Celts, along the north Mediterranean littoral, lived the sea traders, among them Greeks, Etruscans, and Romans. Around the fifth century BC, during a period when the ecotone was located far to the south, the Celts advanced on settlements in Italy and Greece. By the end of the second century BC, as the ecotone moved sharply north, the tables were turned dramatically. Rome came to dominate the Greek-controlled shipping lanes and made a province of the southern fringe of Celtic polities in France. By the end of the first century BC, Rome had conquered the entire Mediterranean region and western Europe as far as the Rhine, roughly the northern location of the ecotone (Crumley 1994b:198).

As Crumley points out, "The extent and duration of the Pax Romana in Europe was greatly facilitated by climatic conditions that favored Roman—as opposed to Celtic—economic, social, and political organization. Not only were Roman patterns of settlement and land use in marked distinction to those of Celtic polities, they were especially suited to the med-

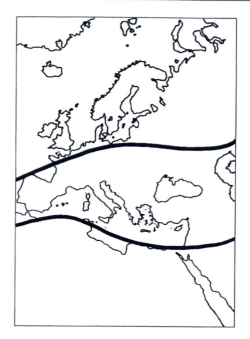

THE ECOTONE'S SHIFTING RANGE IN EUROPE

Figure 3. The ecotone dividing the continental and Mediterranean climatic regimes in western Europe has ranged from 36°N latitude along the North African coast to 48°N in northern Burgundy and Germany, a distance of some 880 km (500 mi) (adapted from Crumley 1994b:195).

iterraneanized climate of Europe." The Romans' use of space, their agriculture and horticulture, their class relations, patterns of inheritance, and forms of government, all associated with Mediterranean ecosystems, moved north along with their legions, following behind the ecotone (Crumley 1994b:198).

As the ecotone retreated in the fifth century AD and continental climate came to dominate most of Europe, Rome's European empire came apart, her legions retreated southward, and northern cultures advanced to the south. The Picts and Scots broke through Hadrian's Wall in Britain in the late fourth century. By the early fifth century, the Visigoths had overrun Rome, and by the end of the century, a Germanic chieftain had deposed the last emperor of Rome (*Encyclopedia Britannica* 1976:VIII, 656–657).

The present work is not the venue to argue the rise and fall of the Roman Empire, but it is the place to note the close association between the advance of Roman military, political, economic, and, most especially, agricultural power and the advance of a mediterraneanized climatic regime into western Europe. We should also note the retreat of Roman power along with the retreat of the mediterraneanized climate to the south. Surely many factors played a role in Rome's boom and bust. Although climate was certainly one of them, and perhaps even a major player, it has only rarely been recognized and discussed in the past.

DESERTIFICATION

Let's look more closely at recent ecotonal shifts, changes in biotic regimes, and humankind's role in those changes. During the 1980s, the southern boundary of the Sahara Desert was believed to be migrating to the south. The consensus conclusion was that in the process of so-called desertification, the advancing desert was changing a living environment to a sterile and barren wasteland. Desertification was supposedly driven by farming marginal lands and overgrazing. In other words, the southward spread of the Sahara Desert was the fault of human beings, the cultivators and pastoralists in the region, as can be seen in the following quotation:

> Desertification, revealed by drought, is caused by human activities in which the carrying capacity of land is exceeded; it proceeds by exacerbated natural or man-induced mechanisms, and is made manifest by intricate steps of vegetation and soil deterioration which result, in human terms, in an irreversible decrease or destruction of the biological potential of the land and its ability to support population. (Monique Mainguet quoted in Nicholson, Tucker, and Ba 1998:816)

Clearly, the humans are at fault. One researcher even went so far as to say that the Sahel drought of the 1970s was, in part, caused by overgrazing. Most of the evidence studied at that time, however, was from locations and time periods that were simultaneously affected by long-term declines in rainfall or outright drought (Charney 1975:200; Nicholson, Tucker, and Ba 1998:818):

> At the heart of the problem was the intentional elimination of climate as a possible cause of desertification. This was unfortunate because nearly all of the few actual assessments extended over periods of drought or rainfall decline. Thus, while desertification itself was defined as anthropogenic, the evidence used to assess it could equally have been a product of climatic variability. (Nicholson, Tucker, and Ba 1998:818)

In order to try to see whether there was a connection between the desert boundary and climate, Compton Tucker, Harold Dregne, and Wilbur Newcomb used satellites to trace the southward spread of the desert into the Sahel. When those images were correlated with precipitation, the results showed that the desert spread to the south as the rainfall moved to the south and it moved back north as the rains moved back north—completely independent of what the humans were doing. In fact, during the period studied, the desert moved to the south and retreated to the north at least three times. The critical factor was not humans but rainfall—and convincingly so (Kerr 1998:634; Nicholson, Tucker, and Ba 1998:815; Tucker, Dregne, and Newcomb 1991:299).

On a smaller scale, scientists from Lund University in Sweden did extensive studies in the Sudan to test some of the basic tenets of desertification. Through a combination of field work and satellite photos, they showed that "there was neither a systematic advance of the desert nor a reduction in vegetation cover, although replacement of forage with woody species was apparent. There was no evidence of a systematic spread of desertified land around villages and waterholes or of reduced crop yield due to cultivation of marginal or vulnerable areas. On the other hand, they clearly demonstrated that changes took place in response to drought, with full recovery of the land productivity at the end of the drought." These same conclusions, of course, were reached by Tucker, Dregne, and Newcomb for the Sahel as a whole (Nicholson, Tucker, and Ba 1998:815; Tucker, Dregne, and Newcomb 1991:299).

It became clear that short-term changes during a temporary drought period had been mistaken for a permanent one-way process in spite of the fact that the same changes had been observed forty years earlier and had been reversed in the wet years in between. Despite all the recent evidence to the contrary, however, the myth of desertification lingers on, even though in the end, according to climatologist Sharon Nicholson, "The scenario of the Sahara sands marching southward at the hands of humans is wrong" (de Selincourt 1997:34; Nicholson quoted in Kerr 1998:633).

LAND DEGRADATION

If humans are innocent of desertification, what about our guilt in land degradation? Work in southern New Mexico, reported by Ronald Neilson in *Science*, suggests that humans may not be entirely to blame for land degradation either. Change in the biogeography of plants in the southwestern United States has long been a subject of controversy. In New Mexico, Arizona, and West Texas, the shift from a semidesert grassland to a desert shrubland has been attributed to overgrazing of livestock, with attendant soil losses, and changes in climate. As in the Sahel, however, the areas and periods studied have also been affected by long-term climatic changes. A marked shift in the climate of the region since about 1900 has been coincident with a rapid and extreme rise in stocking rates. Grazing peaked about 1920, the result of World War I livestock markets, and has been declining since then. Temperatures warmed from 1900 to about 1940, then entered a long-term decline until about 1980, when they began to rise again (Neilson 1986:29).

In the study by Neilson, he demonstrated that the desertification which occurred in southern New Mexico in the twentieth century is not necessarily the result of overgrazing—in other words, the fault of human beings—but is more likely the result of a major shift in basic weather patterns from the Little Ice Age to the twentieth-century warmth. He proposed that "the 'pristine' vegetation of the northern Chihuahua Desert, recorded one hundred years ago, was vegetation established under and adapted to three hundred years of 'little ice age' and is only marginally supported under the present climate." Changes in climatic patterns, like increased winter rainfall, have favored the growth of woody plants rather than forage species like grass. In particular, during the 1930s, a series of climatically favorable winters led to a significant increase of woody plants like creosote bush and the subsequent decrease of grassland (Neilson 1986:232–233).

The implication of the studies both in the Sahel and in New Mexico is that the effect of human mismanagement on the productivity of the land is minimal compared to the effect of climate.

That is not the same as saying that mismanagement of our environment has no effect whatsoever. Other human intervention, like the suppression of fire, has clearly played an important role in the growth of trash plants on rangeland. We are certainly aware of the drastic environmental effects of forest clearance. But who's to say how much more or less greasewood and acacia would clog southern New Mexico under the present climatic regime if buffalo had been grazing the area rather than cattle? After all, a large, concentrated herd of buffalo moving across the land can graze it as close as cattle do. On a large regional scale, the shifts in ecotones appear to play a much greater role in desertification and land degradation than do the agricultural and pastoral practices of human beings.

ECOTONES IN THE MAYA LOWLANDS

Joel Gunn, William Folan, and Hubert Robichaux have proposed that an ecotonal shift on the Yucatán Peninsula played a major role in the Classic Collapse. They believe that the great cities of the Lowlands, which were primarily in the central semikarst geological band, flourished when the warm-cool climatic band coincided with the semikarst geological band. In other words, when the ecotone between the dry north and the wet south (figure 4) was located over the semikarst, surplus agricultural production would have risen sharply and produce would have poured into the Maya cities. When it shifted either to the north or the south, however, the *milpas*,

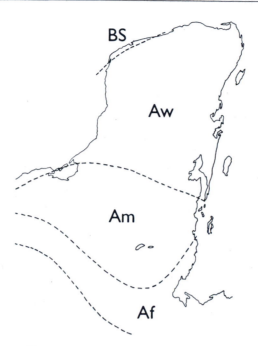

ECOTONES IN THE MAYA LOWLANDS

Figure 4. Climates of the Yucatán Peninsula, showing the approximate modern positions of the ecotones dividing different climatic regions. A southward shift of the semiarid/savanna (*BS/Aw*) ecotone across distances comparable to those seen in Europe would have had devastating consequences for the Classic Maya. The regions are labeled using the Köppen system: *BS*, semiarid; *Aw*, tropical savanna; *Am*, tropical monsoon; and *Af*, tropical rainy (adapted from Folan 1983a:42).

or cornfields, switched off and food resources were limited to the more reliable but labor intensive canal farming. In the off status, the surpluses necessary to maintain hierarchies and public works diminished (Gunn, Folan, and Robichaux 1995:36).

CLIMATE AND HUMAN EVOLUTION

While we are on the subject of interactions between climate and people, there is one short, fascinating digression we can make: climate may have affected human evolution itself. In fact, the relationship between climate and human history may be so deep that the existence of our species may be due to catastrophic climatic change. We will look briefly at two proposed hypotheses.

Johns Hopkins palaeobiologist Steven Stanley proposed in his book, *Children of the Ice Age,* that *Homo sapiens* evolved as the result of drastic climatic changes which occurred as the Earth's climate moved into the current Ice Age. When the weather turned sharply colder at the beginning of the modern Ice Age, the warm, wet climate of Africa became cold and dry. *Australopithecus,* the ancestor of our own species *Homo,* was a tree dweller that also dropped to the ground to get around. As the forests shrank, the Australopithecines were forced to survive exclusively on the ground, which Stanley calls the terrestrial imperative. A change in basic behavior frequently precedes a major evolutionary shift of bodily proportions. No longer needing their hands and arms for tree climbing, they were freed up to carry helpless infants. During the early phases of drought and cold associated with the changing climate, most Australopithecines succumbed to predators or to famine or otherwise died. In a small, localized population, however, the newly found freedom from climbing permitted the evolution of larger brains by allowing parents to carry their babies with them during the long, helpless phase of human infancy. Stanley calls the resulting speciation the catastrophic birth, the birth of the species *Homo* due to a climatic disaster (Stanley 1996:167–168).

Stanley has postulated that the mechanism through which the new species arose was a process called bottlenecking or peripheral isolation. When the environment turned against *Australopithecus,* the ancestral species shrank to become a small population confined to a narrow geographic area. A drastic reorganization of the gene pool is far most easily accomplished in a small founder population. Drastic genetic changes do not occur in widespread, populous species. From the Ice Age bottleneck, then, *Homo* emerged by the evolutionary transformation of a small, beleaguered population of Australopithecines (Eldredge and Gould 1972:94; Mayr 1988:461; Stanley 1996:169).

A second proposal by anthropologist Stanley Ambrose suggests that the subsequent differentiation of *Homo sapiens* into separate races may also be tied to a climatic catastrophe. He believes that once modern humans had evolved in Africa, they spread throughout the world around 100,000 years ago. About 70,000 years ago, the second most devastating volcanic eruption on record occurred at Mt. Toba on the Indonesian island of Sumatra. (It erupted 800 km^3 of rock, compared with El Chichón's 1982 eruption of 1 km^3.) The resulting six-year volcanic winter was followed by a thousand years when "the earth witnessed temperatures relentlessly colder than during the Last Glacial Maximum" (Ambrose 1998:623, 633).

Human populations contracted to small, localized founder-type groups around the world in another episode of bottlenecking driven by severe famine. Ambrose believes the volcanic winter and the thousand years of cold destroyed the primary productivity of the land resulting in widespread starvation. The numbers of possible survivors in each isolated group have been estimated to range between 40 and 10,000 individuals by different researchers. From the small, geographically dispersed founder populations on different continents our modern races emerged (Ambrose 1998:627, 635).

Stanley's and Ambrose's theories represent their own points of view in the debate over our human origins, and there are certainly other points of view as well, but they indicate the extent to which climate is being very seriously considered as a major factor in the evolution of *Homo sapiens*.

OCKHAM'S RAZOR

As we have seen, changes in the environment are very direct causes of human social and perhaps even physical change. Yet they run counter to a recent trend in archaeological thought that simple solutions are inadequate. Ockham's razor is not in fashion. The principle, used by scholastic William of Ockham in the fourteenth century, holds that "entities are not to be multiplied beyond necessity," in other words, that the simplest of competing theories be preferred to the more complex. Lately, however, more is believed to be better and very complex, intricate explanations are believed to be philosophically more acceptable than simple, direct arguments. Complex explanations can play an important role in solving problems, and in certain cases may well be the superior form of explanation, but not in all cases. In the theory presented in this book, a simple, inexorable, driving cause results in a cascade of complex effects which result in the death of a civilization (*Encyclopedia Britannica* Online 1995: Ockham's razor; WWWebster Online 1998: Ockham).

A PROPOSED SYNTHESIS

From the perspective of a Hegelian dialectic, if we began with the thesis of environmental determinism and moved to the antithesis of internal processes alone, perhaps we can now accept the synthesis that internal processes and external perturbations both play a major role in the history of societies, each in their own way, each in their own time. We will investigate this approach more closely in the next chapter.

I want to emphasize the following point very strongly, because I seem to be frequently misunderstood: I do not claim in this book that multicausal explanations of cultural change are invalid. I do claim that multicausal explanations are not necessarily *always* valid. Sometimes, unicausal or monocausal explanations, in fact, fit the available data better than do multicausal ones. There is a role, therefore, for both multicausal and unicausal explanations. In the next chapter, I will try to provide a theoretical foundation for unicausal explanations and propose how both kinds of explanations play their respective roles within the synthesis.

2. ENERGY AND ENVIRONMENT

Having looked at the relationship between climate and human populations, let us turn our attention to the relationship between humans and the physical environment and its most important manifestation, the way humans organize themselves to extract energy from the environment.

Most—though not all—archaeological and anthropological theories are constructed from the inside out. Many theorists seem to believe that in order to understand the functioning and development of social organizations, it is only necessary to look at the humans involved. The present work, on the other hand, espouses an ecological view of human societies and their relationship to the physical world in which the flow of energy generated from the physical world is a critical factor.

The term *ecology* was coined by German zoologist Ernst Haeckel who defined it as "the relation of the animal both to its organic as well as its inorganic environment." Human beings live in a physical world, and like laboratory systems, ant colonies, and monkey troops, interact constantly with the physical environment. We are subject to its laws, its constraints, and its catastrophes. There has been a strong line of research in the past by Maya archaeologists on the effect that human beings can have on their environment, but there have been scant studies of how the environment, when it is changed by the forces of nature, can affect human beings and, in particular of course, the Classic Maya (Haeckel quoted in *Encyclopedia Britannica* 1976 6:197).

Many writers have recognized the role the environment plays in shaping the evolution of cultures and societies. L. van Valen, for example, suggested, "Evolution is the control of development by ecology." Gordon Childe asserted that "adaptation to the environment is a condition of survival for societies as much as for organisms (Childe 1951:172; van Valen quoted in Salthe 1985:x)."

Gregory Bateson wrote that it was no longer "the survival of the fittest," rather "the survival of organism-*plus*-environment." He added (Bateson 1972:502):

> I suggest then that a healthy ecology of human civilization would be defined somewhat as follows:
> A single system of environment combined with high human civilization in which the flexibility of the civilization shall match that of the environment to create an ongoing complex system, open ended for slow change of even basic (hard-programmed) characteristics. (Bateson 1972: 507)

From a Mesoamerican point of view the ecological approach was championed by, among others, archaeologists William Sanders, Barbara Price, Richard MacNeish, Joel Gunn, and William Folan and ethnologists Angel Palerm and EricWolf. Kent Flannery established the ecosystem as a basic model for viewing the adaptive changes between man and his environment. Gordon Willey and Jeremy Sabloff defined an ecosystem as "the interactions involving energy and matter between one living population (such as man) or all living populations of an area (an ecological 'community') and the non-living environment." As can be seen then, a thermodynamic ecological approach to analyzing the relationship between human beings and the physical world, in which energy is the critical resource, is not a new idea in archaeology and other disciplines. It has been raised often in the past by a number of distinguished writers (Flannery 1968a; MacNeish 1958; Palerm and Wolf 1957; Sanders and Price 1968; Trigger 1989b:11; Willey and Sabloff 1980:189–192, 201–203).

The ecological approach, however, has not been universally embraced by all archaeologists. Arthur Demarest, for example, summarized the confrontation over ecological determinism.

> From systems theory, Marxism, and even cultural ecology another series of criticisms accused cultural materialists and most cultural ecologists of having committed the so-called "organic fallacy," another common ailment of functionalist explanations. The Marxists were more aggressive in pointing out that society does not consist of a coordinated uniform organism responding to environmental pressures. Rather, it consists of conflicting individuals, groups, families, and classes whose goals are not necessarily

identical and whose interests (and actions) are often not in agreement with the "adaptive" or "functional" needs of the cultural system as a whole. The unequal distribution of power in complex societies can often result in the dominance of interests of specific individuals or small elites, even in cases where these interests are maladaptive for the society as a whole.

The inability to deal with maladaptation and collapse became another common criticism of most of the "adaptive" functionalist interpretations prevalent in archaeology. Marxists and systems theorists criticized such "vulgar" materialist approaches for their failure to recognize the conflicting forces within society which were, ultimately, the cause of most systemic collapses of civilizations. As Friedman (1974:466) has noted, "History is built upon the failure of social forms as much as on their success." The assumption that institutions and societies are ecologically adaptive only allows for "conquest" (in a Darwinian usage) as an explanation of collapse. Yet it is clear from history that internal maladaptation, conflict, and inefficiency have more often been the cause of the disintegration of civilizations. (Demarest 1989:96)

THERMODYNAMICS, ECOLOGY, AND ARCHAEOLOGY

Thermodynamics, the study of heat, energy, and matter, was introduced to ecology by Alfred Lotka, a physical chemist by training who worked for a chemical company. In his spare time, over a twenty-year period, he developed a new science which he called physical biology and published his famous work, *Elements of Physical Biology*, in 1925. Lotka's basic thesis was that the organic and inorganic worlds function as a single system with all the components linked through thermodynamics in such an intimate way that it is impossible to understand the part without understanding the whole. An ecosystem includes not only other species and societies, other individuals of the same species or society, but the physical environment as well. Lotka felt that biologists took too narrow a view of evolution by focusing on individual species. He believed that natural selection must operate on the energy flow of the undivided system. "It is customary to discuss the 'evolution of a species of organisms,'" he wrote. "As we proceed we shall see many reasons why we should constantly take in the view of evolution, as a whole, of the system (organism plus environment)" (quoted in Lewin 1992:117; Odum 1993:72).

Eugene P. Odum, called by some the father of ecology, is one of a number of ecologists who believe the answers to ecological questions are more often found in physics than in biology. In his view, the single most important factor to analyze in order to understand an ecological system is the flow of energy. He has adopted his brother Howard Odum's maximum power principle: "That system survives which gets most energy and uses

energy most effectively in competition with other systems." Those systems that survive in the competition among alternative choices are those
that develop more power inflow and use it best to meet the needs of survival. To survive and prosper, natural and human made ecosystems require a continuous input of high quality energy, storage capacity (for
periods when input is less than needed), and the means to dissipate entropy (Chaffin 1998:8; Odum 1993:70–72; Odum and Odum 1976:39–40).

> If one were asked to pick out a single common denominator
> of life on earth, that is, something that is absolutely essential and
> involved in every action large or small, the answer would have to
> be energy. (Odum 1993:68)

Ethnologist Leslie White defined human social organizations as thermodynamic systems: "A culture, or sociocultural system, is a material, and
therefore a thermodynamic, system. Culture is an organization of things in
motion, a process of energy transformations." He formulated a concept of
technological determinism as his "basic law of evolution." All things being
equal, he proposed, culture evolves as the amount of energy harnessed per
capita increases, or as the efficiency of putting energy to work is increased.
His law is summarized in the formula: Culture = Energy × Technology
(Leslie White 1959:45, 47, 56).

According to White, the amount of energy per capita per year obtain-
able from human beings is both small and limited, about $\frac{1}{20}$ horsepower
(37 watts) per capita, which sets a limit on the ability of cultures to advance. In order to augment their energy resources, therefore, cultures
turned to domesticated animals, thereby harnessing solar energy in nonhuman biological forms. This led White to two basic principles of cultural
development: "culture advances as the proportion of nonhuman energy to
human energy increases" and "as the efficiency or economy of controlling
energy is increased" (Leslie White 1959:45, 47, 56).

> The degree of organization of a system increases as the con-
> centration of energy within the system increases. Social systems
> are but the social form of expression of technological control over
> the forces of nature. Social evolution is therefore a function of
> technological development. Social systems evolve as the amount
> of energy harnessed per capita per year increases, other factors re-
> maining constant. This is to say, they become more differentiated
> structurally, more specialized functionally, and as a consequence
> of differentiation and specialization, special mechanisms of inte-
> gration and regulation are developed. Thus human social evolu-
> tion becomes intelligible in terms of entropy, in terms of a
> corollary of the second law of thermodynamics: the degree of
> organization of a system is proportional to the concentration of

ergy within the system. We may thus view social evolution against the background of a principle fundamental in nature and cosmic in scope. (Leslie White 1959:144–145)

Thus, it was White's belief that the amount of energy harnessed by a society is fundamental and that technological changes are the prime movers in determining the amount of energy harnessed and even in determining other cultural characteristics (Service 1962:179; Leslie White 1959:45, 47, 56).

Following White's work, Betty Meggers proposed her "law of cultural evolution as a practical research tool." Because nonhuman sources of energy were absent in small-scale societies, she argued, White's Law, as it applied to them, could be rewritten in the following form: Culture = Environment × Technology (Meggers 1955:121, 129; 1960).

Meggers's Law suggested that any archaeologist who could reconstruct the environment and technology of a prehistoric culture could determine what the key features of the rest of the culture were like. Furthermore, any shortcomings were not the responsibility of archaeology but resulted from the failure of ethnologists to elaborate adequate theories relating technology and environment to the rest of culture (Meggers 1955:121, 129; 1960; Trigger 1989b:293–294; Willey and Sabloff 1980:182).

In the case of Classic Maya culture, the environment, including climate, determined the energy resources available for the culture to exploit. For over fifteen hundred years, the environment provided substantial exploitable energy—although with periodic restrictions of various degrees of severity. As their agricultural technology increased, as they learned to exploit more marginal areas and to increase the amount of irrigation water available during the dry season, the Maya were able to increase their energy resources and support greater populations and greater levels of social complexity. When the environment drastically changed, the energy was cut off, and the complexity collapsed.

Environment and Culture

Anthropologist Julian Steward observed that anthropologists have been so preoccupied with culture and its history that they have accorded environment only a negligible role. "Environment is relegated to a purely secondary and passive role. It is considered prohibitive or permissive, but not creative." No culture has achieved so perfect an adaptation to its environment that it is static. He therefore proposed his theory of cultural ecology which introduced "the local environment as the extracultural factor in the fruitless assumption that culture comes from culture." Cultural types, he concluded, "must be conceived as constellations of core features which arise out of environmental adaptations and which represent similar levels of integration" (Steward 1955:5, 35–36, 42).

In his superb, Pulitzer Prize winning survey of the last 13,000 years of history, *Guns, Germs, and Steel*, Jared Diamond investigated the relationship between environment and culture:

> History followed different courses for different peoples because of differences among peoples' environments, not because of biological differences among peoples themselves.
>
> Naturally, the notion that environmental geography and biogeography influenced societal development is an old idea. Nowadays, though, the view is not held in esteem by historians; it is considered wrong or simplistic, or it is caricatured as environmental determinism and dismissed, or else the whole subject of trying to understand worldwide differences is shelved as too difficult. Yet geography obviously has *some* effect on history; the open question concerns how much effect, and whether geography can account for history's broad patterns.
>
> The time is now ripe for a fresh look at these questions.... (Diamond 1997:25–26)

Diamond believes that the interaction between culture and environment plays a major role in determining the success with which people can establish themselves and prosper in different areas of the world. To take one example, as the Austronesians spread out across the Pacific Basin from their homeland in Taiwan, they replaced the resident hunter-gatherers in those places like Indonesia and the Philippines where their Austronesian farming culture could flourish. The culture failed to take root, however, in those places where their suite of cultivars and their farming techniques could not adequately exploit the environment or where the local residents had already developed successful farming cultures, areas where the Austronesian culture had no competitive advantage (Diamond 1997:336–352).

To take another example, in Africa, Bantu farmers overran the hunter-gatherer Khoisan throughout large areas of the continent, but they could not extend into those areas unsuitable for Bantu summer rain agriculture. As the Bantu farmers spread to the south, the southernmost Bantu, the Xhosa, stopped at the Fish River, 800 km (500 mi) east of Capetown. The Fish River was approximately the ecotone between the tropical, summer rain province of most of sub-Saharan Africa and the Mediterranean-like, winter rain province of South Africa. Those areas of South Africa with a Mediterranean climate south of the Fish River were not successfully farmed until Dutch settlers arrived in 1652 with their suite of winter rain crops of Middle Eastern origin. The Bantu culture was developed for a specific climatic environment and could not exploit or survive in the region across the ecotone. The way the Bantu and the Khoisan could interact with their environment was constrained by their culture (Diamond 1997: 396–397).

Why, then, do some people develop a culture which more successfully exploits their environment and others don't? According to Diamond, "the long-term history of peoples of the different continents have been due not to innate differences in the peoples themselves but to differences in their environments." Those cultures and peoples that are the most successful in history are not genetically superior to others, but rather had the good fortune to be living in the right place and the right time to acquire domestic plants and animals, which let them multiply and replace other peoples (Diamond 1997:405).

Diamond's hypothesis is that societies which advanced more rapidly were those that had the advantage of living in a locale where there were plants and animals which could be domesticated, like wheat, yams, maize, cattle, pigs, goats, horses, and so on. Such advantages permitted the growth of large interacting populations which could spurt ahead technologically. The populations of Europe and Asia had such advantages, therefore domesticates diffused widely, and populations grew rapidly. By contrast, no modern domesticates are native to Africa south of the Sahara or to Australia. In Africa, neither Bantu nor modern farmers have been able to develop sub-Saharan African native plants into food crops. Those cultures had the poor fortune of living in an area where neither plants nor animals could be easily domesticated. Their cultures, therefore, remained small, compared to Eurasia, and the technological gap grew (Diamond 1997:388).

On the continents with the good fortune to have domesticatable plants and animals, those species were originally concentrated in small homelands, representing only a fraction of the continent's total area. As a result, diffusion and migration played very important roles. Thus, the second set of factors consists of the ecological and geographical barriers which may have impeded the diffusion of new domesticates by land, like in Africa and the Americas, or the diffusion between continents and islands across the water.

Eurasia, for example, is organized on an east to west axis while the Americas are laid out north to south. In Europe, domesticates can be diffused more easily throughout large geographical regions of similar climatic regimes. In contrast, the range of climates is more extreme in the Americas where diffusion is impeded by the tropical bottleneck of Panama, by deserts in northwestern Mexico, in the southwestern United States, in Peru and Chile, and by high mountain ranges. Those geographical barriers made difficult the regular interaction between different population groups and slowed the diffusion of cultural advances from one area to another. Maize, for example, which was domesticated in Mesoamerica perhaps as early as 3500 BC, did not arrive in the eastern US until about AD 200 and did not become a major crop until about AD 900. Llamas never did make it from the Andes to central Mexico, Mesoamerican writing was never adopted in Peru, and agriculture never crossed the mountains and deserts to California and Oregon (Diamond 1997:406–408).

Luck played an important role not only in which species were available, but also in the ease or difficulty with which they could be domesticated. In Mesoamerica, for example, maize was a more difficult plant to domesticate than wheat, requiring much more significant genetic mutation for it to be suitable for agriculture. In addition, no native animals were present which could be domesticated for either food or work, except, perhaps, dogs and turkeys (Diamond 1997:406–408).

The final set of factors consists of continental differences in area or total population size. As Diamond points out, "a larger area means more potential inventors, more competing societies, more innovations available to adopt—and more pressure to adopt and retain innovations, because societies failing to do so will tend to be eliminated by competing societies.... All human societies contain inventive people. It's just that some environments provide more starting materials, and more favorable conditions for utilizing inventions, than do other environments" (Diamond 1997:406–408).

As important as the interaction is between culture and environment, the major books written about Classic Maya society and the Collapse during the last two decades contain very little discussion of the physical environment and climate—generally little more than a cursory description of the geography and geology of the Lowlands—and almost no discussion of their relationship to Maya culture or the role they may have played in shaping Maya culture. As we have seen, the interaction between physical environment, climate, and culture has been a major factor in the development and spread of other cultures and societies. According to Diamond, "Again and again, when a single wave of colonists spread out over diverse environments, their descendants developed in separate ways, depending on those environmental differences" (Diamond 1997:352).

ENERGY FLOW

For the growth of complex civilizations, then, successful exploitation of the environment is a function of a culture's ability to generate energy from the physical world in which it lives.

Complex structures must be open to their environment, at a minimum importing energy and exporting entropy, a process we will examine in greater detail in the next chapter. Laboratory experiments have demonstrated that under suitable conditions, a constant and rich energy flow passing through a system drives it toward states characterized by a higher level of free energy and a lower level of entropy. In other words, it achieves greater organization. A flow of energy passing through a nonequilibrium system organizes its structures and components to access, use, and store more and more free energy. In social systems, as energy flows increase, the hierarchical complexity also increases and if the energy flow is reduced or even cut off, the hierarchy collapses. The entire hierarchical, complex structure depends on a consistent flow of energy (Laszlo 1987:28).

What counts is how much of the free energy flux density available in the environment is captured, retained, and used in the system. (Free energy flux density is defined as the free energy flow per unit of mass, ie, erg/second/gram.) A living system, for example, retains more than a complex chemical system. A complex farming culture retains more than a hunter-gatherer society. This indicates a basic direction in evolution toward more efficient energy use (Laszlo 1987:28).

Astronomer Eric Chaisson proposed that living organisms tend to maximally utilize both their energy intake from the Sun and the use of free energy by dissipative processes occurring within them. This maxim applies to all of cosmic evolution: organized structures everywhere seem to maximally utilize the flux of energy passing through them. During the course of biological evolution, each succeeding species becomes more complex and thus better equipped to capture and use available energy. The higher the species in the chain, the greater the energy density fluxing through that species (Chaisson 1987:122, 173).

Chaisson's maxim applies in social as well as biological systems. Complex civilizations are characterized by their ability to maximize their use of energy, with greater levels of complexity requiring greater levels of energy. On each level, systems in an energy flow progressively exploit the free energy fluxes in their environment. As the density of the free energy retained in the systems increases, the systems acquire structural complexity (Laszlo 1987:34–35).

Alfred Lotka grasped as early as 1922 a fundamental principle of the self-organization of biological and social systems. "In every instance considered, natural selection will so operate as to increase the total flux through the system, so long as there is presented an unutilized residue of matter and available energy." In 1924, he expanded on his ideas, "so long as there is an abundant surplus of available energy running 'to waste' over the sides of the mill wheel, so to speak, so long will a marked advantage be gained by any species that may develop talents to utilize this 'lost portion of the stream'" (see figure 5) (Lotka quoted in Richard Newbold Adams 1988:36).

"I have a hunch," ventures biologist Stuart Kauffman, "that higher order things emerge because they can suck more flow of stuff into themselves, faster, whether we're talking about *E. coli*, prebiotic evolution, or firms. So what I'd like to see all this lead to is a theory of coupled processes that build themselves up into things that compete for and win the flow—and that get themselves to the edge of chaos at the same time." Kauffman admits that his ideas are only intuition at this point. "If I can just show that those entities that happen fastest and suck the most flow through them are what you see, with some characteristic distribution, that will be it" (quoted in Waldrop 1992:318).

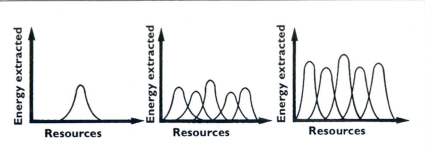

ENERGY EXPLOITATION

Figure 5. In an ecosystem, evolution will lead to filling an empty resource spectrum and to maximizing the efficiency of energy exploitation by developing organisms which are progressively better adapted for extracting energy from the environment (adapted from Allen 1985:14).

Is there a limit to complexity? Prigogine and Allen respond, "The
question...may have a less clear-cut answer than those that have been considered up to the present. According to our results, an important aspect of
the answer would be that complexity is limited by stability, which in turn
is limited by the system-environment coupling." One must add that complexity is limited by the raw materials and energy available to support it.
The higher the level of organization, the more intense the material and energy requirements become. The higher levels will not develop unless the
materials and energy are available. Nor will they survive if the material
and energy sources are lost (Prigogine and Allen 1982:36).

ENERGY IN HUMAN SOCIETIES

Marvin Harris has recognized the same principle in cultural systems:
"Anthropologists have long recognized that, in broadest perspective, cultural evolution has had three main characteristics: escalating energy budget, increasing productivity, and accelerating population" (Harris quoted
in Richard Newbold Adams 1988:37).

Complex civilizations, then, emerge not only because there is more energy available to them, but also because they have organized themselves,
in Kauffman's words, "to suck more flow" of energy through the system.
What are as important as the availability of energy are the necessity, the
will, and the ability to exploit the available energy.

Thus, we saw that Bantu farmers in Africa, with their relatively advanced agricultural techniques, displaced the Khoisan hunter-gatherers
who lacked the requisite technology to achieve the same level of energy
exploitation as the Bantu. It is an oft repeated story in human history. Aus-

tronesian farmers replaced hunter-gatherers throughout the Pacific and Indo-European farmers, with their superior suite of Middle Eastern cultivars and agricultural techniques, spread from India to northern Europe. The key to each of these displacements was a superior ability to exploit the environment and extract greater quantities of energy, which, in an archaeological context, means the ability to generate greater quantities of food from the environment.

The very fact, however, that civilizations have organized themselves to exploit the available energy means that they are dependent on the consistent availability of that energy. The complexity cannot be sustained if the flow of energy is interrupted.

Anthropologist Robert Redfield has said that cities were made possible by the labor of peasants and by the agricultural surpluses they produced. Cities and urban life would be impossible if the surpluses of energy produced in rural areas were suddenly unavailable (Redfield 1953).

Turning to archaeological theory, Betty Meggers proposed in 1954 an important law which integrates ecological and thermodynamic approaches, relating directly to concepts of energy flow: "The level to which a culture can develop is dependent upon the agricultural potentiality of the environment it occupies." She added that if this potentiality is improved, the culture will advance. If it cannot be improved, the culture will become stabilized at a level compatible with the food resources. Even today, the dependence of agricultural activity on natural phenomena will vary inversely with technological input. As we saw earlier, the complexity of a system is limited by the energy and raw materials available to support it. In most archaeological cultures, the primary source of energy flowing through the system is food, followed way behind by fuel for fires, primarily cooking fires, and for heat. Most of the energy in archaeological cultures is used by humans and animals to provide muscle power. Only in recent centuries have machines and fossil fuels become important sources of energy and power (Wolde Mariam 1984:12; Meggers 1954:815).

Meggers further proposed, "If an increase in energy resources or their control results in increased cultural complexity, a decline in energy resources should result in a decline in cultural complexity." She pointed out that in Mesopotamia, in the southwestern United States, at the mouth of the Amazon, and in other parts of the world, regions at one time occupied by rather highly developed cultures are now sparsely inhabited by scattered, more primitive types. She believed that climatic shifts or insufficient technical knowledge could alter the agricultural potential of the local area in the direction of declining yield with a resulting decline in cultural complexity. Her concept is illustrated by the cycle of cultural complexity which occurred in the Teotlalpan of highland Mexico as it moved from Otomí hunting, gathering, and limited agriculture, to Toltec intensive agriculture, back again to an Otomí style regime before the reintensification of Aztec times, in response to changing climatic regimes (Meggers 1960:310–311).

According to Richard Newbold Adams, there is a critical negative aspect to the energy flow identified by Meggers:

> The principle—i.e., the favoring of some forms over others—can only operate when appropriate free energy forms are available, and its reverse is likely to occur if such resources are closed. That is, life forms that succeed in developing structures that channel great amounts of energy can be readily doomed if the necessary energy sources are cut off. (Richard Newbold Adams 1988:38)

The energy and raw material flow, primarily in the form of food and water, was cut off from the Classic Maya as the result of severe drought. Without a strong flow of energy through the system, it was unable to maintain its multilayered complexity, and it imploded. In some areas, the cutoff was so drastic that the populations disappeared entirely. In other areas, as along the east coast, around the Petén lakes, and in the cenote zone, the energy flow was reduced but still able to support a reduced level of social complexity. The society collapsed, therefore, to the level which could be sustained by the energy flow.

3. SELF-ORGANIZATION

Human social structures are not merely sets of human beings but are, rather, assemblages of interdependent dissipative and equilibrium structures. Moreover, it is assumed that
the combinations vary from one society to another—some including and some excluding, for example, domesticated animals, or
pickaxes, or books, or nuclear bombs, or internal combustion engines, etc. Every society is a unique assemblage, a dissipative
structure that is different in some manner from all others.
—Richard Newbold Adams (1988:24)

Although there is disagreement among archaeologists over the role
played by the environment, the theory presented in this book provides for
an active and indispensable role for the environment in human affairs. The
underlying theoretical basis is drawn largely from the Nobel Prize winning work of physicist Ilya Prigogine and his theory of dissipative structures and self-organization, which we will examine in greater detail
shortly. As an introduction to the ideas that follow, he and Grégoire Nicolis
explain how the theory can be applied to human organization:

A dynamical model of a human society begins with the realization that in addition to its internal structure, the system is firm-
ly embedded in an environment with which it exchanges matter,
energy, and information. Think, for instance, of a town in which

raw materials and agricultural products arrive continuously, finished goods are exported, while mass media and professional
communication keep the various groups aware of the present situation and of the immediate trends.

The evolution of such a system is an interplay between the behavior of its actors and impinging constraints from the environment. It is here that the human system finds its unique specificity.
Contrary to the molecules, the actors in a physico-chemical system, or even the ants or the members of other animal societies, human beings develop individual projects and desires. Some of these
stem from anticipations about how the future might reasonably
look and from guesses concerning the desires of other actors. The
difference between desired and actual behavior therefore acts as a
constraint of a new type which, together with the environment,
shapes the dynamics. A basic question that can be raised is whether, under those circumstances, the overall evolution is capable of
leading to some kind of global optimum or, on the contrary,
whether each human system constitutes a unique realization of a
complex stochastic process whose rules can in no way be designed
in advance. In other words, is past experience sufficient for predicting the future, or is a high degree of unpredictability of the future the essence of human adventure, be it at the individual level
of learning or at the collective level of history making? The developments outlined in the preceding chapters suggest that the answer to this question should lean toward the second alternative.
(Nicolis and Prigogine 1989:238)

THE GROWTH OF COMPLEXITY

Robert Carneiro has pointed out that during the Neolithic period, the
autonomous political units in the world numbered several hundred thousand. Today, there are only about one hundred ninety, while the numbers
of humans living has exploded. As recently as AD 1500, less than 20 percent
of the world's land area was marked off by boundaries into states run by
bureaucrats and governed by laws. Today, all the land is, except, perhaps,
for Antarctica which is governed by international treaty. Elman Service
noted that "the evolution of culture as measured by changes in social
structure consists of a movement in the direction of greater size and density of the social body, an increase in the number of groups, greater specialization in the function of groups, and new means of integrating the
groups." These include centralized decision making, high information
flow, great coordination of parts, formal channels of command, and pool-
ing of resources. As the units have become fewer, they have become larger
in terms of population, areal extent, and complexity. How has this process
developed? Are there underlying principles (Carneiro 1978:205–206;

Diamond 1997:266; Service 1962:111; Tainter 1988:50; US State Department 1998)?

The fundamental, underlying argument made in this book treats the flow of energy through organized systems, which leads to greater levels of complexity and treats the disaster that occurs when the flow of energy is cut off. In archaeological societies, the principal source of energy was food, and in the Maya Lowlands, the most critical resource was water. William Sanders and Barbara Price noted that there is an extraordinary correlation between cereals (including maize), dense populations, and complex social systems. The most fundamental interaction of humans with their environment is their ability to secure food and water and a plentiful supply of both fuels the growth of complexity. If their interactions with their environment fail to produce sufficient food and water, on the other hand, they die. We will look further at circumstances under which human beings are unable to procure food and water from their environment during periods of drought, famine, and thirst. Energy flows in human societies are directly related to the interaction between humans and the organic and inorganic environment. When that interaction is not fruitful, there is trouble (Sanders and Price 1968:90).

In social systems, order is not imposed from the outside. It is the human beings within a society, from kings to commoners, that work out the internal ordering. Societies, therefore, are internally self-ordered and, surprisingly, their organization bears much in common with the self-organization that appears in simple laboratory processes. Having said that, it is important to remember that human processes are not laboratory processes and that they may well display their own special characteristics (Peter Allen, personal communication, 1987).

Many anthropologists and archaeologists are offended by the notion that theories developed in the natural sciences could be applied to human processes as well. One need only introduce the idea in any anthropology classroom to provoke instant animosity. Yet humans live in the natural world and are often powerless in the face of its laws. Many theories developed in physical sciences have applications in understanding and describing human beings and society.

[Ross] Ashby's self-stabilizing and self-organizing model known as the "homeostat" applies equally well to artificial servomechanisms and to the human brain. Norbert Wiener's cybernetics describes processes of control in animals as well as in machines; Ludwig von Bertalanffy's general system theory applies to the behavior of systems regardless of the nature of their parts or components; and the laws of contemporary thermodynamics apply to all energy-processing systems whether they are natural or artificial, living or nonliving.

The fact that a theory branches over several fields does not make it any the less valid than theories that stay within single disciplines. Nature does not observe disciplinary boundaries even if scientists do. (Laszlo 1987:115)

We start by looking at self-organization and dissipative structures, theoretical approaches to systems of organization ranging from laboratory dishes to universes. By looking at the process of building higher levels of complexity in organized systems, we can better understand what can bring them down. We will see that higher levels of complexity depend on flows of energy and raw materials, most fundamentally food and water. If those flows are cut off, the system will disintegrate. After all, as White noted:

A society of human beings is a material system. If, therefore, there be principles applicable to material systems in general, as science is obliged to assume, they must be applicable to human social systems in particular. And an interpretation of human social organization and evolution in terms of principles cosmic in scope must be more fundamental and significant than an interpretation limited to human society itself. (Leslie White 1959:147)

As the twentieth century opened, the biological and social sciences saw the world through principles of determinacy and equilibrium. Factors of chance and instability were underemphasized in favor of stability, control, and predictability. The development of the New Archeology and processual archaeology in the second half of the century built on the concepts of determinacy inherited from classical physics. As the twentieth century progressed, science focused on disorganized complexity, via statistical mechanics and quantum mechanics. Physicists advanced views of the world in which the probability of outcomes was substituted for certain knowledge of the result. In the late twentieth and early twenty-first century, science is confronting organized complexity. Starting from simple organizing principles, order is seen to emerge in creative and unpredictable ways in systems ranging from atoms and molecules to civilizations. We will turn our attention to these new concepts of organization and how they describe human societies (Laszlo 1987:19–20; Kauffman 1993:173).

SELF-ORGANIZATION

Self-organization as conceived by Prigogine, part of the emerging science of complexity, seeks to explain the spontaneous emergence of order among unstructured elements. It is not order which is imposed from without, rather order which emerges on its own from within a system. According to the second law of thermodynamics, entropy (the tendency towards disorder in the universe) is increasing, yet organization appears spontaneously, a process which would on the surface appear to be antientropic. Instead of being designed from the top down, self-organizing systems, like living systems, emerge from the bottom up, spontaneously. Although many archaeologists and historians like to focus their investigations on the role played by elites in the formation and dissolution of societies, both integration and disintegration can also proceed from the bottom up—not just from the top down. By concentrating on generative principles, complexity theory seeks to explain the appearance of order in the world.

DISSIPATIVE STRUCTURES

In 1977, Prigogine, a physicist at the Free University of Brussels and The University of Texas at Austin, was awarded the Nobel Prize in Chemistry for his theory of dissipative structures, in which he described the self-organization of relatively simple chemical systems. The theory provides a framework for examining self-organization in more complex systems.

A dissipative structure derives its name from its ability to achieve greater internal order, or self-organization, by dissipating internally produced entropy to the environment. It can be thought of as the self-organization of an unorganized system into a higher level of order or complexity. The so-called dissipative structure is really a dissipative process, an irreversible process, which is caught at a point in time exhibiting structure and coherence, like various chemical reactions or a human body. According to Prigogine, classical and quantum physics are the physics of being, the physics of stability and structure, while self-organization and dissipative structures, both irreversible processes, are part of the physics of becoming, the physics of processes (Prigogine 1980:xviii).

Human society is itself a process. Although we like to think of societies and cultures in terms of snapshots in time, they are ongoing processes in constant contact and interaction with their environment and with other cultures. They are not static. At times they change very slowly, at times very rapidly. A human society, whether Maya or European, is not organized from the outside, but rather from the inside. The humans themselves do the self-organization, and the principles that govern the organization bear much in common with organization in many other systems.

THE EDGE OF CHAOS

Our form of existence, our structure, as humans and as cultures, is quite different from that of a crystal of quartz, which exists in an equilibrium state. A dissipative structure exists far from equilibrium. It is never at rest. If rest ever comes and the system goes to equilibrium, the dissipative structure disappears. According to Prigogine and Peter Allen, life is sandwiched between the dangerous uniformity of equilibrium and the dangerous chaos of turbulence. It exists, as artificial life researcher Chris Langton baptized it, at the edge of chaos. It is the point where the components of a system never quite lock into place and never quite dissolve into turbulence, either. Cell membranes, for example, are barely poised between a liquid and a solid state. The edge of chaos is where life has enough stability to sustain itself and enough creativity to deserve the name of life. Furthermore, according to Langton, "The edge of chaos is where information gets its foot in the door in the physical world, where it gets the upper hand over energy" (Langton quoted in Lewin 1992:51; Prigogine and Allen 1982:14; Waldrop 1992:12, 230).

INTERACTION WITH THE ENVIRONMENT

If the entropy of the universe is increasing, in other words, if everything is tending towards greater disorder, how does organization occur? How do human bodies develop or civilizations emerge without violating the principles of the Second Law of Thermodynamics?

Prigogine proposed that if enough entropy is exported to the environment, then the total entropy change in the system could actually become negative and decrease (figure 6). Negative total entropy change would signify increasing order, which would lead to self-organization. By exporting, or dissipating, its entropy to the environment, a dissipative structure increases its internal order. Simple dissipative structures, then, can import energy and raw materials or other matter and export entropy and waste products. This is, in fact, the metabolism of a system in its simplest form. Human societies, of course, import large quantities of energy and raw materials from the environment and export large amounts of waste products. For early societies, the energy imported was largely in the form of food. Modern societies, of course, import large quantities of animal, fossil, direct solar, wind, tidal, and other forms of energy and export large quantities of waste to the environment (Jantsch 1980:31; Prigogine and Allen 1982:6).

CRITICAL MASS OR CONCENTRATION

Nonequilibrium structures, in laboratory experiments, are characterized by a scale that is much larger than a few molecules and involves gigantic numbers of entities in interaction. A certain critical size or critical concentration must be reached before the process will start. There is no difference, however, whether the environment is barely adequate for the structure or is vast. A nucleation process occurs in which the self-organization starts in a limited region and from there invades the whole space. It doesn't occur everywhere simultaneously in the entire system (Jantsch 1980:31; Prigogine and Allen 1982:8; Prigogine and Stengers 1984:187).

Sociologist Georg Simmel noted in 1950 that groups show certain characteristics only below or above certain sizes. Carneiro noted in 1967 that social scientists have long been aware that a relationship exists between the size of a society in terms of population and its degree of socio-

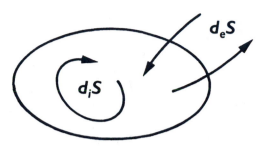

TOTAL ENTROPY

Figure 6. The total entropy production of a system is composed of the internally produced entropy and the entropy that crosses the system's boundaries:

$$dS = d_i S + d_e S, \qquad d_i S \geq 0,$$

where S stands for entropy, dS stands for the total change in entropy in the system, d_iS stands for the internal entropy production and must be equal to or greater than zero, and d_eS stands for the entropy flow across the boundaries of the system. If outgoing d_eS is large enough to offset incoming d_eS and constantly increasing d_iS, then the entropy within the system will decrease and order will increase. The system will dissipate entropy to the environment and organize itself, thus the name dissipative structure (adapted from Allen 1985:6).

cultural complexity. Critical mass is necessary in social systems. An advanced civilization cannot be built by a tribe of a hundred individuals. It takes millions of people supported by an elaborate network of trading and supply channels for food and raw materials. Our modern, technological society requires at least hundreds of millions and probably billions of people. Jared Diamond argued that one of the critical factors spurring the development of civilization in Europe was the relatively large size of the interacting population across Europe and Asia. In the Americas, on the other hand, the populations were isolated from each other by physical barriers, were therefore effectively very small, and were functioning as many small isolated continents. The development of certain aspects of civilization, like technology, was therefore not as fast as in Europe (Carneiro 1967:234; Diamond 1997:262–263; Simmel 1950:174).

ORDER, CHAOS, AND BIFURCATIONS

Systems that are able to escape the type of static order governing equilibrium must be far from equilibrium or stability. At or near equilibrium, instabilities tend to be damped and the system returns to stability. A small fluctuation is born and dies. Far from equilibrium, however, fluctuations can attain major importance, and relatively minor fluctuations can have catastrophic effects on the system. This is the state of criticality. At this point, random chance enters the picture.

If we draw a picture depicting the pathway of the evolution followed, we would see, in figure 7, that as the system reaches an instability, it is presented with a choice or bifurcation. It can proceed down any of two or more paths. The examples of bifurcations shown in figures 7, 8, and 9 indicate two paths leading beyond a bifurcation point. In reality, though, there could be multiple paths along which a system could evolve.

The system follows either one path or another, allowing the amplification of some small, random fluctuation to occur and to carry the system off to one of the possible, new branches of solution. These bifurcation points, these moments of crisis, are regions of instability and chaos. The choice that will be made and the exact path that will be taken cannot be predicted. Crossing a bifurcation point is a stochastic or random and unpredictable process. Nor is there necessarily a right answer. The total system evolution could occur through many different paths and structures. In this *pattern* of development, there is deep unity among widely diverse physical, biologic, and social systems. The passage toward greater complexity, then, is intimately related to the bifurcation of new branches of solutions following the instability of the original state (Nicolis and Prigogine 1989:73; Prigogine and Allen 1982:9; Prigogine and Stenger 1984:177).

The periods of crisis and chaos allow individuals to play major roles in influencing the choices made and the outcomes achieved, roles that aren't even contemplated in other theories. In the New Archeology, according to Bruce Trigger, it was maintained that intentional acts of individuals were not the causal force standing behind history. In the self-organization of human society, however, an individual or a group of individuals can be the source of the fluctuation which spreads throughout the system and leads the organism along a particular path of evolution. In self-organization, therefore, individuals or groups can play very important roles (Trigger 1989a:58).

In looking at the periods of stability and chaos, however, we should remember Leslie White's caution that we not confuse history and evolution. History, he wrote, has been mistaken in the past for evolution and evolution for history. But history occurs during the periods of stability and evolution occurs during the chaos of bifurcation points (Leslie White 1960:viii).

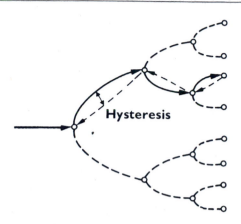

BIFURCATION PATHWAY

Figure 7. An evolutionary pathway showing bifurcation points. The dashed lines represent deterministic processes while the circles represent points of chaos and choice. The solid line represents one path through the possibilities. Although bifurcations are usually depicted as choices between two alternatives, multiple alternatives may be possible. Hysteresis occurs when a collapsing system does not follow the same trajectory on the way down that it did on the way up. Rather, it retains characteristics of the higher level as it collapses to a lower level (adapted from Jantsch 1980:49).

Furthermore, in some cases, especially in living and social organisms, the succession of bifurcations forms an irreversible evolution. Thus historicity is critical in determining the final outcome of the system. An omnipresent observer might be able to see an entire range of final outcomes, only a few of which will be accessible by the system under investigation because of the prior path of evolution. A system in crisis, however, can rarely see beyond the turbulence of the moment (Prigogine and Stengers 1984; Salthe 1985:97–98).

Sanders and Price have observed, however, that convergence after divergence is not only possible, but, given certain specified conditions, is extremely probable. Within the context of cultural-ecological systems with similar characteristics, some adaptations will be more likely to occur than others. Thus, systems which seemed to be evolving differently at lower levels may be seen to come back together again as the complexity increases and as they attempt to respond to similar organizational challenges (Sanders and Price 1968:223, 228).

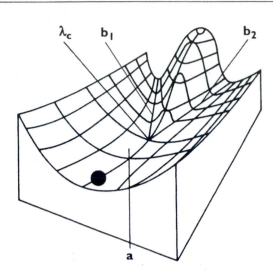

THREE DIMENSIONAL BIFURCATION

Figure 8. A three dimensional mechanical illustration of bifurcation. A ball moves along a valley a until it reaches a branching
point λ_c, where it must follow either valley b_1 or b_2. Nicolis and
Prigogine have speculated that a group of our ancestors, about
to settle on either an ideographic or symbolic mode of writing,
reached such a bifurcation point (adapted from Nicolis and
Prigogine 1989:73).

Bifurcations are the points of maximum entropy production. During
the transition, the system doesn't seem to spare any expense for the creative building of a new structure, as long as the energy is available. This
leads to what Prigogine calls order through fluctuations. A fluctuation or
crisis occurs, spreads through the system, and organizes a new order
(Jantsch 1980:50; Prigogine and Stengers 1984:178).

Progress along an evolutionary path, then, is characterized by periods
of stability in which deterministic processes produce predictable results
which can be modeled, interrupted by periods of chaos in which the choices to be made are determined by chance and cannot be described in advance. Complex, multifactorial models and system analyses, therefore, can
be very useful for depicting the periods of instability. The sources of instability or crisis, on the other hand, can be internal to the system or can be
the result of external shocks. In this work, of course, I propose that Maya
civilization suffered massive external shocks, brutal droughts. Bifurcation
theory thus synthesizes the roles of internal multifactorial models and ex-

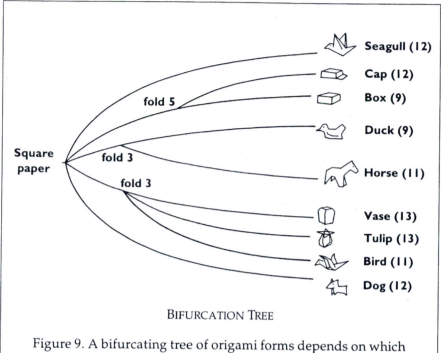

BIFURCATION TREE

Figure 9. A bifurcating tree of origami forms depends on which folds are made at each bifurcation point. Note the role that historicity plays in the origami forms. Because of the prior folds made, a dog cannot become a duck (adapted from Allen 1985:11).

ternal catastrophic shocks and shows how both can contribute to the growth of a complex system like a civilization.

Francis Fukuyama's analysis of the diverging paths of social development between England and France illustrates how bifurcation can be seen in human social evolution:

In the sixteenth and seventeenth centuries, England and France experienced a series of wars between the monarchy and the various nobles, independent cities, and ecclesiastical authorities among which sovereignty was divided at the time. In England, the monarchy lost the struggle and was ultimately forced to accept a series of constitutional constraints on its power that in time became the foundations for modern parliamentary democracy. In France, the monarchy won and began a long-term process of centralizing authority around the absolute power of the state. There is no deep historical reason I know of why the monarchy should have lost in England and won in France; one could easily have imagined the opposite outcome. But the fact that it happened as it did had profound consequences for the political culture of both countries subsequently. The centralization of political authority in France undermined the autonomy of voluntary associations and made the French more dependent on centralized authority in later generations, whether that authority was monarchical or republican. In England by contrast, society became far more self-organizing because people were not dependent on centralized authority to adjudicate their differences, a habit that was carried over by English settlers to the New World (Fukuyama 1995:39).

A Poet's View of Bifurcation

I have tried to describe the processes of stability, bifurcation, and historicity in describing the evolution of societies and civilizations with language as literate as I could muster. As humans we all reach bifurcation points in our own lives as well, and no one has described the process of bifurcation as elegantly as Robert Frost did in 1916:

The Road Not Taken

Two roads diverged in a yellow wood,
And sorry I could not travel both
And be one traveller, long I stood
And looked down one as far as I could
To where it bent in the undergrowth;

Then took the other, as just as fair,
And having perhaps the better claim,
Because it was grassy and wanted wear;
Though as for that the passing there
Had worn them really about the same,

And both that morning equally lay
In leaves no step had trodden black.
Oh, I kept the first for another day!
Yet knowing how way leads on to way,
I doubted if I should ever come back.

I shall be telling this with a sigh
Somewhere ages and ages hence:
Two roads diverged in a wood, and I—
I took the one less travelled by,
And that has made all the difference. (Frost 1916)

STABILITY

The processes at work during periods of stability are more deterministic in nature and their description can be quite useful in explaining those processes. To take one example, system analyses of Maya culture, analyses of internal processes, have been developed by archaeologists. An excellent example is shown in figure 10 describing the relationship between food and monument construction. The difficulty with a system analysis as a complete description of cultural dynamics, however, is that it is a static model and not a dynamic one. The internal relationships of the model do not change. There is no provision for external shocks or for chance occurrences of any kind, and there is no role for an individual. It is essentially self-contained and operates on itself. Nor does the model permit specific, unique individuals to play a role in the ongoing evolution of a society. As can be seen, roles are assigned only to groups or classes of individuals, but never to a great leader.

FLUCTUATION OF THE ECOLOGY

When examining an ecosystem made up of interacting entities which are themselves complex organized systems, we are faced with the fluctuation of the ecological entity itself. Its form may not be completely stable. Following some internal or external event, a new type of entity may evolve, with different behavioral or structural characteristics. We have to worry, then, not only about the fluctuation of the human society, but about the fluctuation of the environment itself. A changed environment, like a period of unusual aridity, could have devastating consequences on its constituent components (Prigogine and Allen 1982:28).

EQUILIBRIUM SHIFTS

When it comes to self-organization in ecosystems, there is a new consideration: innovation. As geographer Karl Butzer has noted, complex cultures frequently respond to novel inputs by relatively sudden equilibrium shifts, leading to fundamental sociopolitical transformations, with or without a change of adaptive strategy. It appears that the trajectories of high civilizations over time have tended to resemble a pattern marked by thresholds at which negative or positive shifts of equilibrium levels have taken place, as illustrated in figure 11 (Butzer 1980:517).

Examples of Butzer's concept are available from Mesoamerica. In the Mexican Highlands, episodes of population surge were associated with developments in agricultural technology: floodwater and diversion flow control in the Terminal Formative, canal irrigation in the Classic, and drainage or chinampa agriculture in the Aztec periods. As we will see in the Maya Lowlands, the increasing sophistication in water management technology appears to have permitted population booms during the Preclassic and Classic periods (Butzer 1980:518; Santley 1990:328; Scarborough 1994:186–187, 197–198).

COMPLEXITY

We have seen what constitutes self-organization and dissipative structures, but what is complexity? The field of complexity theory is itself in the process of emerging. It is not surprising, then, that there is as yet not a clear definition of the term. Grégoire Nicolis and Ilya Prigogine urge that we should not be speaking of complex systems and structures, but of complex behaviors. They are technically correct. We have already seen, in discussing dissipative structures, that they are, in reality, processes. The terms *structure* and *system* are so widely used, however, that it is next to impossible to avoid them (Nicolis and Prigogine 1989:8).

There is a difference between complex and merely complicated. According to Mitchell Waldrop, computer chips and snowflakes are merely complicated. Complex systems are more spontaneous, disorderly, and more alive. They exist at the edge of chaos, the constantly shifting battle zone between stagnation and anarchy, the one place where a complex system can be spontaneous, adaptive, and alive. Nicolis and Prigogine add that, in complex systems, the individual agents are interacting with each other. In contrast, a cloud of gas molecules contains billions of individual molecules, but they are all moving randomly, not interacting (Nicolis and Prigogine 1989:6; Waldrop 1992:12).

In fact, the basic laws underlying complicated systems in both physics and biology are quite simple. The complexity arises from the simultaneous interaction of many simple components. The complexity lies in the organization, the myriad possible ways the components of the system can interact. Living systems—organisms, communities, coevolving ecosystems—are the paramount examples of organized complexity (Kauffman 1993:173; Wolfram quoted in Waldrop 1992:86).

Physicist and Nobel laureate Murray Gell-Mann has suggested that no single concept of complexity can adequately capture our intuitive notions of what the word ought to mean and that several different kinds of complexity may need to be defined. Is computational complexity, for example, the same as ecological complexity (Gell-Mann 1994:28)?

MAYA FOOD/MONUMENT ALLOCATION

Figure 10. (*Opposite*) Flow diagram of food/monument allocation in the Maya Lowlands during the Terminal Classic (adapted from Hosler, Sabloff, and Runge 1977:575).

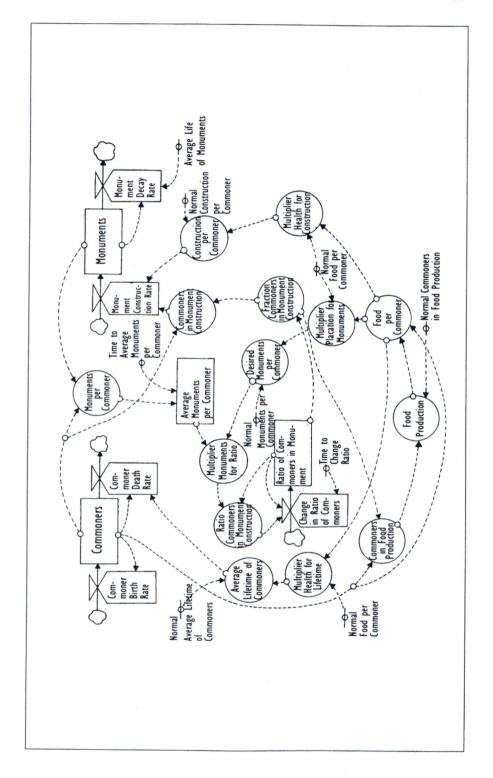

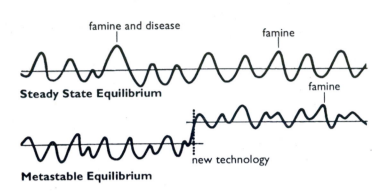

EQUILIBRIUM SHIFT

Figure 11. One common type of equilibrium is steady state (*upper*), in which recurrent famine and epidemic disease lead to repeated population fluctuations without long-term directional change. In more complex societies, new adaptive strategies allow one or more jumps in equilibrium level (*lower*), and subsequent demographic oscillations may be of smaller amplitude. Examples from the Maya Lowlands would include the adoption of intensive maize agriculture or the development of water reservoir technology. Negative or environmental inputs can also have a reverse impact (adapted from Butzer 1980:518).

He believes at least one way of defining the complexity of a system is to make use of the length of its description. But what if a description is unnecessarily long because words are being wasted by a verbose describer? One type of complexity can be called *crude complexity,* defined as the length of the shortest message that will describe a system at a given level of coarse graining, to someone at a distance, employing language, knowledge, and understanding that both parties share beforehand (Gell-Mann 1994:34).

Physicists use the term *coarse graining* to signify the level of detail to which the system is described, with finer details being ignored. A description of an army may include descriptions of the high command, the regiments, and the battalions but ignore the companies, platoons, squads, and individual soldiers. The concept is probably inspired by images of grainy photographs (Gell-Mann 1994:29).

Gell-Mann believes, however, that the most helpful concept is one he terms *effective complexity.* In general, the most useful characteristics of a system to describe are its regularities. Knowing the infinite myriad of random details in a system is not as useful as understanding its regularities at a certain level of coarse graining. Crude complexity fails to correspond to what we usually understand by complexity because it refers to the length of a complete description, including all the random details, rather than just the regularities. Effective complexity, then, is related to the description of the regularities of a system (Gell-Mann 1994:50).

HIERARCHICAL ORGANIZATION

The growth of organization in nature is the result of the interplay between hierarchy and heterarchy, fueled by a consistent flow of energy, as we will see below.

In a hierarchical, complex system, components of lower or inner levels of organization are combined into higher levels. In nature, for example, subatomic particles are organized into atoms, atoms into molecules, molecules into amino acids and proteins, proteins into cells, cells into animals including humans, humans into families, bands, tribes, nations, and civilizations.

Each lower level of organization retains its own autonomy of action. In a human body for example, cells carry out the process of metabolism quite independently of instructions from the brain. Similarly, within large societies, families procreate and nurture their young without specific instruction from government.

Herbert Simon has suggested that in the actual world the only kinds of complex systems possible are hierarchical. "Among possible complex forms hierarchies are the only ones that have time to evolve." Hierarchies are evolutionarily advantageous because they are built up by stages which are themselves stable. A disruption at any particular level will not necessarily disrupt the lower levels. The system will not need to start from the beginning to rebuild. The rebuilding process will start from the level of the highest remaining stable component. In biological and cultural evolution, where large-scale disruptions have repeatedly occurred, hierarchically organized systems can rebuild comparatively quickly. Hierarchical organization provides a way of making complexity manageable (Simon quoted in Salthe 1985:46).

There is a danger, however, to the ever increasing complexity of higher levels of organization. Evolution to higher and higher organizational levels involves a gamble: the exchange of the kind of stability typical of the simplest forms is surrendered, and its absence is compensated for by greater dynamism and autonomy—but at the risk of the mortality of the individual and the risk of the sudden destabilization and ultimate extinction for the species. The fossil record testifies to the poor odds in this gamble: more than 96 percent of the biological species that at one time populated this planet have ultimately disappeared (Laszlo 1987:83, 127).

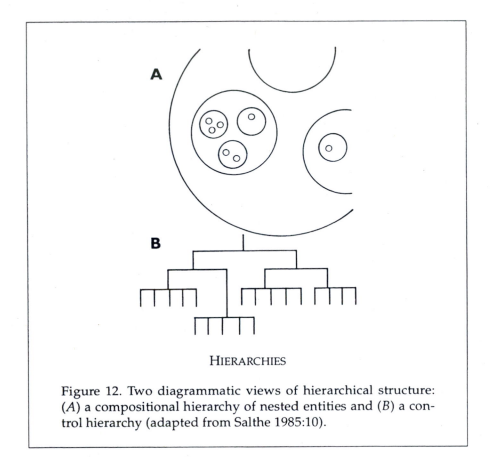

HIERARCHIES

Figure 12. Two diagrammatic views of hierarchical structure: (A) a compositional hierarchy of nested entities and (B) a control hierarchy (adapted from Salthe 1985:10).

EMERGENCE

It is extremely important to recognize that one cannot predict the characteristics of the next level by knowing those of the lower level. In far from equilibrium structures, the characteristics of a particular level are a property of the collectivity and cannot be inferred from a study of its individual elements in isolation. Reductionism, then, long a strongly criticized attitude in the social sciences, is found to be inadequate even in the physical sciences in predicting the characteristics of higher levels of organization (Prigogine and Allen 1982:7).

Knowing the nature of molecules, for example, does not allow us to predict the self-replicating nature of DNA. The nature of unicellular life does not permit us to predict the nature of mammals. Each new level develops entirely new and unexpected characteristics. This process is known as emergence. (See Durkheim 1895:69–71 for an early discussion of emergent properties.) By the same token, as it is not possible to predict emergent properties from the characteristics of their components, neither is it possible to understand higher levels by analyzing the lower level components. Reductionism, while useful in understanding the underlying constituents and how they work, is not a method of understanding higher levels.

Whatever analysis of the emergent properties is made, however, must take into account the fact that the lower levels of organization continue to exist and operate autonomously within the higher level. A full understanding of human reproduction, for example, requires a knowledge of atoms and molecules. But a knowledge of atoms and molecules, in and of itself, will not predict the remarkable qualities of DNA and how it works to guide the development of human beings.

Complex behavior need not have complex roots. In very complicated systems in physics or biology, the basic components and the basic laws are quite simple. Tremendously interesting and beguilingly complex behavior can emerge from collections of extremely simple components. The complexity arises because a great many simple components are interacting simultaneously. Complexity deals with systems that have many, many agents. At each level, new emergent structures form and engage in new emergent behavior. Complexity, in other words, is really a science of emergence (Langton and Wolfram quoted in Waldrop 1992:86, 88, 279).

CONTROL VERSUS EMERGENCE

Artificial life researchers using computer simulations have found that top down control systems, with rules telling each agent precisely what to do in every situation, are impossibly cumbersome and complicated. Since it is effectively impossible to cover every conceivable situation, top down systems are continually running into combinations of events they don't know how to handle. They tend to be touchy and fragile. All too often, they grind to a halt in a gridlock of indecision (Waldrop 1992:279–281).

A similar form of social pathology has been proposed by Kent Flannery, who used R. A. Rappaport's term, *hypercoherence*. Flannery cautioned that although archaeologists have typically applauded settlement patterns which show "a high degree of integration," they may be reporting a case of hyperintegration or hypercoherence, which he defined as a highly centralized but sometimes unstable condition resulting from the breakdown of whatever autonomy the various small subsystems in a larger system may have. "Enough centralization, promotion, and linearization may move the state toward hypercoherence and instability. Finally, hypercoherence can lead to collapse and devolution" (Flannery 1972:420, 423).

The way to achieve lifelike behavior in computer simulations is to simulate populations of simple units, instead of one big complex unit, and let the behavior emerge from the bottom up. As Los Alamos physicist Doyne Farmer explained, "Evolution thrives in systems with bottom up organization, which gives rise to flexibility. But at the same time, evolution has to channel the bottom up approach in a way that doesn't destroy the organization. There has to be hierarchy of control—with information flowing from the bottom up as well as the top down" (Farmer quoted in Waldrop 1992:294).

The role of higher levels, then, should be to set norms, standards, and even desired outcomes—and to make sure they are observed and accomplished. The lower levels, however, should be allowed the autonomy to achieve those standards and goals on their own.

HETERARCHY

If hierarchies can be visualized as growing vertically, then heterarchies spread horizontally. They represent the network of relationships among elements in a particular level. Hierarchies are characterized by the asymmetrical, one-way nature of their relationships. The relationship between a general and a soldier, for example, is asymmetrical. Heterarchies, on the other hand, consist of reciprocal, two-way relationships carried out among equals.

To pursue the geometrical metaphor a little further, we have defined two dimensions of social organization, vertical and horizontal, hierarchies and heterarchies. The third dimension, which is analogous to depth, is critical concentration or population size. The self-organization of complex societies, therefore, requires horizontal heterarchical relationships to organize vertical hierarchical levels, with the level of complexity achieved depending on the depth or size of the population, all fueled by a consistent flow of energy through the system.

The organization of hierarchies does not occur by itself. It depends on the functioning of heterarchies. Heterarchies can exist within hierarchies, but the reverse is true as well: hierarchies can exist within heterarchies. For self-organizing systems, the constituent elements must interact with each other in heterarchical relationships before another level can be self-organized.

DEFINING HETERARCHY

The term *heterarchy* was first used in its modern sense by Warren McCulloch, a medical doctor, an early cyberneticist, and a student of the brain and mind, in an article he wrote in 1945 describing conduction between one parallel neural circuit and another and the representation of values by the brain. His study is written in the language of topology. Unfortunately, McCulloch did not formally define the term. Most writers who use the term, therefore, provide their own definition. The result has been varying concepts of heterarchy and differing definitions. It would be worthwhile to return to McCulloch's writings to try to rebuild a definition of the term from its origins.

According to McCulloch, we commonly suppose that ends or goals can be arranged in a hierarchy of values increasing, as he put it, *"ab infimo malo ad summum bonum*," from the lowest bad to the highest good. The values or ends in a hierarchy are ordered by the right of each to inhibit all inferiors. The order is such that some end, the highest, is preferred to all others and another, the lowest, is always preferred least. Thus in a situation in which A dominates B and B dominates C, A will also dominate C, and a clear hierarchy is established (McCulloch 1945:92; 1956:196).

But what about the situation where A dominates B, B dominates C, and C dominates A? There is no clear *summum bonum*, or highest good, and no clear hierarchy. The elements in this grouping of values alternately dominate each other and this is the situation which McCulloch called a heterarchy (McCulloch 1946:256–257).

He described it as the consequence of the interconnection of elements in a net. Thus, the term has gained considerable popularity in the world of cybernetics where it is defined as a form of organization resembling a network or fishnet. The Internet, for example, is often described as a heterarchy (Principia Cybernetica Web 1999).

McCulloch provided an illustration from real life to explain his idea. In animal behavior studies, a hundred male rats, deprived of food and sex for a specified period of time, will all prefer food to sex, sex to avoidance of shock, and avoidance of shock to food, in other words, A to B, B to C, and C to A. In another example, McCulloch found in his own studies of experimental aesthetics, when examining paired comparisons of three rectangles divided into 2, 3, and 5 equal smaller rectangles, people preferred the division into 2 over 3, 3 over 5, and 5 over 2. In both of these situations there is no *summum bonum* (McCulloch 1956:196).

The term *heterarchy*, as used by McCulloch, consists of lateral relationships among elements in which no single element dominates all others and no single element is dominated by all others. The elements take turns dominating each other.

The definition of a heterarchy, then, based on McCulloch's use of the term, would be a set of elements participating in a network of relationships in which no single element dominates all others, even though one element may consistently dominate another and may, in turn, be consistently dominated by yet another. Further, the elements behave autonomously in their interactions. McCulloch's use of the term will inform the discussion in this book.

EXAMPLES OF HETERARCHY

Let's turn our attention to the human realm. A prototypical example of a heterarchy among modern humans consists of the customers of a telephone company. They are linked together in a network through which they interact with one another. At times one particular customer initiates telephone calls, at other times he or she receives calls. Most importantly, there is no higher level of authority which is controlling the customers in their interactions with one another. The customers connect and disconnect autonomously.

Douglas Hofstadter proposed a further example of heterarchy in his Pulitzer Prize winning book, *Gödel, Escher, Bach*. Take a hypothetical, hierarchically organized computer program which is comprised of lines of code which are organized into subroutines which are organized into routines which comprise the program. If the routines were able to call each other without going through a higher level of control, they would be elements in a heterarchy within the hierarchical structure of the overall program. Each would alternately use the other as a subroutine. There would be a degree of rerankability among the routines as one after another performed the role of controller, calling other routines, and then being in turn called by other routines. The relationship between them, then, would be flexible and shifting (Hofstadter 1979:133–134; Minsky and Papert 1972:20).

HETERARCHY IN ARCHAEOLOGY

Heterarchy was introduced into archaeology by Carole Crumley who defined it as a complex system in which elements have "the potential of being unranked (relative to other elements) or ranked in a number of ways, depending on systemic requirements." As she quite rightly points out, complex systems—human, environmental, or mechanical—are characterized as much by their relations as by their structure (Crumley 1979:144; 1994a:12; 1994b:183).

Since Crumley introduced the term, archaeologists have been trying to come to grips with the concept and have used it with differing meanings. At the 92nd Annual Meeting of the American Anthropological Association in 1993, a symposium was held wholly dedicated to heterarchy. The participants used the term heterarchy in the following ways:

1. an array of independent, homogeneous elements;
2. the membership of elements in many different unranked interaction systems with participation in each system determined by the needs of each element;
3. the membership of elements in many diverse systems of ranking where the same element occupies a different rank in different systems;
4. the existence of two or more functionally discrete but unranked systems that interact as equals;
5. the existence of two or more discrete hierarchies that interact as equals; and
6. a flexible hierarchy and horizontal or lateral differentiation (Brumfiel 1995:126; Joyce White 1995:104).

Let's try, then, to clarify the meaning of the term, relying on McCulloch's definition and its usefulness for archaeologists. A heterarchy, in particular, is characterized by the interaction between its elements. It is, as McCulloch emphasized, a network of relationships. A mere collection of non-interacting elements cannot constitute a heterarchy, nor, for that matter, organize a higher level of hierarchy.

The growth of hierarchical self-organization could not occur without heterarchies. Through the heterarchical relationships among elements at the top level of a hierarchy, a nucleation event occurs and spreads throughout the heterarchy organizing the elements into a new level of hierarchy. In the same fashion, the continued existence of a self-organized hierarchy requires the autonomous functioning of the constituent elements at each level, in heterarchical relationships, in order to maintain the next higher level of organization. Self-organization, then, depends on the interplay between heterarchy and hierarchy, the interplay between coordination and subordination, all fueled by a consistent flow of energy through the system. Neither hierarchies nor heterarchies are static entities. Both are constantly evolving within themselves and both are coevolving together (Goertzel 1998:11). (See table 1 on page 64.)

This concept is similar to one proposed by Richard Blanton, Stephen Kowalewski, Gary Feinman, and Jill Appel in *Ancient Mesoamerica*. According to them, the hallmark of complexity is the functional differentiation among societal units, which can be decomposed into vertical differentiation and horizontal differentiation. Vertical differentiation, of course, corresponds to hierarchical levels of control and horizontal differentiation, which they define as functional specialization among parts of equivalent rank in a system, to heterarchical relationships (Blanton et al 1981:21-22).

Elements in hierarchies, therefore, can be elements in heterarchies and vice versa. By the same token, heterarchies can exist within hierarchies, and hierarchies can exist within heterarchies. Heterarchies at times subsume hierarchies, and at times hierarchies subsume heterarchies, depending on the perspective of the analysis. The city states of the Maya Lowlands were hierarchical, structured organizations which formed a heterarchy in their relations among themselves, that is, independent hierarchically or vertically organized states which interacted heterarchically, or laterally, with one another through warfare, trade, marriage, and other relations.

Crumley and William Marquardt have emphasized the organizational role of heterarchies:

> Heterarchy has been introduced as a more general term to be used in conjunction with hierarchy in the analysis of organizational structures. This is not to imply that hierarchies do not exist, for indeed they abound; but we caution against viewing any society as having a single dominant or nested hierarchy, rather than crosscurrents of interests and allegiances at a number of scales, with in-

dividuals interacting in some more fully than in others. Insofar as is possible, a collective assessment of individual rank in various activities must be used to discover social networks, offering a means of identifying and studying social relations.

The commonly held assumption of hierarchichal structure can seriously affect one's understanding of history. If hierarchy stands as the only representative of order and organization in so-called complex societies, then collapse of a hierarchy must inevitably be seen as a reversal or setback on the road to increasing complexity, and the perceived lack of structure (lack of hierarchy) be assumed to indicate chaos. We object to this way of thinking. Instead, we argue that the structure in question (secular administrative, commercial, etc.) must be explicitly identified, along with the extent of its organizational connectivity with other aspects of the society. If our definition of *effective scale* is accepted, then hierarchy and heterarchy are simply patterns of relations to be recognized at certain (necessarily explicit) scales....

Put simply, the ranking of priorities by an ostensibly authoritative decision-maker is not itself sufficient to result in hierarchization. What is hierarchically organized at one scale can be heterarchically organized at another, and this is true both spatially and temporally. (Crumley and Marquardt 1987:613–615)

An implication of these dynamics is that control and regulatory mechanisms can be dispersed rather than centralized and contextual rather than structural. In business management theory, for example, new heterarchical concepts of management are gaining popularity in which managerial capabilities, responsibility, and decision making are dispersed throughout the organization, rather than concentrated at the top; lateral relationships between subsidiaries are encouraged; and activities are coordinated along multiple dimensions, typically geography, product, and function (Birkinshaw and Morrison 1995:737; Joyce White 1995:117).

In Stanley Salthe's conception of hierarchies, the elements of lower levels could interact with homologous elements in another hierarchy only through the interaction of the entire hierarchy. Thus, soldiers in opposing armies interacted only if the armies clashed. It would appear, however, that heterarchical relationships can be formed by homologous elements in separate hierarchies. Thus, some hydrogen atoms bound in molecules can still form bonds with other electronegative atoms in other molecules through hydrogen bonding. Individual cities within states within nations can form sister-city relationships with cities in foreign countries. Cities in neighboring nations can have extensive trade relationships without the active participation of higher levels of hierarchy. In Mesoamerica, for example, the pochteca class of traders and merchants regularly interacted with their homologs in other states.

Although the essential organizational structure of the universe is hierarchical, from quarks to humans to galaxies, it is heterarchies which organize the universe and, therefore, enable it to function. Yet that organization requires the interplay of hierarchies and heterarchies. Heterarchies allow new levels of hierarchy to evolve which create new heterarchies which allow new levels of hierarchy to emerge and so on, as the interplay between vertical and horizontal defines the organization space.

In the Maya Lowlands, Daniel Potter and Eleanor King have applied the concept of heterarchy to the Classic Maya. They believe the use of a heterarchical approach allows them to uncover the distinctive workings of two cultural subsystems: one self-organized and economic and the other politico-ritual and centrally administered. For them, the Maya economy had both elements of hierarchy and heterarchy. Utilitarian goods were traded and exchanged laterally through trading networks, and there appears to have been no central control of these trading activities. In contrast, luxury items were used and exchanged primarily by the elite. Thus they traded vertically within an economy, from the artisans to the elite, and laterally or heterarchically between elite peers in different polities. Although the items of exchange undoubtedly possessed great intrinsic value, the route of exchange itself was of equal or greater value (Potter and King 1995:29).

MISCONCEPTIONS OF HETERARCHY

Some archaeologists try to define a heterarchy-hierarchy continuum as though heterarchies were at one end and hierarchies at the other. They then try to class societies as either heterarchies or hierarchies and use the term *heterarchy* to mean an egalitarian society and the term *hierarchy* to mean a more structured, complex society. Thus, some Southwestern cultures in the United States are called heterarchies while the Aztec polity is called a hierarchy. (See Rautman 1998 for a discussion of this tendency in Southwestern archaeology.)

The concepts, however, are complementary rather than polar. Any human organization worthy of the name society is hierarchical in its structure, and its elements participate in heterarchical relations. All human societies, therefore, exhibit organizational characteristics of both hierarchies and heterarchies.

Let's look at one example of an egalitarian society: the Fayu of New Guinea, a society made up of about four hundred hunter-gatherers. They normally live as single families scattered through a remote, swamp filled basin many miles apart from one another. They come together only once or twice a year to negotiate the exchange of brides in gatherings of a few dozen people. Yet within Fayu society, they are divided into four clans, which in turn are divided into families. Even within such a tiny society, they recognize a hierarchical structure and are held together by heterarchical relations (Diamond 1997:265–266).

HUMAN HIERARCHIES

It is important to understand how human societies build up complex hierarchical states and how those states ultimately collapse if we are to understand the dynamics of the Maya Collapse. In order to do so, we need to focus on hierarchies. In 1959, Leslie White proposed a hierarchical theory of human social organization which he called *segmentation*. White's concept of segmentation parallels the principles of emerging self-organization.

> A segment is, in fact, a mechanism of integration; a segment is a part, and *part* implies a *whole*. Segmentation, as a process, is a means of increasing the size of systems while preserving at the same time a high degree of inner cohesion or solidarity....It makes possible an increase in size; no system, physical, biological, or social, can increase its size beyond a certain point without resort to segmentation. By means of the segmentive process any type of system may be enlarged, for not only is an increase made possible by the integration of one class of segments on one level, but the segments of one level may become integrated into units that constitute segments of a higher level of organization, and so on indefinitely. But at the same time that the process of segmentation operates to increase the size of the system, it functions to maintain its inner cohesion or solidarity. (Leslie White 1959:145)

Elman Service proposed a hierarchy of social systems for human beings in which lower levels act as segments of higher levels. In human societies, the size of the regional population is the single strongest predictor of the level of social organization, although not a perfect one. Building on his ideas, I have outlined the hierarchical organization sequence presented below. Of course, six categories are insufficient to describe all the world's so-

---

HIERARCHICAL VERSUS HETERARCHICAL DYNAMICS

Table 1. (*Opposite*) An awareness of heterarchy opens new avenues of social analysis. Joyce White proposed differing characteristics of social organization in hierarchies and heterarchies (adapted from Joyce White 1995:118).

HIERARCHY	CHARACTERISTICS	HETERARCHY
Rigid proscribed rules; strong sanctions against violation	**Rules of behavior**	Flexible, preferred rules; social ties not permanently broken if rules are violated
Marked gender stratification and role definition; male dominance	**Gender relations**	Women have realms of or access to economic and/or political power; role flexibility
Controlled, centralized	**Economy**	Multimodal, self-organizing, market based, commercial
Ascribed, hereditary, or rigid class system; vertically differentiated	**Social status**	Flexible, includes personal "achievement," multiple avenues to status enhancement, horizontally differentiated
Violence focused; control oriented; imposed solutions	**Conflict resolution**	Peace focused; cooperation or alliance oriented; negotiated solutions
Global; cultural imperialism seeks to reduce or eliminate intergroup differences	**Social ideology**	Localized, pluralistic, horizontally differentiated; ethnic differences accepted and/or functionally integrated
Autocratic, authoritarian	**Political relationship of leaders and followers**	Consensus oriented; democratic, in the literal sense, or in the sense that it is economically and socially viable for individuals and/or groups to "vote with their feet," centripetal, attracting
Linear, progressive, steady state	**Temporal dynamics**	Oscillating, cyclical, pulsating

cieties, but they give us an idea of progressive complexity. Starting with estimates made by William Sanders and Barbara Price and by Jared Diamond of approximate population sizes for each hierarchical level, I indicate a range of sizes for each level.

Spectra, of course, are continuous while categories are discontinuous. The population ranges listed below are meant to give a relative idea of where along the population spectrum these types of social organizations occur. They should be viewed through a prism of fuzzy logic, a system of thinking devised by Berkeley's Lofti Zadeh which recognizes that reality is made up of spectra of gray rather than sharply defined black and white categories.

Societies occur which maintain lower levels of organization at much larger populations and others which adopt higher levels with smaller populations. There is no clear break between one level and the next. Rather, there is a continuum of organizational characteristics that start with small numbers and grow into huge numbers in which the lower levels organize and then are incorporated into the higher levels.

1. *Nuclear families*. The fundamental social grouping of human beings.
2. *Bands* (30 to 100 people). Family bonds of kinship and marriage by their nature can integrate only the relatively small and simple societies that we call bands. Their settlement pattern is generally nomadic and decision making is egalitarian. Conflict resolution is informal.
3. *Tribes* (100–2,000). Tribes can integrate several bands into one. The problems of social order are resolved in terms of etiquette, normative ideology, and customs. In rare circumstances, family authority may be called on, but there is very little occasion for the political use of force. The settlement pattern is normally fixed in one village, relationships are through kin-based clans, and decision making is egalitarian or big-man.
4. *Chiefdoms* (2,000–10,000). Specialization, redistribution, and the related centralization of authority integrate still more complex societies. Chiefdoms have centralized direction, hereditary, aristocratic hierarchical status arrangements, but no formal, legal apparatus of forceful repression. Their organization seems to be universally theocratic. Chiefdoms have been reported from Polynesia with populations of 30,000. Settlement patterns are fixed with one or more villages and may include a paramount village, relationships are based on class and residence, conflict resolution is centralized, and decision making is centralized and hereditary. Bureaucracy and elaborate public architecture first appear.
5. *States* (10,000+). A bureaucracy employing legal force can further integrate a state. Civil law and formal government are distinguished by the fact that they are institutionalized, enacted, and official, and they employ, threaten, or imply the actual use of force. Although Diamond would put the threshold for states at 50,000 people, Sanders

and Price believe statelike characteristics have been seen in Mesoamerica for populations as small as 5,000 people. Settlement patterns are fixed in many villages and cities, with one capital city; relationships are based on class and residence; conflicts are resolved by judges applying laws; and decision making is centralized.

6. *Industrial societies.* They are integrated not only by a state apparatus, but also by a complex network of specialized, interdependent occupations (Diamond 1997:268–269; 274, 284; Kosko 1993; Sanders and Price 1968:41, 81–82, 207; Service 1962:181; 1975:14–16).

Society evolves through convergence to progressively higher organization levels. As the flows of people, information, energy, and goods intensify, they transcend the formal boundaries of the social system. Thus, neighboring tribes and villages converge into ethnic communities or integrated states, these in turn become colonies, departments, provinces, states, cantons, or regions of larger empires and ultimately of nation states. In today's world, this process is leading to the creation of various regional and functional economic and political communities and blocs among developed as well as developing nations (Laszlo 1987:88–91).

In his widely acclaimed book, *Trust,* Francis Fukuyama, one of today's most insightful social analysts, described the role of hierarchies in modern industrial states:

> When the information age's most enthusiastic apostles celebrate the breakdown of hierarchy and authority, they neglect one critical factor: trust, and the shared ethical norms that underlie it. Communities depend on mutual trust and will not arise spontaneously without it. Hierarchies are necessary because not all people within a community can be relied upon to live by tacit ethical rules alone. A small number may be actively asocial, seeking to undermine or exploit the group through fraud or simple mischievousness. A much larger number will tend to be free riders, willing to benefit from membership in the group while contributing as little as possible to the common cause. Hierarchies are necessary because all people cannot be trusted at all times to live by internalized ethical rules and do their fair share. They must ultimately be coerced by explicit rules and sanctions in the event they do not live up to them. This is true in the economy as well as in society more broadly.... (Fukuyama 1995:25)

MAYA ORGANIZATION

Complex society appears to have emerged in the Basin of Mexico and in the Maya Lowlands by the same time, around 300 BC. The earliest evidence for Maya regional integration may have been the Preclassic city of

El Mirador, which collapsed around AD 150 during the Preclassic Abandonment (Pyburn 1996:237).

After El Mirador's demise, Maya populations began to rebuild, and regional integration increased. Simon Martin and Nikolai Grube have proposed that the Maya lowland states were organized at a macropolitical level during the Classic by a limited number of powerful polities in a hierarchical system. They believe the central area was dominated by two state formations: one led by Tikal, especially during the Early Classic, and the other by Calakmul, especially during the Middle to Late Classic. The picture they see emerging from their epigraphic research is neither a centralized administration of regional states nor a political vacuum populated by weak ones. Instead, a few powerful kingdoms held lesser ones in their sway, a system not unlike others seen throughout Mesoamerica in which dominant states integrate empires through tribute relationships rather than direct administration. In fact, Martin and Grube believe that Calakmul tried to consolidate the whole Maya Lowlands under its sway but overreached. Tikal fought back and frustrated the strategy. According to their scenario, Tikal in turn was unable to consolidate its hold over former Calakmul territory. In the end, the organizational level collapsed to scores of small city-states claiming independence (Appenzeller 1994:734; Martin and Grube 1994:29–30; 1995:46).

The collapse of various regions in the Maya Lowlands seems to follow the principle that the system will collapse to the highest remaining stable component, the highest component that can be supported by the energy flow through the system. The Classic Collapse at Copán, for example, stopped at the level of lineage head. Cobá dropped from state to chiefdom. At Colha, the society apparently dropped to subsistence farming as the city was abandoned, and only rural populations survived. At Tikal, however, the collapse was complete. The society, both urban and rural, disappeared entirely (Folan 1983b; Fry 1969; Tom Hester, 1994, personal communication; Fred Valdez, Jr., 1994, personal communication; Wingard 1996:231).

INTERNAL VERSUS EXTERNAL

Ilya Prigogine, Peter Allen, Ervin Laszlo, Lewis Binford, Richard Newbold Adams, and others have emphasized the importance of external shocks to a system. Some archaeologists have proposed external shocks to explain the collapse of cultures and civilizations and the Maya in particular. Other archaeologists, however, and, in particular many Maya archaeologists, remain adamantly opposed to finding explanations for the disappearance of Maya civilization in anything other than internal processes. In recognition of that tendency, Jeremy Sabloff and Gordon Willey made the following admonition:

Too often, as will be shown below, workers in the Maya area have attempted to explain the collapse in terms of internal processual events alone, a sort of consideration of Maya culture and its environmental setting *in vacuo*. External forces, such as Mexican incursions, were relegated to a secondary role and were used to fill in gaps in the internally focused hypothesis. What we are saying here, in essence, is that in the Maya area processual factors, such as the ecological effects of population increases in a "type X environment," or the long term inviability of a "theocratic state," can be understood only after external historical factors are controlled. (Sabloff and Willey 1967:312)

I think it is important to emphasize, at this point, that the theory of self-organization presented here as the model for human social development does not negate the value of processual hypotheses or system analyses or so many of the other worthwhile concepts that have been advanced to explain particular aspects of Maya culture. Rather, it presents a more robustly encompassing framework which incorporates the other concepts as special cases. Processual explanations and system analyses, for example, can describe the periods of stability between the storms. But they will fail in describing the path taken through times of turmoil and turbulence. These paths are random in nature and are not analyzeable in advance.

SUMMARY AND DISCUSSION

The organization of human societies has much in common with organizational systems throughout nature. It exhibits characteristics of self-organization and dissipative structures, concepts for which physicist Ilya Prigogine won a Nobel Prize in 1977. The fundamental perspective discussed in this chapter is the view of human societies as dissipative structures. In general, dissipative structures exhibit the following characteristics:

- There must be a certain critical mass or critical concentration of organizing units.
- They form in response to the external application or the importation of energy to the system.
- They must be in open interaction with the environment, importing energy and raw materials and exporting reaction products, waste, and entropy.
- They exist far from equilibrium at the edge of chaos.
- Their evolutionary path is a series of alternating regimes of stability and chaos in which chance plays a large role in the ultimate path followed after periods of turmoil.

Complex systems arise from the interaction of many self-organizing constituent components. They exist at the edge of chaos. In biological and social systems, as complexity increases, information processing plays an increasingly important role.

Complex, self-organized systems exhibit hierarchical organization in which the lower level constituents retain their autonomy of action and generate the creative potential for organizing the next higher level. The higher levels provide a regulatory or control function, setting norms and standards and, at times, establishing goals or desired outcomes.

When a group of unorganized constituents organizes itself, totally new properties and characteristics emerge which cannot be predicted from knowledge of the components themselves, a process known as emergence. Relatively simple components can lead to complex properties and behaviors. One can identify hierarchies in the world around us ranging from elementary particles to galaxies.

The elements in one level of a hierarchy engage in a network of reciprocal, two-way relationships known as a heterarchy. The elements of heterarchies operate autonomously, and they can alternately dominate one another. Most importantly, there is no dominant element. The heterarchy, then, is the network of autonomous elements.

Heterarchies exist within hierarchies and hierarchies within heterarchies. It is the self-organization of elements within a heterarchy which allows the next level of hierarchy to emerge. They are complementary concepts which coexist and coevolve.

Complex processes evolve to maximally utilize the energy available to them, thereby organizing greater levels of complexity. The greater levels of complexity require greater levels of energy and raw materials. Complex systems continually organize themselves to states of self-organized criticality thereby maximally exploiting the available energy resources.

The most successful complex processes rely on bottom up responses to environmental change, rather than top down control. Ecosystems, and the biosphere as a whole, are constantly changing. The individual species and organizations are constantly coadapting to each other and to the environment and therefore coevolving. The most successful species and societies are those that optimize the ability to evolve and the ability to use the available energy.

The critical concept for the hypothesis presented in this work is that complex organizations require a constant flow of energy and raw materials to support them. If that flow is cut off or severely restricted, they collapse level by level. As Alfred Lotka and others have pointed out, we should always take in the view of evolution as a whole, of the organism plus its environment, or in contemporary terms, the view of coevolution and coadaptation.

Human organizational systems exhibit the following characteristics:
• Human societies are self-organized and complex, yet exhibit characteristics different from simple laboratory systems. Basic organizing principles that describe the characteristics of self-organized systems

in other fields can be used to describe the characteristics of human systems as well.

- Human beings are bound together through their interaction with each other in both hierarchical and heterarchical relationships. A society is bounded by its interaction with its environment, which includes not only the physical environment but also other societies.

- Human societies are self-organized in a nonequilibrium state at the edge of chaos. Their development follows an evolutionary path of repeated, alternating cycles of order, chaos, and bifurcations.

- Societies are coevolving systems constantly adapting to each other and the environment. Like all systems at the edge of chaos, they are subject to destabilization and bifurcation.

- Individuals and groups can have an important effect on the outcome of the society at bifurcation points.

- As the complexity of the society grows, it requires larger and larger amounts of energy and raw materials to sustain itself. In human societies especially, as the complexity increases, information processing takes on a more vital role and selection processes themselves act on cultural information pools more than on genetic characteristics.

In ecological theory, Betty Meggers proposed that the cultural advance of a civilization is dependent on its agricultural potential because, as Leslie White postulated in his thermodynamic approach, the degree of organization of a system is proportional to the concentration of energy in or its flow through the system. Along these lines, Sanders and Price recognized the extraordinary relationship among cereals, dense populations, and complex social systems.

As we have seen, a complex society must not only have ample agricultural potential, it must organize itself to efficiently exploit that potential. Having done so, however, it is then dependent on a consistent level of agricultural energy flow to support its higher levels of hierarchical complexity. If the energy flow is reduced or cut off, the society will collapse to a level that the available energy can support, if only a level of subsistence cultivation. If agriculture fails and the energy flow stops, the society will disappear altogether.

4. Famine and the Individual

Have you ever seen a man—a good honest man who has worked hard, a "law abiding citizen," doing no serious harm to anyone—when he has had no food for more than a month? It is a most agonising sight. His dying flesh hangs from him in wrinkled folds; you can clearly see every bone in his body; his eyes stare out unseeing; and even if he is a youth of twenty he moves like an ancient crone, dragging himself from spot to spot. If he has been lucky he has long ago sold his wife and daughters. He has sold everything he owns—the timbers of his house itself, and most of his clothes. Sometimes he has, indeed, even sold the last rag of decency, and he sways there in the scorching sun, his testicles dangling from him like withered olive seeds—the last grim jest to remind you that this was once a man!

Children are even more pitiable, with their little skeletons bent over misshapen, their crooked bones, their little arms like twigs, and their purpling bellies, filled with bark and sawdust, protruding like tumours. Women lie slumped in corners, waiting for death, their bladelike buttocks protruding, their breasts hanging like collapsed sacks. But there are, after all, not many women and girls. Most of them have died or been sold. [description of a famine in Suiyuan, northwest China, 1929]

—Edgar Snow (1937:216–217)

Drought destroys. Famine is ugly, mean, and cruel. Those who abstractly argue that societies organize themselves to handle famine have never experienced the hopeless, endless cruelty of drought and death.

In this chapter we look at how communities and states can be devastated by drought. Our goal is not to develop a full theory of social collapse, instead to look at the question of how drought destroys.

Extremely heavy mortality is usually caused either by famine or by disease. A famine based crisis affects a large area all at once, often recurring in successive years. Disease, on the other hand, not associated with famine, would spread gradually across a continent, affecting areas in turn, but only comparatively small numbers would suffer at any one moment (Hollingsworth 1980b:21).

Cornelius Walford's search of historical sources, published in 1879, uncovered mention of three hundred fifty famines in various parts of the world between 1708 BC and AD 1879, but he merely scratched the surface. Shêng-Han later discovered references to over 1,800 in China alone. It has been estimated that Britain, France, and the German states suffered famine in one region or another every two or three years from the beginning of the Christian era until the latter half of the nineteenth century. In Russia and Ukraine, the situation was not very different through the 1930s (Dando 1980:vii; Davies 1977:400).

Mesoamerica, and in particular the Yucatán Peninsula, has seen repeated episodes of famine. Nancy Farriss listed eighteen episodes in northern Yucatán during the Colonial era alone, and as she pointed out, the Maya chronicles indicate that famine had a venerable Precontact history as well. Colonial historian Diego López de Cogolludo reported heavy mortality, for example, during the drought, famine, and epidemics which scourged the Peninsula from 1648 to 1656 when almost half of the Maya inhabitants died. Reports of famine in the chronicles of the Mexican Highlands are so frequent, in fact, that Nigel Davies dismissed them on the basis that they are part and parcel of the standard Mesoamerican formula for describing periods of disaster! The most complete record of famine, however, is that compiled by William Dando, a data bank of information covering more than 8,000 famines over the last 6,000 years. Virtually every part of the world has seen famine in the past, and much of the world remains famine prone today (Cogolludo quoted in Farriss 1984:426; Dirks 1980:22; Farriss 1984:61–62).

No two episodes of famine have ever been identical, and no two societies have ever responded to famine conditions in the same way. Nonetheless, certain phenomena have occurred with sufficient regularity to suggest some universal features of famine. Plainly the circumstances found in diverse famines vary greatly. One need only consider, for example, the range of causes found in the siege of Leningrad (1941–1942); the refugee situation in the cassava eating populations in the Kasai, Congo (1960); the families of the Donner party snowed-in high in the Sierra Nevada (1846); the Irish potato famine (1846); the Nigerian Civil War (1967–1970); and the drought driven famines of Ethiopia in the 1980s to understand the wide variety of causes of famine (Golkin 1987:20; Jelliffe and Jelliffe 1971:54).

MORTALITY

Historical records of famines in pre-industrial societies usually paint pictures of death on a massive scale. Harvard sociologist Pitirim Sorokin had a particularly unique insight into the workings of famine. A former high official of the Czarist government of Russia, he lived through the social turbulence and famine following the Bolshevik Revolution and subsequently devoted a significant part of his academic career to studying the effects of famine on societies. He described the horrific loss of life caused by historical famines and demonstrated that death rates in affected areas sometimes reached 200, 500, or even 800 for every 1,000 population compared with normal rates of 10 to 30. In the Soviet famine of 1921, he maintained, regional death rates reached 600 per 1,000. As with all famines, excessive mortality is brought about not only by outright starvation. Famine induced malnutrition leaves the population relatively defenseless against any infections that might be encountered. Thus, even though the recorded cause of death may be an infectious disease, famine and malnutrition are usually the more fundamental causes (Hugo 1984:14–15; Sorokin 1942).

Northeastern India has seen the horror of famine all too often. Some estimates put the mortality of the Bengal famine of 1769–70 alone at 10 million. There is no doubt, however, that the pain of famine falls disproportionately on the poor and landless. A case study in Bangladesh showed that the 1975 Crude Death Rate among landless families was three times higher than that for families with 1.2 or more hectares (3 ac) of land (Arnold 1988:20; Hugo 1984:18).

In centuries past, Europe was regularly afflicted by famine. Every peasant in seventeenth-century France probably experienced a major subsistence crisis at least once during his or her lifetime. Even more striking was the Russian famine of 1932–34 in which several million peasants died not as a result of any climatic freak or Malthusian check but because of virtual civil war between the peasants and the Soviet state. Between 1930 and 1937, at least 11 million peasants died in the Soviet Union and maybe more. In 1933 alone, perhaps 7.2 to 8.1 million died of starvation (Arnold 1988:16, 98; Becker 1996:46).

The famine with the highest known mortalities occurred in the People's Republic of China in the years 1958–1961. As near as imperfect census data can be projected into these years, mortalities were probably 30 million. (The official government figure is 16 million.) A most remarkable aspect of the famine was that for over twenty years, no one outside of China was sure whether it had taken place. At least 30 million people had starved to death, far more than anyone, including the most militant critics of the Chinese Communist Party, had ever imagined. Mao Zedong refused to accept that there was a food shortage, and since he was convinced that the peasants were hiding grain, he refused to open the state granaries. His government officials falsified reports, doctored photographs, and transplanted massive amounts of plants when he went to inspect the countryside (Becker 1996:xi, 81; Seavoy 1986:395).

We will examine the history of Mesoamerican famine in great detail in chapter 11. Suffice it to say, the mortality in famines during the Colonial period in Yucatán was very heavy. The levels of death may have reached as high as 40 to 50 percent. According to historical reports during the Colonial era, famine repeatedly devastated the Maya, as well as Mesoamerica in general.

It is clear, then, that famine causes death in huge numbers, but the next question for the purposes of our inquiry should be: can drought cause famine? One would think that the answer to this question would be straightforward. Surprisingly, theorists are very divided on this topic.

FOOD TRANSPORTATION

There may be dangers in reading the complexities of modern famine into the famines of other times, other places, and other peoples. Perhaps, the famines of an earlier age were less complicated affairs. Without the pressures of international capitalism to distort local economies, without railways and trucks to speed foodstuffs into drought stricken areas, and without international aid and medical relief operations to lessen famine's impact, climate had a more immediate and brutal impact. When the rains failed or the floods swept away crops and houses, people starved for simple want of food (Arnold 1988:33).

Obtaining food for famine relief obviously does not depend on the mere distance between the famine area and areas where food is available. It depends on the communications between these areas. An abundant harvest in Madras, for example, would be of no use in a famine in Rajputana when the only means of transportation was by bullock cart. During the drought driven famine of AD 362–363 in Antioch (in modern Turkey), the city was unable to avail itself of grain located a mere 80km (50mi) away. Until about a century and a quarter ago, before the coming of the railways, communities whose crops failed usually starved in isolation (Aykroyd 1974; Finley1985:245n 8; Neville Morley 1996:65).

In Mesoamerica, prior to the arrival of the Spaniards, the transportation system relied entirely on human porters. There were no wheeled vehicles or beasts of burden to pull them. Robert Drennan examined the energy requirements of human porters in Mesoamerica and proposed a transportation limit based on the nutritional needs of the porter of approximately 550 km (330 mi), calculated on a round trip basis. The transportation of maize beyond this limit, for example, results in a net energy loss. In other words, the porter would eat more than he delivered. He believed, however, that the effective limit, taking into account overhead and profit, was 275 km (165 mi), and ordinarily we would expect the transportation of such staples to be restricted to substantially shorter distances. On this basis, he concluded that the transportation of food staples would have been profitable only within such archaeological regions as the Basin of Mexico, the Valley of Oaxaca, or the Petén (Drennan 1984:107).

Whereas Drennan made his calculations on the basis of a single porter alone, Ross Hassig made calculations on the basis of the nutritional needs, not only of the porter, but of his family of five as well. He estimated that a single human porter, or *tlameme* as they were known in Nahuatl, could carry a load of about 25 kg (55 lb) of maize. He calculated, however, that the per day overhead burden of a porter, taking into account the nutritional needs of the porter and his family, was about 30 percent of the value of the load, based on a round trip for the porter. This places an absolute limit on the transportation of corn of 3.3 days or 100 km (60 mi). In other words, if a porter carried a load of corn 100 km (60 mi), he would have used it all to feed himself and his family. The effective limit for a commercial distribution system, of course, would have been considerably less, say 50 percent of the absolute limit or 50 km (30 mi). During the period of Aztec dominance in the Mexican Highlands, basic foodstuffs, other than gourmet items, were normally drawn from within a restricted radius of one day's journey or approximately 30 km (18 mi) from the major centers (Hassig 1985:128; 1986a:135–136; 1986b:309).

We can compare these theoretical limits for food transportation from Mesoamerica with real data compiled for preindustrial, nineteenth-century Europe. Johann von Thünen published an analysis of German agricultural economics in 1826, *Der Isolierte Staat* (*The Isolated State*). As part of his analysis, he determined that the absolute transportation limit for cereals carried by a horse and wagon was about 80 km (50 mi). At that point, the horses and drivers would have eaten all of the grain during the round trip, which, according to von Thünen, would have taken twenty days (Thünen 1826:13).

Farming, as von Thünen made very clear, is a business and as such it has costs other than transportation. Thus the farmer not only had to get his crop to market, he also had to spend to rent his land, plant, cultivate, and harvest his crop. He determined, therefore, that the limit of economical viability from a city, for most kinds of agriculture, was 46 km (28.6 mi), although certain kinds of agriculture could be economically viable as far as 50.5 km (31.4 mi). Because of factors like transportation, perishability, and spoilage, the farther a farmer was from the city, the less price he received for his crop (Hall 1966:xxviii; Thünen 1826:44).

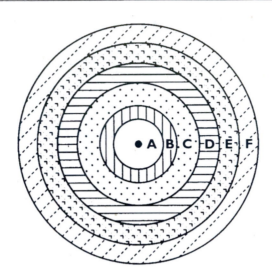

VON THÜNEN'S ZONES OF AGRICULTURAL VIABILITY

Figure 13. Johann von Thünen proposed a series of concentric rings around an idealized, isolated major city representing the economic viability of different types of agricultural activity. The most intensive agriculture was found closest to the city and the least intensive farthest away. The idealized rings could be distorted by the presence of highways, rivers, or sea ports which would change the economics of transportation. • central market, A horticulture and dairying, B forest, C intensive arable, D long ley arable, E three field arable, F ranching (adapted from Neville Morley 1996:62).

For an idealized isolated state, located in an idealized plain, von Thünen proposed a major city would be surrounded by a series of concentric rings of farming systems (figure 13), with the most intensive, like horticulture and dairying, at the center, with the least intensive, like ranching and animal husbandry, at the farthest distance. The important considerations are the bulk of the product, its transportation costs, and its perishability. The products in the outer rings are cheap to transport in relation to their value (Thünen 1826:8; Neville Morley 1996).

The idealized pattern of the rings can be affected by local geography and by the availability of highways, rivers, and sea ports. It was estimated, for example, in early eighteenth-century England that the costs ratios of different forms of transport were of the order of 1 for sea, 4.7 for river, and 22.6 for land. In other words, a given good could be transported 5 miles overland, 25 miles by river, and 115 miles by sea for the same cost. Rome was able to grow to such an enormous size for its time by its access to sea transport through its port at Ostia, 30 km (20 mi) down the Tiber River, which enabled it to bring in foodstuffs from throughout the Mediterranean Basin. Thus, large distant regions of coastal farms were as economically accessible to Roman populations as nearby inland farms. In similar fashion, the construction of highways in Europe and *sak beob*, elevated caliche roadways, in the Yucatán Peninsula had very clear economic implications (Neville Morley 1996:63–65).

The result of these studies, then, is a realization that the region a pre-industrial city can draw on for its day to day sustenance, and even more importantly for famine relief, is circumscribed. Thus, other writers have described the phenomenon of frequent famine in the midst of glut, as occurred in Antioch. When a Maya city fell victim to regional drought and famine, there was no way to bring relief supplies from more distant regions.

Furthermore, we will see in chapter 11 that during times of famine, shipments of food are likely to be attacked by starving people, making any attempts at organized food distribution futile. Although it is theoretically possible to transport food staples during times of famine over longer distances, such a theory must assume that a large region remains under tight military control that would assure the safe passage of the relief convoys. This does not apply to ancient cultures alone. As recently as 1995 in northern Mexico, for example, grain trains and warehouses were attacked and robbed by famished *campesinos* during a serious drought (Institute for Agriculture and Trade Policy 1996; Sluyter 1993).

One can see that during the Classic, the ability to redistribute foodstuffs to famine stricken areas in the Lowlands from areas that still had ample supplies of food was most likely non-existent. When the crops failed in an area and the reserves ran out, there was nowhere to go to get food because of the severe limitation of the transportation system and the size of Maya polities. This limitation points to a serious vulnerability in Classic society to drought and famine. When people ran out of food, they died.

FAMINE TYPOLOGIES

It is not our goal in this book to develop a full theory of famine. That topic has received extensive treatment by numerous other writers. It will be sufficient for our purposes to demonstrate that drought does cause famine. We begin, however, by looking at how other writers have categorized famine and its causes.

Leftwich and Harvie, for example, proposed the following taxonomy of famines based on their underlying causes:

1. Food availability decline
    1.1 Population increase (Malthus)
    1.2 War
    1.3 Climatic factors
2. Ecological mismanagement
3. Socioeconomic and political dislocation in the course of change or development
4. Economic theories
    4.1 Market failure
    4.2 Exchange entitlements
5. Government mismanagement/political or institutional failure
6. Anthropological or sociological explanations
7. Multi-causal or eclectic approaches (Devereux 1993: 31).

William Dando, on the other hand, proposed a scheme of geographically determined famines, arguing that certain regions of the world were prone to specific types of famines. Of course, a specific famine type could occur anywhere in the world, given the appropriate conditions:

1. *Physical (or Egyptian) famines* in regions where the physical environment was naturally hostile to intensive forms of sedentary agriculture but man developed techniques which enabled him to temper natural hazards in all but their extreme form.
2. *Transportation (or Roman) famines* in highly urbanized, commercial, or industrial food deficit regions dependent upon distant food sources and supplied normally by a well developed transportation system.
3. *Cultural (or West European) famines* in food surplus regions induced by archaic social systems, cultural practices, and overpopulation.
4. *Political (or Eastern European) famines* in regions that are nominally self-sufficient in basic foodstuffs but where regional politics or regional political systems determine food production, food distribution, and food availability.
5. *Overpopulation (or Asian) famines* in drought-prone or flood prone, overpopulated, marginal agricultural regions with primitive agricultural systems, whose inhabitants' perennial food intake was only slightly above starvation levels (Dando 1980:87).

Stephen Devereux finds all of the above taxonomies to be inadequate and proposes that famine theories should be arranged in three broad groups: climatic, demographic (Malthusian), and economic (entitlements and market failure) (Devereux 1993:31–32).

There exists a certain tension between those famine theorists who see the cause of famine in events external to the culture and those who see the causes as internal, a distinction Devereux defines as between precipitating factors and underlying processes:

EXTERNAL	INTERNAL
Natural disasters	Social processes
Declining natural resources	Declining political and economic influence
Transitory food shocks	Increasing vulnerability
National / regional analysis	Household / individual analysis
Supply failure	Demand failure

Ross Hassig considered the question of famine typologies in the context of Mesoamerica and concluded that the multiple categories customarily used are neither conceptually complete nor logically exhaustive or exclusive. He feels they are a hodgepodge of empirically based categories of limited theoretical utility. To attempt to place some order upon the array of famines in Central Mexico, he proposed a conceptual framework that permits some logical structuring of the chronology of events. He prefers to separate famines into (1) ecological, those caused by natural events such as floods, insects, droughts, or frosts; and (2) social, those caused by government edict, hoarding, profiteering, and the like. Hassig believes that this dichotomy separates those famines caused by factors beyond the immediate control of the society in question and those that could be controlled but are not. He adds that most famines incorporate elements of both types (Hassig 1986:305–306).

I find Hassig's analysis very useful because I propose the Collapse of Classic civilization was not the Mayas' fault. They did not cause the devastating climatic catastrophe that overtook them. Their food producing system was designed for their normal climatic conditions. Neither they, nor anyone else, could have overcome the hunger and thirst to which they succumbed. In Hassig's terms, it was an ecological disaster beyond the immediate control of Maya society.

Nancy Farriss prepared a list of famines reported during the Colonial era in Yucatán together with the causes attributed to them by Colonial sources when available. (See page 306 for a full list of Colonial Yucatecan famines.) Of the twenty-five famines listed, about half are attributed to drought. In fact, in only two cases was famine attributed to a hurricane, and in other cases, the cause was not given in the historical reports. Mesoamerica, like India, Africa, and so many other regions of the world, was repeatedly afflicted by climatically induced famine (Farriss 1984:61–62).

WHAT IS A CAUSE?

At this point it is necessary to clarify the role of a "cause." Lewis Binford proposed that all cultures tend towards equilibrium or homeostasis unless perturbed by an external shock, which he referred to as an extra-systemic selective pressure. The internal workings of the culture will continue to function adequately as long as the conditions of the external environment in which the culture exists do not change radically or change slowly enough for the culture to adapt. These are the periods of stability (Lewis Binford 1972:106, 112; Trigger 1989a:296).

The normal variability of a system's components controlled by homeostatic regulators, then, do not constitute evolution. Homeostasis is an important force in demographic history. Without it there is no equilibrium population and population does not forget the catastrophes of the past. In other words, a 10 percent loss of the population in the past would render the current population 10 percent lower than otherwise forever more (Lee 1993:2, 28).

On the other hand, when there is a radical external shock, the internal, homeostatic processes of the culture may be incapable of coping with the new demands placed on them. When drought comes and crops fail, for example, a transportation system, which may be adequate under normal circumstances, may be completely incapable of handling the demands of moving large quantities of food into the stricken areas. These are the periods of crisis and chaos.

Which, then, is the cause of the ensuing famine, the drought or the transportation system? Some famine theorists would say the drought, others transportation, others the interaction between the two. Certainly all three factors play a role in this simplified hypothetical example.

I claim, however, that the cause is the factor without which a situation would not exist. In other words, if the factor is not present, the result does not occur. Unfortunately, stating the idea in positive terms implies a degree of determinacy which is unwarranted.

In the above example, the transportation system may have functioned satisfactorily for years without a concurrent famine. The fact that it could not handle the extraordinary demands of famine relief should not be sufficient to make it the cause. Except for the drought, the transportation system could have continued to operate for years handling the normal transportation needs of the society. Without the drought, the transportation system would not have overloaded nor would any of the rest of the cascade of effects have occurred. Without the drought, the breakdown in the system would not have occurred. The cause, then, is the drought, even though the drought itself does not kill. It produces a cascade of other processes which result in death, as we shall see.

It should be noted that the above argument in favor of the causal role of severe droughts does not exclude the possibility that in other situations, at other times, demographic disaster may be the result of a multitude of interrelated causes and effects.

EXTERNAL VERSUS INTERNAL

Binford viewed cultures as humanity's extrasomatic means of adaptation. Changes in all aspects of cultural systems were therefore interpreted as adaptive responses to alterations in the natural environment or in adjacent or competing cultural systems. He described evolution as "a process operative at the interface of a living system and its field." It is not enough to describe how societies evolved from one level to the next, archaeologists must also explain how each society has been influenced by its neighbors. He treated cultures as normally tending towards equilibrium or homeostasis, with change being induced by external factors. He insisted that the change had to be understood in terms of the responses that occurred within cultural systems. He shared the tendency, already evident in settlement archaeology, to concentrate on understanding cultural change from an internal point of view. Thus external factors induced internal response (Binford 1972:106; Lamberg-Karlovsky 1989:27; Trigger 1989a:295–302; Willey and Sabloff 1980:188).

Along similar lines, Elman Service summarized his views regarding what he called the classic civilizations, the Indus, Egyptian, and Maya, as follows:

> The virtue of our present perspective on adaptation and its relationship to evolutionary potential is that it removes the focus from internally caused rises and falls, suggesting the usual cyclical tautologies and Toynbeean mysticisms, toward outside environmental factors that are real, true-to-life events that can be found in recorded history and investigated archaeologically.
>
> The causes of the rise of a civilization lay in its solution of problems posed by the outside environment by means created inside itself—i.e., inside its bureaucracy. The explanation of its decline, however, lies within its environmental sphere but outside itself. And even most of the modern environmentalists (or "cultural ecologists," like Julian Steward), in combatting this tendency, confined their attention too much to the geographic environment, never enough to reciprocal, intersocietal adaptations....
>
> The many theories of cultural evolution reviewed in this book [Origins of the State and Civilization] never took enough account of a culture's interactions with its environment....

The first classic civilizations, therefore, did not fall; they were pushed. (Service 1975:321–322)

Not all famines are caused by external shocks like drought. The Soviet famine of 1932–1933 was the result of Joseph Stalin's decision to collectivize agricultural production throughout the Soviet Union, regardless of the cost in human lives. Eleven million people died. The Chinese famine of 1958–1961 was the result of Mao Zedong's obsession with Lysenkoist agricultural programs which effectively destroyed food production in China. Mao was misled by those under him who told him that China had surpassed the US in food production, that rich peasants were hoarding food, and that no one was really hungry. Thirty million people died. Both famines originated from effects internal to the systems.

When an external shock perturbs a system, the system must respond. In some instances the system will be able to deal with the external shock, in others, it won't. Where does the blame lie? Is it the fault of the external shock or is it the fault of the system's response. Is it reasonable to expect a system to be able to deal with a serious shock that was out of the ordinary? Will the same system always respond to the same shock in the same way? Let us turn to these questions.

SELF-ORGANIZED CRITICALITY AND THE EDGE OF CHAOS

In terms of organizational theory, as we saw in the last chapter, all self-organized systems depend on a constant flow of energy to maintain their structure. Life is sandwiched between the dangerous uniformity of equilibrium and the dangerous chaos of turbulence. It exists at the edge of chaos. It is the point where the components of a system never quite lock into place, and never quite dissolve into turbulence, either (Prigogine and Allen 1982:14; Waldrop 1992:12, 230).

How, then, do such systems respond to external shocks? Is there a predictable pattern? Does twice as much external shock result in twice as much internal damage?

Per Bak, a physicist at Brookhaven National Laboratory, together with his colleague, Kan Chen, studied complex systems in nature. He argued that complex behavior reflects the tendency of large systems with many components to evolve into a poised, "critical" state, way out of balance at the edge of chaos, where minor disturbances start a chain reaction that affects any number of elements in a system, leading to events of all sizes. He refers to all such events as avalanches because most of the changes in the system take place through catastrophic events rather than following a smooth, gradual path. The evolution to this very delicate state occurs without design from any outside agent; it is self-organized. According to Bak, self-organized criticality is the only known general mechanism to generate complexity (Bak 1996:1–2).

Complex systems, therefore, naturally evolve to a critical state in which a minor event starts a chain reaction that can affect any number of elements in the system.

Bak believes that insight seldom arises from messy, complicated modeling. It more often results from gross oversimplifications which allow us to see underlying processes. Once the essential mechanism has been identified, we can check for robustness by tagging on more and more details (Bak 1996:132).

What are the effects, then, of an external shock on a system? In order to illustrate their theory with a simplified model, Bak and Chen have conducted laboratory experiments using a pile of sand. If you run a thin stream of sand onto a round plate, a pile steadily builds, reaching the edge of the plate. The grains of sand on the surface of the pile are just barely stable, a state of self-organized criticality. The pile itself gets bigger and bigger until suddenly one more grain of sand triggers an avalanche. One time the avalanche will be a small one, one time a medium one, the next time, perhaps, a big one. Over a period of time there will be avalanches of all sizes—all provoked by the same size disturbance: one additional grain of sand. Perturb such a system and you might get some small response. Perturb it again with the same degree of disturbance and the thing might collapse completely. Perturb it many times while it is poised at the critical state and you will get a range of responses which can be described by a power law: big responses are rare, small responses are common, and intermediate responses fall in between. Complex systems, then, never reach equilibrium, but evolve from one metastable, or nonequilibrium, state to the next. Large, interactive systems perpetually organize themselves to a critical state (Bak and Chen 1991:46; Bak quoted in Lewin 1992:61 and in Waldrop 1992:304).

A theory describing such systems and their responses to shock must be statistical in nature. Because of their composite nature, complex systems can exhibit catastrophic behavior, where one part of a system can affect many others by a domino effect resulting in a system collapse. Frequently, the system responds to an external perturbation with small events, infrequently with large events. Medium sized events fall somewhere in between. The occurrence of such events, it turns out, can be plotted on a log-log, or double log, graph as a straight line and are therefore said to behave according to a power law. The theoretical concept, then, is illustrated by the avalanches in the pile of sand, which leads to the conclusion that large catastrophic events occur as a consequence of the same dynamics that produced small ordinary everyday events (Bak 1996:10, 12, 32).

In self-organized critical systems, most of the changes concentrate within the largest events, so self-organized criticality can be thought of as the theoretical underpinning for catastrophes, the opposite philosophy to gradualism. Real change comes, as Karl Marx predicted, by revolution and not by gradual change because the systems are poised at the critical state. Self-organized criticality is nature's way of making enormous transformations over short time scales (Bak 1996:60–61, 131).

Power law phenomena can be identified throughout nature, manifesting themselves in things as diverse as earthquake magnitudes, stock market prices, extinctions, sandpile avalanches, or the sizes of cities in the United States. Richard E. W. Adams and Richard Jones, for example, have applied power law analysis to cities in the Maya Lowlands and have determined that the distribution of Maya city sizes can be described by a power law (Bak 1996:12–19, 60, Adams and Jones 1981:312).

The prevalence of power law phenomena throughout nature leads to two important speculations with regard to the Maya Collapse. The first is that the severity of droughts may well respond to a power law distribution and the second that the response of the system will also follow a power law distribution: sometimes the response will be moderate, other times catastrophic. The notion that droughts have occurred in the past, then, really doesn't tell us much about the next one. The fact that a society survived the last ten droughts does not indicate how they will deal with the next one.

Furthermore, because the magnitude of droughts follows a power law distribution, the nature of the last ten droughts does not tell us anything about the severity of the next one, which may be the most severe drought ever seen. Most importantly, however, the response of the system to an external shock is unpredictable. One time it may survive a drought while the next time it may collapse from a drought of the same magnitude. When destabilized, a society normally transforms and renews itself or is absorbed by other societies. When it suffers a massive external shock to which it cannot adequately respond, however, it can disappear and become extinct.

The Maya Lowlands have seen repeated episodes of demographic disaster: the Preclassic Abandonment, the Hiatus, the Classic Collapse, and the Postclassic Abandonment are the ones large enough to show up in the archaeological record. How many more of lesser degree occurred that don't show up in the record is impossible to say. The ones noted resulted in the total abandonment of various cities. The archaeological record does not easily distinguish, for example, demographic disasters in which 20 percent of the population died but the surviving society recovered quickly. The various disasters have occurred in widely ranging environments of Malthusian population pressure ranging from the density of the Classic Collapse to the relative emptiness of the Postclassic Abandonment.

We know from historical records after the Spanish conquest that famine was a frequent recurrence in the Yucatán Peninsula, but the society recovered and continued. By that time, the Spanish had introduced a transportation system unavailable to the Precontact Maya including draft animals and wheeled vehicles. Nonetheless, the mortality appears to have approached 50 percent in one or more of the Colonial famines.

One is tempted to speculate that Maya demographic disasters followed a power law distribution, although specific data are obviously not available. It is also tempting to speculate that Maya society was prepared to cope with disasters up to a certain size, but could not cope with the severity of those which only occurred every three hundred years or so.

MALTHUS

The idea of an overcrowded and worn out planet has surfaced and resurfaced many times throughout history. Ecological pessimism, for example, was a part of the early Christian Fathers' view. Sixteen centuries before Malthus, around AD 200, Tertullian, the North African Christian theologian, lamented the great "density of human beings" on the earth:

> Plowed fields have replaced forests, domesticated animals have dispersed wildlife. Beeches are plowed, mountains smoothed and swamps drained. There are as many cities as in former years there were dwellings....Everywhere there are buildings, everywhere people, everywhere communities....Proof [of this crowding] is the density of human beings. We weigh upon the world; its resources hardly suffice to support us. As our needs grow larger, so do our protests that already nature does not sustain us. In truth, plague, famine, wars, and earthquakes must be regarded as a blessing to civilization, since they prune away the luxuriant growth of the human race. (Tertullian 200)

But it is with Thomas Malthus that the overpopulation theory is most commonly identified. In the late 1790s, he was an Anglican parson of a small country church. As a bachelor, he appears to have spent considerable time in his parents' home where he got into a friendly argument with his father over the future course of society. The result was *An Essay on the Principle of Population*, published in 1798 (Gilbert 1993:vii).

His theory is based on two postulates: "First, That food is necessary to the existence of man. Secondly, That the passion between the sexes is necessary and will remain nearly in its present state." From these postulates, he concluded, "Population, when unchecked, increases in a geometrical ratio. Subsistence increases only in an arithmetical ratio." Malthus believed that agriculture could only increase its productivity slowly and, as a result, human fecundity would rapidly outstrip its food supply. Inevitably, therefore, population will always expand to the limit of subsistence and will be held there by famine, disease, and war. "This implies a strong and constantly operating check on population from the difficulty of subsistence. This difficulty must fall some where, and must necessarily be severely felt by a large portion of mankind."(*Encyclopedia Britannica* 1976:11:395; Gilbert 1993:xxv; Malthus 1798:12–13).

Malthus's views were attacked by most of literary England. Lord Byron, Shelley, Coleridge, and evens Dickens, among others, ridiculed his work. Thomas Carlyle was prompted by the essay to dub economics "the dismal science." But his work found a receptive audience among the social and natural scientists of the day. In fact, Charles Darwin maintained that his theory of evolution came to him while he was reading *An Essay on the Principle of Population*. It was at that moment when he realized existence was a constant struggle for survival and "that under these circumstances favourable variations would tend to be preserved and that unfavourable ones would be destroyed. The result would be the formation of a new species. Here, then, at last I had got a theory by which to work" (Darwin 1859:v–vi; Gilbert 1993:viii, xx–xxi).

One of the problems with Malthus's theory is that population growth and food supply per capita feed back on one another. He could not see the new technology that would be invented in the future, nor did he see the changes that had occurred in the past (see figure 14). His views were based on a static view of agricultural technology and, of course, the level of agricultural technology which surrounded him in the late 1790s. In his mind, agricultural productivity would be increased by hiring more agricultural laborers and bringing more land into cultivation.

BOSERUP

In contrast, United Nations economist Ester Boserup analyzed the changes in agricultural technology and practices over time. She concluded, in her 1965 book, *The Conditions of Agricultural Growth*, that cultivation techniques responded to changes in population pressure. Population growth spurred agricultural intensification, and intensified agriculture allowed populations to increase yet further. By the same token, if population density decreased, agricultural intensity would decrease. Thus, German immigrant farmers to very lightly populated areas of Brazil in the 1800s reverted to swidden agriculture, even though they knew well the intensive techniques of European cultivation (Boserup 1965:63,118).

Our investigation in the preceding pages lends no support to this conception of an agrarian surplus population emerging as the result of population growth. We have found that it is unrealistic to regard agricultural cultivation systems as adaptations to different natural conditions, and that cultivation systems can be more plausibly explained as the result of differences in population density: As long as the population of a given area is very sparse, food can be produced with little input of labour per unit of output and with virtually no capital investment, since a very long fallow period helps to preserve soil fertility. As the density of population in the area increases, the fertility of the soil can no longer be preserved

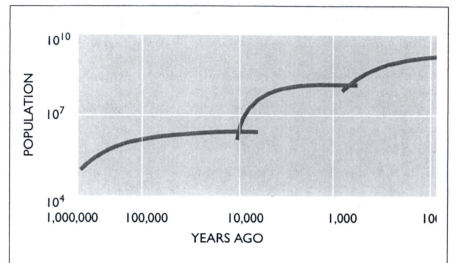

TECHNOLOGY AND POPULATION GROWTH

Figure 14. Edward Deevey proposed three surges in population based on broad technological advances: first, the toolmaking revolution among hunter-gatherers; second, the agricultural revolution; and third, the scientific-industrial revolution. Each technological advance allowed greater populations to be supported. Narrower technological advances, like water collection and distribution systems, affected Maya populations in a similar way (adapted from Deevey 1960:198).

by means of long fallow and it becomes necessary to introduce other systems which require a much larger agricultural labour force. By the gradual change from systems where each cultivated plot is matched by twenty similar plots under fallow to systems where no fallow is necessary, the population within a given area can double several times without having to face either starvation or lack of employment opportunities in agriculture. (Boserup 1965:117)

In Boserup's view, then, population growth, in and of itself, would not be the cause of recurring demographic calamities, since increased population would lead to increased agricultural production.

FAMINES

From a neo-Malthusian point of view, however, Ronald Seavoy has pointed out that, during long periods of peace without an increase in agricultural technology, peasant populations increase to the maximum densities that can be fed from the land they control. When this occurs, they become vulnerable to famines during periodic recurrences of poor weather conditions. For Malthus, famine was the most important check on population size. "Famine seems to be the last, the most dreadful resource of nature" (Malthus 1798:61; Seavoy 1986:8).

On the other hand, Rolando Garcia and Pierre Spitz studied a number of modern famines and reached the conclusion that population pressure was not the determining factor in today's famines.

a.   In none of the case studies we made was "population pressure" at the root of the problems. To say it in our own terminology: population pressure was not a factor playing a leading role in determining the instability of the system.

b.   Population pressure did play a role as an *aggravating* factor in catastrophic situations, the roots of which are to be found elsewhere.

c.   Population pressure has been used as a "scapegoat," as an easy way out to "explain" situations that in order to be properly explained would require going deeply into the analysis of prevalent socio-economic and political conditions in extended regions of the world.

d.   Population pressure is *becoming* a most serious problem. Unless some remedies are found, population pressure that exceeds certain limits may trigger off irreversible processes that will get entirely out of control. (Garcia and Spitz 1986:xvii)

According to Arnold, Malthus was surely wrong in postulating a single and universal law linking population and subsistence. In a modern context, population growth, in combination with technological stagnation, social conservatism, and political inertia or oppression, forms an integral part of a complex of forces responsible for causing famine (Arnold 1988:42).

Demographer and economist Ronald Lee has suggested a synthesis of Malthus's and Boserup's theories. He made two assumptions, which he admits are controversial. First, diminishing returns will eventually set in as both labor and technology increase while resources remained fixed. Second, there is a cost associated with maintaining any technological level and higher costs with higher levels, due to the need for maintaining the human and physical capital stocks without which the technology would soon be forgotten. With these two assumptions, then, the system does not move onward and upward forever, but rather comes to rest at a high technology/high population equilibrium. One can see Lee's assumptions at work in technologically advanced modern societies. As the cost of educat-

YEAR	LOCATION	DEATHS
1865–1867	Madras, Orissa, Bengal, Bihar	1,300,000
1868–1870	Central Provinces, Northwestern Provinces, Punjab	1,410,000
1876–1878	North Madras, Mysore, Central Provinces, Punjab	6,135,000
1877–1879	Northwestern Provinces, Oudh, Punjab	1,600,000
1896–1898	Bombay, Central Provinces, Northwestern Provinces, Punjab, Bengal	5,150,000
1899–1901	Central Provinces	3,250,000

SEVERE NINETEENTH-CENTURY INDIAN FAMINES

Table 2. All the major famines in India in the nineteenth century were preceded by drought (*Source:* Seavoy 1986:242).

ing children rises, the number of children per family has fallen (Lee 1986:128).

The Maya Lowlands have been repeatedly devastated by the cruelty of demographic collapse. These have occurred without regard to the population density, agricultural techniques, agricultural productivity, or the social complexity of the time. Although each episode could have had a different cause, there is evidence that they may have been drought induced, as we will examine in greater detail in chapter 11. Given the range of population densities and pressures, it is unlikely that population pressures alone induced the famines in the absence of sudden changes in the environment—especially climate.

DROUGHT INDUCED FAMINES

Some famines are unquestionably drought induced. Some writers have, in fact, argued that most catastrophic famines have been produced by drought. All the famines during the second half of the nineteenth century in India, as listed in table 2, occurred during peacetime when there were two or more consecutive poor crop years because of drought. British observers of famine in India estimated that acute hunger occurred when harvests were 50 percent of normal. They also observed that when rainfall was half of normal due to a failure of the monsoon rains, crop yields were one-third of normal, producing severe famine conditions (Hidore 1996:94; Seavoy 1986:242, 278).

In Africa, the specter of drought appeared in 1980. The area worst affected was the Horn of Africa. As in the previous drought of 1968–1974, the rains failed for a succession of years. Based on the total number of people affected, it was the worst disaster in the modern history of Africa. In 1984, twenty-seven countries needed food aid and not a single African country produced a food surplus. By 1985, famine was rampant on the African continent. By March of 1985, as many as 35 million people were persistently short of food and over 1 million had already died. Not only was famine severe, it was widespread (Hidore 1996:100).

People began to migrate. In Chad, thousands died, infants and the elderly were abandoned as there was nothing to feed them, and hundreds of thousands of people were wandering over the country looking for food. In Mauritania, the capital Nouakchott grew in size from 100,000 to 400,000 between 1982 and 1984. Three hundred thousand people had come off the grasslands looking for help. In the spring of 1985, 3,000 refugees from famine were crossing the border from Ethiopia to Sudan every day. There were approximately 1.5 million Ethiopians in Sudanese relief camps or trying to get into them and, in addition, refugees were streaming in from Uganda, Chad, and Zaire (Hidore 1996:100).

THE ROLE OF CLIMATE IN FAMINE

Alexander de Waal argued, based on the perception of the locals, that the 1984–1985 famine in Sudan was caused by drought, not politics or the economy. Along the same lines, Robert Dirks examined the ethnographic and historical record for the reported causes of famines in the Statistical Cross-Cultural Sample (SCCS) and found that factors such as drought, warfare, and crop failure were among nineteen identified causes (table 3). Most of these causes were mentioned less than ten times. Drought, however, received 41 out of the 114 mentions. Clearly, those who suffered these famines believed that insufficient rainfall was to blame the highest percentage of the time (Devereux 1993:35; Dirks 1993; McIntosh 1996:162; Waal 1989).

During the 1970s, many academics tended to place great emphasis on the vagaries of the earth's climate in assigning causes of famine. While this may not be true in every case, climatic changes frequently precipitate a famine. Several years of drought, or flooding, can greatly reduce available food supplies. In fact, as seen above, monsoon rain failure preceded every major famine in India during the nineteenth century (Cox 1981).

REASON FOR FAMINE	FREQUENCY
Drought	41
War	11
Hunting or fishing failure	11
Insects	10
Rats and other pests	7
Economic problems (collapse of trade, inadequate supply, etc)	5
Flood (riverine and tidal)	5
Hurricanes and other tropical storms	5
Crop disease	4
Livestock disease	4
Frost	3
Unfavorable weather conditions	3
Civil disturbance	2
Human disease	1
Transportation failure	1
Undomesticated crop failure	1
Land shortage	1
Inadequate storage	1

REASONS GIVEN BY SCCS SOURCES FOR FAMINE
AND FREQUENCY OF MENTION

Table 3. An analysis of causes of famine offered by sources in the Standard Cross-Cultural Sample (*Source:* Dirks 1993:34).

A related argument to climate suggests that external forces such as insects, plant disease, and a deteriorating environment also cause famines. When we look more closely at Yucatán, we will see that some famines may have been caused in this way. Ecological constraints, such as soil degradation due to overcropping, overgrazing, and deforestation, have been said to lead to reductions in food output. While present in many cases, they generally are not a sufficient condition in and of themselves for severe famine. The effects are slow enough to allow the system to adapt. They can, however, serve to exacerbate a famine underway from other causes.

The idea that some famines are drought induced is not universally accepted. As Stephen Devereux insists, "'Single cause' explanations are no longer valid, but no one has yet suggested a 'multiple cause' model which incorporates all the factors that combine to create famine conditions" (Devereux 1993:29).

> As a generalization, which view individual writers hold tends to be compatible with the discipline in which they were trained. If an economist writes about famine, then famine is caused by market failure or lack of purchasing power. If a climatologist writes about famine, then famine is caused by drought or desertification. When a Marxist sociologist explains famine, colonialism and international capitalism are to blame. (Devereux 1993:29)

Devereux adds, however, that "we must conclude that there is an evident association between climate and famine, but whether droughts and floods are a *sufficient* explanation of famine is another matter....Just because drought is not *invariably* associated with famine does not mean that drought and famine are not causally related" (Devereux 1993:40, 42).

THE EFFECT OF DROUGHT

How, then, does drought affect a culture? What are the specific steps that lead from sunny skies to starvation and death?

Of course, a pretty, sunny day does not kill anyone in and of itself. Death is caused by the cascade of effects that result from a seemingly unending string of rainfree days. The immediate cause of death will always be something other than a sunny day. Yet the engine that drives the train of cascading effects along is drought. Were it not for the drought, the chain of events leading to death would not have occurred.

An analogy exists in HIV infection. No one ever dies from an HIV infection itself. The immediate cause of death is always from some consequence of HIV infection such as malignancy, an opportunistic infection, or a general system collapse as a result of multiple opportunistic infections. Were it not for the HIV, however, and the resulting impairment of the immune system, the opportunistic diseases would most likely not have killed the organism (Virginia Pittman-Waller, MD, December 1997, personal communication).

What, then, is the role of HIV? Is it a trigger or a cause? Many of today's famine theorists would argue that HIV is merely a trigger, that the real cause of the organism's death lay in the inadequacy of the immune system.

HIV strikes with deadlier results among societies in which the people carry heavy chronic disease loads as in many tropical countries. In addition, it appears to strike more often in societies in which the males are not circumcised. High chronic disease loads and uncircumcised males seem to predispose societies to higher risk of HIV infection. But is the cause of a particular individual's death his or her predisposition to HIV infection, or the HIV infection itself? After all, similarly predisposed individuals not infected by HIV will live for many more years with their predispositions intact (Caldwell and Caldwell 1996:63–66; Root-Bernstein 1992:148–183).

It seems clear today that HIV drives the cascade of effects that ultimately result in the death of an individual from AIDS by slowly destroying the immune system thereby allowing opportunistic diseases to kill the individual. HIV, itself, however, is not the immediate cause of death.

By the same token, in the case of drought, certain famine theorists argue that the cause of famine is the predisposition of the society to famine and not the drought itself which is at fault. According to them, famine is not the result of the drought which is occurring, but the result of an inadequate transportation system which cannot handle relief supplies, or the result of a government which withholds food aid as a punishment to rebellious provinces, or the result of inept relief programs, or a combination of many such factors.

In this book, I take the position that the cause of drought-induced famine and the ensuing deaths is the drought itself; that without the drought, the society would have continued to function with all of its predispositions intact. I further maintain that the massive mortality from a severe drought is mediated by a cascade of processes which result in death through starvation, thirst, disease, and conflict.

In the end, when an archaeological society ran out of food and water because the rains and crops failed, it didn't matter what the predispositions were. Before modern transportation systems could transport food around the world, the people in that society would starve to death by themselves. It seems odd to me that this point is argued about. But it is. The basic, fundamental premise of this book is that when a society runs out of food and water, the people die.

FAMINE

In order to define famine, let us start with what famine is not. Individuals or individual families may struggle for existence in a state of extreme deprivation, of almost continuous undernourishment and malnutrition, in most parts of the world. We may even find, amidst affluence, pockets of communities that may be suffering from chronic malnutrition in varying degrees. Yet ordinary hunger is not famine, malnutrition is not famine, even though all these terms are often used interchangeably as if they were synonymous. In defining famine, then, we are not concerned with specific hunger, but with general hunger (Wolde Mariam 1984:4, 9).

Famine is the most negative state of food consumption under which people, unable to replace even the energy they lose in basal metabolism, consume whatever is stored in their bodies. They literally consume themselves to death. To use Mesfin Wolde Mariam's definition, famine is a general and widespread, prolonged and persistent, extraordinary and insufferable hunger lasting for several months and affecting the majority of the rural population over a more or less extensive area, resulting in total social and economic disorganization and mass death by starvation (Wolde Mariam 1984:9).

Famines are woven into the fabric of history, as David Arnold has noted. We have become accustomed to thinking of them as a particularly horrific kind of disaster, replete with human misery on a massive, almost unimaginable scale. Famines are clearly disasters and catastrophes. Through their sheer magnitude and through the extent of the devastation and disruption they cause, famines have been powerful engines of historical transformation, driving some societies to the verge of extinction, impelling others into wholesale migration or radical economic, political, and social change (Arnold 1988:5).

The most prominent signs of famine are widespread death from starvation, migration, social disruption, and the spread of epidemic diseases. Famine is a multifaceted process which includes changes in eating patterns, declines in the demand for employment, and profiteering by merchants. Economic confusion is pronounced, as hoarding occurs, and costs of staple foods rocket to three, five, or one hundred times the normal price. Personal possessions and property, such as household goods, tools, domestic animals, and land, are sold to buy food. They may never be recovered. Markets disappear. Seeds needed for the next year's planting are eaten, sold, or destroyed. Increasing debilitation and death within the human and animal work forces, as well as population migrations, diminish prospects for renewed food production. Marriage and birth rates decline, while mortality rates rise. As the social order breaks down, people in famine stricken communities resort to virtually any activity to obtain food. Theft, brigandage, prostitution, progressive abandonment of the sick and immobile, migrations in search of work and food, sales of women and children, and cannibalism have been recorded. Social chaos is evident everywhere, as refugees flock to cities or roads seeking food. Almost all normal functions are reduced or halted (Carlson 1982:8; Golkin 1987:21).

Only a small proportion of severe famines has been resolved by comparatively rational and painless methods. A much larger proportion, as Sorokin wrote, "has been liquidated by the scythe of death disguised in the form of riots, revolutions, wars, pestilence, and starvation." Famines have been brought to a close in many societies by the terrible mortality of the population, not only from starvation, but also from epidemics and other satellites of extreme poverty. "All famines," he wrote, "have been terminated either by the removal of their necessary and supplementary causes or by the catastrophic exhaustion of the famine after it has taken its full toll of suffering and death." The removal of the necessary cause means the restoration of society's ability to produce the required minimum of food for its members. Sorokin concluded that the great losses from death and from frequent reductions in the birth rate bring the surviving part of the population into an equilibrium with the available food supply. This appears to have occurred along the east coast of the Maya Lowlands during the Collapse when the cities were emptied but rural populations survived (Sorokin 1942:296, 298).

Sorokin has pinpointed an idea that is critically important to understanding the arguments over the disappearance of Classic Maya civilization in the Lowlands. When crisis and chaos strike a system, the end result is not necessarily the disappearance of the system. After reviewing over a hundred theories, explanations, and hypotheses of the Classic Collapse, however, it would appear that most of those writers believe disappearance is the only resolution to social stress and chaos. The rational end result of most of the theories proposed in the past, however, is not the disappearance of the people, but a lower level of social complexity. It is a new equilibrium, perhaps achieved after great mortality, between population levels and the available food supply or energy flow.

Declining agricultural productivity, to look at one competing theory, argues for a lower level of social complexity with smaller populations. It does not provide a theoretical framework for the complete disappearance of the entire population in large regions of the Lowlands. As agricultural productivity declined, so would populations until a balance was reached between the carrying capacity of the land and the population. A society will use the energy resources available to it. If the society disappears entirely, then, its energy source was probably cut off.

The loss of trade routes and reduced commerce, to take another, would not explain why the subsistence peasants stopped growing corn and disappeared. It might explain why urban centers would have decreased in size, but it does not explain the disappearance of the subsistence farmer. A theory explaining the disappearance of subsistence farmers must explain the cessation of all agriculture.

HOW DO MILLIONS DISAPPEAR?

At the time of the Classic Collapse, regardless of whose estimates are used, millions of people vanished from the Maya Lowlands. How does a culture vanish? How do millions of people disappear?

Either they fail to reproduce, they move, or they die. There are no other reasons.

No one has ever proposed a theory which would specify a failure to reproduce as the mechanism for the Collapse, and I cannot think of how that might happen. In fact, the Collapse at individual cities appears to be so abrupt, that failure to reproduce cannot account for it. It should be noted that in the case of the Taino culture, Sheldon Watts has suggested a failure to reproduce as the ultimate reason for their disappearance, but he does not specify how that might have transpired (Watts 1997:88).

Although Lorenzo Ochoa proposed a theory of the Maya Collapse based on migration, there is no evidence of great population movements involving millions of people at the end of the Classic period. There appear to be rapid increases in population in certain northern communities like Chichén Itza and Uxmal in the Late Classic, which may represent arriving refugees from the south, but these increases involve tens of thousands of people, at the very most hundreds of thousands, not millions. Even though migrations are characteristic of famines, there is no evidence for massive migration and resettlement in the Terminal Classic. There are no huge surges in population elsewhere (Ochoa 1980:145).

For millions of people to disappear, therefore, the people must have died. How do people die? There follows a list of general categories of how people die. The categories are meant to be very broad.

1. *Trauma.* They are physically killed, either deliberately as in war and murder or accidentally.

2. *Medical.* This category incorporates everything dealt with by doctors and hospitals in modern times. They die from disease, either the result of infection or the result of an organ or system failure, they are infested by parasites, they ingest toxic substances, they succumb to chronic problems, including those conditions we label "old age," or they die during childbirth, especially a thousand years ago.

3. *Exposure.* They freeze to death or get heat stroke.

4. *Famine and Thirst.* They run out of food and water and die of starvation and thirst.

Of the above causes of death, only war, infection, and famine and thirst can account for mortality measured in the millions.

Were millions of people murdered over a hundred-year period? One would have to postulate a series of military invasions in which the end goal was to murder millions of people one by one over a hundred-year period instead of conquering, ruling, and exploiting them. Even though warfare may be implicated in the fall of individual cities, murder is an unlikely explanation for how the Collapse as a whole developed. While it is true that Genghis Khan laid waste to many Persian cities, numerous examples exist in the historical record of societies that lived in constant, unending warfare with their neighbors without disappearing.

Ross Hassig has estimated that the operational radius for a Mesoamerican army was about three-days' march, if supplied from their home base. Local foraging, of course, could have extended that limit. Simon Martin and Nikolai Grube, on the other hand, have suggested, based on epigraphic references, that Calakmul twice attacked Palenque, once in AD 599 and again in 611—a distance of one hundred fifty miles if the army was raised at Calakmul itself. Of course, the hieroglyphic texts they analyzed say nothing about where the army was from, or its size, or how it was provisioned, or even what constituted an attack. Regardless, Hassig estimates that the sizes of armies were quite small. He believes, for example, that Tikal could have fielded an army of only 1,055 soldiers. In short, Maya warfare was circumscribed and was primarily important in legitimating political rule. The size armies he proposed would certainly be incapable of murdering millions of people (Hassig 1992:23, 77–78; Martin and Grube 1995:45).

What about disease occurring by itself in the absence of famine, could that account for the Collapse? From historical sources, there is no record of a disease that succeeded in wiping out an entire civilization elsewhere in the world. Even the Black Death resulted in the deaths of no more than 30 percent of the population of Europe. While a devastating death toll, it did not result in the almost complete disappearance of European civilization. In modern times, neither AIDS nor the Ebola virus kills everyone. Further, there was no reservoir of endemic disease left in the native populations of Mesoamerica which would account for such incredible mortality. Disease without famine is a theoretically conceivable cause, even though there is no evidence that it has ever wiped out an entire civilization elsewhere, and there is no evidence for it in the case of the Maya. It should be noted, however, that disease is one of the cascade of effects of drought and famine (Watts 1997:1).

Having said that, it is important to recognize the devastating, murderous power of epidemics. During the first century of the arrival of 200,000 Spaniards in the Americas, between 60 and 80 million people disappeared from the Indies, Mexico, and Central America—a truly staggering sum. While factors such as war, wholesale murder, slavery, *encomiendas*, droughts, and famines played important roles in that terrible tragedy, nevertheless it appears that a major part was reserved for disease. A particularly virulent form of smallpox may have virtually destroyed individual communities. Death rates, sometimes exceeding 85 percent, were reported for certain tribes in North America. In fact, according to Watts, the extinction of "whole groupings" was common in North America, the Caribbean Islands, and Brazil, although not in Mesoamerica. Smallpox did not destroy by itself, however. Other diseases like colds, influenza, measles, mumps, German measles, whooping cough, plague, yellow fever, and malaria may all have been introduced into native populations within a very short period of time. It is important to note, however, that those diseases which killed so many in the Colonial past have still been endemic recently, approximately four hundred to five hundred years later, whereas there do not appear to have been any endemic infectious diseases present in the native populations at Contact which might explain the Classic Collapse six hundred years before (Ramenofsky 1987:147–159; Stannard 1992:94–95; Watts 1997:92, 107).

During the first century after Spanish contact, the death rate among the Maya from all causes appears to have been around 95 percent. As we will see, however, disease was not the only factor at work. Drought and famine also devastated the peninsula during the first hundred years causing an enormous loss of life (Stannard 1992:94–95).

Returning to the mortality of millions, the only remaining cause of death with the potential to kill millions of people is starvation and thirst, which has been implicated in the disappearance or severe contraction of other civilizations like the Akkadian in Mesopotamia, the Tiwanaku and Moche in South America, the Anasazi in North America, the Toltec in Mesoamerica, and others around the world. Among all the potential causes of the death of millions of Maya, famine and thirst is the only explanation that accounts for the pattern of their survival around long-term, stable sources of drinking water and their death elsewhere. Drought, in fact, has been associated before with the demise of Maya cities like El Mirador and Calakmul (Armillas 1964:76; Folan et al 1995:330; Gibbons 1993:985; Kerr 1998:325; Larson et al 1996:219; Wright 1998:99).

It is important to repeat, however, that drought rarely, if ever, results in starvation and thirst by themselves. They are inextricably intertwined with disease, so that it is often difficult to determine whether a person died of starvation or disease. The cascade of effects driven by a drought often incorporates all three large-scale causes of death: starvation and thirst, disease, and conflict.

THE PHYSIOLOGY OF STARVATION

The way to death is nasty and brutish and often not short.
                              —W. R. Aykroyd (1974:12)

As we examine the steps between a drought and the disappearance of a culture, we should look at the effect of famine on individuals and then the resulting effects on a famine stricken society. Famine, of course, destroys cultures through its effect on individuals.

Human beings have developed adaptive mechanisms in the form of energy reserves to help survive periods of extreme hunger. Among individuals who have been well fed, physiologic reserves can avert death from starvation for months as their bodies adjust to steady weight losses. Consumption of small amounts of proteins and carbohydrates will permit them to function normally until about 10 percent of their body weight has been lost. Their bodies then begin to make downward adjustments in energy demands. As body weight is reduced, fewer calories are required to sustain physical activity. At the same time, a curtailment of normal activity occurs, which explains why the rate of weight loss declines during periods of time on relatively small amounts of food. In mobilizing its reserves, the body progressively selects fat over muscle as fuel, allowing life to be sustained for one to three months in acute starvation. Anything short of total fast greatly prolongs resistance. People who have limited nutritional reserves, however, can exhaust them within two days when food is absent. They are the first to starve (Dirks 1980:23; Golkin 1987:110).

During a severe famine in Madras during 1877–1878, Alexander Porter performed autopsies on men and women who died of starvation. He found that when human beings had lost approximately 33 percent of their normal weight, "life is held by a slender thread which the least untoward circumstance is sufficient to snap." On the other hand, during the Dutch famine of 1944–1945, the threshold weight loss was about 40 percent among the normally better fed populace (Aykroyd 1974:14).

Actual starvation, the most severe form of hunger, is manifested in extreme physical depletion. It is the paramount sign of famine when it occurs on a wide scale. Individuals who are starving complain of weakness, hunger pains, dizziness, blackouts, and increased urinary frequency. They are depressed, irritable, withdrawn, and emotionally unstable. They become emaciated. Their skin develops the consistency of paper, becomes dull and inelastic, and may show dusty brown splotches. The skin is dry, scaly, inelastic, and very thin with a tendency to ulcerate. The skin at first is pale, probably because of a reduced peripheral blood flow, and subjects tend to complain of the cold. A later dirty brown darkening of the skin has been frequently reported in light skinned famine victims. This discoloration may particularly occur in areas of the skin most traumatized. It is not due to exposure to the sun, although there is also an increased sensitivity of the skin to sunlight. Their hair becomes dry, lackluster, and sparse. Folliculitis, inflammation of the hair root, is generally present (Golkin 1987:110; Harrison 1988:78–79).

Skeletal muscles are slack, movements are slow and clumsy. Even before there is a detectable loss of cardiac tissue, the pulse rate and the cardiac volume are reduced when measured at rest, but disproportionately increased by mild exercise. As weight loss continues, the resting pulse is further reduced and blood pressure falls. There is a progressive fall in the basal metabolic rate (Harrison 1988:78–79).

The alimentary canal is thinned, but gut function is generally normal in mild starvation. In severely starved subjects, however, gut function is disturbed so that feeding may be associated with severe diarrhea, and food passes through the gut undigested. The intestinal wall becomes thin and loses its ability to absorb nutrients. Urine volume is often reported as increased, possibly because reports come from situations where large volumes of soup have been consumed. Nocturia and polyuria, frequent and copious urination, are a common complaint, but no convincing kidney abnormalities have been demonstrated, even though kidney mass is lost (Golkin 1987:110; Harrison 1988:78–79).

In moderate starvation, extra cellular fluid volume is somewhat increased, and some individuals, especially adults aged over forty years, get hunger edema or swelling. As greater amounts of weight are lost, the prevalence of hunger edema rises, and all age groups become affected. The skeleton is radiologically normal, but there is some reduction in bone marrow which is replaced by water, which, being more radiologically opaque, makes the skeleton radiologically dense, and may mask demineralization (Harrison 1988:78–79).

In adolescents, puberty is delayed and may not occur. When it does it has unusual features. In boys, the voice may not break and, in both sexes, there is a curious tendency in the more severely starved for a luxuriant growth of hair on the face and in the genital regions and excessive amounts of a fine lanugo hair on the face, trunk, and limbs have been described. Severely starved adults from the age of thirty onwards may lose hair even in the armpits and genital regions (Harrison 1988:78–79).

Women experience amenorrhea, the cessation of menstruation, and men become impotent. Pregnancy rates decline and miscarriages increase. The reasons for the short-term decline in births in famine situations are fairly well understood. As with mortality change, malnutrition plays a critical role. There is a decrease in fecundity when the nutritional value and quantity of food consumed falls below minimal levels, and women stop ovulating and male sperm mobility and longevity are reduced. Moreover in times of famine there is likely to be increased fetal wastage due to the deteriorating condition of mothers, while women may breast-feed children for longer periods and in so doing prolong postpartum amenorrhea. Infant risk is increased in other ways. Undernutrition interferes with prenatal development, raising chances of mortality, and poorly nourished women typically endure prolonged birth labor, which increases the hazard for both mother and infant (Dirks 1980:23; Golkin 1987:110; Hugo 1984:20).

Speech is usually lucid, though a little slow; starving people almost at the point of death can often answer questions clearly. Hearing remains unimpaired. In fact, there are reports that it becomes especially acute in starvation, an impression probably arising from increased sensitivity to noise and general irritability. But while, in the physiological sense, the brain continues to function, the psychological effects of deprivation of food are distressing. An obsession with things to eat—what has been called "the persistent clamor of hunger"—takes charge of the mind (Aykroyd 1974:15).

During the Bengal famine of 1943, many of the patients in the famine hospital were picked up in a state of extreme weakness and collapse, often on the point of death. They were for the most part emaciated to such a degree that the description "living skeletons" was justifiable. Many suffered from mental disorientation, showing a very marked degree of apathy and indifference to their surroundings. When taken to the hospital, such patients made very little effort to help themselves and received medical attention with an indifference which sometimes amounted to passive obstruction. They did not care how dirty or naked they were. Those with famine diarrhea would repeatedly soil their beds and pay no attention to the protests of the attendants. In a few cases maniacal symptoms were present. The mental state of many starving destitutes indeed sometimes disconcerted workers in famine hospitals, who were not aware that it was a pathological condition induced by starvation. There was some tendency to regard starving cases as needlessly dirty and uncooperative, and, since they made little effort to help themselves, not worth helping (Aykroyd 1974).

Comparative time and motion studies in Guatemala have established that peasants with lower caloric intakes work more slowly and rest longer than those fed protein calorie supplements. At the cellular level, activity also declines. There is a marked decrement in basal metabolism per unit of tissue and a concomitant drop in body temperature. Blood pressure and velocity decline, and heart rate slows gradually, becoming less responsive to stimulation. In sum, savings go beyond what might be expected solely from loss of mass. Research has shown that a weight loss of 10 percent reduces energy expenditure by about 25 percent; a weight loss of 20 percent reduces caloric demand by about 50 percent. As much as 60 percent of these reductions is due to a decrease in tasks undertaken. Reductions in caloric expenditures due to reduced activity help explain why the rate of weight loss declines during semi-starvation and why life can be maintained for extended periods (Dirks 1980:23).

Distinct stages of starvation can usefully be distinguished in adults on the basis of weight loss: moderate starvation, when up to 25 percent of the normal body weight is lost; severe starvation, when 25 to 50 percent of the body weight is lost; and a terminal stage when weight loss exceeds 50 percent and the condition has so deteriorated that death often occurs despite treatment. Death from starvation usually occurs when about 33 to 50 percent of the body weight has been lost, depending on the initial nutritional condition of the individual. Intractable diarrhea is the most common terminal event (Golkin 1987:111; Harrison 1988:78).

Some individuals resist terminal starvation better than others. Previous experience boosts subsequent resistance, and females withstand starvation longer than males. Because of their relatively high protein demands, children are at a disadvantage. Nursing infants usually are spared disease in early stages of famine, but later on lactation is liable to decrease or cease entirely, leaving them no longer protected (Dirks 1980:24).

If water is available, but no food is consumed, death may not come for three months or more, depending on initial body fat. The cause of death in total starvation is obscure; it may be due to electrolyte depletion, especially magnesium depletion, or it may be due to loss of vital body protein, particularly heart muscle (Harrison 1988:63).

DEHYDRATION

Absolute thirst kills in a few days.
—W. R. Aykroyd (1974:15)

If nothing whatever is consumed, the limiting factor in survival is water. Death from dehydration occurs in a few days when water losses are high, as in a hot environment, at high altitude, or when sweating is profuse, and always before any other nutritional deficiency appears. Primary dehydration, due to inadequate intake, has rarely been observed among famine victims, not least because those without water are unlikely to reach a relief feeding center where most observers are. Secondary dehydration as a result of diarrhea is the most likely cause of death. In both cases, the clinical signs are the same: the subject is weak and apathetic with sunken features, oliguria, or sparse urination, is present, the eyes are sunk into the orbits, the skin is loose and inelastic, and when pinched stands up away from the subcutaneous tissue. The victims of severe dehydration show signs of oligemic shock due to an inadequate quantity of blood, severe vasoconstriction, high pulse rate, and low blood pressure (Harrison 1988:62–63).

The Maya survived close to water and died away from it. The common thread that runs through those cities that survived the Collapse is the availability of long-term sources of fresh drinking water. While it is true that survivors of demographic catastrophes tend to congregate around local water sources, the total depopulation of extensive areas of the richest, most fertile agricultural areas of the Classic period suggests that a different dynamic was at work in the case of the Classic Maya. Those cities that had water survived and those that did not died. This fact leads to a presumption that water played an important role in the Maya Collapse and that thirst and dehydration was as serious a factor as famine in determining who lived and who died. Thirst may, in fact, have been the determining factor. We will examine Maya water resources in greater detail in chapter 9.

MAYA MALNUTRITION

The studies done on Maya skeletons retrieved from formal burials indicate changes that might have occurred over long periods of time. Unfortunately, in periods of famine, formal burials rarely occur, especially in the segments of society that suffer the most. The survivors themselves are starving to death and too weakened to exert the energy required. The result is that people die in the streets, in the plazas, on the roads, or in their homes. The vultures, dogs, and varmints eat the corpses and the bones. Those bones that are not eaten deteriorate rapidly in the tropical environment. In fact, in the Maya Lowlands, bones and teeth in formal burials often decompose (Fred Valdez Jr., February 1998, personal communication).

In short, there is no direct evidence of physiological starvation from the Maya Lowlands, nor should we expect there to be.

Skeletons from several Maya lowland sites do give us an indication of changes that were occurring in the nutritional status of Maya populations through time. Stress levels increased dramatically during the Classic. At Tikal, there was a marked reduction in non-elite adult male stature during the Late Classic, a pattern that also occurs at Altar de Sacrificios, Barton Ramie, and perhaps Copán. At Tikal, mortality was particularly high for infants and females entering childbearing age, a pattern also seen at Copán. At Altar de Sacrificios and Copán, the incidence of porotic hyperstosis also increased markedly during the Late Classic. Porotic hyperstosis consists of pitted lesions of the cranial vault and orbital roof and spongy thickening of the parietal boss area of the skull. It occurs in populations suffering from chronic anemias that are often caused by inadequate amounts of iron intake, although prolonged breastfeeding, diarrheal infections, and parasitic disease infestations due to population aggregation also play a role. To date, apparently no studies have been carried out looking for Harris lines which form when a person's bone growth is temporarily halted because of stress caused by famine or malnutrition. Harris lines are internal and can only be seen in X-ray or cross sectional examinations of human long bones. Some kinds represent periods of short stress, others periods of longer stress. They are generally found in the bones of farming cultures (Angel 1966:760; Vaughan Bryant 1994:121; El-Naijar and Robertson 1976:141; Holland and O'Brien 1997: 184; Santley 1990:329–330).

DISEASE

There is no doubt that famine and pestilence—in that order—have been evil partners through the ages and outbreaks of disease in the course of famine have often killed more people than starvation itself. Starvation and epidemic diseases occur together for two reasons. First, extreme hunger impairs defense mechanisms and increases susceptibility to disease. Second, the social disruption, crowding, lack of sanitation, and virtual absence of medical facilities, which are characteristic among starving communities and refugee congregations, accelerate the spread of diseases. The combination results in epidemic outbreaks (Aykroyd 1974:20; Golkin 1987:113).

One of the earliest Indian famine enquiry commissions, reporting in 1868, made a brave attempt to produce a rational statement about famine and epidemic disease: "We think it is impossible to distinguish between the mortality caused by starvation and that due to disease, directly or indirectly connected with starvation....In truth, want and disease run so much into each other that no statistics and no observations would suffice to draw an accurate line" (quoted in Aykroyd 1974:22).

Typhus, or "famine fever," was a major cause of famine deaths in Europe. Smallpox and cholera have taken uncounted lives during periods of famine in Asia. Plague, diphtheria, typhoid, whooping cough, scarlet fever, measles, and tuberculosis also have been associated with famine deaths for centuries. During recent decades, African famine victims have died of bronchitis, cholera, diarrhea, measles, and pneumonia as well as from the effects of extreme undernutrition. Historical records of famine conditions have not distinguished deaths caused by starvation from deaths due to epidemic disease. However, a United Nations Food and Agricultural Organization report published in 1967 expressed a growing consensus that, during most periods of famine, deaths from epidemic diseases have exceeded deaths from starvation (Golkin 1987:113; Masefield 1967).

James Waller spent a year and a half at a refugee camp in Sudan between 1985 and 1986. The following descriptions of disease in the midst of famine are drawn from his observations of a real world famine refugee camp as recounted in his book, *Fau: Portrait of an Ethiopian Famine* (Waller 1990).

The severely malnourished Ethiopian peasants arriving at Tuklebab were susceptible to all sorts of diseases that normally would be fought off by the body's immune system. The higher susceptibility of malnourished individuals to tuberculosis is well documented in medical textbooks. Tuberculosis spread rapidly at Tuklebab. Measles rampaged through the camp in the winter, killing untold numbers of children. Pneumonia was common in both adults and children as was typhoid. Beriberi and scurvy were not uncommon. Blindness from vitamin A deficiency was frequently encountered. Simple falls resulted in broken legs—bones brittle from lack of calcium and vitamins (Waller 1990:42).

Prolapsed rectums in children were sickeningly common. Diarrhea-producing intestinal parasites, along with simple bacterial diarrhea, were the biggest killers of all. Diarrhea, lack of water, 50°C (120°F) heat, and blasts of desert winds combined to dehydrate their victims with frightening speed. Hundreds of hungry children developed diarrhea for a few hours, vomited a couple of times, and then went into convulsions and died. Dehydration kills by draining the body of salt-containing fluid (Waller 1990:42–43, 67).

The graveyard at Tuklebab was the camp's most distinctive feature....The dead were carried out to the graveyard in an early morning ritual. Days were spent fighting the soft, dull ache of hunger and the desperate, piercing agony of thirst. Women watched their children die. Men watched their women mourn. The only sound was the interminable coughing of those who were dying. The entire spectacle seemed as though it had been conjured by some demon as a vision out of hell. (Waller 1990:43)

Those most vulnerable to disease are the children. In addition, if diseases spread faster, children will catch them when they are younger and more vulnerable. Disease is a major cause of undernutrition in children (Waal 1989:192).

Although epidemics are historically inevitable, there have been noteworthy exceptions. Despite widespread starvation in Greece in 1942 and in Holland in 1945, no real epidemics developed. Even in the Warsaw Ghetto, with extreme malnutrition and almost 300,000 deaths, epidemics were very rare (Foege 1971:67).

There is no specific evidence of disease at the time of the Maya Collapse. As already noted, porotic hyperstosis is present in many skulls. In addition, Frank Saul and Julie Mather Saul found a great variety of disorders in the bones they examined ranging from dental decay on through lesions of greater medical interest—similar to those possibly associated with treponemal diseases like syphilis or yaws, tuberculosis, and Paget's disease—as well as a series of lesions related to malnutrition. Although it is not possible to make definitive diagnoses from the bones, the Sauls conclude that "skeletal lesions indicate the presence of important health problems throughout the known past as well as in modern times, and a chronic precarious health status would be likely to magnify the impact of invasions or crop failures or any similar sudden negative occurrences and thus could set the scene for the 'collapse' of the Classic Maya" (Saul and Saul 1989:296–300).

Although specific evidence from the Maya Lowlands is scarce, analyses of mummies and coprolites, mummified or fossilized feces, from other regions of the New World indicate that the major health problem faced by Native American populations was most likely parasites. Thus, hunters in the Arctic perished from heart failure as armies of nematodes invaded their muscles. In the Great Basin of the United States, thorny-headed worms pierced the intestinal walls of foragers. In the Andes, protozoans ulcerated and rotted farmers' throats, mouths, and lips. In modern times, 18 million inhabitants of Central and South America suffer from Chagas' disease. Other studies have identified roundworms, pinworms, tapeworms, and wireworms. According to parasitologist Karl Reinhard, "The hard data of paleopathology show that many people were as sick as dogs." Yet, populations tend to live with their parasite infections. There is no evidence that parasites have been responsible for acute epidemics. Interestingly, of sixteen species of parasites found by Reinhard and his colleagues in archaeological contexts, eleven were almost certainly native to the Americas and the rest were probably transported within themselves by the pioneers arriving from Asia (Pringle 1998:76–78).

5. Famine and Social Dissolution

F amine throughout history has generally been class famine, in the sense that the poor died while the rich secured enough food for survival. It is, indeed, reported that in a famine in India in 1344, the Mogul emperor could not obtain enough food for his household, but chroniclers more often tell of abundant meals behind the palace walls, while the king's ministers make fortunes buying and selling grain, and the peasants die (Aykroyd 1974:10–11, 52).

In the Maya Lowlands, Frederick Wiseman wrote that "the Collapse was not only a hierarchical phenomenon, but also a general catastrophe that affected the bottom of the social pyramid, the Maya farmer." He based his conclusions on palynological evidence from the central Petén lakes indicating a total cessation of agriculture (Wiseman 1978:114).

The first in the society to feel the effects of drought are the peasants and farmers. Either their crops fail to germinate or they wither and die. In either case, they cannot harvest a crop—the first step towards disaster. The way from crop failure to starvation for the poor can follow three routes:

1. by reducing their own production of food and any sales they might make;
2. by reducing their ability to get cash or in kind wages through work;
3. and by raising the price they pay for food, thereby reducing the purchasing power of what wages they do get, and assets they have accumulated (Devereux 1993:39, 42).

109

We will look in this chapter at the effect of drought and famine on peasants and their communities. Peasants can be defined as small producers on land, who, with the help of simple equipment, their own labor, and that of their families, produce mainly for their own consumption and for meeting obligations to the holders of political and economic power. They reach nearly total self-sufficiency within the framework of a village community. Peasants are small, usually family oriented, agricultural producers, who own, rent, or hold through contract the land they cultivate, for example, as sharecroppers. With little or no capital at their disposal and a generally low level of technology, peasants rely on the land and their family's labor to meet household subsistence needs. According to Eric Wolf, peasants are different from farmers. Farmers operate a business; peasants run a household. Robert Redfield emphasized that a peasant's agriculture is a livelihood and a way of life, not a business for profit (Arnold 1988:50; Garnsey 1988:44; Redfield 1956:18; Wolf 1966:3–4).

If they are not farmers, then how are peasants distinguished from primitive peoples? In primitive society, producers control the means of production, including their own labor, and exchange their labor and products directly for the goods and services of others. As societies grow and develop, however, such simple systems are replaced by others in which control of the means of production, including the disposition of human labor, passes from the hands of the primary producers into the hands of groups that are not directly engaged in the production process themselves, but assume instead special executive and administrative functions, backed by the use of force. Instead of direct exchange, goods and services are furnished first to a center and then redistributed by a dominant group that uses the surpluses to underwrite its own standard of living. They then distribute the remainder to groups in society that do not farm but must be fed in return for the specific goods and services which they produce. "There were no peasants before the first cities," Redfield wrote, "and those surviving primitive peoples who do not live in terms of the city are not peasants." Peasants are rural natives whose order of life takes important account of the cities. In fact, urban life would be impossible without peasants and their agricultural surpluses. Cities in nonindustrialized states, therefore, cannot exist without peasants and peasants cannot exist without cities. The presence of cities in a nonindustrial society indicates that the rural population lives as peasants (Redfield 1953:18, 31; Wolf 1966:3–4).

As Sanders and Price have pointed out, the economic and social aspects of the existence of cities imply that means exist not only for the production of a surplus, but for distributing it to feed people who themselves are not primary producers. "In other words, it is insufficient for the peasantry to produce a surplus; there must also be some incentive for them to spend it in this particular way. Surplus is channeled into the cities in the form of taxation, tribute, tithes, rents, and market exchanges" (Sanders and Price 1968:236).

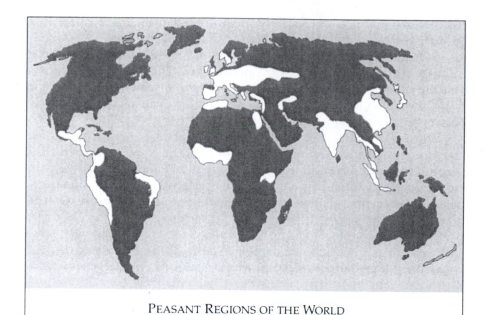

PEASANT REGIONS OF THE WORLD

Figure 15. Peasant regions of the world, *light areas*, as defined by Eric Wolf (adapted from Wolf 1966:2).

Wolf wrote in 1966 that there were still large areas of the world in which peasants who cultivated the land not only formed the vast majority of the population, but also furnished the funds of rent and profit which underwrote the entire social structure. In such societies, all other social groups depended upon peasants both for their food and for any income that might accrue to them (Wolf 1966:12).

Peasant society has often been divided into three layers, and these internal divisions are of particular importance in understanding the differential impact of food crises and famines on rural households. First, there are the rich peasants who cultivate sufficient land to meet their own needs and may hire additional labor to help them to produce a marketable surplus. Secondly, the middle peasants whose holdings are sufficient for their family subsistence needs but little more. Thirdly, the poor peasants who, holding insufficient land to satisfy their needs, have to find employment as laborers on the lands of others or perhaps outside the village as seasonal and plantation workers (Arnold 1988:50–51).

PEASANT FAMINE

Paradoxically, since they are one of the most long lived forms of human organization known to recorded history, peasants seem always to walk a razor thin line between survival and extinction. This appears to be an almost universal characteristic of peasant life. Peasants push against the very margins of subsistence, risking death not just in the tens and hundreds like nomads, but in the millions (Arnold 1988:54).

To better explore this widespread trait, it will be useful to frame the discussion by asking some important questions. The following questions and the discussion of the vulnerability of peasant cultures to famine is drawn from an insightful analysis by Ronald Seavoy in his book, *Famine in Peasant Societies* (Seavoy 1986).

Why are peasant societies vulnerable to famine in ways that commercial farmers are not? Why don't peasant societies grow an assured food surplus so that hunger can be avoided when there are consecutive poor crop years? Why don't densely populated peasant societies that have experienced peacetime famines stabilize their birth rate so that those who are born can always be fed? Why are peasant societies, which have 60 to 90 percent of their populations engaged in food production, the very same societies that are constantly vulnerable to periodic famine? Stated another way, during long periods of peace, why do peasant populations increase their numbers to the maximum carrying capacity of the land during normal crops years and periodically endure seasonal hunger or famine during consecutive poor crop years? According to Seavoy, this question is seldom or never asked, yet annual periods of hunger and periodic famine affect all peasant societies, regardless of their race, religion, climate, population density, subsistence crop grown, or geographic area. As difficult as it is to understand, even peasant societies that have low population densities and cultivate fertile soils experience famine (Seavoy 1986:9–10).

The answer to all the questions, according to Seavoy, lies in the peasants' outlook on life, the subsistence rationality, and their practice of the subsistence compromise which defines those who are peasants. Under the subsistence compromise, the peasants attempt to grow sufficient food for their own consumption and additional meager needs with the least expenditure of labor on the assumption that all crop years will be normal. The concept explains the low level of material welfare and nutritional safety in peasant societies and why peasant societies universally have persistent food shortages regardless of population densities, regardless of soil fertility, and regardless of the cultivation techniques used (Seavoy 1986:10).

There is a revolutionary difference in the motivations of farmers, who produce food for market sale, and peasants, who produce food for subsistence consumption. The chief difference is the amount of labor that farmers and peasants expend in food production. Farmers maximize labor inputs, and thereby maximize profits, peasants minimize labor inputs and thereby maximize their free time (Seavoy 1986:10).

Commercial cultures use money to facilitate the production and exchange of almost all the material goods and services that the entire population consumes. This is especially true of food. In commercial cultures, almost all labor is performed for money in the form of wages, salaries, or a money income earned from entrepreneurial profits. Market institutions force cultivating households to measure their social security by the amount of their money incomes. Commercially motivated households voluntarily stabilize their numbers at a level that is in balance with the marketable food surplus available to feed them (Seavoy 1986:9).

Commercial rationality places a high social value on physical labor and rewards it with a scale of money incomes depending on individual skills, discipline, and hours worked. The social goal of commercial cultures is the production of a maximum amount of goods, services, and profits by maximum labor inputs (Seavoy 1986:11).

Subsistence rationality, on the other hand, places a low social value on physical labor and seeks to minimize its expenditure or to transfer it to the weakest members of society. In the subsistence compromise, the peasantry's primary social goal is the least expenditure of physical labor to achieve a satisfactory level of material welfare and nutritional safety. Peasant societies are part of cultures that desire a minimal level of material wealth and nutritional safety because this is the easiest way to reduce labor expenditures. The marginality of peasant subsistence is most easily observed by the small number of material possessions owned by each peasant household, but it is more accurately measured by the low margin of nutritional safety that peasants have in normal crop years. Even though peasant societies have a high percentage of their population engaged in food production, they produce only a small food surplus in normal crop years, and frequently there is no food surplus. The subsistence compromise is a calculated risk that peasants make at every planting on the assumption that every year will be a normal crop year (Seavoy 1986:11–12).

There are, thus, two types of rationality: subsistence rationality practiced by the peasants and commercial rationality practiced by farmers. Subsistence rationality places a low social value on the labor of cultivation, and commercial rationality places a high value on it. The difference in labor expenditures explains the vast difference in nutritional safety between peasants and wage laborers in commercial societies. It also explains why peasant societies are vulnerable to periodic peacetime famines and commercial societies are not (Seavoy 1986:388).

The technological limitations and slender resource base that plague peasant societies is borne out by another almost universal phenomenon, the hungry gap, which occurs every year between the exhaustion of the previous harvest and the ripening of the new crops. It is hardly ever due to lack of effort or foresight. No one chooses to be hungry for two or three months of the year, especially as the hungry gap leaves peasants physically weakest at the very time when they need to muster fresh energy for plowing and planting the new season's crops (Arnold 1988:54–55).

Yet, peasants have minimal motivation to expend the necessary labor to grow an assured food surplus or to limit the fertility to those who can be fed from existing food resources. In normal crop years, minimal labor expenditures provide all households with adequate nutrition, and during most periods of hunger, harvest sharing allows all households to subsist on a minimum diet until the next harvest. The production of a marginal food supply, when it is possible to produce an assured food surplus, is the single most important cause of the subsistence standard of welfare found in all peasant societies. Ester Boserup phrased it succinctly: "It seems that the people who employ land-using systems would also be able to produce surpluses if they were to make labor investments and work longer hours" (Boserup quoted in Seavoy 1986:11).

Peasants are little motivated to accumulate commercial wealth, measured in money, by producing commodities for market sale. They measure their welfare by the amount of free time they can enjoy after satisfying their subsistence food needs and other communal obligations. Peasant households are unwilling to expend any more labor than is necessary to grow enough food to feed themselves, produce seed for the next crop, pay a tithe to the clergy or moneylender, satisfy their exchange needs, and pay their tax or rent obligations that require money (Seavoy 1986:22, 24, 387).

To summarize, Seavoy has concluded that minimal labor expenditures in food production, the subsistence compromise, cause hunger regardless of climate, soil fertility, population density, crops grown, cultivation techniques used, or geographical area (Seavoy 1986:387).

According to historian Sir Moses Finley, the subsistence compromise has been noted by other economic geographers and named the "law of minimum effort" or "the principle of least effort." In Mesoamerica, the inclination to avoid labor has been reported among modern peasants as well. Redfield, for example, reported that, among the Maya peasantry of Yucatán, "leisure is also desirable and that hard work is, if possible, to be escaped." As Eric Wolf put it, "the peasant aims at subsistence, not at reinvestment. The starting point of the peasant is the needs which are defined by his culture." In general, according to Kent Flannery, primitive farmers don't produce a surplus unless they are forced to. In fact, the people with the most leisure time are the hunters and gatherers, who also have the lowest productivity (Finley 1985:127; Flannery 1972:405–6; Redfield 1956:68; Wolf 1966:504).

According to Seavoy, after each famine, peasant societies again increase their populations to the maximum carrying capacity of the land, to a state of criticality, and in effect, reprogram themselves for another famine, just as Malthus would have predicted. Famine and famine conditions are frequent occurrences and well within the memories of many persons in each village in all peasant societies. The peasantry know the value of enough food in storage to feed them until the next abundant harvest. Yet, after each period of hunger or famine, they do not produce an assured food surplus and population densities soon equal or exceed the previous numbers (Seavoy 1986:11).

An example is available from recent history which illustrates the point that peasants only produce what they need. Crop yields dropped in Ethiopia in 1975 when peasants were relieved from contributing a share of their harvest to feudal landholders. The Marxist military regime that overthrew the feudal government deprived the feudal landholders of their share of the harvest in the expectation that the peasantry would produce the same quantity of food and increase its profits by selling the food that had formerly gone to the feudal landholders. It did not happen. The peasantry was not interested in profits. It was interested in reducing labor expenditures. Food production declined an estimated 40 percent, the amount formerly paid to the feudal landholders. The peasantry lessened labor expenditures by cultivating less land, doing less weeding, and transferring the labor of cultivation to landless or near landless households on a sharecropping basis (Seavoy 1986:19–20).

Periodic peacetime famines occur in all peasant societies, including those with low population densities, but their greater impact is on dense populations. Famines usually ensue when there are two or more consecutive poor crop years. According to Seavoy, the usual cause of poor crop years is abnormal weather, with drought being the most common. Substantially deficient harvests, however, are also caused by excessive rains, floods, locust swarms, and cold and shortened growing seasons. Weather, together with marginal labor inputs, results in recurring famine (Seavoy 1986:27).

Those persons who lament malnutrition in peasant societies do not understand subsistence motivations for food production. They assume that peasants are inadequate food producers who practice high fertility because they are peasants. Yet, the nations of Western Europe that are now commercial food producers were once subsistence food producers that experienced periodic peacetime famines. The European nations became commercial food producers by restructuring land tenure and forcing cultivators to adopt commercial social values (Seavoy 1986:393).

MAYA PEASANTS

Most analysts of Maya settlement patterns have argued that the Classic Maya farmers were basically subsistence farmers working plots of land at their own discretion. Richard E. W. Adams and W. D. Smith, on the other hand, proposed a feudal model for Classic Maya society which Adams now believes has structural and processual similarities to Late Classic society. Small and large country estates developed with client peasant families living in clusters around the manor houses or minor palaces. Adams believes the Río Bec, Río Azul, and La Milpa zones show this process as does Copán. Population was spread thickly over the countryside as well as in proximity to the urban centers (Richard E. W. Adams 1997a:8–9; 1997b:56; Adams and Smith 1977; Pyburn 1996:239).

According to historian Terry Rugeley, Maya peasants in Colonial Yucatán did not begin to turn from subsistence to commercial agriculture until the mid eighteenth century in the northwestern part of the peninsula. From there, it gradually spread southward and eastward, although subsistence farming was still practiced in the twentieth century (Rugeley 1996:xiv).

Although we cannot know for sure, there is evidence enough to allow us to speculate that the rural, agricultural population of the Maya Lowlands lived as peasants. The presence of large cities, as we have seen, indicates that the rural population participated in a redistributive network for food surpluses, the primary indicators of a peasant society. Adams's and Smith's work suggests they lived in a subservient position to landlords who inhabited manor houses. The presence of lineage heads at Copán also suggests rural fiefdoms. The fact that well developed cities existed during the Classic indicates that systems of distribution and redistribution had to be in place. At the time of Contact, they did not practice commercial agriculture. And finally, the fact that commercial agriculture did not begin in the northern Lowlands until the eighteenth century suggests that subsistence agriculture was practiced before that time.

If the Maya did live as peasants and if Seavoy is correct that subsistence rationality is universal in all peasant societies, then the Maya peasants lived in constant danger of famine in normal times. They would have been particularly vulnerable to severe, extreme drought.

SOCIAL DISINTEGRATION

Let us turn our attention now to how peasant communities respond to the stress of drought and subsequent famine. Nobel laureate economist Amartya Sen studied the sequence of destitution in drought stricken farming communities through interviews with relief camp refugees. As the crisis deepens, he learned, crops and grazing are reduced. Servants and dependents of farmers begin to be evicted, and they are among the first to move to look for work elsewhere. Next the tenants are evicted from the land, and they too are set on the move. Both the tenants as well as small-scale family-land holders are gradually forced to sell livestock, in addition to losing many to the drought. Farmers run out of seeds when a second planting becomes necessary after a false start of the rains. There begins an unusually large movement in search of employment for daily labor or harvest work. The wives and children of the migrating men either stay with relatives, or come to town to beg for a living, or seek shelter in the relief camps (Sen 1981:98–99).

Piecing together the available information, the destitution groups in the 1973–1974 famine in Wollo, Ethiopia, would seem to include at least the following occupational categories (and their dependents):

1. pastoralists;
2. evicted farm servants, rural laborers, and dependents of farmers;

3. tenant cultivators, sometimes evicted, but often simply squeezed by economic circumstances;
4. small land owning cultivators;
5. male daily laborers in urban areas;
6. women in service occupations;
7. weavers and other craftsmen; and
8. occupational beggars.

Such occupational categories as weavers, craftsmen, service sellers, urban laborers, and beggars suffer mostly from straightforward derived destitution. The economic decline of the peasantry leads to shrinking demand for goods and services sold by other groups, in this case, clothing, craft products, services, and even general labor power. Also, of course, living on charity is made that much more difficult. One decline leads to another through the multiplier effect. Some occupations become more competitive, with the influx of displaced rural men and women seeking work for survival, after migration into urban areas. Trade entitlement failures, then, are the indirect result of agricultural decline. As the destitute lose their economic support, they cannot purchase food and they join the ranks of the famished (Sen 1981:103).

A similar effect was seen in a study of the impact of famine that was carried out following the Bengal famine of 1943. The Indian Statistical Institute surveyed 15,769 households, a sample regarded as representative of the entire Bengali population. The researchers constructed a destitution index and found that those at the lowest levels of society, fishermen, agricultural laborers, paddy huskers, and craft and transport workers, suffered the greatest incidence of destitution. The main cause of destitution was given as the death of the principal income earner of the household (Hugo 1984:19).

GOVERNMENT RESPONSE

As a drought develops, we have seen what the effect is on those most seriously harmed by the developing crisis. Now we turn our attention to the higher levels of the social hierarchy. The response of the ruling class to an impending famine appears to be remarkably the same everywhere. Officialdom has a characteristic propensity to receive any information on famine with scornful disbelief. The attitude is best manifested by the British official who refused to believe the fact of the Irish Famine and wrote with an air of authority, "There is such a tendency to exaggeration and inaccuracy in Irish reports that delay in acting on them is always desirable." In Ethiopia, the Ministry of the Interior, informed of the deaths by famine, requested a list of the names of the dead. At another time when the complaint that field rats were destroying crops reached the Ministry of the Interior, the response was: "Send a sample of the rats." During the Indian famine of 1974–1975, a famine crisis was not officially declared until September, when starved bodies were common items of litter on the side streets of the city of Dacca (Wolde Mariam 1984:10; Seavoy 1986:267).

Even when famine is finally accepted as a fact, the scornful disbelief merely turns into an astonishing underestimation of the magnitude and the intensity of famine. The net result is some perfunctory and ineffectual decision which gets more and more ineffectual as it goes down the bureaucratic ladder (Wolde Mariam 1984:10).

The most astounding example of scornful disbelief comes from the People's Republic of China. Not only did Mao Zedong refuse to accept the signs of severe famine during 1958–1961, but his subordinates went out of their way to prove to him that his obsession with Lysenkoist agricultural policies was justified by faking photographs of lush fields and actually transplanting millions of plants to fields he was scheduled to visit in order to give him the impression that agriculture was flourishing. In addition, they reported to him that China had surpassed the United States in agricultural production when in fact his Lysenkoist policies were destroying agriculture and tens of millions of people were dying from the resulting food shortages. Apparently, Mao never released the substantial food reserves held in government granaries (Becker 1996:xi, 81).

However, once the reality of famine is finally accepted, Sorokin wrote, the next stage of response is an expansion of governmental regulation, regimentation, and control of social relationships. The expansion of governmental control and regulation assumes a variety of forms, embracing socialist or communist totalitarianism, fascist totalitarianism, monarchical autocracy, and theocracy. It is imposed at different times by revolutionary regimes, by counterrevolutionary regimes, by military dictatorships, or by dictatorial bureaucracies (Sorokin 1942:122).

The shift may take place peacefully, the existing government itself effecting the change, or it may assume a violent form, the existing regime incapable of carrying out the process, being replaced by a revolutionary regime. Other conditions being equal, the greater the contrast between the rich and the poor, the sharper the increase of governmental regulation (Sorokin 1942:127).

The Bible gives us one of the oldest records of government imposed control, the terrible famine that devastated Egypt during the time of Joseph. As a result of the famine, the money failed, and Joseph gathered up all the money, the cattle, and all the land of ancient Egypt which "became Pharaoh's." He removed all the people to the cities throughout the country. The entire economic life began to be controlled by the government (Genesis 47:13–26, King James Version). In modern terminology, everything was nationalized. Similar examples, says Sorokin, abound from Egypt, China, Greece, Rome, and numerous other countries (Sorokin 1942:128–134).

RITUAL

As predictable as increased regulation is an intensification of ritual. Since the heavens were thought to control the elements, it was logical to appeal for a god's help, or to seek to atone for the sins that had manifestly provoked divine displeasure. Victims of disaster often view it as a consequence of divine disturbance, and government authorities, acting as religious and ritual leaders, frequently take extraordinary steps to bring relief supernaturally (Arnold 1988:76; Dirks 1980:27–28).

One of the principal duties of the emperors of China was to pray for rain on behalf of their people. One anguished emperor addressed heaven in the following moving terms:

> This year the drought is most unusual. Summer is past and no rain has fallen. Not only the crops and human beings feel the dire calamity, but beasts and insects, herbs and trees almost cease to live. I, the Minister of Heaven, am placed over mankind and am responsible for keeping order and peace in the world. I am scorched with grief and tremble with anxiety, but no genial and copious showers have been obtained.
>
> Some days ago I fasted, and offered rich sacrifices on the altars of the gods, and had to be thankful for gathering clouds and slight showers, but not enough to cause gladness. Summer is past and autumn has arrived; to wait longer will really be impossible. Knocking head, I pray Imperial Heaven to hasten and confer gracious deliverance—speedy and divinely beneficial rain, to save the people's lives and in some degree redeem my inequities. Alas! Oh Imperial Heaven, be gracious to them. I am inexpressibly grieved, alarmed and frightened. (quoted in Aykroyd 1974:83)

The emperor's distress is echoed in the Maya Lowlands. *The Book of Chilam Balam of Maní*, for example, tells us:

> Lahun Chablé will establish, to the south, a Katún 8 Ahau. With his eyes on the heavens, the ruler will implore food and drink. The warrior will thank him who will give him food and drink. The fields having been impoverished, shall be searched for food and water which will not be found anywhere in the Petén or in the entire land, wherever there are Bacabs. (Craine and Reindorp 1979:83)

> Lahun Chan established the Katún 8 Ahau and directed his powerful gaze toward heaven, imploring hard bread and water. No one entertained the soldier with bread or water. The people, on the plain and in the forest, were chilled. Everything was searched,

but nothing [neither food nor water] could be found on the plains, or in the forest, or in the whole world, or in all of Petén. (Craine and Reindorp 1979:156)

In Katún 6 Ahau they shall eat trees and rocks as they shall be dying of starvation. Seated on their beds, on their mats, the dying governors, with their relatives besides them, shall speak of food and they will talk incessantly, wishing the trees would fructify. (Craine and Reindorp 1979:84–85)

When rituals fail to bring relief, more divisive or desperate responses follow. Scapegoats are sought out and punished for "holding the rain" for their own ends, especially those who, at least initially, profit from a lack of rain like grain traders and brickmakers (Arnold 1988:77).

REBELLION AND CONFLICT

Sorokin pointed out that once in a while, each of the four calamities of the Apocalypse occurs alone and spreads without the company of the others, but more often than not they ravage in various combinations. Many a famine did not produce either revolution or war. Many a war or revolution has occurred in prosperous societies. The number of famines that have occurred in the history of any great nation has been much greater than the number of wars and revolutions caused by famine. What are the conditions, then, under which famine and impoverishment may lead to riot, revolution, or war? First, for a given society there must be no other means except revolution or war to alleviate its impoverishment. Secondly, in a famishing society there must be a notable contrast between the starving and the non-starving groups. Thirdly, the rich and the ruling classes or the rich societies must be poorly organized and poorly armed. Fourth, the most important condition is the disintegration of the system of norms and values—moral, religious, juridical, and others—in a considerable part of the starving masses or the poverty stricken society (Sorokin 1942:289–291).

Many famines have ended in tragic ways. First, they have resulted in internal disturbances and conflicts which, except in mild and superficial revolutions, have hardly ever alleviated the famines. Instead, practically all the great revolutions have enormously aggravated starvation, to say nothing of generating various epidemics, civil wars, and revolutionary terrors. Revolutions, therefore, have greatly increased the death toll and the death rate in famine. If, after months or years of revolution, the famine ended, it did so mainly because of the decrease of huge numbers of victims claimed by starvation, pestilence, and civil strife (Sorokin 1942:297–298).

On the other hand, other observers maintained that famines have rarely stimulated upheavals. Rebellious activities such as food riots or looting may occur during the early stages of famine, but people facing starvation are too weak and too concerned with basic survival to summon the energy or the organization needed to undertake either rebellious or revolutionary activities. They believed that food riots and looting needed to be understood for the limited phenomena they generally are, that such eruptions seldom prove overtures to revolution (Arnold 1988:85; Golkin 1987:21).

In order to reconcile these views, Ancel Keys and his colleagues proposed the following measure of the increase in civil strife as famine worsens: at an average 5 percent weight loss for the population, the chance for incidents of political disorder is slight, at 10 percent moderate, at 15 percent serious, and at 20 percent very serious. Thereafter, the probability declines (Keys et al 1950:917).

Anthropologist Robert Dirks, however, pointed out that these estimates are extremely gross and that Keys and his colleagues did not distinguish between organized rebellions and revolutions and disruptions of a more spontaneous, less broadly organized sort like rioting, banditry, and looting. They also did not adequately reconcile the proposed mounting tendency for strife and disorder with the simultaneously declining capacity for members of the population to exert themselves. Therefore, Dirks believed rebellion and revolution are more likely to occur during the first phase of the famine than later, and the overthrow of government is more likely to be attempted by mildly affected segments of the population than by those seriously affected. The events surrounding the overthrow in 1974 of Emperor Haile Selassie and the 2,000-year old dynasty in Ethiopia is a good case in point (Dirks 1980:27).

As obtaining food from familiar sources becomes more and more difficult, efforts to procure nourishment expand into previously unexploited niches, competition intensifies, and conflict increases. Aggression is enhanced in situations where food concentrations present hungry individuals with attractive and defensible sites. Dirks listed several examples of conflict around the world during famines. Gardens, for example, are guarded closely. During the famines of the past, the residents of Wuppertal, Germany, took great precaution against theft, householders taking turns day and night to watch crops. The Ik's gardens in northeastern Uganda were equipped with watchtowers, gardens in Ireland with watchhouses. The watch over crops in China became a permanent institution. On Tikopia in the Santa Cruz Islands of the Pacific, brothers who usually shared garden land set up boundaries between them, and neighbors accused one another of moving boundary markers. Theft became so rampant in both Ireland and Tikopia that people began to despair of gardening altogether. Popular sentiment on Tikopia demanded the execution of thieves. Successive famine years in the Trobriand Islands of Papua New Guinea caused inland dwellers to attempt fishing on the shores, where local residents responded by hunting down and killing the interlopers (Dirks 1980:29).

A question frequently asked regarding the droughts during the Classic Collapse is: why didn't the people go where there was food and water, if they had run out at home? According to the above examples, those who had food and water during a time of famine would most likely have run off refugees searching for food, or perhaps even killed any interlopers like the Trobrianders.

Perhaps the great Somali poet, Mohamed Abdile Hassan, best described the spirit of conflict that surges during famine:

Charred plants, stumps of burned trees,
the hot air rising from them,
the burnt branches and tree trunks
through which you pass in pain....

Who welcomes you like a kinsman in your day of need
and who, at the height of the drought, does not bar his gate against you,
Is not he who never fails you in your weakness one of the brethren? (quoted in Cahill 1982b:39)

MIGRATION

Most famines lead to peaceful or violent exodus. In contradistinction to the gradual, orderly, and voluntary character of migration and mobility in normal times, catastrophes render these processes sudden, violent, chaotic, largely involuntary, and essentially tragic. They disrupt the existing network of social relationships, and make the social structure chaotic, fluid, and "protoplasmic" (Sorokin 1942:106–107).

Mass emigration is often diagnostic of famine. The Indian Famine Commission in 1901 identified "unusual wandering" as the first unambiguous sign of famine in India. The pattern, direction, volume, and personnel involved in these early and often panic-stricken movements appear highly varied, depending in part on the nature and location of available relief (Aykroyd 1974).

In the famine of 1921–1922 in Russia, the majority of the population of the famine regions became nomadic. The city population markedly decreased—for instance in Moscow from 1,854,426 in 1917 to 1,023,000 in 1920, in St. Petersburg from 2,420,000 in 1917 to 740,000 in 1920, contractions of 45 and 70 percent, respectively. These wandering hordes often traveled considerable distances in what Sorokin called their "mapless migrations." Vast areas were depopulated to such an extent that the few who remained behind were sometimes able to subsist on the existing food stock. Fairly representative are the cases where from 20 to 70 percent of the total population of large areas fled. In France during several eighteenth-century famines, the famine *emigrés* numbered as many as one million (Hugo 1984:23; Sorokin 1942:108).

Whatever the situation, migrants rarely can be assured of success in obtaining relief. Overcrowded towns, shelters, and transportation facilities frequently become disease hazards and the journey itself so exhausting that death is the only relief at the end. Among famished Russian peasants in 1921, those who remained in their villages had a better chance of survival than those who fled (Dirks 1980:27).

Famine reaches disaster levels when the starving muster their last energies to flee to other areas. This eliminates the last hope of a new crop. The refugees rapidly drain the resources of nonfamine areas, hoarding increases, and food supplies disappear (Weissman 1974:7).

In the end, no adjustment can prove sufficient without some measure of relief. Exhaustion overtakes all and brings silence. Visitors to Russian villages in 1921–1922 found many completely quiet, their inhabitants having either died or fled. Centuries earlier, a similar scene greeted travellers to Ireland:

> Ireland...now lay void as a wilderness. Five-sixths of her people had perished. Women and children were found daily perishing in ditches, starved. The bodies of many wandering orphans whose fathers had embarked for Spain and whose mothers had died were preyed upon by wolves. In the years 1652 and 1653 the plague and famine had swept away whole counties, that a man might travel twenty or thirty miles and not see a living creature. (Pendergast quoted in Dirks 1980:31)

MESOAMERICAN FAMINE MIGRATION

The collapse of Tula occurred during a drought in the twelfth century when farmers on the agricultural frontier of northern Mesoamerica began retreating from their scorched fields, falling back on Tula, and overwhelming the drought strained resources of the city (Armillas 1964:76).

In Tenochtitlan, during the famine of 1 Rabbit in 1454, Moctezuma Ilhuicamina distributed food from the royal granaries to the poor. When the stores ran out, he gave permission for the populace to leave the city to find food elsewhere and people left. The populations of Texcoco, Chalco, Xochimilco, and Tepanecapan also fled their cities. The Maya Lowlands appear to have suffered a famine at the same time, and the cities of Chichén Itza, Mayapán, and Uxmal appear to have been all abandoned simultaneously (Edmonson 1982:xvi, xx; Hassig 1981:172; Kowalski 1987:59, 62–63; Tozzer 1957:49–50).

The Books of Chilam Balam and Spanish Colonial reports of famine in Yucatán indicate that the people repeatedly abandoned their homes and fled into the forest or to the towns to look for food. During the famine of

1769–1770, for example, Juan Francisco Molina Solís reported that "entire towns are deserted because their inhabitants emigrated en masse, begging bread which would free them from death....At the gates of Campeche, throngs of people from more than sixty leagues came in search of alms and help to sustain life." (Sixty leagues is a distance somewhere between 250 and 300 km [150 and 200 mi], depending on whether a *legua legal* or a *legua común* was intended.) During the famine of 1822–1823, bands of beggars overran towns and took over haciendas and villages by force of arms, employing very violent methods to obtain anything to eat. Historian Eligio Ancona believed that in the Yucatán Peninsula, "the frequent migrations of the Mayas and most of the wars the different tribes waged against each other were caused by the want" of water. Migration during drought was as common in the Lowlands as in the rest of the world (Ancona quoted in Casares 1905:228; Molina Solís quoted in Molina Hübbe 1941:26, 28–29).

DEPRAVITY

In studying many reports of the disintegration of society during periods of famine, there are numerous reports of aberrant behavior, behavior that would be considered depraved in normal times. These sensational reports are repeated so frequently that one is led to believe they are commonplace. But are they?

Accounts of the sale of men, women, and children are prevalent. Such sales have been justified on the basis of providing them with the opportunity to survive, and at the same time, helping to assure the survival of their families. A man, woman, or child who is sold may be able to avoid starvation in the home of strangers, while the cash or food realized from the sale may give the rest of the family a similar opportunity. Such sales were reported among the Aztecs during the famine of 1 Rabbit, although it is not possible to determine the percentage of the population involved.

Survival cannibalism is the most difficult famine response for well-fed people to understand or accept. However, famine records compiled over many centuries tell of cannibalism in Egypt, Italy, England, Hungary, Ireland, India, China, the United States, Chile and many other places. Golkin believes that the number of famines which have produced conditions so extreme that people were driven to eat human flesh has probably been underestimated rather than exaggerated. Yet such cannibalism most likely involves less than 1 percent of the people who die in a famine (Golkin 1987:23).

Not only acts of murder, robbery, theft, maltreatment, and crimes against fellow citizens occur during periods of starvation, but also the conduct of people sometimes becomes bestial, particularly among the children. Brutal people are ready to see anyone as the cause of their hunger and to seek salvation by all possible means. Hence the beating and killing of shopkeepers appear first during a famine. Thereafter follow a series of tragic ways of sacrificing intimates in order to keep from dying of hunger. Hunger makes a norm of abnormality, and the sacrilege becomes a tolerable and permissible act. According to Sorokin, starvation mercilessly rips off the social garments from man and shows him as a naked animal, on the naked earth (Sorokin 1922:114, 137).

However, in order to try to bring some perspective to the sensationalist reports of depravity repeated by so many writers, Sorokin attempted to quantify the degree to which people engage in aberrant behavior during a famine, as shown in table 4. While admittedly subjective in nature, the table does give us a better understanding of the general frequency of such deviant behavior.

One of the principal patterns to emerge from Sorokin's work is a set of apparent contradictions. Recognizing this himself, Sorokin concluded that the effects of famine are highly variable and may be opposite for different individuals and groups. He postulated his "Law of Diversification and Polarization" which, simply put, states that disaster brings out the very best and the very worst in people. It exaggerates what is already there. When one compares various pieces of research, the descriptions and contradictory conclusions appear to confirm his law. For example, some have come away from their studies convinced that a dearth of goods and perceptions of scarcity make people generous, while data reported by others point to precisely the opposite (Dirks 1980:22).

Yet, if starvation provokes antisocial and brutal behavior in one part of the population, it engenders an opposite reaction in another part. The demoralization of the one is counterbalanced by the ennoblement of the other. Side by side with the desocializing processes, there appear conspicuous deeds of altruism, heroism, and religious devotion. Instead of becoming cannibals, the majority share their last crumb of bread with their fellows. We have heard of religious leaders, ascetics, and political prisoners who have faced death by starvation rather than yield their cherished convictions to their captors (Sorokin 1942:80–82).

In the end, it is clear that starvation and semistarvation alter behavior and social interactions. Remarkably, behavioral disturbances similar to those described for humans are also reported in other starved or undernourished mammals, including mice, rats, pigs, dogs, and other primates. Famished people are not interacting with what can be considered a viable human environment, and it may be that as things grow worse what is necessary to attempt survival in one energy depleted ecosystem is in general much the same as in any other, not only for animals, but also for humans in different parts of the world. Therefore, the reports of famines in Mesoamerica which we will read in chapter 11 could be the reports from so many other famines from so many parts of the globe (Dirks 1980:40; Franková 1980:36).

ACTIVITIES INDUCED BY STARVATION	PERCENT SUCCUMBING	PERCENT RESISTING
Cannibalism	< 0.3%	>99%
Murder of members of the family and friends	<1.0%	>99%
Murder of other members of one's group	<1.0%	>99%
Murder of strangers—not enemies	<2–5%	>95%
Infliction of various bodily and other injuries on members of one's social group	<5–10%	>90%
Theft, larceny, robbery, forgery, and other crimes against property, which have a clear-cut criminal character	<7–10%	>90%
Violation of various rules of strict honesty and fairness in pursuing food, misuse of rationing cards, hoarding, and taking unfair advantage of others	20–99% depending on the violation	1–80%
Violation of fundamental religious and moral principles	<10–20%	>80–90%
Violation of less important religious, moral, juridical, conventional, and similar norms	50–99%	1–50%
Surrender or weakening of most of the aesthetic activities irreconcilable with food-seeking	50–99%	1–50%
Weakening of sex activities espec. coitus	70–90%	1–30%
Prostitution and other dishonorable sex activities	<10%	>90%

INCIDENCE OF DEPRAVITY DURING FAMINE

Table 4. The incidence of depravity and aberrant behavior during famines as proposed by Sorokin (1942:81).

COLLAPSE IN PEASANT COMMUNITIES

We saw in the last chapter how complex societies are built up level by level through consistent flows of energy. As that energy flow becomes restricted, the collapse of peasant society appears to proceed level by level as well, from community to family to individual.

Having analyzed disintegrating, famine stricken societies, Dirks has concluded that, regardless of environment, culture, or previous experience, many of the recursive changes that occur during food shortage exhibit universal tendencies which suggest to him "the existence of motive forces at deep infrastructural levels, including the neurophysiological." In other words, the way a community responds to stress is very similar to the way individuals respond to stress (Dirks 1980:26).

In describing the process of collapse in a famine stressed community, he has found useful the notion of a general adaptation syndrome to stress in individuals—as developed by the originator of the concept of stress, McGill's Hans Selye, MD, PhD, DSc (plus forty-three honorary doctorates). In particular, he noted that one of the theory's fundamental features, its three phase organization—alarm, resistance, and exhaustion—paralleled the three phases of response to famine in peasant communities. When taken in the abstract, what the Selye-Dirks approach appears to describe is the basic process by which all living things adjust to drastic environmental change: first, the manifold reactions to the initial shock, in famine, aimed at stabilizing the system communitywide; next, more specific and economical means as the system girds itself for protracted resistance, in famine, family by family; finally, a last ditch effort to sustain life after previous defenses collapse, in famine, on an individual basis. As we can see, the phases proposed by Dirks exhibit a clear hierarchical structure as well, the collapse proceeding from the community, to the family, to the individual. We will look below at how Selye's concepts have been applied to famine by Dirks (Dirks 1980:26).

Alarm/Community. Selye has characterized the first phase of the syndrome as the "alarm reaction." With the onset of famine stress, in Dirks's concept, the initial response is systemwide with the emphasis being on protecting the community. General hyperactivation takes place as a broad spectrum of mechanisms is mobilized to sustain the traumatized system. Famine that begins under cover of annual hunger or expected fluctuations in the weather at first does not excite alarm. Yet there is an initial reaction, as has been seen in experiments where subjects have shown increased gregariousness following fasts of less than twenty-four hours. One can hypothesize, then, a relationship between hunger and affiliation: in extreme hunger, gregarious tendencies first increase, then decrease. In other words, victims of famine at first seek help and give aid in an altruistic manner (Dirks 1980:26–27).

Resistance/Family. If relief is not forthcoming, the response moves into a second phase, the "stage of resistance." Here an energy conserving strategy ensues as the scope of defense narrows. In this phase, the emphasis in a famine stressed community is on protecting and ensuring the survival of the family, and there is no longer any concern for the community as a whole (Dirks 1980:26, 28).

The second stage marks the beginning of a strategy characterized by decreasing physical activity. Social ties erode. The effective unit of resistance narrows to the family. Conservative measures are introduced which are antithetical to widespread generosity and broadly based group action. In this phase, there is a tendency for the division of labor to collapse as everyone turns their attention to the quest for food. Time allocated to anything but food-related activities soon approaches zero. As a resistance measure, family bonds generally remain intact, though the extent of active relations, indexed by food sharing, shrinks considerably. Under continued stress, individuals drop friends and extended kin from food sharing networks, restricting generalized reciprocity to close relatives (Dirks 1980:28; Sorokin 1922:94–95).

Exhaustion/Individual. If the famine continues, the syndrome finally enters a third phase, the "stage of exhaustion." Selfishness increases in direct proportion to the degree of starvation until only personal survival remains important. In the most severe famines, reciprocity eventually constricts to a point at which the family ceases to function as a redistributive, protective entity, and individuals begin to fend for themselves. This does not happen all at once. Nutritional inequities within the family during the stage of resistance and earlier foreshadow its collapse. In the middle of distress, with the family circle fully closed off, the elderly are liable to be the first pushed out. As with the aged so with the young. The relief workers responding to emergencies in places as culturally dissimilar as Austria and Uganda have found it necessary to take steps to prevent mothers from appropriating their children's rations. Of course, cases of extreme altruism toward children also occur, but these attract less attention because indulgence toward children is expected. It is the growing tendency toward parental selfishness that seems remarkable to those entering a famine region (Dirks 1980:26, 30).

> The inescapable conclusion seems to be that, in the prolonged, severe food shortages that are labelled famines, the range of compassion progressively decreased—from the community to the family to the individual. As starvation presses in on a society, mutually helpful behavior and other niceties are eroded and eventually disappear. The weak are neglected and left to die. Personal survival ultimately dominates all else. Ritual and mutual obligation disappear progressively—the social creature, man, is re-

placed by the individual, snarlingly determined on survival. (Jelliffe and Jelliffe 1980:36)

LARGE-SCALE SOCIAL COLLAPSE

We have focused primarily on modern peasant communities, and we have seen how they collapse from community to family to individual. Social scientists have not been able to study collapse in modern times at the level of states or civilizations. The understanding of large-scale collapse, therefore, must draw on scant archaeological data and on analogies with the process in small communities. In the larger societies, however, there also appears to be a process of collapsing levels, analogous to the level by level collapse seen in peasant communities, with the collapse stopping at a level that can be sustained by the available energy flow.

Copán, thus, appears to have collapsed in the first phase of its ultimate descent into oblivion from the hierarchical level of a monarchy to that of lineage heads. At Cobá, William Folan described the collapse as reducing a state to a chiefdom in the initial phase, before it was finally abandoned later in the Postclassic. Along the rest of the East Coast, the peasantry could no longer provide the agricultural surpluses to support urban life, and a few cities, like Lamanai, were severely reduced in population, while most others, like Colha, were abandoned altogether. Farmers, however, continued to cultivate their fields. The flow of energy in those areas could support only subsistence farming and minimal urbanization. Around Tikal, on the other hand, everything collapsed. Rural and urban populations both disappeared at the time of the Collapse. Evidently, agriculture ceased altogether. We will return to the fate of these cities with more detail in chapter 12. For our present purposes, it is worth noting that societies are built up to the hierarchical levels that can be sustained by the available energy, and when the energy is reduced, they appear to collapse to a level which the reduced energy will support—just as peasant communities collapse level by level as a famine worsens.

6. METEOROLOGY

There are brief droughts and long-continued droughts, local droughts and widespread droughts, and there are droughts preceded by good rains and droughts preceded by scanty rains.

Drought is too persistent a phenomenon to be the result of mere chance. Coincidences can occur, of course, but it is too much to believe that the juxtapositions of rainless days in long sequences can happen as frequently as they do without some real cause behind them. We must look for the causes in the great elemental forces of the sun, atmosphere, continents, and the oceans. We must examine the records of weather and climate and identify the withering hand that falls upon our farms and ranges every few years.
—Ivan Ray Tannehill (1947:22)

In the jungle, near Tikal, the forest towers 30 m (100 ft) or more overhead, water drips from the leaves, enormous bromeliads droop off the branches, parrots and toucans fly among the tree tops, while monkeys chatter and howl overhead. Standing in the jungle, it is very difficult to imagine that drought might have even once, much less repeatedly, ravaged the area. In this chapter we will look at the basic concepts of meteorology and present a model of North Atlantic weather patterns, which will demonstrate how drought can occur in the Yucatán Peninsula, the Petén, and the tropical jungle surrounding Tikal.

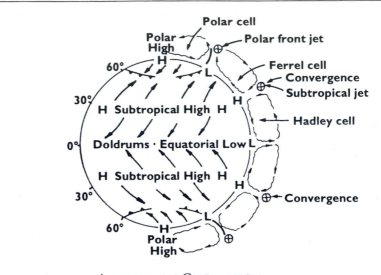

ATMOSPHERIC CIRCULATION

Figure 16. An idealized model of atmospheric circulation over a uniformly water covered Earth. Note the three principal cells of north-south, or meridional, atmospheric circulation with the subtropical highs located under the descending arm of the Hadley cells (adapted from Ahrens 1988:321).

Let's begin with the end. The meteorological concept I propose is as follows: when the North Atlantic high pressure system is displaced far to the southwest, over a multiyear period, cold weather occurs in Arctic Europe or North America and drought occurs in the Yucatán Peninsula. Evidence of severe cold in the Northern Hemisphere, then, *might* indicate periods conducive to drought in Yucatán.

> Research has demonstrated the unity of the general circulation of the atmosphere and that climatic changes in one zone are accompanied by changes in all the other zones. (Bryson 1973:366)

The atmosphere is a large, rotating thermodynamic system, heated by the sun, in which convective flow has developed, similar to Bénard cells in laboratory systems. The convective flow is divided into three cells. The first, closest to the equator, is known as the Hadley cell, named for English meteorologist George Hadley who first proposed the idea in 1735 (figure 16). The Hadley cell is the primary thermodynamic cell, driven by energy from the sun, in which air is heated at the equator, rises, and flows poleward to about 30° where it descends and returns to the equator as the trade

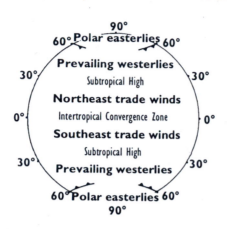

SURFACE WINDS

Figure 17. The names of surface winds over a uniformly water covered Earth which correspond to the three cells (adapted from Ahrens 1988:321).

winds (figure 17). The middle cell is the Ferrel cell, a secondary cell driven by the circulation of the Hadley cell in which air subsides at 30°, flows along the surface towards the pole, rises at about 60°, and flows back to 30°. The third cell is the polar cell in which air subsides near the pole, flows equatorward to about 60° where it rises and returns to the pole. The Hadley cell is the most important of the three for the purposes of our present study.

In the Hadley cell, air is heated near the Equator. As the air rises, it expands and cools. Water vapor then condenses, forming thick clouds and frequent, heavy rain in the intertropical convergence zone along the Earth's thermal equator. When the air reaches the tropopause, the point at which the atmosphere no longer cools as altitude increases, it can rise no further, and it begins to flow towards the pole. As it flows poleward, it gradually subsides until it reaches the surface. The area of subsidence, around 30°, is indicated by the presence of the subtropical highs around the world and is known to sailors in the Northern Hemisphere as the "horse latitudes." Because the subsiding air is very dry, the area between 20° and 40° includes many arid zones around the world, like the Sahara, Atacama, Kalahari, Outback, and the Sonora cell over northern Mexico, South Texas, and the Southwest. It includes, in my opinion, Progreso on the northern edge of the Yucatán Peninsula and the arid offshore islands like Cayo Arenas and Arrecife Alacrán, areas of very low rainfall. Without delving too deeply into questions of atmospheric physics, it is important

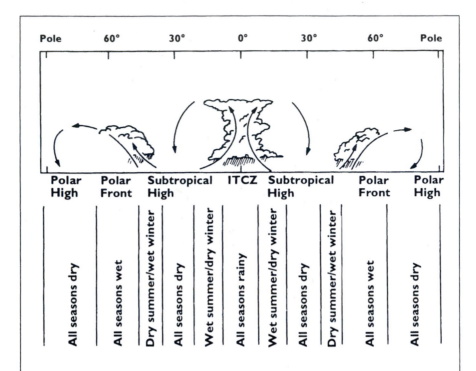

| Pole | 60° | 30° | 0° | 30° | 60° | Pole |

REGIONS OF RISING AND SINKING AIR

Figure 18. A vertical cross section along a line running north to south illustrates the main global regions of rising and sinking air and how each region influences precipitation. A small shift of the circulation patterns to the south, especially in Mesoamerica, could move the boundary between wet/dry and all dry to the south, causing severe problems to cultures dependent on wet summers to provide them with water. In modern times, the boundary between wet/dry and all dry passes through northern Yucatán. The *ITCZ* is the intertropical convergence zone (adapted from Ahrens 1988:480).

to note that factors related to the Earth's rotation, the Coriolis effect, and the conservation of angular momentum prevent the flow from being directly north-south and deflect it to a northeast-southwest orientation. (Figures 18 and 19 indicate the relationship between atmospheric convection and climate at the surface.)

As the circulation moves northward in the Hadley cell, it gradually descends towards the surface. The result is the creation of an inversion layer of warm tropical air which comes closer and closer to the surface. The convection of warm, moist air is stopped by the inversion layer. If the in-

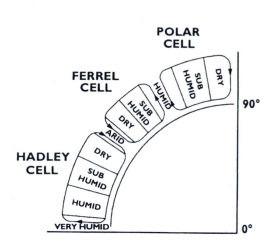

ATMOSPHERIC CONVECTION CELLS

Figure 19. The idealized latitudinal distribution of the Hadley circulation and the zones of humidity within each cell. Note that the boundary between subhumid and dry at the margin of the Hadley cell is located at the latitude of northern Yucatán (adapted from Perlmutter and Matthews 1992:381).

version is low enough, humid air will not be able to rise high enough to cool sufficiently to form thick clouds. Rainfall, therefore, will be strongly suppressed, as is demonstrated in figure 20. The extension of the descending branch of the Hadley cell to the southwest will bring lower inversion layers over Yucatán. The inversion layer over the Caribbean is normally present during about 80 percent of all days during the winter, but only 30 to 40 percent during the summer. Its height during the winter is approximately 1,500m (4,900ft), which is low enough to prevent rainfall. During the summer, its normal height is 2,000m (6,500ft), high enough to allow convection to form cumulus clouds in the atmosphere below the inversion. The presence or absence of the inversion layer is the main reason for the dry season/rainy season weather patterns in the Caribbean area. The returning flow at the surface towards the equator produces the trade winds (Nieuwolt 1977:164–165).

Between the latitudes of 20° and 40°, the mean surface pressure maps are dominated by a number of elliptical areas, elongated in the east-west direction, with relatively high pressure, called the subtropical highs. In the high pressure cells themselves, the predominant vertical motion is downward. The result is horizontally divergent air flow at the surface as the air

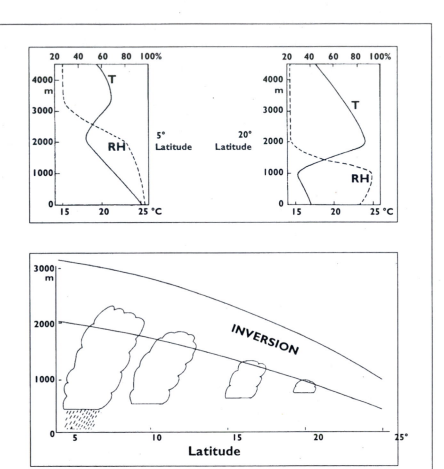

INVERSION LAYER

Figure 20. The development of an inversion layer from the equator to 25° latitude. Note how convection is impeded by the presence of the inversion layer and rainfall is prevented as the inversion layer drops lower. The upper graphs depict the change of temperature and relative humidity with altitude at 5° and 20° latitude. *T*=temperature, *RH*=relative humidity (adapted from Nieuwolt 1977:45).

moves away from the high pressure cell. The highs tend to develop well over water areas where mountain effects, heating, and other surface effects do not disrupt the idealized flow. The North Atlantic, the North Pacific, and the southern oceans, for example, all have well developed subtropical highs, as seen in figure 21. The Hadley cell circulation is a major contributor to the presence of the North Atlantic High in the Atlantic Ocean (Nieuwolt 1977:43; Trewartha 1981:74).

The most cloudfree area in the North Atlantic is the southern half of the subtropical high. In January, a belt with less than 20 percent frequency of cloudiness is centered on 20°N and extends across the width of the ocean. (Chichén Itza is at 20.40°N.) In July, the cloudfree area is limited to the central and western areas and is located slightly farther north. We should note how close the cloudfree area is to the Maya Lowlands (Tucker and Barry 1984:237).

Since the Hadley cell is a thermodynamic structure supported by solar energy, it is possible that its areal extent is dependent on the amount of solar energy arriving at the troposphere. Locating the position of the subsiding branch of the cell, as indicated by the position of the North Atlantic High, would indicate the areal extent of the Hadley cell and changes in the long-term position of the downward flowing high would indicate changes in the long-term areal extent of the cell. Presumably, an increase in the cell's energy would cause the cell to expand and the North Atlantic High to be displaced in a northeast direction. A decrease of energy would cause a contraction in the Hadley cell and a retreat of the North Atlantic High to the southwest. If this is true, those processes which reduce the energy of the troposphere, like reduced solar heating, would result in a southward displacement of the North Atlantic High (Haigh 1996:983).

Roger Barry and Richard Chorley have pointed out that the major droughts in the African Sahel, along the same latitude as the Maya Lowlands, during the 1970s have been attributed to an eastward and southward extension of the North Atlantic High. As is reflected in figure 25 on page 142, the center of the North Atlantic High moved to the south during the 1970s while maintaining its far eastward position. Furthermore, they conclude that "global climate is closely related to the position and strength of the subtropical high-pressure cells" (Barry and Chorley 1987:110, 380).

It should be added that this concept is a subject of debate among meteorologists, not all of whom are in agreement. J. S. Sawyer, for example, proposed that the position of the subtropical jet streams and the size of the main Hadley cell are fundamentally determined by the Earth's rotation and they are restricted in their ability to move north or south in response to changes in heating and cooling. Stefan Hastenrath is not comfortable with the idea that the north and south movements of the high represent an expansion and contraction of the Hadley circulation. Nevertheless, some investigators of the evidence of past climates have concluded that the subtropical anticyclone belt was nearer the equator and narrower in ice ages and that it underwent significant displacement poleward in warm epochs. Others have proposed that the intertropical convergence zone (ITCZ) was located farther to the south during the last ice age, and it shifted north during the deglaciation as the trade winds weakened. A northward position of the ITCZ brings rainy conditions to the circum-Caribbean, region and a

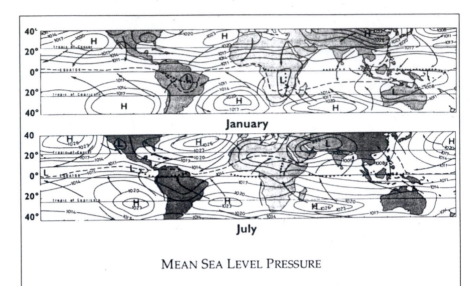

January

July

MEAN SEA LEVEL PRESSURE

Figure 21. Mean sea level pressure and surface winds for January and July. The dashed lines indicate the intertropical convergence zone and the dotted lines secondary convergence areas. Note the presence of the subtropical highs at about 30°(adapted from Nieuwolt 1977:37).

southward position brings dry weather. Anomalously dry years have been associated with the ITCZ remaining farther to the south. Such a position, of course, would have affected the location of the North Atlantic High (Curtis and Hodell 1993:143; Hastenrath, 1993, personal communication; Islebe et al 1996:269–270; Lamb 1972b, 1:119; Leyden et al 1993:176; Sawyer 1966:222). (See figure 26 on page 143 for past positions of the North Atlantic High.)

NORTH ATLANTIC HIGH

For the purposes of this study, I have chosen to use the position of the highest pressure reading in the Atlantic Ocean as the center of the North Atlantic High. This, of course, is only a rough estimate. The area of the central pressure of the subtropical highs is not always neatly organized. Sometimes it is small, sometimes it spreads over large areas. Sometimes it is L shaped, sometimes it looks like a dumbbell.

Using information provided on magnetic tape by the National Center for Atmospheric Research and with the help of Ray Gay, Director of Academic Computing at The University of Texas at San Antonio, we prepared printouts of the monthly averages of sea level pressure around the world on a five degree grid from 20°N to 80°N. From these printouts, I visually chose the location of the central pressure in the Atlantic Ocean. There was

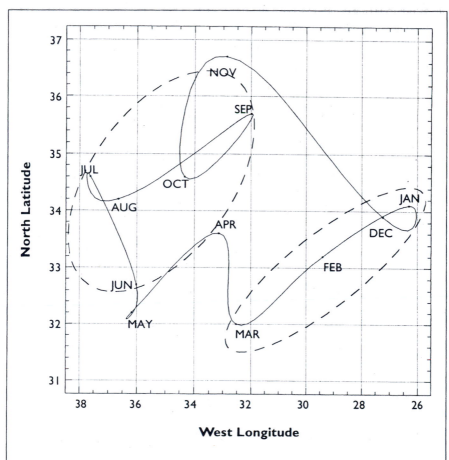

NORTH ATLANTIC HIGH AVERAGE MONTHLY POSITION

Figure 22. The average monthly position of the North Atlantic High central pressure at sea level. The spline connecting the points shows the movement around the North Atlantic during the course of a year. The winter position lies to the southeast and the summer position to the northwest, as indicated by the *dashed lines*.

an occasional element of subjectivity in the choice of the central pressure location. In trying to choose the center of an L or a dumbbell, for example, I had to make a subjective decision where to locate the center for purposes of tabulating the data. Some decisions could be questioned, but they generally represent a subjective leeway of only 2.5°. They also represent a small number of the 1,056 monthly averages tabulated.

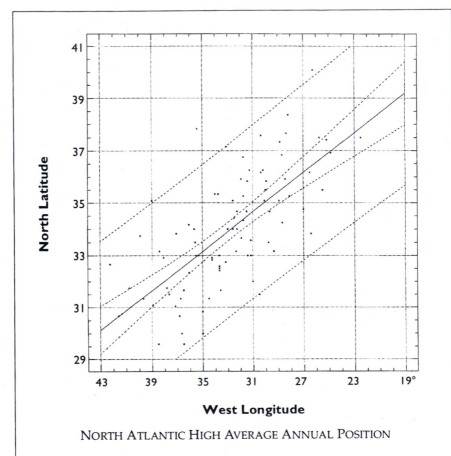

NORTH ATLANTIC HIGH AVERAGE ANNUAL POSITION

Figure 23. The annual average location of the North Atlantic High central pressure between 1900 and 1988 indicates a narrowly defined track in the Atlantic Ocean within which the high normally traveled in the twentieth century.

The normal movement of the North Atlantic High during the course of a year is shown in figure 22. In general, it moves northwest during the summer and southeast during the winter. The average position of the North Atlantic High central pressure in the twentieth century was about 34°N 33°W.

NORTH ATLANTIC HIGH POSITION

The movement of the center of the North Atlantic High during the twentieth century followed a northeast-southwest track as seen in figure 23. Its annual average position moved between 30°N and 40°N and between 25°W and 42°W. Of even more interest is how the movement tend-

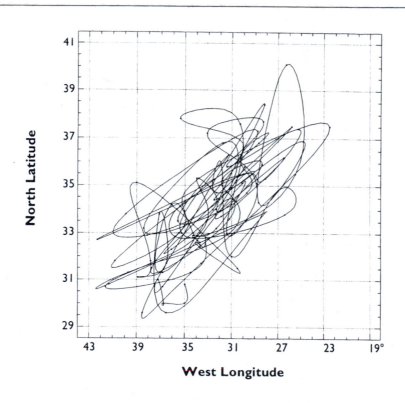

North Atlantic High Consecutive Annual Position

Figure 24. In this spline, a line is drawn through consecutive positions, from one year to the next. It is clear that the North Atlantic High annual average position generally moves back and forth within its track in a northeast-southwest direction.

ed to be northeast-southwest on an interannual basis, as seen in figure 24. There is a positive correlation coefficient of 0.68 between north-south and east-west movement. Through the century, the center migrated to the north and east as seen in figure 25.

As the North Atlantic High moved to the north in the twentieth century, so the Icelandic Low moved north by about 3°. Correlations between the four times series of latitudinal position and central pressure of the two centers were calculated for each month (figure 26). They demonstrated that the Icelandic Low and the North Atlantic High both tend to intensify if they move northward and that they tend to move in the same direction. Both centers, then, are responding to changes in the general circulation of

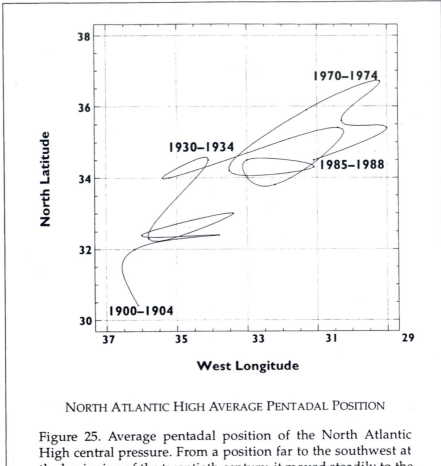

NORTH ATLANTIC HIGH AVERAGE PENTADAL POSITION

Figure 25. Average pentadal position of the North Atlantic High central pressure. From a position far to the southwest at the beginning of the twentieth century, it moved steadily to the northeast until 1970–1974, when it started moving to the south.

the North Atlantic, if not far more widespread circulation changes (Glowienka 1985:160, 164).

An even more impressive correlation is shown in figure 27. Between 1894 and 1958, the North Atlantic High and the South Atlantic High moved north and south more or less together. The worldwide nature of climatic fluctuations is emphasized in this graph, especially the north-south movement of the intertropical convergence zone. It appears that both the northern and the southern Hadley cells and the ITCZ tended to move north and south together during the time period of the study. As we can see, the whole system moved far to the south in the first decade of the twentieth century, the farthest south in the last hundred years.

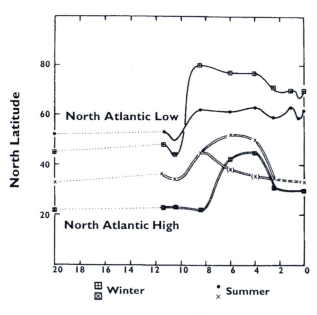

NORTH ATLANTIC HIGH AND LOW

Figure 26. Estimated average latitudes of the lowest and highest barometric pressures (at sea level) in the European sector of the Northern Hemisphere since the latter part of the last ice age. In Lamb's reconstruction, at the end of the last glaciation, a period of extreme cold, the North Atlantic High was located far to the south. As the global atmosphere warmed to the Altithermal period, the high moved to the north. As the atmosphere cooled to today's temperatures, the high retreated towards the south. The two lines to the north represent the Low and the two to the south represent the High (adapted from Lamb 1972a:386).

To summarize, then, the North Atlantic High moves back and forth across the North Atlantic in a northeast-southwest channel. In the early decades of the twentieth century, it was located far to the southwest, closer to Yucatán, and moved generally to the northeast, closer to Europe, during the course of the century.

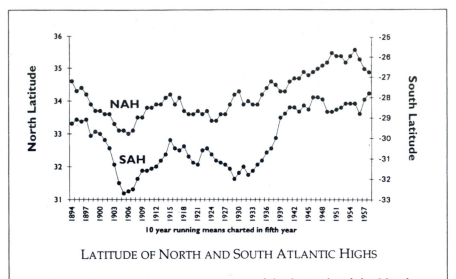

LATITUDE OF NORTH AND SOUTH ATLANTIC HIGHS

Figure 27. Ten-year running means of the latitude of the North Atlantic High and the South Atlantic High charted in the first year of the ten years. Note how they have moved north and south more or less together (*Source*: Lamb and Johnson 1966:120–121).

TROPICAL COLD

Temperature variations are more dramatic towards the poles than at the equator. Changes in Arctic temperature are greater in magnitude and more rapid. When the temperature turns colder, it turns more dramatically colder in Arctic areas, increasing the temperature difference between the poles and the equator. A stronger meridional, or north-south, temperature gradient causes an equatorward shift of the high pressure, although, in fact, it may be the equatorward shift in high pressure which causes the increased temperature gradient. The latitude of the subtropical high pressure belt is correlated to the meridional temperature difference between the equator and the poles. On the one hand, some researchers have suggested that despite major changes in the meridional temperature difference, tropical temperatures will always remain fairly stable. On the other, recent evidence presented by a number of researchers indicates that the Tropics cooled significantly during the last glacial maximum, by as much as 5°C (9°F) around 19,000 years ago. In fact, Barbara Leyden and her colleagues have shown a cooling of 6.5°C (11.7°F) to 8°C (14.4°F) in the Petén. A review of the recent literature indicates a general cooling of at least 5°C from 40°N to 40°S. The key indicator, nonetheless, of meridional temperature differences are the Arctic temperatures rather than the tropical temperatures (Barry and Chorley 1987:140, 155; Bradley 1973:398; Colinvaux et al 1996:19; Guilderson, Fairbanks, and Rubenstone 1994:663; Kelly et al 1982:71; Kerr 1994:173; Lindzen 1993:26; Stute et al 1995:379).

Temperature changes in Arctic areas, then, are important clues to the position of the North Atlantic High. The greater the temperature difference, the colder the Arctic areas, the more southwestward is the location of the North Atlantic High, as seen in figure 28 which is the central conclusion for the meteorological model presented in this book. The more southwestward the North Atlantic High is, the lower the inversion layers are, and the less likely convection will develop cumulus clouds and rainfall.

Barry and Chorley have estimated that a significant warming of the Arctic troposphere, say +10°C in winter and +3°C in summer, or about 7°C annually, would be associated with a northerly displacement of the North Atlantic High of some 5° latitude, or about 100 to 200km (60 to 120mi) in the summer and as much as 800km (480mi) in the winter, bringing serious drought to the Mediterranean, California, Middle East,Turkestan, and the Punjab. Similarly, a cooling of the Arctic would have the reverse effect, moving the North Atlantic High farther south and bringing drought to Yucatán, in accord with the model presented here (Barry and Chorley 1987:380).

In analyzing the colder conditions of the last ice age, a period of extreme aridity in Yucatán, M. D. Perlmutter and M. D. Matthews estimated a 10° southerly displacement of the North Atlantic High to a position about 25°N. In my analysis of the North Atlantic High's position during the period of historical weather records in the twentieth century, the southerly displacement associated with the terrible drought of 1902–1904 in Mérida was 6° south of its 1970–1974 position (Gates 1976:1142; Perlmutter and Matthews 1992:383).

It must be emphasized that long-term trends appear to be more important than the annual position of the high. Year to year fluctuations occur around more important long-term trends in the general circulation.

PAST CHANGES

Geoffrey Lemdahl has demonstrated that temperatures in Arctic Sweden cooled by 5°C over an 800-year period from 11,600 BP to 10,800 BP and then warmed again by 4°C by 10,200 BP at the end of the Younger Dryas period. More recent work on Greenland ice cores has shown that temperature shifts of 7°C or so, accompanied by changes from dusty, dry glacial conditions to warmer weather, may have occurred in a year or two in Greenland. In short, very rapid large temperature changes in the Arctic, reflecting significant changes in general circulation patterns, have been seen again and again since the end of the last ice age. Over the last 3,000 years, numerous fluctuations have occurred, some lasting up to a century (Lemdahl 1991:313; Monastersky 1992c:404; Nicolis and Prigogine 1989:39).

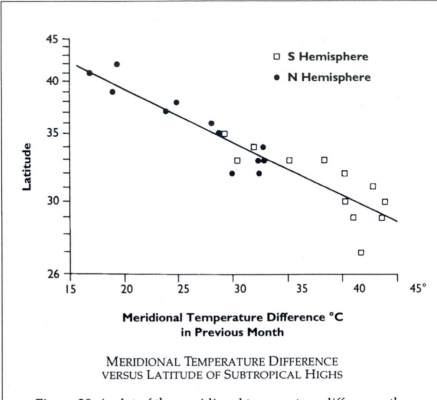

**Meridional Temperature Difference °C
in Previous Month**

MERIDIONAL TEMPERATURE DIFFERENCE
VERSUS LATITUDE OF SUBTROPICAL HIGHS

Figure 28. A plot of the meridional temperature difference, the difference between equatorial and arctic and antarctic temperatures, at the 300-700 mb layer ($\cong$ 3–9 km, 10,000–30,000 ft) in the previous month against the latitude of the center of the subtropical high pressure belt. A larger meridional temperature difference indicates colder arctic and antarctic temperatures. Note the correlation between cold arctic temperatures and the north-south position of the North Atlantic High (adapted from Barry and Chorley 1987:144, after Flohn in Flohn and Fantechi 1984).

The low temperatures for the twentieth century in the Northern Hemisphere occurred during the first decade and were accompanied by a southwestward displacement of the North Atlantic High central pressure and presumably by a contraction in the Hadley cell over the North Atlantic. Subsequently, there was a broad trend of increasing temperatures during the century. Global temperatures warmed 0.5°C (0.9°F) during that period as shown in figure 29. Northern Hemisphere temperatures followed the global trend. Warming began during the first decade and jumped between

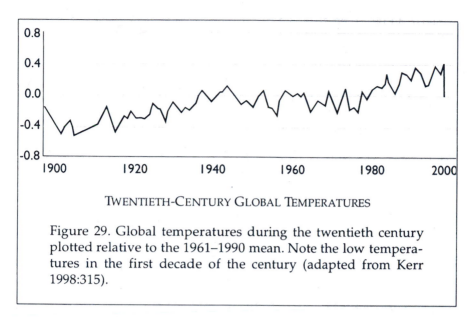

TWENTIETH-CENTURY GLOBAL TEMPERATURES

Figure 29. Global temperatures during the twentieth century plotted relative to the 1961–1990 mean. Note the low temperatures in the first decade of the century (adapted from Kerr 1998:315).

1919 and 1921. There was a cooling trend which began about 1960, continued until about 1980, then reversed itself.

ECOTONAL SHIFTS

Are there examples of large-scale circulation shifts from other parts of the world? Let's look across the Atlantic at the same latitude in Saharan Africa. Derek Winstanley proposed a correlation between general circulation changes and the advance and retreat of the Sahara Desert to the south. He estimated that the southern limit of the desert could advance between 150 and 180 km (90 and 110 mi) during the next century. Compton Tucker, Harold Dregne, and Wilbur Newcomb mapped the north-south movements of the Sahara desert between 1980 and 1990 using satellite images. They calculated that the desert's southern boundary was shifted towards the south by 242 km (150 mi) between 1980 and 1984 due to a shift in precipitation patterns. As the rains shifted to the south, so did the desert. As they moved back north, however, so did the desert. Peter Lamb identified tropical Atlantic surface features which are located 300 to 500 km (180 to 300 mi) farther south during extremely dry years in Subsaharan Africa. These studies indicate that major atmospheric and oceanic circulation patterns can shift over substantial distances in relatively short periods of time with important effects on precipitation (Lamb 1978:482; Tucker, Dregne, and Newcomb 1991:299; Winstanley 1973:194).

Such shifts in weather patterns are known from Europe as well. As we saw in chapter 1, Carole Crumley has demonstrated how the ecotone representing the northern boundary of the Sahelian climatic regime has shifted over the course of the last two millennia from along the North African

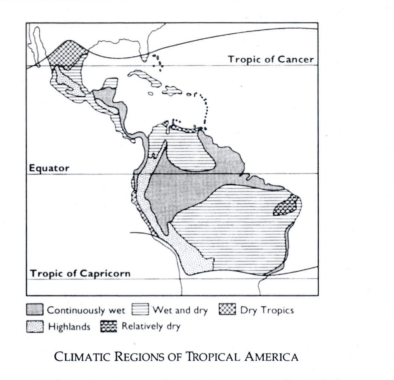

Tropic of Cancer

Equator

Tropic of Capricorn

■ Continuously wet   ☰ Wet and dry   ▨ Dry Tropics
▧ Highlands   ▨ Relatively dry

CLIMATIC REGIONS OF TROPICAL AMERICA

Figure 30. Climatic regions of tropical America. The shift from continuously wet to wet and dry rainfall regimes occurs in the southern Maya Lowlands (adapted from Nieuwolt 1977:163).

coastline to northern France and Germany and back—a distance of a thousand kilometers or hundreds of miles (Crumley 1994b:193–196).

In fact, the wetter and drier climates known to occur in northern intertropical Africa due to shifts in the ITCZ have parallels in the Caribbean and Central America. The cited studies demonstrate that major displacements in climatic regimes can and do occur. A southward displacement of the northern Yucatecan aridity into the Petén, due to circulation changes, would have had devastating consequences for those depending on rainfall for their supply of drinking water, like most Classical Maya cities and towns (Islebe et al 1996:269–270).

MAYA LOWLANDS WEATHER

Weather in the Maya Lowlands is part of the North Atlantic weather system. The only weather with possible origins in the Pacific are the *nortes*, or northers, which occasionally blow in during the winter. They are brief cold air outbreaks from the cold interior of the wintertime North American

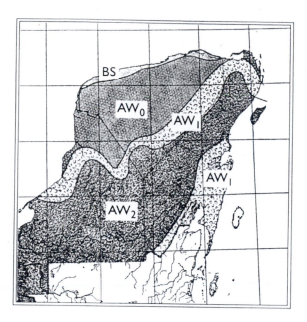

Climates of Yucatán

Figure 31. Climates of the Yucatán Peninsula classified by the Köppen system, as modified by Enriqueta García. Note the increasing aridity towards the north. In García's modification, BS, the most arid along the northern coast, represents a steppe climate where evaporation exceeds precipitation. Aw climates have a pronounced dry season with one or more months in which precipitation is less than 60 mm (2.4 in). Aw_0 is the driest and Aw_2 is the wettest (adapted from García 1964:35).

continent. The Lowlands normally lie in the belt of easterly trade winds. They are characterized by a six-month rainy season and a six-month dry season. Temperature variation is nominal between seasons. Interannual variability, therefore, is mostly a matter of rainfall differences. The Lowlands lie at the northern margin of the tropical rainfall belt, as seen in figure 30. To the north lies a zone of aridity over the northwest coast and the offshore islands (figure 31). In the Yucatán Peninsula itself, as seen in figure 32, rainfall varies from over 4,000 mm (157 in) at Ilusión, Petén, in the south, to approximately 2,000 mm (80 in) at Flores near Tikal, to 945.5 mm (38.6 in) at Mérida, to 440 mm (17 in) at Progreso, to below 330 mm (13 in) at the lighthouse on Cayo Arenas, one of the offshore islands 150 km (90 mi) to the north: a twelvefold difference! A southward extension or displace-

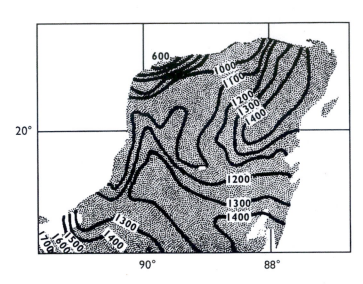

AVERAGE ANNUAL RAINFALL

Figure 32. Average annual rainfall for the Yucatán Peninsula in mm. Note the isohyets run roughly east-west, indicating increasing aridity towards the north, except for a slight increase in precipitation along the northeast coast probably due to the local double sea breeze effect (adapted from Trewartha 1981:80).

ment of the arid regime in the north would have serious consequences for those farther to the south relying on rainfall for their drinking water.

We saw in chapter 1 that ecotonal boundaries between climatic regimes have moved more than 880 km (500 mi) in Europe (figure 3 on page 19), and that large-scale movements of the Sahara/Sahel ecotone have been seen. The north-south extent of the Maya Lowlands is roughly 900 km (560 mi). If an ecotonal shift of the same magnitude seen in other parts of the world occurred in the Maya Lowlands, the effects would have been disastrous. (See figure 4 on page 23 and figure 31 for maps of ecotones in the Maya Lowlands.)

Climatologists Pedro Mosiño and Alfonso Contreras Arias attribute the northern aridity to its leeward location on the peninsula. S. Nieuwolt, however, attributes the dry area around Progreso not only to its leeward location on the Yucatán Peninsula, but also to its far northward position. The leeward effect is most pronounced during the cooler, drier months when the rainfall isohyets run roughly north-south. During the summer months of maximum rainfall, the isohyets are lined up in an east-west direction, indicating decreasing rainfall from south to north, not a pattern related to leeward position. Glenn Trewartha suggested that an upwelling of subsurface waters along the north coast contributes to the aridity of the offshore islands. Such an upwelling would, of course, play a contributory role in the Gulf, but it would not explain the south to north decrease of rainfall on the peninsula as a whole during the rainy season. Richard Sands has described the rainfall in Yucatán as decreasing from the Guatemalan border to the northwest coast and the port of Progreso, continuing out to the center of the Gulf of Mexico, for all months. He proposed that the northward decrease is related to geographically larger controls in the atmosphere than a factor operating parallel to or at the north coast of Yucatán. He suggested atmospheric subsidence, the descending arm of the Hadley cell circulation, as the cause (Nieuwolt 1977:168; Mosiño, 1991, personal communication; Mosiño and Contreras Arias quoted in Trewartha 1981:81; Sands 1960:20).

Figure 33 shows that, contrary to the leeward position theory, the decrease in thunderstorms in Yucatán is paralleled by a decrease in thunderstorms along the mainland Gulf Coast as well, suggesting an involvement of more widespread general circulation. The number of thunderstorms is broadly representative of precipitation levels. In contrast, one might propose that the unusual local effect is not so much the dryness of the west coast of Yucatán, but the raininess of the northeast coast. The raininess of the East Coast, however, is part of a pattern of progressively increasing precipitation from Veracruz northeast towards Florida. As one can see from figures 33 and 34, the pattern of rainfall over the Yucatán Peninsula is not a localized phenomenon, but rather part of a much larger regional and global circulation pattern. Certainly local onshore breezes play a part, but so do regional and hemispheric circulation patterns.

Bruce Hewitson and Robert Crane studied the large-scale atmospheric controls on local precipitation in tropical Mexico. They found that the degree of relation between the large-scale circulation and the local precipitation was surprising, with the circulation demonstrating about a 65 percent control over the smoothed daily local precipitation. Their analysis indicated that the onset of the rainy season was controlled by the large-scale circulation. In midseason, the phase of the precipitation events is controlled largely by changes in the location of the North Atlantic High, which controls the direction of airflow over the region and thus the availability of moisture. Local effects play an important role in determining the final variability of rainfall (Hewitson and Crane 1992:1837).

One very important local effect is the double sea breeze. When sea breezes from the north coast of Yucatán converge with the prevailing easterly trade winds, a line of thunderstorms tends to form. The double sea breeze effect sweeps across the peninsula every day during the warm season and more frequently as global temperatures warm. Evaporation over water is still significant even during cool and cold periods, even though at

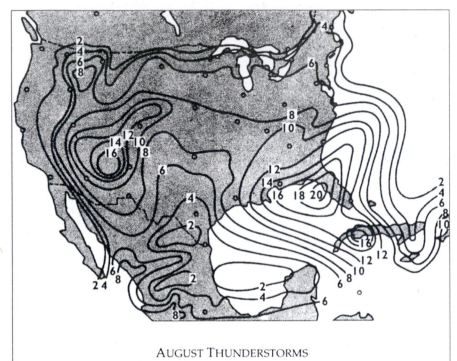

AUGUST THUNDERSTORMS

Figure 33. Average number of thunderstorms in North America in August. Note the decrease in thunderstorms towards the north in Mexico along the Gulf Coast and the increase across the Gulf of Mexico towards Florida. The pattern of rainfall in the Yucatán Peninsula is part of a larger regional pattern not satisfactorily explained by relying on local effects. The number of thunderstorms is broadly similar to the pattern of precipitation (adapted from Trewartha 1981:315).

a reduced rate. The sea breeze movement over land, however, is reduced during periods of global cold such that it is less likely to trigger precipitation (Gunn, Folan, and Robichaux 1995:25).

MÉRIDA RAINFALL

The only long-term rainfall record which exists in the Lowlands area is from Mérida, Yucatán. The record begins in 1894 and extends to the present, with 1894, 1899, and 1901 missing several months. Figure 35 shows the Mérida annual rainfall record beginning in 1900. The average rainfall for 1900–1987 is 945.5mm (37.2in). The data through 1919 I gathered from the original reports archived at the Observatorio Meteorológico at Tacubaya in Mexico, DF, for the year 1920 from data provided by the Na-

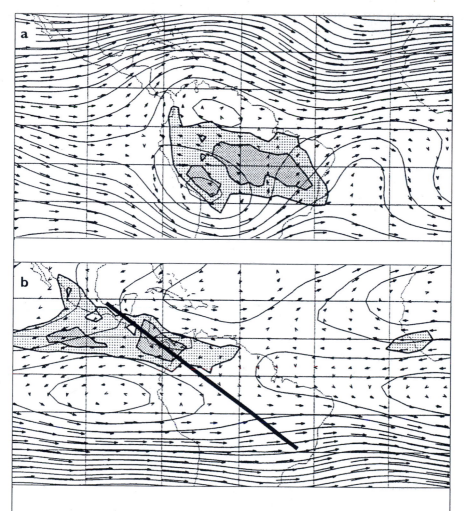

AREAS OF MAXIMUM TROPICAL RAINFALL

Figure 34. *a.* January *b.* July. *Shaded* areas represent intense convective activity characteristic of heavy rainfall in the American Tropics. *Dark shading* represents the heaviest activity, as indicated by outgoing longwave radiation. Note that most of the Maya Lowlands do not lie in the zone of heavy tropical rainfall. Those southern areas closer to the tropical rainfall zone receive more rain than the more distant northern areas. The *solid line* in *b* approximates the path of maximum convective activity during the year as the maximum rainfall zone shifts with the seasons. *Arrows* represent the vector wind (adapted from Horel, Hahmann, and Geisler 1989:1390).

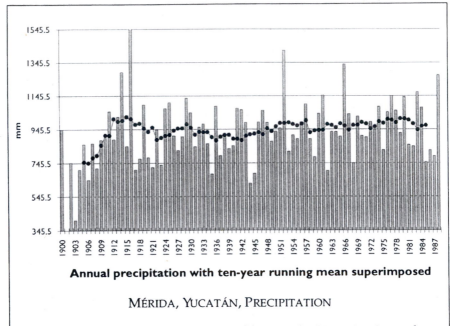

Annual precipitation with ten-year running mean superimposed

MÉRIDA, YUCATÁN, PRECIPITATION

Figure 35. Rainfall totals by year for Mérida, Yucatán. Annual average rainfall is 945.5mm (37.2in). Severe drought is defined as rainfall below one standard deviation or below 738mm (29in). Note the three-year severe drought between 1902 and 1904 and the comparative aridity of the first decade.

tional Climatic Data Center of the National Oceanic and Atmospheric Administration in Asheville, NC, and from 1921 to 1991 from tabulations of the original reports provided by the Observatorio Meteorológico.

Rainfall averaging can be tricky in northern Yucatán because occasional hurricanes introduce wild fluctuations in the year to year numbers which obscure the underlying trend. Figure 36 shows the ten-year running means for the twentieth century. Except for the first decade of the century, rainfall has tended to fluctuate in a close range around the 1900–1991 average. The first decade, however, was significantly below the average.

DROUGHT

The motivation for this study is an attempt to understand weather patterns in the Lowlands and to appreciate their archaeological implications. Of primary interest, of course, is the question of severe drought. When does it happen and what are the circumstances surrounding its occurrence?

The first problem is to define what drought means. There is no accepted standard definition. In fact, Barry and Chorley compiled over one hun-

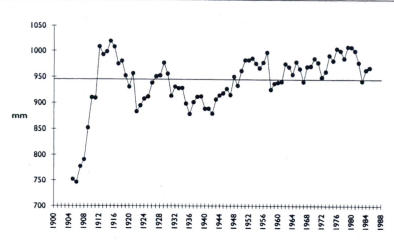

Ten-year running means plotted in fifth year

MÉRIDA, YUCATÁN, MEAN PRECIPITATION

Figure 36. Ten-year running means, plotted in the fifth year, of Mérida, Yucatán, rainfall. Note the severely reduced levels of precipitation in the first decade of the century. After about 1910, annual rainfall varies narrowly around the annual average of 945.5mm (37.2in), *solid line*. Since the 1940s, rainfall has been mostly above the long-term average.

dred fifty different definitions from the literature. Drought is, of course, partly contingent on its effect on society and on the economy, but that is difficult to measure quantitatively. I have chosen to arbitrarily define a mathematically severe drought in Mérida as a year in which the total rainfall is below one standard deviation, or below 734mm (28.9in) (Barry and Chorley 1987:110; Namias 1981:117).

The conditions associated with drought are multifactorial and include local, hemispheric, and global effects. Among the possible factors, then, are the location of the North Atlantic High, a tendency for lower tropospheric divergence and subsidence, the height of the tropical inversion layer, the temperature of the sea water, and the abundance of moisture in the atmosphere.

The average global temperature influences regional moisture through the atmospheric circulation. One particular cause of drought is an increase in area and persistence of the subtropical high pressure cells. Extreme dry years in the Caribbean area have been associated with an equatorward extension of the North Atlantic High (Barry and Chorley 1987:110; Gunn, Folan, and Robichaux 1995:6; Hastenrath 1976:202; 1985:300).

> Rainfall variations during the Northern summer half-year in the Central American-Caribbean region are related to the position of the North Atlantic high. During drought years, the pressure on the equatorward side of the subtropical high is enhanced, the trades appear stronger albeit in a band farther South, and most of the North Atlantic waters are anomalously cold. The approximately inverse departure configurations are characteristic of abundant rainfall years.... (Hastenrath 1985:317)

There is a slight statistical correlation between the position of the North Atlantic High and rainfall in Mérida during the century. A linear regression analysis calculates a weak positive correlation of 0.14. In other words, there has been a slight tendency for rainfall to increase with the northward position of the North Atlantic High. On the other hand, there seems to be a stepwise position far to the southwest which is associated with diminished rainfall in Yucatán. Once the high moves away from the extreme southwest location to the northeast, the exact position appears to be of relatively little importance. This stepwise phenomenon is also apparent in the correlations between cold global temperatures and discharge from the Río Candelaria seen in figure 37.

The position, extension, and intensity of the North Atlantic High affects those places located at its southwestern and northeastern margins. One can expect abundant rainfall in Yucatán when: (a) the center of maximum pressure is displaced towards the east, (b) the band of high pressure moves towards the north, (c) the zonal circulation increases (strong trades and westerlies). This coincides with warm summers in the northern latitudes of the Northern Hemisphere. Jáuregui Ostos believed there was a very strict relationship between the mean position of the highs and the rainfall in the Mexican Highlands (Armillas 1964:78; García 1974:35; Jáuregui Ostos 1979:51).

Decreases in rainfall in Mexico are associated with a southward regression of the subtropical high pressure cell and a cooling of the northern latitudes. J. K. Angell and J. Korshover have suggested a possible correlation between the mean surface temperature and the latitude of the subtropical high in the Northern Hemisphere. In other words, a more northerly position of the North Atlantic High would be associated with warmer surface temperatures. (See figure 28 also.) Over the twentieth century, in fact, there has been a general trend towards the north and a general warming (Angell and Korshover 1974:674; Wallén 1956:148).

Joel Gunn, William Folan, and Hubert Robichaux have analyzed the discharge data from 1958 to 1984 of the Candelaria River which flows into the Laguna de Términos on the southwest Gulf coast of the Yucatán Peninsula in Mexico. (See map on page 253.) When they compared the flow data with the Global Energy Balance—worldwide temperatures—for the same period, their results indicated that hot global temperatures result in

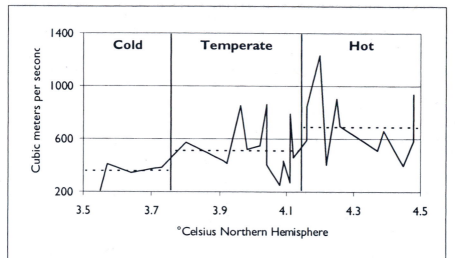

RÍO CANDELARIA ANNUAL DISCHARGE

Figure 37. A plot of annual discharge from the Río Candelaria in the southwestern Yucatán Peninsula versus Northern Hemispheric temperatures from 1958 to 1990. Note the consistently low discharge rates for cold temperatures indicating reduced precipitation in the river's drainage basin. *Dashed lines* represent average annual discharge for each temperature group (*Source:* Gunn, Folan, and Robichaux 1995:19).

maximum discharge in the area, with the least precipitation being produced as global temperatures turn the coldest, in a stepwise fashion, as can be seen in figure 37. The cold years appear to have a delayed onset and earlier termination of the rainy season, in other words, a short wet season. The end result is a significant decline in precipitation which results in lowered streamflow. The results, therefore, support the stepwise function of the meteorological model proposed (Gunn, Folan, and Robichaux 1991:1; 1995:19–20).

The effects of shifting the onset of the wet season can have a significant impact on planting and harvesting corn as seen in figure 38. For planting techniques employed in the state of Campeche, the best time to plant a *milpa*, or cornfield, is in May when it is planted on upland surfaces. If the rains come later, the corn will be planted on lower surfaces facing the sea. As a final alternative, if the rains have not started by September, the milpa is planted on the floor of a *bajo*, or marsh. There is a progressive loss of productivity at each decision. Milpa productivity, therefore, will generally increase as the climate heats from cold to warm. In sum, cold global climate

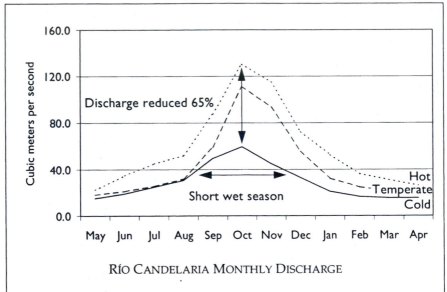

RÍO CANDELARIA MONTHLY DISCHARGE

Figure 38. Río Candelaria average monthly discharge plotted by climate type from 1958 to 1990. Note the long wet season for hot, wet years, the short wet season for cold, dry years, and the 65 and 47 percent reductions of the maximum discharge from hot and temperate to cold years (*Source:* Gunn, Folan, and Robichaux 1995:20).

will reduce the productivity of the corn harvest because of the delayed onset of the wet season (Gunn, Folan, and Robichaux 1995:26).

The general relationship noted above between global temperatures, moisture levels (as reflected in moisture levels in the Rio Candelaria watershed by our model) and major cultural events in the watershed and surrounding areas suggest that prehispanic Maya culture fared best during globally warm-cool periods with moderate precipitation and a distinct dry season. They tended to decline during cold (dry) and hot (excessively wet) periods. (Gunn, Folan, and Robichaux 1995:35)

Gunn and Crumley have suggested that years of global cold temperatures are dominated by ice age circulation patterns and years of hot temperatures are dominated by interglacial patterns. In other words, there is a clear relationship between global temperatures and Yucatecan rainfall, with cold temperatures associated with low rainfall (Gunn and Crumley 1991:580).

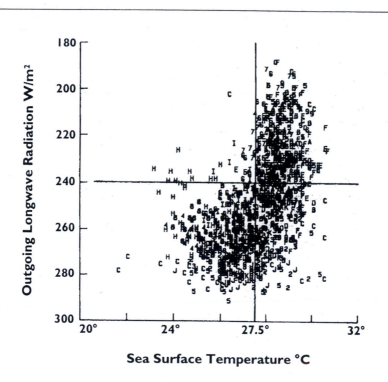

PACIFIC OCEAN CONVECTION, PRECIPITATION,
AND SEA SURFACE TEMPERATURES

Figure 39. Scatterplot of outgoing longwave radiation (OLR), associated with deep convection and rainfall, versus sea surface temperature. Note the on/off switch at 27.5°C, marked by the vertical line. OLR values above 240W/m², marked by the horizontal line, are associated with deep convection. Most of the deep convection and resulting precipitation is seen in the upper right quadrant, above OLR values of 240W/m² and over sea surface temperatures in excess of 27.5°C (adapted from Graham and Barnett 1987:658).

OCEAN TEMPERATURES

Hastenrath has associated an equatorward extension of the North Atlantic High with the advection of cold water in the eastern part of the Atlantic Ocean, particularly in the realm of the Canary Current. He has associated drought in the Central American-Caribbean region with an equatorward extension of the North Atlantic High and anomalously cold water across the North Atlantic Ocean. Along the same lines and across the ocean, William Gray has associated Sahelian drought with cold North Atlantic waters. There seems to be an association, then, with cold Atlantic water in the Tropics and drought in Central America and the Caribbean (Gray 1990:1255; Hastenrath 1976:202, 207; 1978:2224).

One reason may be an on/off switch for deep convection in the tropical Pacific at 27.5°C, as seen in figure 39. When water temperatures are above 27.5°C, deep convection occurs. When they drop below 27.5°C, convection is suppressed. Temperatures progressively greater than 27.5° do not result in progressively greater rainfall and the exact temperature above 27.5° is not important. When sea surface temperatures are above 27.5° in the Pacific, surface wind divergence is closely associated with the presence or absence of deep convection. Deep convection is required for thunderstorms which provide most of Mesoamerica's summer rains. Data from the tropical Atlantic show a slightly lower critical temperature at about 27°. Water temperatures in the Caribbean off Yucatán rise above 27° during the summer rainy season and fall below 27° in the winter dry season. Although the effect has been identified specifically over the oceans, the principle holds true for regions relying on ocean winds for their rainfall, like Yucatán (Graham and Barnett 1987:657).

The dominating feature of the general circulation in the Caribbean area are the trade winds, which originate over the Atlantic Ocean. The trades reach Yucatán after a journey of 6,500 to 8,500 km (4,000 to 5,000 mi) across the tropical Atlantic and the Caribbean Sea, which normally maintains water temperatures of around 27°C throughout the year. As the trades cross the tropical Atlantic and the Caribbean, more water vapor will evaporate from warmer water than from cooler water. Thus, the combination of cooler water, less evaporation, a reduction of the double sea breeze effect, a southwestward extension of the North Atlantic High, and a lower inversion layer will result in less rainfall in Yucatán (Nieuwolt 1977:164).

THE COLDEST YEAR OF THE TWENTIETH CENTURY

One very unusual event occurred during the period of historical weather records. Returning to the definition of a severe drought in Mérida as a year in which annual rainfall totals less than 734 mm (28.9 in), the twentieth century saw fourteen such years. Five of them occurred during the first decade and three occurred together, 1902, 1903, and 1904, following the eruptions of Santa María, Mt. Pelée, and La Soufrière-St. Vincent in 1902. Unfortunately, the rainfall records for 1901 are missing. This three-year drought was not only severe, it was brutal. The three years' rainfall totals are 747.9, 407.4, and 706.0 mm (29.44, 16.0, and 27.8 in), compared with an average of 945.5 mm (37.2 in). The rainfall for 1903 was only 43 percent of normal. There was a basic failure of the summer rains from 1902 to 1904. In 1903, the June–September rainfall was only 39 percent of normal.

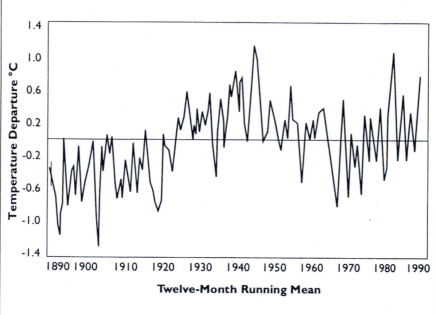

NORTHERN LATITUDE AIR TEMPERATURES

Figure 40. Areally averaged temperature anomalies for the region poleward of 55°N. The line represents a twelve-month running mean of northern latitude air temperature differences. Note the deep low in 1903 (adapted from Walsh 1991:19).

Of the fourteen years of severe drought in the century, five occurred in the first decade, three between 1917 and 1923, and only six were spread over the ensuing sixty-eight years. There was a significant increase in mean Northern Hemisphere temperatures, on the order of 0.35°C at the beginning of the 1920s. A general global warming of this nature would help explain the increase in rainfall apparent in Mérida since then (Ellsaesser et al 1986:769-770).

What were the conditions in the North Atlantic weather system at the time of the drought? There was a coincidence of a number of unusual events between 1901 and 1904—at least unusual in terms of the rest of the twentieth century.

As seen in figure 40, air temperatures in the region north of 55°N reached a severe low for the century in 1903. Spring, summer, and autumn air temperatures in the Arctic plummeted to their lowest levels of the century, as seen in figure 41. According to P. M. Kelly and his colleagues, 1902 was the coldest year on record in the Arctic. As can be seen from figure 42,

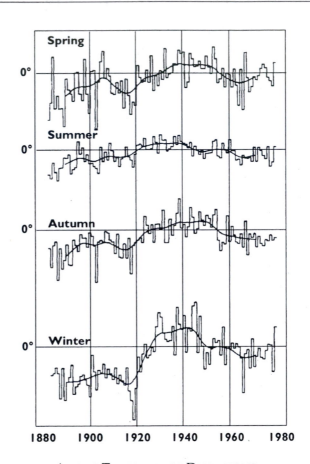

ARCTIC TEMPERATURE DEVIATIONS

Figure 41. Seasonal temperature deviations from the reference period 1946–1960 averaged over the Arctic. Note the deep spring, summer, and autumn lows around 1903 (adapted from Kelly et al 1982:75).

summer sea surface temperatures reached their lowest levels of the century (Kelly et al 1982:74–75).

Between 1880 and 1910, the temperature of the waters of the tropical North Atlantic fell about 1°C (1.8°F). As can be seen from figure 42, summer sea surface temperatures in the Northern Hemisphere reached their low point for the century in 1903 (Paltridge and Woodruff 1981:2432; Tucker and Barry 1984:199).

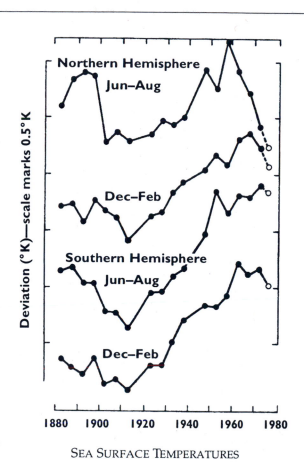

SEA SURFACE TEMPERATURES

Figure 42. Pentadal average deviations of winter and summer sea surface temperatures for each hemisphere. Note that summer sea surface temperatures in the Northern Hemisphere reached their low point for the century about 1903, as shown by the top graph (adapted from Paltridge and Woodruff 1981:2432).

As we saw in figure 25 on page 142, the North Atlantic High was displaced far to the southwest during 1900–1904.

A significant drop in solar radiation took place at ground level in 1902 and 1903, a 26 percent reduction in intensity between 1901 and 1903 as measured at Warsaw by Ladislas Gorczýnski. According to him, similar reductions in radiation were independently measured in Lausanne, Heidelberg, Warsaw, and Washington by different scientists. In Washington, S. P. Langley of the Smithsonian Institution recorded up to a 20 percent drop in the atmospheric transmissibility, depending on the wavelength measured. Writing in *Nature,* he also commented on the "unusual coolness of the summer" in 1903, the year of least rainfall in Mérida (Gorczýnski 1904:255–258; Langley 1903:5).

These factors coincided with the most severe multiyear drought in Mérida since weather records have been kept.

The frequency of occurrence of natural processes is inversely proportional to their magnitude. One event does not have statistical significance for forecasting. There is no guarantee that the same coincidence of air temperature, sea temperature, and North Atlantic High position will once again result in drought in Mérida. A single event, however, can demonstrate an actual set of circumstances under which a meteorological anomaly can occur. Furthermore, one event does have one enormous statistical significance: it did occur once, at least once. If it occurred once, it may have occurred more than once, and it may occur again. One event demolishes the argument that such circumstances could never occur. The events of 1902–1904 demonstrate clearly that extreme drought can occur in Yucatán. Because it did. An extreme drought will only occur infrequently, so we were lucky to have seen it at all in the weather records of the twentieth century (Hsü 1990:309).

THE COLDEST YEARS OF THE NINETEENTH CENTURY

Although detailed weather data were not kept for most of the world during the nineteenth century, we do have access to ample historical records which give us a qualitative description of exceptional weather events. We cannot determine the exact rainfall for Mérida, for example, but there is much of value that we can glean from historical descriptions of the times.

The most massive volcanic eruption of recorded history began when the Indonesian volcano, Tambora, on the Sangarr Peninsula of Sumbawa Island near Bali, first erupted on April 5, 1815. The sound was heard in Jakarta and Ternate, 1,250 to 1,400 km (775 to 850 mi) away. Minor activity continued for five days until the early evening of April 10, 1815, when a truly massive eruption exploded into the atmosphere, the most massive historically documented eruption known since New Zealand's Taupo in about AD 130. It was heard on Sumatra, over 2600 km (1600 mi) distant. It blew a column of ash and aerosols 50 km (30 mi or 165,000 ft) into the atmosphere. The nearby city of Madura was shrouded in darkness for three days (Sigurdsson and Carey 1988:67:68; Stothers 1984a:1191–1192).

At about 7:00 PM, the eruption intensified. The sultan of Sangarr saw three fiery columns climb into the sky above the volcano and merge at a great height. Moments later, the entire volcano was like a sea of liquid fire in what the sultan described as "a whirlwind on the southeast slope of the volcano which hurled whole forests and villages with people and cattle, in short everything, into the air and devastated the country." Following the firestorm, the 4,500m (15,000ft) summit collapsed, forming the modern caldera of Tambora (Sultan of Sangarr quoted in Sigurdsson and Carey 1988:69; Stothers 1984a:1191).

Around the world, brilliant red sunsets and twilights were seen throughout the summer and fall, probably inspiring Turner's striking landscapes from that time. The most dramatic effect, however, was climatological. The summer of 1816 was so cold that it was known colloquially in New England as "eighteen hundred and froze to death" and the "year without a summer." In June, on Nantucket Island, the temperature plunged to minus 5.5°C (22°F) and three to six inches of snow fell there and in other parts of New England and New York. In Vermont, crops were damaged by frost. A second cold wave struck on July 9, when water in Maine froze "thick as window glass," killing crops again. A third cold wave hit on August 21. Frost killed corn, potatoes, beans, and vines in New Hampshire, Massachusetts, and Maine, while snow covered the mountains of Vermont. A final storm struck the region on August 30, destroying most of the remaining crops. Although systematic meteorological weather records are not available outside of New England, similar weather patterns can be documented for almost the entire eastern portion of North America. Complaints of frost and drought during the spring, summer, and autumn, with ensuing harvest deficiencies and fears of dearth, were widely expressed from Québec to Pennsylvania. Even in the South, cool, dry weather was reported in the Moravian colonies of North Carolina, in South Carolina, Alabama, and Louisiana. Food scarcities also developed in the Caribbean islands (Post 1977:11–14; Sigurdsson and Carey 1988:71–72).

Lord Byron, who spent the summer of 1816 in Switzerland on Lake Geneva, described it in the following verses from his poem, "Darkness":

The bright sun was extinguished, and the stars
Did wander darkling in the eternal space,
Rayless, and pathless, and the icy earth
Swung blind and blackening in the moonless air;
Morn came and went—and came and brought no day....
(quoted in Sigurdsson and Carey 1988:72)

For the rest of 1816 and 1817, grain prices rose sharply in North America and Europe, where similar climatic aberrations caused similar crop failures, resulting in social and economic disorders and famine in the last widespread European subsistence crisis. July of 1816 was the coldest in England's two-hundred-year weather record, and snow fell near London in August. According to Emmanuel Le Roy Ladurie, "In 1816 the subtropical high pressures which normally lap over onto Europe during the summer scarcely reached it at all....All Europe spent the summer seeking refuge from the rain round the fire." Atmospheric haze was still being noted at Glasgow Observatory in September of 1817, two and one-half years after the eruption. We will examine in detail the climatological effects of volcanoes in chapter 8. At this point, it is sufficient to note that the eruption occurred and the climatic effects ensued consistent with the meteorological model presented in this chapter (Le Roy Ladurie 1971:64; Post 1977:xiv; Sigurdsson and Carey 1988:71–72; Stothers 1984a:1195).

According to the model, a period of severe cold in the Northern Hemisphere should be accompanied by drought in Yucatán and, indeed, Ricardo Molina Hübbe reported that the year 1817 is described in Spanish colonial documents as one of drought and famine. He reports that Maya first fled from the towns and villages to the cities and then into the forests looking for something to eat. It was a year, as he put it, of "mortal suffering" (Molina Hübbe 1941:27).

The next episode of severe cold in the nineteenth century in New England, according to reliable observations made at Williamstown, MA, was 1836–1837, following the enormous eruption of Cosegüina Volcano in Nicaragua in 1835. As Molina Hübbe and John Lloyd Stephens reported, this was a period of drought and famine in the Yucatán Peninsula, which may have started as early as 1834, but intensified in 1835 and 1836 (Molina Hübbe 1941:29; Post 1977:7; John L. Stephens 1843 (2):187; Williams 1952:21).

The model, then, of severe cold in the Northern Hemisphere resulting in drought in the Maya Lowlands is confirmed by well documented historical events. One such event might be ascribed to a sheer coincidence between cold and drought. Two and three such events, however, begin to suggest a pattern. Not all droughts in the Maya Lowlands are necessarily tied to periods of cold. There are undoubtedly different sets of circumstances which also result in drought. Furthermore, not all years of European cold can be tied to drought and famine in the Lowlands, and not all droughts and famines can be definitively tied to hemispheric cold, especially as we go back in time and the data get sparser and less reliable. We have, however, identified a repeating pattern of hemispheric cold and drought in the Maya Lowlands, and we have seen that the coldest years of the nineteenth century and the coldest years of the twentieth century were coincident with serious drought in Yucatán.

While we are talking about historical confirmation of the model, it should be noted that severe cold has been identified in tree ring data for the Northern Hemisphere at the beginning of the 1450s, both in North America and Europe, as we will see in detail in chapter 10. Historical documents, various Aztec chronicles, indicate that the early 1450s were a time of severe cold and famine in the Mexican Highlands, including the terrible famine of the year 1 Rabbit, in 1454. In the Maya Lowlands, the *Book of Chilam Balam of Maní* indicates severe cold, drought, and famine at roughly the same time, coincident with the fall of Mayapán. It should also be noted that there was a very large eruption of Kuwae Volcano in Indonesia in about 1452. Although, as mentioned above, the historical details become sparser and less reliable as we go farther back in time, the events of the early 1450s in Mesoamerica appear to conform to our model and might well provide yet a third historical confirmation of its predictions. We will return to the topic of repeated famines in Mesoamerica in greater detail in chapter 11 (Craine and Reindorp 1979:83; Kovar 1970:28–31; Witter 1999:1).

RANDOM NATURE OF DROUGHT

One very important point needs to be made about the spatial characteristics of drought. Even though drought may afflict a region in general, its specific effects in a particular locale can be very unpredictable. Texas suffered a terrible drought during the 1950s. The most severe drought occurred during the year 1955–1956. Figure 43 shows the severity of the drought for the state as a whole during that year. As can be seen, in the middle of areas of severe drought, there were areas of only moderate drought. One cannot assume that a drought, therefore, will strike a whole region uniformly. There can be areas where drought is devastating, surrounding areas where it is merely difficult. In thinking about the Maya Lowlands, then, we need to realize that severe drought may not have affected all areas equally in every episode of drought. Some cities and regions would have been harder hit than others one time, with a different pattern of severity the next time.

PALAEOCLIMATES

According to Nils-Axel Mörner, short term climatic changes tend to last on the order of 50 to 150 years. Keith Briffa and his colleagues have identified quasi-cyclical climatic changes lasting about 70 to 90 years that have occurred regularly since 1700. Hastenrath has pointed out that the climatic variability characteristic of the outer Tropics to Subtropics around the Atlantic is concentrated at the scale of two to three decades. With only one hundred years of weather records available for study, it is not likely that we would see more than one shift in short term cycles. In fact, we are lucky to have seen even one event. The early part of the twentieth century saw such a shift from cooler to warmer. Worldwide, the average change in global temperatures during the century was only about 0.5°C (0.9°F). Changes during the last 1,500 years, on the other hand, are estimated to have varied as much as 3°C. We did not see the kind of dramatic weather change in the twentieth century that has occurred in the past two millennia (Briffa et al 1990:436-437; Hastenrath 1985:315; Lamb 1982:310-311; Mörner 1984:646).

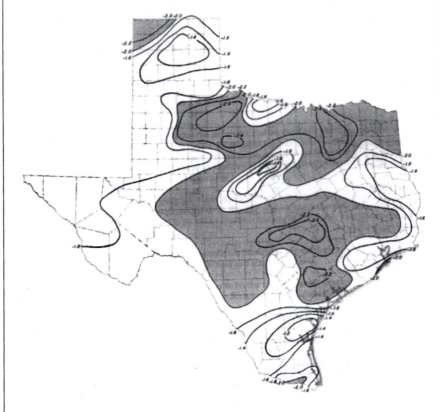

DROUGHT SEVERITY IN TEXAS 1955–1956

Figure 43. The severity of drought during the years 1955–1956 for the state of Texas as a whole. The areas of severe drought are indicated in *gray,* moderate drought in *white*. Note the random distribution of severe drought over the state, with areas of moderate drought within areas of severe drought (Hatfield 1964).

SCANDINAVIA

According to Edward Lorenz, true teleconnections seem to qualify as features of the general circulation. Yucatán and Lapland are located at the southwestern and northeastern corners of the Atlantic weather area. As pointed out by García, Armillas, Jáuregui Ostos, Hastenrath, and others, when the North Atlantic High moves to the northeast, humid conditions would be expected in Yucatán and warm conditions in northeast Europe. If the high has moved far to the southwest, cold would prevail in Europe, as the Siberian High moved in across northern Europe. As the North Atlantic High moved south, dry conditions would prevail in Yucatán. A Scandinavian tree ring record, then, might well serve as a proxy record for Yucatecan palaeoclimates. It would at least indicate periods of cold in Arctic Sweden during which conditions would be propitious for Yucatecan drought. Such a tree ring record will be examined later in the palaeoclimatology discussion in chapter 10 (Brian Goodman, 1993, personal communication; Gribbing 1976:58; Lorenz 1991:13).

A Blind Alley

Before leaving the topic of lowland meteorology, it is necessary to discuss a line of articles that are often referred to by archaeologists and are often raised as counterarguments to the meteorological model presented in the present work. This path was first blazed by Ellsworth Huntington in papers written in 1913 and 1915 in which he tied the florescence of Maya civilization to dry periods and its collapse to the return of wet weather when "the bushes could not be burned; the jungle grew thick; fevers became ominously severe; and the stagnant air became more enervating than ever before" (Ellsworth Huntington 1913:558–561; 1915:160).

W. A. Sanchez and J. E. Kutzbach wrote an article in 1974 in which they analyzed a ten-year series of weather data from 1961 to 1970. Taking the years 1931 to 1960 as a baseline, they then used the 1961 to 1970 data to determine that a cooling had occurred. That cooling, they concluded, was accompanied by increased precipitation over the Yucatán Peninsula. The ten years of meteorological data used, however, were much too short to be meaningful. The article spawned progeny which were based on the Sanchez and Kutzbach research, therefore suffering from the same shortcomings, and are often cited by archaeologists (Sanchez and Kutzbach 1974).

Joel Gunn and Richard E. W. Adams, for example, proposed in 1981 that the Collapse may have occurred during a time of cold weather in the Northern Hemisphere when a band of wet tropical air was present over the Maya Lowlands, resulting in increased precipitation, in accordance with Sanchez's and Kutzbach's conclusions. William Folan and his colleagues, relying on Sanchez's and Kutzbach's work and Gunn's and Adams's work, proposed in 1983 that the ninth century AD was a cool, wet period followed by a warm, dry phase in the tenth century. I, of course, believe that a cold, dry period occurred from about AD 800 to 1000 followed subsequently by a period of increasing temperatures and precipitation (Folan et al 1983; Gunn and Adams 1981).

Joel Gunn has since retracted his earlier conclusions reached in the Gunn and Adams (1981) article based on the findings reported in Gunn, Folan, and Robichaux (1995), as discussed earlier on page 156 of this book. In that article they clearly determined that global cooling *reduced* rainfall in the Yucatán Peninsula. William Folan, as one of the coauthors of the

Gunn, Folan, and Robichaux article, also seems to have implicitly, if not explicitly, retracted the conclusions of his 1983 article. Messenger's 1990 survey of climate studies relating to Mesoamerica also relies heavily on Sanchez and Kutzbach and Gunn and Adams. It merely repeats the flaws of those articles on this topic and adds nothing new (Folan et al 1983; Gunn and Adams 1981; Gunn, Folan, and Robichaux 1995).

Since both Gunn and Folan, two of the lead authors of the often quoted articles, participated in doing and reporting the research which refutes this whole line of thought, the matter would seem to be closed. Looking down what ultimately turns out to be a blind alley is, however, an important part of the work of science.

DISCUSSION

A particular concatenation of climatic factors occurred in the first decade of the twentieth century. The meteorological hypothesis of this book is that the coincidence of these events was responsible for drought in Mérida and may provide a model for understanding how drought can occur in the Maya Lowlands.

1. There was an abrupt Northern Hemispheric cold spell, especially in the Arctic, which occurred during the first few years of the twentieth century.
2. This cold spell was accompanied by a severe southwestward displacement of the North Atlantic High, relative to the rest of the century.
3. Solar radiation measured at ground level fell up to 20 percent.
4. Sea surface temperatures hit their lowest levels in the last hundred years.
5. The coincidence of these factors was associated with the longest and most severe drought in Mérida, Yucatán, in the past hundred years, lasting from 1902 to 1904.
6. The June–September rains in 1903 were only 39 percent of normal.

These observations outline a model which explains how drought occurred in the Maya Lowlands at least once and perhaps repetitively. Since it happened once, therefore, it *may* have happened more than once.

The coincidence of a southwestward displacement of the North Atlantic High and cold ocean water are conducive to drought, and both are likely to occur during cold periods. Gunn, Folan, and Robichaux have demonstrated that cold global temperatures accompany periods of reduced rainfall in the Yucatán Peninsula. During past periods of severe cold in the Northern Hemisphere similar coincidences of factors *may* have occurred which would have been associated with terrible drought in Yucatán and the Petén. This would make possible the use of tree ring records from the White Mountains and Lapland to identify cold periods in the Northern Hemisphere which *might* be conducive to drought in Mesoamerica.

Greater temperatures swings are known to have occurred during the last 2,000 years than occurred during the last hundred years. Therefore, the coinciding anomalies over the past 2,000 years may also have been more severe, and the coinciding droughts could have been more severe and longer lasting than during the last century, although we do not have specific data to establish this as a fact.

We looked at two additional incidences of severe cold which occurred in the nineteenth century. You may have noticed, as I did, that each of the three coldest episodes of the last two hundred years followed major volcanic eruptions and resulted in drought in the Maya Lowlands. We will turn our attention in chapter 8 to volcanic eruptions and see whether they have an identifiable effect on Yucatecan weather.

The concepts presented in this chapter demonstrate that severe drought can occur in a seasonal tropical forest at the northern limit of the tropical rainfall regime. Such drought would have inflicted unimaginable suffering and death on a population living a millennium ago who could expect no help from anywhere.

7. Thermohaline Circulation

About four million years ago, trees grew along the shores of the Arctic Ocean and the northern ice caps did not exist. North and South America were separated by a waterway and currents flowed between the Atlantic and the Pacific. About three million years ago, however, the Isthmus of Panama rose out of the sea, blocked off the interocean passageway, and prevented the equatorial current from transporting water from the Atlantic to the Pacific. The time can be dated from near shore marine fossils present in Panamanian sediments. At about this same time, the Earth began its plunge into the Ice Age, a period from which we have not yet emerged, as can be attested by the presence of ice caps and glaciers around the world (Stanley 1996:179, 184).

Evaporation and Salinity

There is a major difference between the Atlantic and the Pacific Oceans today. The Atlantic is saltier and warmer and the Pacific is fresher and cooler. Not by much, but by just enough to make a big difference—a difference that has enormous climatological consequences. To be specific, between 45°N and 65°N, the Atlantic has an annual mean sea surface temperature of 10°C (50°F) and a salinity of 34.9 parts per thousand, while the Pacific has an annual mean sea surface temperature of 6.7°C (44°F) and a salinity of 32.8 parts per thousand. The difference in salinity is about 6 percent (Street-Perrott and Perrott 1990:608).

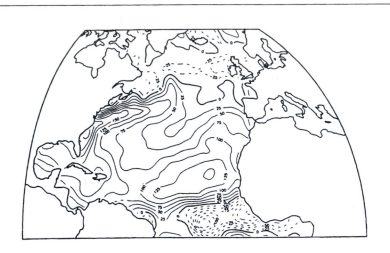

EVAPORATION MINUS PRECIPITATION

Figure 44. Annual evaporation minus precipitation for the North Atlantic in cm per year. The areas where evaporation exceeds precipitation are shown in *dashed lines* (adapted from Schmitt, Bogden, and Dorman 1989:1211).

Compared to the Pacific, the Atlantic Ocean is long and narrow. A greater fraction of its surface area is under the influence of dry continental air, making the Atlantic a net evaporative basin. This river of air, the dry return flow of the Hadley circulation, is very arid as it blows off of the Sahara desert. As it crosses the Atlantic, it absorbs a tremendous amount of water vapor from the warm sea surface, leaving the salt behind. Warmer waters lose more water vapor to the air through evaporation than do cooler waters. When it reaches the Isthmus of Panama, the water laden air crosses readily into the Pacific. The isthmus is low enough that the winds can transport the water across Panama to the Pacific Ocean, without losing it to mountain ranges. Once over the Pacific, it precipitates out over the relatively cool waters.

The process of evaporating water in the Atlantic and precipitating it in the Pacific creates a salinity imbalance between the two oceans. The Atlantic loses more water through evaporation and transport across the Isthmus of Panama than it gains through precipitation and continental runoff. Additionally, the more northerly westerlies transport more water vapor out of the Atlantic across Eurasia than they bring in across the North American cordillera (figures 44 and 45). The waters left behind, therefore, are enriched with salt. The excess salt in the Atlantic is then redistributed to the world's oceans in a circulation system that geologist and geochemist

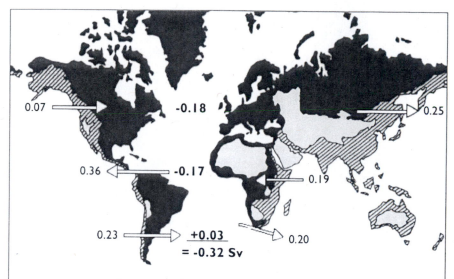

ATLANTIC OCEAN HYDRAULIC BUDGET

Figure 45. The hydrolic budget, the gain or loss of water vapor, of the Atlantic Ocean. Its continental drainage basin is shown in *black*. Drainage to the Pacific and Indian Oceans is shown in *hatching*. Deserts from which no drainage occurs are shown in *gray*. *Light* numbers give the inputs and losses in three latitude zones: north temperate, equatorial, and south temperate. *Bold* numbers give the net loss or gain for each zone in the Atlantic and the total for the Atlantic as a whole. As can be seen, easterly tradewinds carry more water vapor out across Central America than enters across Africa. Westerly winds in the Northern Hemisphere transport more water vapor across Asia than enters across the American cordillera. *Sv*=Sverdrup, $10^6 m^3/s$ (adapted from Broecker 1997:1583).

Wallace Broecker has dubbed the ocean conveyor belt (figure 50). He emphasizes that the most vulnerable attribute of the conveyor system is the water vapor transport across the Isthmus of Panama (Broecker 1987:77–79; 1997:1583; Graeme Stephens 1990:634, 644; Weyl 1968:46).

CONVECTION AND DEEP WATER FORMATION

In both the Atlantic and the Pacific there are great, swirling, subtropical ocean gyres which rotate clockwise between 10°N and about 45°N around a center of about 30°N latitude. In the North Atlantic, the gyre is the principal transporter of surface water. It is driven by the Coriolis force, due to the Earth's rotation, and by the prevailing westerly winds to the

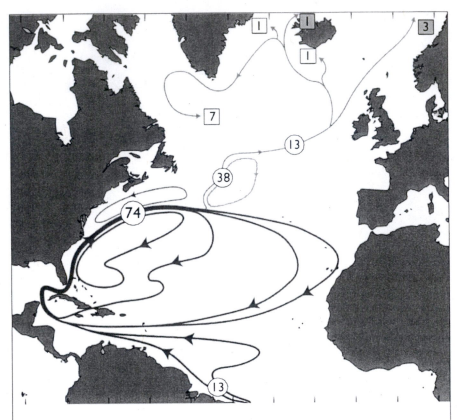

NORTH ATLANTIC CIRCULATION

Figure 46. A simplified rendition of the system of linked gyres and flow pathways of imported warm water from the equator to the subpolar basins of the North Atlantic. Flow rates in millions of cubic meters per second are indicated by *circles*. Deep water production is indicated by *squares*, deep water production farther north in the Nordic Seas is indicated by *dark gray squares* (adapted from McCartney 1994:7).

north and the tradewinds to the south, which impart a torque to the ocean currents. The center of the North Atlantic gyre's circulation is known as the Sargasso Sea, named for its abundant seaweed. It is a region of calm winds and warm temperatures (figure 46). The water circulating in these massive systems reaches to about 2 km (1.2 mi or 6,300 ft) below the surface (Duxbury 1971:211, 219; Pedlosky 1990:316).

With the passageway between the Americas blocked by Panama, the saline waters of the tropical Atlantic flow north, mostly through the Yucatán Strait, and into the gyre's Gulf Stream where the warm water

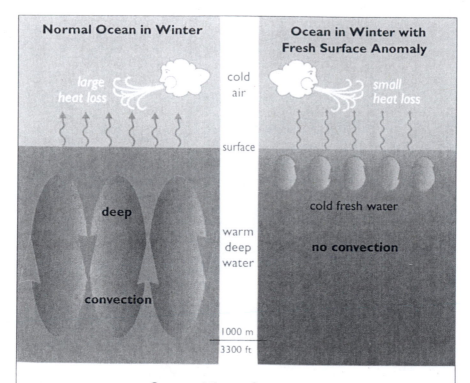

Normal Ocean in Winter

Ocean in Winter with
Fresh Surface Anomaly

large
heat loss

cold
air

small
heat loss

surface

deep

cold fresh water

warm
deep
water

no convection

convection

1000 m

3300 ft

CHILLED WATER CONVECTION

Figure 47. Deep convection is essential for deep water formation. Otherwise only the surface layer is cooled. Strong winter
chilling of the surface waters causes them to become denser
than the water below and they sink. Deeper warmer water then
rises and releases its heat as well. If the surface waters are too
fresh, deep convection does not occur and the heat of the deep
water is not released (adapted from Schmitt 1996:5).

flows at about 800m (2,640ft) depth. Most of the Gulf Stream waters continue around the gyre, but a portion veers off into the northern parts of the
North Atlantic. As it flows farther north, around Iceland and Greenland,
winds sweep the surface waters aside and the warm water rises to the
ocean surface.

At the surface, it encounters very cold winds, especially during the
winter. Heat, of course, can only flow from warm to cold, not the other
way around, so the warm waters from the south give up their heat to the
cold winds blowing across them. As the warm, southern, saline waters are
chilled by the Arctic winds during the winter, they become as dense as any
water in the deep sea and they start to sink, setting up convection cells (fig-

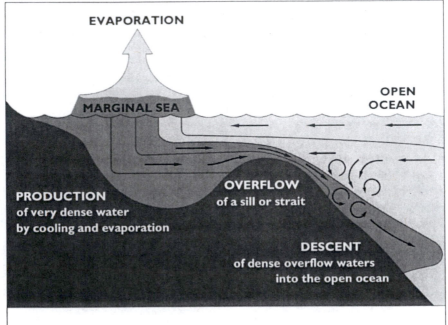

EVAPORATION

MARGINAL SEA

OPEN
OCEAN

PRODUCTION
of very dense water
by cooling and evaporation

OVERFLOW
of a sill or strait

DESCENT
of dense overflow waters
into the open ocean

DEEP WATER FORMATION IN A MARGINAL SEA

Figure 48. Three stages in the formation of deep water in a marginal sea. A shallow and confined marginal sea acts as a concentration basin that produces a comparatively small volume of very dense water which descends the continental shelf and slope, mixing with oceanic waters along the way. The final deep water may be quite different from the water that first poured across the sill (adapted from Price 1994:10).

ure 47). As they sink, warmer water from below flows to the surface and gives up its heat to the atmosphere as well. The arriving water from the south has a temperature of about 11°C (52°F) and the departing deep water about 3°C (37.4°F). The quantity of heat released to the atmosphere is approximately equal to 25 percent of the solar energy reaching the Atlantic, roughly north of Africa, during the year—during the winter, the released heat may even rival the sun's heat (Broecker 1997:1588; Broecker and Denton 1989:2489–2490; 1990:54; Broecker, Peteet, and Rind 1985:24).

Surface water cools almost to the freezing point throughout the northernmost parts of the Atlantic Ocean during the winter. Only where the salinity is high enough, however, and therefore the density great enough, does it sink into the abyss (figure 48). Those places are in the Labrador Sea, in the North Atlantic west of the Faroe Islands, in the Denmark Strait, in the Greenland and Norwegian seas, and, perhaps, the Arctic Ocean (figure

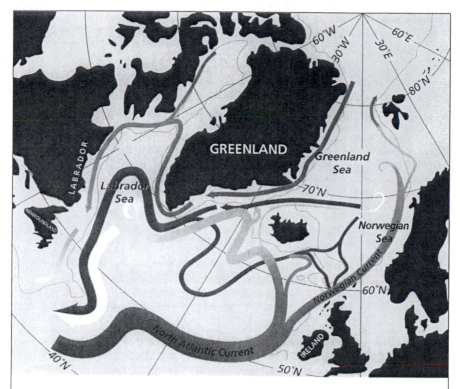

NORTH ATLANTIC DEEP WATER FORMATION AREA

Figure 49. The area and pathways associated with the transformation of warm subtropical waters into colder subpolar and polar waters (McCartney, Curry, and Bezdek 1996:19).

49). Because this process is driven by temperature and salinity, and therefore density, it is known as the thermohaline circulation (*thermo* for temperature and *haline* for salinity) (Broecker and Denton 1990:54; Jones, Anderson, and Rudels 1998:1; McCartney 1994:6; Rahmstorf 1997:825).

The process of deep water formation and the tremendous release of heat to the atmosphere result in northern Europe enjoying a far warmer climate than comparable latitudes in North America and Asia. Cities like Dublin, London, Copenhagen, and Berlin, not to mention Oslo and Stockholm, lie farther north than any major city in the United States and Canada. Rome, we should remember, lies slightly north of Chicago. Were the conveyor belt to shut down, Dublin would have a summer climate like Spitsbergen, 1,000 km (600 mi) north of the Arctic circle, and London would experience the winter cold of Irkutsk in Siberia. The heating effect

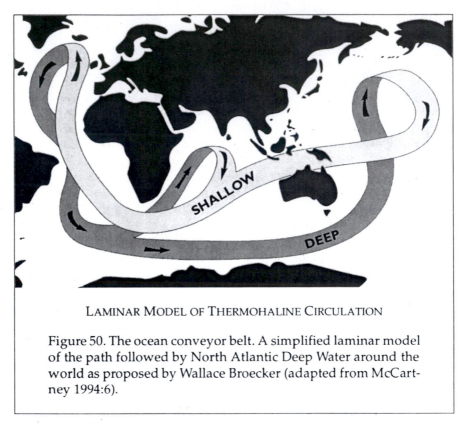

LAMINAR MODEL OF THERMOHALINE CIRCULATION

Figure 50. The ocean conveyor belt. A simplified laminar model
of the path followed by North Atlantic Deep Water around the
world as proposed by Wallace Broecker (adapted from McCartney 1994:6).

of the deep water formation is often mistakenly attributed to the Gulf
Stream flow, which is well to the south (Broecker 1995:63, 68).

OCEAN CONVEYOR BELT

Once the cold saline waters sink into the abyss of the North Atlantic,
they begin to flow south, as can be seen in figure 50, under the Gulf
Stream, into the South Atlantic, and then into the circumpolar current
around Antarctica, known as the raceway. There, they rise, are again
chilled to the freezing point, and sink. Since there are no land obstacles to
break the raceway's flow around Antarctica, the resulting strong current
flows in a circle around the continent. In the raceway, the North Atlantic
Deep Water is joined by an equal amount of deep water formed in the
Weddell Sea. As it circulates around Antarctica, some of it peels off into the
Indian Ocean and some of it peels off into the Pacific, from which it then
returns at progressively shallower depths until it flows into the Atlantic.
No deep water is formed in either the Indian or Pacific Oceans. The round
trip takes between 1,000 and 1,600 years. The conveyor belt runs deep and
slow (Albarède 1997:908; Broecker 1995:62; 1997:1582–1583; 1998:121;
Kunzig 1996:86; Schmitz 1995:167; Talley 1996:631; Weyl 1968:53).

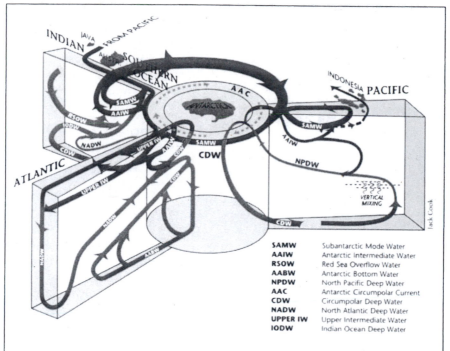

THREE DIMENSIONAL OCEAN CIRCULATION MODEL

Figure 51. The actual flow in the world's oceans is more complex than the laminar model would suggest, as can be seen in this more intricate yet still simplified circulation schematic of the world's major water masses. North Atlantic Deep Water flows through linked circulation systems in the world's oceans (adapted from Toole 1996:34).

Broecker has dubbed this circulation system the ocean conveyor belt—a conveyor belt which redistributes salt throughout the world's oceans. It is a self-reinforcing and self-stabilizing system. As the surface water sinks and spreads southward, it draws in more shallow water to the North Atlantic. The conveyor belt distributes tropical warmth to the northern latitudes in the Atlantic and carries cold surface waters southward in the Pacific, pushing warm water back towards the equator. At steady state, it transports just enough salt out of the Atlantic to compensate for the excess created by evaporation. In effect, the conveyor belt reunites the salt left behind in the Atlantic with the water vapor which was transported across the Isthmus of Panama and precipitated in the Pacific. Although not a large current when compared to the strength of the Gulf Stream or the southern circumpolar current, the conveyor belt carries 15 times as much water as all the rivers of the world combined. Of course, the actual flow in the world's oceans is more complex that the simplified laminar model suggests, as can be seen in figure 51—which is itself a simplification (Broecker 1987:77–78; 1997:1588; Broecker, Peteet, and Rind 1985:24; Gordon 1986:5037).

BROECKER'S THEORY

The world's first thermodynamicist was Benjamin Thompson, an American royalist who moved to England after the Revolutionary War where he became Sir Benjamin before moving to Bavaria and becoming the Count of Rumford. In 1797, he posited the idea that waters in the North Atlantic sank when chilled and that a current of warm water from the south flowed north to replace them. The process of deep water formation, therefore, has been known for two hundred years. By the early 1960s, oceanographer Henry Stommel, then director of the Woods Hole Oceanographic Institution, became concerned that the currents might stop flowing if too much fresh water was released to the ocean surface in the northern Atlantic (Calvin 1998(Part 1):12; Warren 1981:8).

In 1984, Wallace Broecker made a connection between the conveyor belt and climate change (while he was listening to a lecture by physicist Hans Oeschger, of the University of Bern, discussing the climate record in an ice core from Greenland). He saw that the cessation of the conveyor belt would play a major role in the abrupt shifts between periods of cold and periods of milder weather in the North Atlantic region and between full glacial periods and interglacials. Building on the earlier proposals of Henry Stommel and Claes Rooth, Broecker suggested that there exists an on/off switch to the thermohaline flow. If the salinity of the North Atlantic were altered, then the formation of deep water would shift to the south of Bermuda or to the South Atlantic, and the release of heat in the northern Atlantic wouldn't occur. Temperatures in northern Europe and the North Atlantic would drop dramatically, bringing on colder conditions. He believes this shift can occur quite abruptly. When combined with orbital forcing (figure 53), it is the mode present during glacial maxima (Broecker 1995:64; Broecker, Peteet, and Rind 1985:24; Kunzig 1996:89; Labeyrie, Duplessy, and Blanc 1987:477; Rooth 1982:131, 135; Stommel 1961).

The relationship between fresh water and the thermohaline circulation is non-linear. As fresh water flows into the North Atlantic, little happens at first. The circulation continually removes the fresh water and replaces it with more salty water. There is a well defined critical threshold, however, where the circulation cannot cope with increased amounts of fresh water and breaks down. Broecker has suggested that there are two stable modes of circulation in the Atlantic: the strong mode is the thermohaline conveyor belt described above, which is the principal mode of circulation during glacial minima, and the weak mode is the pattern where

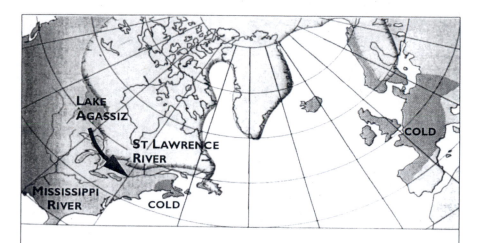

FLOW FROM LAKE AGASSIZ

Figure 52. During the Younger Dryas cold period, meltwater flow from Lake Agassiz was diverted from the Mississippi River across the Great Lakes to the St. Lawrence River, *arrow,* for 700 to 1,000 years, thereby decreasing the salinity of the Atlantic, preventing the formation of deep water, shutting down the conveyor belt circulation, and bringing cold weather to a small area in North America and a broad area in western Europe, *hatching* (adapted from Broecker and Denton 1990:55).

the North Atlantic Deep Water formation is suppressed, the principal mode during glacial maxima (Broecker, Peteet, and Rind 1985:25; Rahmstorf 1997:825).

THE YOUNGER DRYAS

A most dramatic shift, the smoking gun for Broecker's theory, occurred about 9,000 years ago, about 2,000 years after the end of the last glacial maximum. It instigated a very cold period, a return to near glacial conditions in northern Europe. The period is known as the Younger Dryas, named after a flower that covered the tundra landscape during glacial times and which replaced the forests in northern Europe at this time. The Younger Dryas appears in palaeoclimatic records from Europe and the North Atlantic, but not from most of North America. It was a time when temperatures in western Europe plunged. According to Broecker, the villain was the ocean conveyor belt—it stopped functioning (Broecker 1987:80–81; Broecker and Denton 1989:2481).

At the end of the last glacial maximum, as the glaciers began melting, the meltwater at first flowed down the Mississippi River into the Gulf of

Mexico. As the glaciers retreated, passages to the east began opening up and some of the meltwater was diverted in steps to the North Atlantic. After about 800 years of glacial retreat, a lobe of ice blocking off the eastern end of what is now Lake Superior melted or was breached. A catastrophic release of meltwater from the southern end of the Laurentide Ice Sheet, impounded in Lake Agassiz, poured across Lake Superior and Lake Huron, from there into the St. Lawrence River and the North Atlantic (figure 52). The continuing flow of meltwater into the North Atlantic for hundreds of years was approximately equal to the amount of water emanating from the Amazon River today. As a result, the salinity of the North Atlantic dropped; the deep water formation, which depends on high salinity water, was shut down; the release of heat to the atmosphere stopped; and the conveyor belt was turned off. Europe turned severely cold and stayed that way for 700 to 1,000 years until the meltwater was rediverted to the Mississippi and the conveyor belt started up again. A similar catastrophic flood of water was released from Lakes Agassiz and Ojibway, about 8,200 years ago, and rushed through the Hudson Strait into the Labrador Sea creating a flow about 15 times greater than the present discharge of the Amazon River and dropping temperatures in Western Europe for 200 to 400 years. (Broecker 1987:80–81; 1995:65; Broecker and Denton 1989:2492, 2494; Barber et al 1999:344; Yee 1999).

THE BIPOLAR SEESAW

During the Younger Dryas, when heat formation in the North Atlantic was shut off, it appears to have been enhanced in the Southern Ocean. Southern temperatures rose during that time, leading Broecker to propose a bipolar seesaw in heat release, involving a shift in deep water formation from the northern Atlantic to the Southern Ocean. The conveyor belt transfers heat from the South Atlantic to the north, so that as the north warms, the south cools. In other words, when the conveyor belt shuts downs, the north cools and the south warms (Alley and Bender 1998:85; Broecker 1998:119).

There is some evidence that suggests deep water formation can be affected by slight increases or decreases in the salinity of the water in the areas of deep water formation, changes short of what is necessary to shut off the conveyor belt. These slight changes might result in warmer or cooler periods in northern Europe and may have played a role in the onset of the Little Ice Age between the fifteenth and nineteenth centuries. Such modification of the thermohaline circulation, if true, might play a role in periodic cold phases affecting the North Atlantic and, perhaps, leading to drought in the Maya Lowlands. Such a connection, however, remains to be definitively established (Jones 1991:365; Kerr 1998:158).

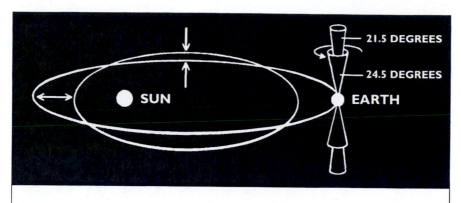

MILANKOVITCH CYCLES

Figure 53. Orbital forcing is the result of the three Milankovitch cycles named for Serbian mathematical physicist Milutin Milankovitch: the shape of the Earth's orbit, the tilt of the axis of rotation, and the precession or wobble of the axis (adapted from Broecker and Denton 1990:50).

MILANKOVITCH CYCLES

Modifications of the Earth's seasons, induced by changes in the shape of the Earth's orbit around the Sun, in the attitude of its tilt, and in the precession of its wobble around its axis, known as Milankovitch cycles (figure 53), can alter the flow of water vapor from the Atlantic to the Pacific. According to Broecker and George Denton, this orbital forcing can change the salinity levels of the Atlantic and disrupt the most vulnerable part of the ocean-atmosphere system, the conveyor belt. The combination of the orbital forcing and the cessation of deep water formation in the North Atlantic would trigger the onset of a glacial maximum and would explain the alternating pattern of glacial and interglacial periods of the current ice age (Broecker and Denton 1990:337).

ATLANTIC CONVEYOR BELT AND CLIMATE

Hurricane researcher and meteorologist William Gray and his colleagues have produced qualitative estimates that suggest conveyor belt alterations may possibly be coincident with multidecadal warming and other climatic effects. As shown in table 5, periods when the global conveyor belt circulation is strong are characterized by different atmospheric general circulation patterns than when the conveyor belt is weak. Weak conveyor belt strength is associated with decreased sea surface temperatures in the North Atlantic, decreased rainfall in the Sahel, and decreased hurricane formation in the western Atlantic. The true role of the thermo-

	1870–1899	1900–1942	1943–1967	1968–1991
Conveyor belt strength	Strong	Weak	Strong	Weak
Sahel rainfall	Wet	Dry	Wet	Dry
Atlantic hurricane activity	Enhanced	Weak	Enhanced	Weak
El Niño	Weak	Enhanced	Weak	Enhanced
Global air temperatures	Decrease	Increase	Decrease	Increase

ATLANTIC CONVEYOR BELT AND CLIMATE

Table 5. Qualitative assessments of the relationship between Atlantic conveyor belt strength and climatic conditions by William Gray and colleagues (*Source*: Kondratyev and Galindo 1997:40–41).

haline circulation, whether cause, symptom, or merely coincidental event, needs much more research to be understood (Kondratyev and Galindo 1997:40).

STANLEY'S ICE AGE HYPOTHESIS

Paradoxically, geologist and palaeobiologist Steven Stanley proposed that the deep water formation may, in fact, be responsible for the current ice age we live in. According to his theory, the rise of the Isthmus of Panama, the narrowness of the Atlantic Basin, the flow of the tradewinds and westerlies and the resulting excess salt, the formation of deep water in the northern Atlantic, and the release of the tremendous amount of heat which warms Europe are the very factors responsible for the ice age which began about 3 million years ago and for the frigid winters which assault the Northern Hemisphere. Were it not for these factors, the warm waters from the south would not achieve adequate density as they cooled to sink near Iceland. They would continue flowing north into the Arctic Ocean, spiral clockwise around, and return to the Atlantic (figure 54). The deep water formation, however, cuts off the northward flow of warm water and turns

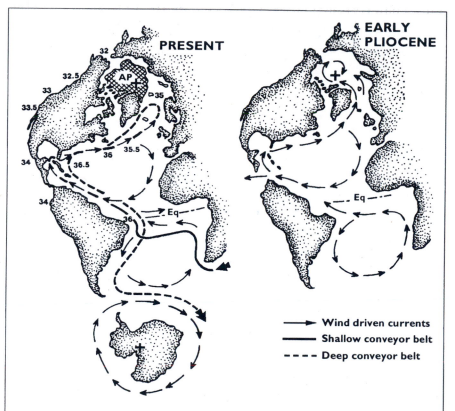

STANLEY'S ICE AGE HYPOTHESIS

Figure 54. The map on the *left* shows today's circulation in the North Atlantic, with the formation of deep water in the vicinity of Iceland and Greenland as a result of the high salinity of the Atlantic. The *numbers* indicate the salinity of the ocean water in parts per thousand. Note the strong difference across the Isthmus of Panama. The map on the *right* shows the circulation during the Early Pliocene, before the Isthmus of Panama closed the passageway between North and South America. At that time, according to Steven Stanley, currents between the Atlantic and Pacific lowered the salinity of the Atlantic and prevented the formation of North Atlantic Deep Water. The flow of southerly water, therefore, continued into, around, and out of the Arctic Ocean, keeping the temperatures higher than today and preventing ice ages. *Crosses* mark the poles (adapted from Stanley 1996:183).

the Arctic Ocean into a frigid pond where the water is entrapped. Prior to the current ice age, Stanley points out, the Arctic Ocean was surrounded by forests, indicating a much warmer climate (Stanley 1996:184–187).

The key, he believes, is the residence time of the water in the Arctic pond. It stays long enough to turn cold enough to freeze. Were warm water to flow in, around, and out again, it would not have enough time to freeze. In addition, the formation of ice in the Arctic increases the albedo of the surface, thus reflecting more of the scant Arctic sunlight back into space, which increases the cold even more (Stanley 1996:184–187).

During the present glacial minimum, the Arctic periodically sends some of its frigidity far south. During the winter, cold high pressure systems penetrate as far as the Maya Lowlands, where they are known as *nortes*. Over the last 3 million years, the low latitudes have been exporting very little warmth to the Arctic, which has retaliated by sending very cold air and water southward, robbing the continents of the warmth they formerly enjoyed, especially during winter (Stanley 1996:184–187).

DISCUSSION

The world's oceans clearly play a major role in climate, especially in northern Europe. The temperature of the sea surface, as we saw in chapter 6, plays a very direct role in atmospheric convection, resulting in precipitation over the ocean and in those coastal areas that depend on ocean breezes for their precipitation, like the Yucatán Peninsula. Oceanography, however, is still in a state of exploration, and the exact flow of the oceans is still being sorted out. The large-scale ocean currents are extremely complex phenomena, consisting of ribbons of flow interlaced with return currents, both horizontally and vertically, which meander over hundreds of miles. The actual flow is not laminar as suggested by the simplified conveyor belt model, but turbulent and labyrinthine. The northward transport of warm water in the North Atlantic occurs through a linked set of gyre flows, rather than along the simple image of the upper limb of the conveyor belt. The scheme presented here of an ocean conveyor belt simplifies the overwhelming complexity of the true ocean to model a concept of the salt diffusion between oceans (Macdonald and Wunsch 1996:436; McCartney 1994:6; Munk 1955).

The position of the North Atlantic's currents is not fixed, but shifts as the climate changes or, perhaps, the climate changes as the currents shift. The thermohaline circulation seems to have remained essentially stable for the last 8,000 years, since the end of the Younger Dryas—although there are hints that some oscillations in the strength of the flow may have occurred during that time and may have affected the weather. The climate of the Maya Lowlands is certainly influenced by the seas that envelop it. So far, however, the only suggestion of a link is Hastenrath's assertion that anomalously cold water lying between Africa and northern South Ameri-

ca is correlated with drought in the Caribbean area. As oceanographers begin to understand better the enormous flow of water that passes by the
Lowlands through the Yucatán Strait, its sources and variations, we may
start to understand more direct oceanic influences on Yucatecan and Mesoamerican weather (Hastenrath 1985:317; Jones 1991:365; Kerr 1998:158;
Rind and Chandler 1991:7437; Tucker and Barry 1984:199).

8. Volcanoes and Climate

W e have seen in broad general terms how weather patterns can shift in the Atlantic weather region between periods of cold and periods of warm weather. We have seen that periods of cold in the Northern Hemisphere *might* indicate periods of drought in the Maya Lowlands. But are there factors external to the climate-ocean system that can trigger a cooling or even a cold response in the climate? We now turn our attention to possible exacerbating factors for some cold periods.

The principal meteorological hypothesis of this book is that cold periods, whatever their origin, can be coincident with drought in Yucatán. It is not necessary to identify the origin of the cold and, furthermore, not all of the cold periods need have the same cause. The hypothesis which links cold and drought does not rise and fall on the basis of identifying the cause of the cold period.

There may be, however, an identifiable trigger for some periods of acute cold and drought. Let's take a look now at the climatic effects of volcanic eruptions and their ability to exacerbate cold periods. We'll look in depth at El Chichón Volcano as an example of what happens in the atmosphere after a volcanic eruption, because of its proximity to the Maya Lowlands and because few eruptions have been as well studied as El Chichón's 1982 eruption. El Chichón and Popocatépetl may have erupted early in the Classic period and may have made a bad situation worse. But the evidence at this point is not clear cut, either for the exact timing of the eruptions or for their climatic impact.

We will see that large volcanic eruptions can be followed by an equatorward movement of the subtropical highs, as would be expected from the meteorological model, which can bring drought to Mesoamerica and could have brought death and suffering to the Maya in times past.

Both El Chichón and Popocatépetl can affect worldwide climate. When they erupt, they produce huge quantities of sulfur which can have global climatic effects. We will look at the possibility that El Chichón and Popocatépetl, or perhaps other volcanoes elsewhere in the world, triggered worldwide climatic reactions which produced drought in parts of Mesoamerica. Finally, we will look at forty-seven large, tropical eruptions which occurred between 1440 and 1840 and see what effect they had on Mesoamerica.

BENJAMIN FRANKLIN'S HYPOTHESIS

The earliest known reference to the possible climatic impact of a volcanic eruption was by Benjamin Franklin in a paper read before the Literature and Philosophical Society of Manchester on December 22, 1784, describing the "dry fog" of 1783 and other atmospheric effects, including cold, which resulted from Iceland's Laki eruption. Although Franklin was apparently only aware of the Laki eruption, at least one other large eruption occurred in 1783, Asama in Japan, along with several smaller ones (Goodman 1984:1, 12).

Because volcanic particles and aerosols are large enough to scatter all visible colors fairly efficiently, the sky appears milky white rather than blue after large eruptions. Franklin assumed that the high altitude dry fog he observed was formed from the solid tephra particles, or volcanic dust and solid material, ejected by the explosive force of the Icelandic eruption. The volume and injection height of tephra produced by an eruption are related to the explosive force of the eruption, the vertical wind structure at the time, and the location. The basic implication of Franklin's observations, that only the most violent, explosive eruptions of volcanic ash or dust would produce a measurable climatic impact, became the basic assumption of all further studies on the relationship between volcanoes and climate until the 1970s (Goodman 1984:1, 12; Kondratyev and Galindo 1997:104).

Many other scientists have studied the relation between volcanic eruptions and weather since Franklin's observations. Most of these studies have consisted of statistical correlations between bad weather and single eruptions or between climatic anomalies and a series of volcanic eruptions. These studies do show that during some years with abnormal weather, such as 1783 and 1816, there were volcanic events; and in addition, that major shifts of the past 500 years occurred many times in parallel with variations in

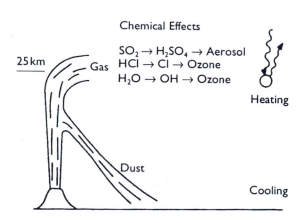

Chemical Effects

25 km — Gas

$SO_2 \rightarrow H_2SO_4 \rightarrow$ Aerosol
$HCl \rightarrow Cl \rightarrow$ Ozone
$H_2O \rightarrow OH \rightarrow$ Ozone

Heating

Dust

Cooling

ATMOSPHERIC EFFECTS

Figure 55. Schematic drawing of the effects of volcanic eruptions on the stratosphere. Silicate particles, volcanic dust, fall
out relatively rapidly while gaseous products remain to form
aerosols, or liquid droplets, and ozone, increasing the atmosphere's albedo or reflectivity (adapted from Hofmann
1987:744).

the level of volcanic activity. On the other hand, there is no evidence that volcanic explosions preceded and initiated the ice age.
Many years of droughts or severe cold occurred without evidence
of any major eruptions. The volcanic eruptions are not responsible
for all climate change nor all years of bad weather, but they may
cause some of them. (Kondratyev and Galindo 1997)

STRATOSPHERIC AEROSOLS

Let us turn our attention, then, to how volcanoes may cause some
years of bad weather. Two important types of ejecta are emitted during an
eruption: tephra particles—solid materials of all types and sizes that are
erupted from a crater or volcanic vent and deposited from the air—and
gaseous aerosol precursors. Direct in situ sampling of the stratosphere
during the 1970s demonstrated that the principal volcanic ejecta introduced to the stratosphere are the gaseous sulfuric acid (H_2SO_4) precursors,
mainly sulfur dioxide (SO_2). The small amount of tephra particles detected
decrease to virtually undetectable levels over a period of three to four
months, while the sulfuric acid droplets remain up to four years (figure
55). Recent studies have indicated that the mass of H_2SO_4 and SO_2 erupted

during the 1970s by Fuego in Guatemala were one to two orders of magnitude (10 to 100 times) greater than the mass of silicate particles, or volcanic dust (Goodman 1984:10; Kondratyev 1988:82).

Direct sampling of the aerosol layer of the stratosphere began in the 1960s, but the in situ measurements were not associated with volcanic eruptions until the 1970s. These measurements clearly demonstrated that, contrary to what had been assumed, the dominant stratospheric aerosols following a large eruption were droplets of highly concentrated solution of roughly 75 percent sulfuric acid and 25 percent water, the exact concentration varying slightly at different altitudes. Droplets of sulfuric acid are formed by gas to particle conversion processes from the gaseous magmatic sulfur emissions introduced into the stratosphere during an eruption. The volume and injection height of the gaseous sulfur aerosol precursors are not solely a function of the explosiveness of an eruption and the vertical wind structure, but also of the eruptive mechanism and the magma chemistry. The eruption plume must be high enough to inject aerosol precursors into the stratosphere, as seen in figure 56, but the actual height reached in the stratosphere is not important in determining climatic effects. Column heights have reached as high as 50 km (30 mi or 164,000 ft) (Goodman 1984:24; Jakosky 1986:247; Kondratyev and Galindo 1997:90).

A certain time lag normally occurs between the eruption and the climatic effect, due both to the time needed for the conversion processes to produce the maximum concentration of sulfuric acid and to the time needed to mix the sulfuric acid throughout a hemisphere (see figure 57) (Goodman 1984:40).

MAGMATIC SULFUR

Although sulfur is relatively abundant in our planet, its distribution is uneven due to its complex chemical and physical behavior. Sulfur is highly concentrated in the core and mantle as dense sulfides, while it is also found in the oceans as sulfate anion. Sulfides in erupted magmas are extremely sparse, in large part due to their high density and their tendency to sink and accumulate at the base of magma bodies (Sigurdsson and Laj 1992:186).

Some eruptions produce far more sulfur than others. In fact, eruptions of basaltic magmas generate one to two orders of magnitude (10 to 100 times) larger volumes of sulfur than silicic magmas. Particularly sulfur rich are the magmas associated with subduction zones where the Earth's oceanic plates, hydrated in contact with sea water, dive under the adjacent overlying plates, as along the Mesoamerican volcanic zone. The incorporated sea water is driven off when the plate reaches about 100 km (60 mi or 330,000 ft) depth. This water rises into the overlying mantle and induces melting to form the magmas that erupt explosively at subduction zone volcanoes like El Chichón and Popocatépetl. The resulting high water con-

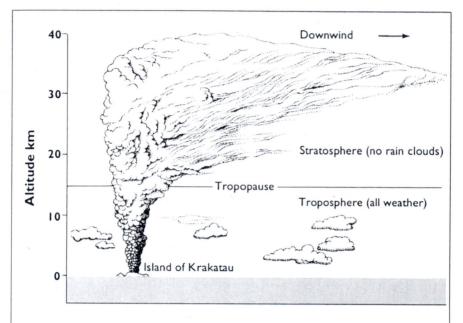

KRAKATAU ERUPTION CLOUD

Figure 56. The Krakatau eruption cloud of 1883 was injected high into the stratosphere. The tropopause is represented by the line separating the high altitude stratosphere and the lower level troposphere, where weather systems occur. The exact altitude of the tropopause can vary according to latitude and time of year. Below the tropopause the atmosphere becomes cooler with increasing altitude, thereby permitting convection and precipitation to occur. Above the tropopause, the atmosphere warms up with increasing altitude, thereby suppressing convection and precipitation. For a volcano to be climatically effective, it must be explosive enough and sulfurous enough to inject large quantities of sulfur above the tropopause into the stratosphere (adapted from Decker and Decker 1989:216).

tent of these magmas is responsible for the explosive nature of the eruptions.

It is possible that changes in the physical and chemical state of the magmas during an eruption would allow free crystals of anhydrite, a mineral containing sulfur, to decompose and release sulfur gases which would contribute to the sulfur yield. Volcanic anhydrite is something of an apparent rarity in volcanic deposits for two reasons. First, the sulfur content of subduction zone magmas varies considerably, and some magmas lack sufficient sulfur to form anhydrites. Second, anhydrite is highly soluble in

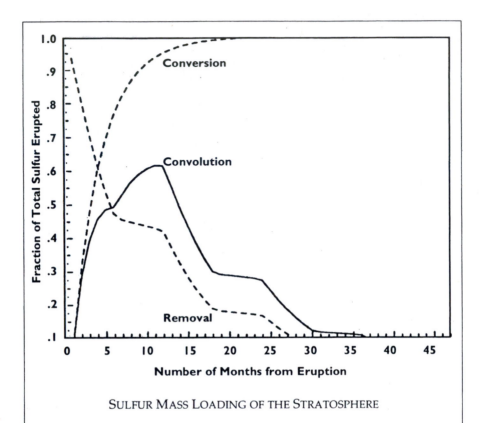

SULFUR MASS LOADING OF THE STRATOSPHERE

Figure 57. The mass loading of sulfur in the stratosphere from a large, explosive eruption is a result of the combination, or convolution, of the conversion processes and the seasonally varying removal processes. This example assumes a January 1st eruption date. Note that the maximum concentration of sulfuric acid in the stratosphere occurs twelve months after the eruption in this example (adapted from Goodman 1984:25).

surface water and will not survive more than a few years at the surface. When compared with other classes of terrestrial magmas, hydrous and oxidized magmas, formed in subduction zones, have a considerably greater ability to store sulfur and to transport it to volcanoes at the Earth's surface, where powerful eruptions can propel it into the stratosphere. Pumice erupted from El Chichón, for example, contains three times as much anhydrite as that from Pinatubo in the Philippines (Devine, Sigurdsson, Davis, and Self 1984:6309, 6315; Luhr 1991:104–105; Minnis et al 1993:1415).

STRATOSPHERIC AEROSOL LAYER

A large eruption introduces various sulfide and sulfate gases, primarily sulfur dioxide, SO_2, directly into the stratosphere where they are converted into sulfuric acid. These gases are exsolved from the magma at the time of the eruption and are carried into the stratosphere in the eruption plume. Once suspended in the lower level of the stratosphere, they settle in a supposedly permanent layer of sulfate aerosols discovered by C. E. Junge, C. W. Chagnon, and J. E. Mason in 1961, now known as the Junge layer. They are converted into sulfuric acid, H_2SO_4, by a variety of photochemical conversion processes driven by solar radiation. These reactions take about twelve months to convert the sulfur dioxide to sulfuric acid. The optimum rate of conversion occurs at about 20 km (12.4 mi or 65,000 ft) of altitude, which corresponds to the maximum stratospheric aerosol abundance (Goodman 1984:10, 13, 16–17; Kondratyev 1988:83–84; Rampino, Self, and Stothers 1988:75).

Once the liquid droplets of sulfuric acid are formed, removal processes begin to eliminate them from the stratosphere. Droplets collect in the vicinity of the troposphere, in the Junge layer, through gravitational settling and are then removed through stratospheric-tropospheric exchange mechanisms. The rate at which the droplets are transported downward out of the stratosphere will vary with the height of the droplets above the tropopause, with the season of the year, and with latitude. Goodman has identified four latitudinal bands with similar removal processes which correspond to the main global circulation zones (Goodman 1984:1516):

Northern Hemisphere subpolar	70° N to 50° N
Northern Hemisphere middle latitude	50° N to 20° N
Equatorial	20° N to 10° S
Southern Hemisphere	10° S to 50° S.

OPTICAL DEPTH

The increased concentration of volcanic aerosols in the stratosphere following a magmatic eruption will decrease the transparency of the atmosphere, or as is more commonly stated, will increase the optical depth of the atmosphere, since transparency and optical depth are related through Beer's Law. The optical depth of stratospheric aerosols is usually quite small. After an explosive eruption, however, the optical depth increases, sometimes quite dramatically. Optical depth, therefore, can be used as a measure of the attenuation of incoming solar radiation. Three months after the eruption of El Chichón in 1982, for example, total solar radiation at Mauna Loa was decreased 7.7 percent, and the optical depth increased from a background value of 0.02 to 0.3. The planetary albedo increased by 10 percent (Goodman 1984:52; Hofmann 1987:747; Kondratyev and Galindo 1997:321; Toon and Pollack 1982:121).

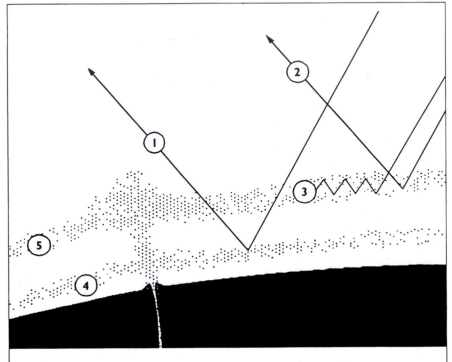

VOLCANIC AEROSOL EFFECTS

Figure 58. The effects of volcanic aerosols from explosive volcanic activity on the Earth's atmosphere and climate include (1)
increased tropospheric albedo and increased cloud formation,
due to an increase in condensation nuclei, which reflects solar
radiation and causes surface cooling; (2) increased stratospheric backscatter of solar radiation by sulfuric acid aerosols, which
causes surface cooling; (3) increased stratospheric absorption of
solar radiation by volcanic aerosols, which also causes surface
cooling; (4) volcanic contribution to the greenhouse gases; (5)
stratospheric ozone depletion due to reactions of stratospheric
ozone with odd-chlorine and hydroxyl radicals from volcanic
sources (adapted from Sigurdsson and Laj 1992:184).

CLIMATIC EFFECTS OF AEROSOLS

The liquid sulfuric acid droplets in the Junge layer are very efficient at
scattering or reflecting the visible wavelengths of incoming solar radiation
and very poor at absorbing the outgoing infrared wavelengths emitted
from the Earth's surface (figure 58). The result is that volcanic aerosols effect a cooling of the Earth's surface by blocking and absorbing incoming

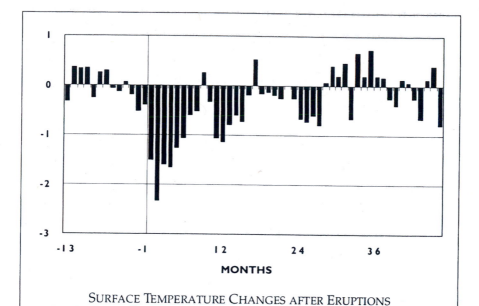

SURFACE TEMPERATURE CHANGES AFTER ERUPTIONS

Figure 59. Mean changes in monthly surface air temperature after volcanic eruptions, measured in standard deviation units,
beginning thirteen months before the eruption and continuing
forty-six months afterwards (*Source*: Budyko, Golitsyn, and
Izrael 1986:14).

sunlight (figure 59). The sulfuric acid in the stratosphere reflects solar radiation, thereby increasing the albedo of the atmosphere, and absorbs it as
well, causing an initial warming of the stratosphere following a major
eruption, followed by a rapid cooling within two years (figure 60), possibly the result of the depletion of ozone which is an absorber of solar radiation. Shifts in the circulation patterns, as they readjust themselves in
response to climatic changes of the surface energy balance, will result in a
pattern of local warming and cooling (figure 61) (Goodman 1984:50–51;
Monastersky 1994:70).

Volcanic eruptions affect the climate system, then, primarily by changing the transparency of the atmosphere to solar radiation. The amount of
solar radiation reaching the lower levels of the atmosphere is therefore reduced. The solar radiation received in the troposphere and at the Earth's
surface provides the primary source of energy to the climate system for
driving the principal atmospheric and oceanic general circulations. These
circulations are responsible for the global distribution of pressure, temperature, precipitation, cloudiness, etc. Any changes in the solar forcing of the
climate system will result in a redistribution of these climatic variables.

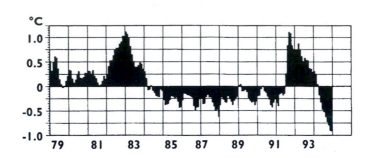

STRATOSPHERIC TEMPERATURE CHANGES AFTER ERUPTIONS

Figure 60. Stratospheric temperatures rise and then plummet after El Chichón and Pinatubo eruptions in April 1982 and June 1991. The sharp drop may be related to the depletion of ozone by sulfur aerosols of volcanic origin (adapted from Monastersky 1994:70).

The result will be climatic change distinguished by localized warmings and coolings.

In fact, the key to understanding volcanic climatic changes may lie in understanding the climatic response in areas where the effects of volcanic aerosol clouds may be amplified by perturbed atmospheric circulation patterns. Such perturbations can be detected in surface temperatures and in palaeoclimatic evidence, such as frost damage rings, narrow tree rings, and changes in the tree line, and in weather anomalies such as unusually cold springs and summers, severe sea ice in polar and subpolar regions, and poor grain years and crop failures. It may well be a mistake to look for a global, monolithic response rather than a pattern of localized responses. Regional and seasonal effects may be the major result of most volcanic eruptions. The negative anomaly in eastern Hudson Bay, for example, in midsummer 1816 was between 5°C and 6°C, substantially greater than the global average. Meridional, or north-south, circulation patterns brought extremely cold weather to the eastern United States and western Europe, while opening a warm area over the usually ice covered Greenland Sea between 74°N and 80°N (Goodman 1984:10–11; Minnis et al 1993:1411; Rampino 1991:12).

During the three months after an eruption, a marked drop in surface pressure occurs across middle latitudes of the North Atlantic sector, suggesting a southward shift in the track taken by middle latitude cyclones and the subtropical high. A major anomaly center is found over the United Kingdom and extending over much of western Europe. Such a change in the atmospheric circulation patterns is likely to give rise to cold, wet summers in Europe. P. M. Kelly and C. B. Sear have reconstructed such a pattern for 1816, following Tambora's 1815 eruption. The severity and distribution of sea ice in Hudson Strait in 1816 suggest prevailing northerly or northwesterly winds, indicative of strong meridional circulation patterns which allow southward penetrations of Arctic air across eastern North America and western Europe (Kelly and Sear quoted in Kelly, Wigley, and Jones 1984:77; Rampino 1988:85).

A study of the effects of volcanic eruptions on tree rings in the United States between 1602 and 1900 determined that the western continental United States warmed, especially in winter, and the central and eastern United States cooled off, especially in summer, after low latitude volcanic eruptions (figure 61). The suggested pattern is supported by four independent proxy temperature series within the study area. Additional support is provided by three independent series lying outside the area, which suggest that the spatial response of temperature may extend to the north beyond the area covered by the tree ring reconstructions (Lough and Fritts 1987:219, 236; Papp 1983:89).

Researchers studying surface air temperature compilations from land and marine data for both the Northern and Southern Hemispheres found that major Northern Hemisphere eruptions have an immediate effect on the Northern Hemisphere average surface temperature, but little or no effect on the Southern Hemisphere. Southern Hemisphere tropical eruptions, on the other hand, affect both the Southern and Northern Hemispheres after a lag of six months to a year. Aerosols from low latitude eruptions tend to remain at low latitudes for several months after the eruption and then diffuse into both hemispheres, whereas high latitude aerosols remain at high latitudes. The volcanic silicate dust in the atmosphere will cause an initial warming after an eruption due to a greenhouse effect of increased opacity at infrared wavelengths. The initial greenhouse heating overwhelms the aerosol induced cooling, but it is followed thereafter by increasing cooling as the silicate particles fall out of the atmosphere (Dyer quoted in Handler 1984:1122; Pollack et al 1976:1071; Sear et al 1987:365).

After adjusting for sea surface temperature changes, the eruptions of the tropical volcanoes El Chichón, Agung, Santa María, Mt. Pelée, La Soufrière-St. Vincent, and Krakatau all appear to have caused a decrease in Northern Hemisphere continental surface temperatures of about 0.3°C (0.54°F) (Kondratyev and Galindo 1997:212).

How much, then, of global temperature changes can be attributed to volcanism? According to Gunn, Folan, and Robichaux there are four major components to the global energy balance, the worldwide temperature: El Niño, which contributes about 33 percent; solar energy, which contributes about 23 percent; CO_2, about 7 percent; and volcanism, which contributes about 12 percent. Absent from the above list, which deals with historical weather records, is orbital forcing, which can have significant effects over longer time periods. As they point out, it is the whole of the global energy balance that drives the thermodynamics of the atmosphere, and volcanism can clearly play an important role (Gunn, Folan, and Robichaux 1995).

Climate Models

A number of studies have been done in recent years attempting to model the climatic effects of volcanic eruptions. Model results, of course, are not actual, real world results, but they do represent the best attempts to calculate the effects of climatic variables. The results of those studies were summarized by Kirill Kondratyev and Ignacio Galindo:

> Although different assumptions about the details of the volcanic forcing in the climate models, and different sets of surface temperature records were used in the studies, all of them agree on one point: large volcanic eruptions cause a reduction of hemispheric or global average temperature for a period of a year or two and may be an important cause of climate change on the interannual to 500-year time scale. (Kondratyev and Galindo 1997:308)

Volcanic Climatic Catastrophes

Michael Rampino has suggested that a super eruption producing on the order of 1,000 Mt (megatons) of stratospheric aerosols might be capable of creating conditions favorable for the initiation of a glaciation, bringing the freezing level over the Canadian plateaus down to the surface in the summer (Rampino 1991:14).

Regional Temperature Changes

Figure 61. (*Opposite*) Average reconstructed temperature differences (°C) between the average of years 0 to 2 after key dates minus the average of years 1 to 5 prior to key dates for low latitude eruptions. Heavy dots indicate stations at which the temperature difference is significant at the 95 percent confidence level. As can be seen, specific temperature effects are localized (adapted from Lough and Fritts 1987:230).

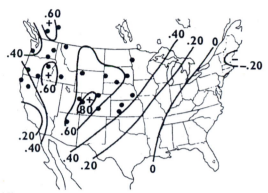

Winter temperature after low latitude eruptions

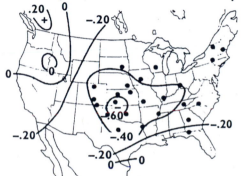

Spring temperature after low latitude eruptions

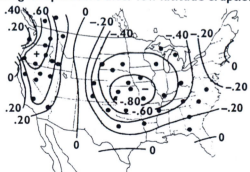

Summer temperature after low latitude eruptions

What would be the temperature effect of 1,000 Mt of sulfur aerosols? A volcanic emission of 1,000 Mt of sulfur would cause a serious climatic event, creating an optical depth of 10 and resulting in a surface temperature decrease on the order of 4.0°C. This would require an eruption of 400 km³ of basic magma, 800 km³ of trachytic, Tambora-type magma, and more than 4,000 km³ of silicic magma.

The silicic Toba eruption in Indonesia, about 75,000 years ago, for example, ejected 2,800 km³ of magma and an estimated 1,000 to 6,500 Mt of sulfur dioxide. The largest historical eruption was the April 1815 eruption of Tambora, also in Indonesia, which emitted 50 km³ of magma in two plinian explosions and threw up eruption plumes of 33 km (20 mi or 108,000 ft) and 43 km (27 mi or 140,000 ft). (Other studies have placed the estimated eruption material at Tambora as high as 175 km³. I have used the most recent estimate, which is lower.) Estimates of the sulfur yield range between 80 and 200 Mt, causing an optical depth of 1.4, compared to a more normal background level of around 0.02, which did not decay to background levels for three years. In March and April 1982, El Chichón in Mexico erupted about 1 km³ of magma and 12 to 20 Mt of sulfur, roughly 1 percent of the total erupted magma. The 1991 eruption of Pinatubo ejected 3 to 5 km³ of dacitic magma and 25 to 30 Mt of sulfur dioxide (Devine, Sigurdsson, Davis, and Self 1984:6318; Kerr 1993:594; Luhr 1991:104; Rampino 1991:13; Rampino, Self, and Stothers 1988:90; Sigurdsson 1990:281–283).

If it is true, then, that volcanoes can affect climate, what does it take to create a dramatic or even catastrophic effect on climate? For volcanic aerosols to be climatically effective, the initial total mass of the aerosol cloud must be on the order of 10 Mt of sulfur dioxide. The thermal inertia of the Earth is, to a large extent, dependent on the heat exchange between the ocean and the atmosphere. Were it not for the thermal inertia of the oceans, the temperature drop after large explosive eruptions would be on the order of 5°C (9°F), not tenths of a degree. Since the residence time of volcanic aerosols in the stratosphere may be as many as ten years, the influence of thermal inertia on temperatures decreases and becomes insignificant in the case of long-term increases of optical depth. Thus, a series of ten explosive eruptions distributed over a period of ten years would induce a climatic catastrophe (although no direct geologic evidence exists of such a series of eruptions ever having occurred, according to Rampino, Stephen Self, and Rhodes Fairbridge). A similar climatic catastrophe could be induced by a single explosive eruption which forms a stratospheric aerosol layer denser by one order of magnitude (10 times) than the 1883 eruption of Krakatau. The United States National Research Council, in a 1985 report, estimated that an eruption one order of magnitude greater than the 1815 Tambora eruption would cause an average temperature drop, for the Earth as a whole, of 10°C over several months. According to Budyko, Golitsyn, and Izrael, it is absolutely certain that an abrupt cooling by tens of degrees would lead to the death of the majority of animals and plants

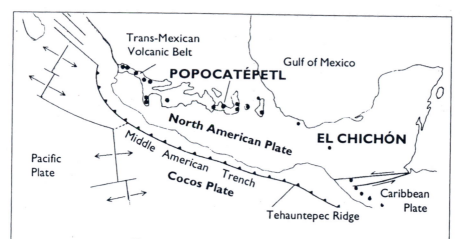

TECTONIC MAP OF MESOAMERICA

Figure 62. Tectonic map of Mesoamerica shows the relation of
El Chichón to the Mexican and Guatemalan volcanic belts and
to local tectonic features. Three major plates of the Earth's crust
meet near this region. The Caribbean plate is sliding past the
North American plate along a series of faults in Guatemala parallel to the Motagua Valley. The Cocos plate is being subducted
under the North American plate at the Middle American trench
off the coast of Mexico. The isolated position of El Chichón may
be the result of a break in the Cocos plate where the Tehuantepec Ridge, an inactive fracture zone with which it is aligned, is
being subducted. • = active volcano (adapted from Rampino
and Self 1984:50).

inhabiting the land (Budyko, Golitsyn, and Izrael 1986:16; Kondratyev
1988:83; Rampino, Self, and Fairbridge 1979:828).

EL CHICHÓN

As first described in 1928, El Chichón was a volcanic peak rising
1,260 m (4,134 ft) above sea level. It is located at 17.33°N 93.2°W in Chiapas, the southernmost state of Mexico, near the Guatemalan border. Three
tectonic plates intersect nearby: the North American, the Caribbean, and
the Cocos. The volcanic activity is related to the subduction of the Cocos
plate under the North American plate (figure 62). El Chichón and several
associated volcanic centers lie in a gap between the trans-Mexican volcanic
belt to the north and the Guatemalan belt to the south. This isolated position may be related to a break in the Cocos plate caused by the subduction

of the Tehuantepec Ridge off the southwestern coast of Mexico (Rampino and Self 1984:48).

In 1928, F. Mullereid reported that El Chichón last erupted in the late Pliocene or early Pleistocene. Decades later K-Ar dating showed it to be at least late Pleistocene. With no documentation of late prehistoric or historic eruptions, volcanic hazards at El Chichón went overlooked. During late 1980 and early 1981, geologists René Canul Dzul and V. Rocha were engaged in a geothermal survey of the region and doing field work in the summit area when they heard frequent loud noises and felt earthquakes. In a report completed in September of 1981, they interpreted these phenomena to be related to subsurface magmatic activity and/or tectonic movements, and they warned that a high volcanic risk existed at El Chichón. Their warning went unheeded (Tilling et al 1984:747).

By happenstance, a seismic network had been set up to monitor fault movements in the area as newly constructed reservoirs filled with water. In February of 1982, the network began to register unusual microseismic activity at depths of 20 to 25 km (12 to 15 mi or 65,000 to 82,000 ft) coming from the zone around El Chichón. Soon there were ten to twenty-five events per day. The earthquakes slowly rose towards the surface until by late March they reached a depth of 2 to 3 km (1.2 to 1.8 mi or 6,500 to 9,800 ft) and their frequency increased to sixty per hour, roughly one per minute. At 9:30 PM on March 28, 1982, the earthquakes abruptly stopped. Two hours later, El Chichón exploded to life after laying dormant for perhaps 500 to 600 years. A series of ten explosions followed. Six days later, on April 4, the largest of the eruptions blew off the top 200 m (720 ft) of its volcanic cone, devastating a circular 155 km² (60 mi²) area around the volcano, partially or totally destroying nine villages, and killing as many as 2,000 persons. It was the worst volcanic disaster in Mexico in historical times (Rampino and Self 1984:48–49; Riva Palacio-Chiang 1983:51; Sigurdsson, Carey, and Espindola 1984:11–12; Tilling et al 1984:747).

Of the ten explosions which produced distinct plumes on NOAA satellite images (figure 63), six were seismically detected. Only three, however, produced significant pyroclastic deposits, which are fragmented rock deposits formed in a volcanic explosion or emitted from a volcanic vent. The first was the magmatic phase of March 29, and the second and third were the phreatomagmatic phases of April 3 and 4, the explosive volcanic eruptions resulting from the interaction of surface or subsurface water and magma. The first plinian eruption began at 11:32 PM on March 28 and lasted for five or six hours. A plinian eruption is an explosive eruption in which a steady stream of fragmented magma and magmatic gases is released at a high velocity, with a large volume of tephra and a tall eruption column. The second, which began at 7:35 PM on April 3, lasted for four hours and produced a large amount of old volcanic rock. The third began at 5:22 AM on April 4, lasted seven hours, and produced ash and pumice deposits including large amounts of old volcanic rock. The eruption col-

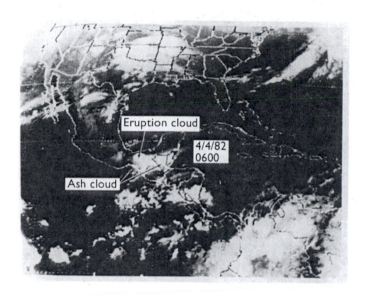

EL CHICHÓN ERUPTION CLOUD

Figure 63. GOES enhanced thermal infrared imagery of the El Chichón eruption and ash cloud. The ash cloud from the April 3 eruption had moved over the lower Yucatán Peninsula, the Petén, and Belize when the April 4 eruption occurred (Matson 1984:7).

umns reached heights of 21 to 25 km (13 to 15.5 mi or 69,000 to 82,000 ft), penetrating the tropopause at 16.5 to 17 km (10 to 10.5 mi or 54,000 to 55,800 ft). The surrounding destruction was carried out by ash fall from trachyandesite magma, by pyroclastic flows or the lateral flows of turbulent mixtures of hot gases and unsorted rock material, by surges or ring-shaped clouds of gas and suspended solid debris that move radially outward at high velocity, and by debris flows. An area in excess of 50,000 km² (20,000 mi²), extending primarily east and northeast towards the Yucatán Peninsula, was blanketed with tephra fall that was transported in the troposphere. Large amounts of fine ash and volatiles, primarily sulfur, were injected into the stratosphere, forming a dense aerosol cloud which circled the globe in twenty-one days (figure 64). The total erupted mass was originally estimated to be between 0.3 and 0.45 km³, but is now believed to have been about 1 km³. A new crater 1 km (.6 mi) wide and 230 m (755 ft) deep was formed (Gutiérrez Coutiño, Moreno Corzo, and Cruz Borraz 1983:78; Rampino and Self 1984:50–51; Sigurdsson, Carey, and Espindola 1984:11–14, 30; Sigurdsson and Laj 1992:185; VolcanoWorld online glossa-

April 25, 1982

EL CHICHÓN'S STRATOSPHERIC AEROSOL CLOUD

Figure 64. Global map of the location of the stratospheric aerosol cloud in the first three weeks after the eruption. The cloud was confined to a narrow range of latitudes by the circulation pattern, remaining south of 30°N for six months. During this time, it had an unexpected significant effect on Northern Hemisphere surface temperatures, even north of 30° (adapted from Rampino and Self 1984:54).

ry, http://volcano.cs.und.nodak.edu/vwdocs/glossary.html, September 16, 1999).

EL CHICHÓN SULFUR

The chemical composition of volcanic magmas varies from silica poor, iron rich basalt, at one end of the spectrum, through intermediate composition andesite, to silica rich, iron poor rhyolite and dacite at the other end. Sulfur, it turns out, is more soluble in iron rich magmas. However, to generate significant amounts of stratospheric aerosol, an eruption must be sufficiently explosive, in other words contain enough silica, to penetrate the tropopause and must contain large amounts of sulfur (figure 65). Intermediate andesites contain enough silica to be explosive and enough iron to dissolve large quantities of sulfur.

The volcanic ash ejected by El Chichón was andesite, a type commonly erupted by subduction zone volcanoes. The ash deposited by El Chichón has a sulfur content, however, that is anomalously high for any eruption. It contains remarkably high values of sulfate, about 1 percent by weight, perhaps the highest concentrations of sulfur known for unaltered eruptive products worldwide. It also contains free crystals of anhydrite, a calcium sulfate mineral rare in volcanic rocks.

An important question, of course, is where does all the sulfur come from? There are two possible sources. First, the anomalously high levels may be explained by the presence of sedimentary deposits of sulfur rich minerals under the volcano, thick layers of sedimentary anhydrite and salt formed by the evaporation of shallow seas some 100 million years ago (figure 66). Several investigators have suggested that the magma rising toward the volcano may have assimilated large amounts of sulfur passing through the sedimentary deposits. Second, as others have argued, the sulfur could have come up from great depth along with the magma (figure

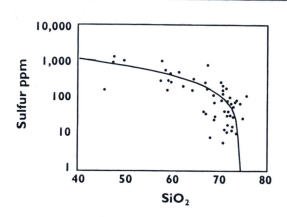

SULFUR VERSUS SILICA

Figure 65. The yield of sulfur to the atmosphere as a function of magma composition. Note the decrease in sulfur yield as the silica content, SiO_2, and thus the explosiveness, of the magma increases. To be climatically effective, a volcano must erupt magma which has sufficient silica to be explosive and sufficient sulfur to affect the climate (adapted from Sigurdsson 1990:280).

67). Large quantities of sulfur in the magma at depth would require a source of sulfur in the subducting plate. At some of the midocean rifts where new crustal plate is manufactured, hydrothermal vents emit hot, sulfur rich solutions that coat the newly formed crust with sulfide deposits. When such a crust is subducted and melted, magmas unusually rich in sulfur may be formed. Trace elements can be followed from sediment input to volcanic output at subduction zones. Thus, some of the characteristics of arc volcanism can be traced back to the sediments at the trench. Initial isotopic studies of the sulfur erupted by El Chichón suggest that it was of mixed origin. How much was contributed by each source has not yet been determined (Plank and Langmuir 1993:739–740; Rampino and Self 1984:53).

Given that the sulfur is from a combination of sources, there are two mechanisms by which the excess sulfur emitted during El Chichón eruptions may be released to the atmosphere: the decomposition of anhydrite crystals and degassing of the magma at depth. The anomalous levels of sulfur are probably due to a combination of both sources (Devine et al 1984:6318).

The large sulfur enrichments of the 1982 eruptions were in no sense unique, but have been a consistent feature of El Chichón eruptions. Chemical data show that its eruptive products have varied within a relatively

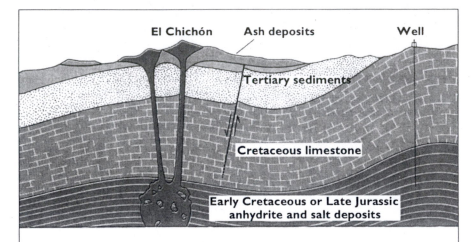

SEDIMENTARY SOURCE OF EL CHICHÓN'S SULFUR

Figure 66. Two sources for the sulfur erupted by El Chichón have been proposed. A deep drill hole near the volcano tapped sedimentary deposits of anhydrite and salt left by the evaporation of shallow seas about 100 million years ago. The magma may have assimilated large amounts of sulfur in passing through these layers on its way to the surface (adapted from Rampino and Self 1984:51).

narrow compositional range. There is little, if any, change in magma chemistry over the last 300,000 years. The very high levels of sulfur released to the atmosphere in 1982, as a percentage of erupted products, is probably characteristic of all prior eruptions as well (McGee, Tilling, and Duffield 1987:85, 105; Rampino and Self 1984:53; Rose et al 1984:164; Tilling 1992; Tilling et al 1987:337, 344).

SULFUR AEROSOLS

All three of El Chichón's plinian eruptions penetrated the tropopause and injected sulfur rich gases into the base of the tropical stratosphere. The third eruption on April 4, however, was by far the largest contributor. Satellite observations of the March 28 eruption suggest that it created a cloud at an altitude of 20km (12mi or 65,000ft). The April 3 cloud was a little lower and the April 4 eruption created a massive cloud centered at 26km (16mi or 85,300ft). The stratospheric cloud, containing perhaps as much as 20Mt of aerosols, spread to the west, while the upper tropospheric cloud of ash spread to the east across the Yucatán Peninsula. As it moved westward, the tongue of densest aerosol was concentrated at about 20°N lati-

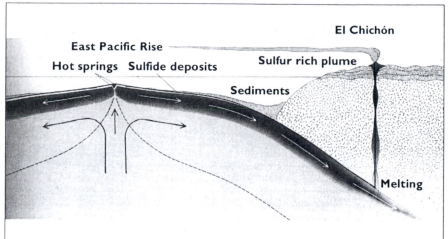

MAGMATIC SOURCE OF EL CHICHÓN'S SULFUR

Figure 67. It is also possible that the sulfur was in the rock that melted to form the magma. In some sections of the midocean rifts where new oceanic crust is manufactured, vents release sulfur rich solutions. When the solutions precipitate, they coat the newly formed crust with sulfide deposits. A plate carrying such deposits may have produced a sulfur rich magma when it was subducted and melted. Initial tests indicated the sulfur in the magma El Chichón erupted may have come from both sources (adapted from Rampino and Self 1984:51).

tude. The cloud took twenty-one days to circle the globe, moving at a speed of 20 m/s, about 45 mph. As it circled around the globe, the bulk of the cloud remained south of 30° N for more than six months after the eruption. A blocking pattern of this kind in the stratospheric circulation was unexpected. It is very intriguing because one analysis of temperature data suggests that El Chichón had its maximum effect on Northern Hemisphere temperature when most of the aerosol was still confined to latitudes only a third of the way from the equator to the pole. It should be noted that in this position, it would have covered the Hadley cell and reduced the solar energy reaching the tropical troposphere. Figure 68 shows the effect of the aerosol cloud on the optical depth, or transparency, of the atmosphere, while figure 69 shows the temperature response of the stratosphere and the troposphere (Handler and Andsager 1989:245; Kelly and Sear 1984:742; Rampino and Self 1984:55–56; Robock and Matson 1983:196–197; Sigurdsson, Carey, and Espindola 1984:34; Sigurdsson and Laj 1992:196).

The latitude at which an eruption takes place is an important factor that determines the strength of the volcanic effects on climate. High lati-

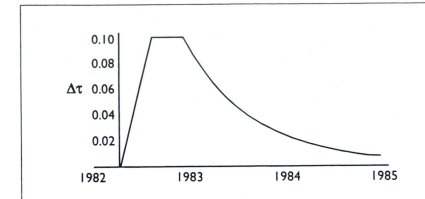

OPTICAL DEPTH AFTER EL CHICHÓN'S 1982 ERUPTION

Figure 68. The variation of the optical depth, or transparency, of the atmosphere, $\Delta\tau$, after El Chichón's 1982 eruption. Compare the changes in optical depth with the surface cooling shown in figure 69 (adapted from Vupputuri and Blanchet as reproduced in Kondratyev and Galindo 1997:315).

tude eruptions are the strongest in high and midlatitudes. The effect of low latitude eruptions tend to be confined mainly to the Tropics and midlatitudes (Kondratyev and Galindo 1997:234).

Returning to El Chichón, Kelly and Sear commented, "The most striking feature of our results is the speed of the climate system's response. Contrary to general belief, the maximum impact occurs when the volcanic cloud is far from being hemispherically distributed." The global stratospheric mass of volcanic aerosol from the eruptions was concentrated between 21 and 25 km (13 to 15 mi or 69,000 to 82,000 ft) altitude and has been estimated to range from 12 to 20 Mt, about 1 percent of the total erupted magma, consisting of 99 percent sulfuric acid. The concentration of the El Chichón aerosol at low latitudes did not fall to background levels even after five years. After the eruption, the temperature of the equatorial stratosphere rose by about 4°C at 20 km and 6°C at 24 km, the warmest since continuous temperature readings were begun in 1958 (figure 69) (Handler and Andsager 1989:245; Kelly and Sear 1984:742; Kondratyev and Galindo 1997:211; Rampino and Self 1984:55–56; Robock and Matson 1983:196–197; Sigurdsson, Carey, and Espindola 1984:34; Sigurdsson and Laj 1992:196).

PREHISTORIC ERUPTIONS

The data indicate that the pre-1982 eruptions also involved sulfur rich magma. Although estimates of the size of the earlier eruptions have not

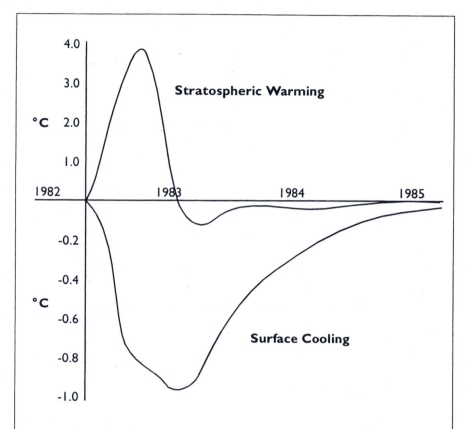

SURFACE COOLING AFTER EL CHICHÓN'S 1982 ERUPTION

Figure 69. Variation of surface and stratospheric temperatures with time after El Chichón's 1982 eruption. Notice the significant cooling, about 0.9°C (1.6°F), at the Earth's surface which occurred as a result of the small 1982 eruption (adapted from Vupputuri and Blanchet as reproduced in Kondratyev and Galindo 1997:319).

been made, consideration of the thickness of the pyroclastic deposits suggest that some of them must have produced ejecta volumes at least several times greater than the total volume of the 1982 eruptions, if not more. According to Robert Tilling and his colleagues, if the comparatively smaller eruptions of 1982 could produce significant and measurable atmospheric effects, then past major eruptive episodes could have contributed to periods of global cooling. Haraldur Sigurdsson has concluded that we do know that El Chichón has had several major eruptions far in excess of the

1982 explosive event (Tilling et al 1984:224; Haraldur Sigurdsson, 1993, letter to author).

It should be noted that there is some question whether the effects of volcanic emissions can be scaled up proportionately as the size of the eruption increases, which is the assumption employed in the arguments here. Joseph Pinto, Richard Turco, and Owen Toon have argued that larger eruptions produce larger sized particles, rather than greater numbers of the same sized particles, which have a smaller optical depth and settle out of the atmosphere faster. They suggest, in effect, that volcanic climatic effects may be self-limiting (Pinto, Turco, and Toon 1989:11,165).

DATING VOLCANIC ERUPTIONS

As important as estimating the size of an eruption is estimating its age. The dates of the ash deposits at El Chichón have been calculated from radiocarbon analysis of the carbonized remains of trees found in the ash. The radiocarbon date of the sample, however, doesn't automatically give the date of the eruption.

In calculating the age of a carbon sample, a laboratory will give its radiocarbon age in years BP, before present, which is actually years before 1950, based on the percentage of ^{14}C remaining in the sample. ^{14}C is an unstable atom which decays at a steady, known rate to ^{14}N. By calculating the percentage of ^{14}C in an organic sample today it is possible to determine when the living sample was created. One fundamental assumption in radiocarbon dating is that the percentage of radiocarbon in the atmosphere is always the same as it was in 1950. Studies of tree rings whose exact ages are known, however, have indicated that the ^{14}C content of the atmosphere varies from year to year and therefore the radiocarbon age must be adjusted, or calibrated, to reflect the amount of ^{14}C present in the atmosphere in the year the sample was formed. The calibrated dates are best written as "cal year" to indicate clearly that they have been calibrated—for example, cal AD 822. The 1σ range, or one standard deviation, a measure of the dispersion of results about the mean, gives a range of years which has a 68 percent probability of containing the year in which the sample was created and the 2σ range, or two standard deviations, has a 95 percent probability of containing the year of formation. Within each range, there is a different probability for individual years. In the 1σ range, the probabilities for each individual year can differ by a factor of 2, while in the 2σ range, the probabilities can differ by a factor of 16. See figure 74 on page 233 for an illustration of how probabilities can vary within a range of calibrated years (Ramsey 1998; Christopher Ramsey, 21 October 1998, e-mail to author; WWWebster Dictionary http://www.m-w.com/home.htm).

Old Wood

Samples taken from the center of a tree for purposes of radiocarbon dating will give results earlier than samples taken from the outside of the same tree. The samples from the center, of course, represent the date when the center was grown, not the date of the last growth on the tree, or the date of the tree's death. In a tree, thin walled cells forming lines or ribbons radiating outward from the pith are called wood rays. They often remain alive for years in the sapwood, the lighter colored, outer, water conducting portion of the stem with living tissue. Metabolic wastes move inward through the living wood rays and are dumped at the point where these cells are no longer living so that the wood inside the sheath of living rays turns darker. The darker-colored central portion of a stem in which the wood rays are dead is referred to as heartwood (Fritts 1976:62, 357, 543).

> The one remaining assumption is that the time of death and cessation of exchange with the biosphere are contemporary events. If not, then the radiocarbon age of the organism at death is not zero. This is one type of 'age offset'....
>
> The outstanding example of age at 'death,' or more usually felling, is wood. It is well known that trees grow by the addition of rings, usually though not always annually. Once laid down, rings cease to exchange with the biosphere. Hence, if one considers a long-lived tree, say a three-hundred-year-old oak, the innermost heartwood will give a radiocarbon result 300 years older than the sapwood. Indeed, this is as it should be. However, if part of that heartwood were found on an archaeological site, the radiocarbon result would not provide the date of usage of the wood, but rather a date 300 radiocarbon years earlier; more if it had been seasoned before use or re-used. This is the 'old wood' problem. (Bowman 1990:15)

A sample nearer the center of a hundred-year-old tree, then, could give a radiocarbon measurement 50 to 100 years earlier than a sample from the outside of the same tree. In order to obtain calibrated dates as close to the eruption date as possible, by getting dates as close to the death of the tree as possible, archaeologists and geologists must take care to recover samples from the outer layers of carbonized tree fragments. Small twigs are very useful because they should date near the end of the tree's life.

During the 1982 eruptions at El Chichón, live trees did not ignite. According to Rampino and Self, temperatures were high enough to ignite dead wood and the wood of houses but generally not high enough to ignite living trees. The carbon samples remaining from burned dead trees and burned houses would have given calibrated dates earlier than the eruption itself (Rampino and Self 1984:50).

DATING AN ERUPTION

There are seven principal problems, then, in trying to date an eruption. The first is the old wood problem—was the tree alive or dead when it burned? The second is the care used in recovering the sample—did the sample come from the outer layers or the inner core of the carbonized remains of a tree? Third is the wide range of dates from samples recovered from the ash deposits. Fourth is the wide range of 1σ dates, which may be spread over hundreds of years. Fifth is the contamination of the sample while it lay in the ground, thus indicating an older or younger date. Sixth is the absorption of volcanic CO_2 which would give an older date. Seventh, one must include laboratory error or improper sample preparation in the laboratory on the list of possible problems.

During the 1982 El Chichón eruption, only dead trees burned. Obviously, dead trees are going to give dates older than the eruption itself—older by as much as the age of the dead tree (depending on how much has burned away) and the number of years it had been dead at the time of the eruption. If anyone has ever watched logs burn in a fireplace, as the outer layers burn away, some get skinnier and skinnier until only the inner layers are left. Obviously the inner layers are going to give an older date than the outer layers. But what if the log barely burned, just enough to create charcoal? It's almost impossible to know.

In rare cases, dates can be anomalously old. Plants growing close to volcanic vents which are emitting CO_2 can absorb the volcanic CO_2, which is low in ^{14}C, rather than atmospheric CO_2, which is relatively higher in ^{14}C. When volcanic CO_2 is incorporated into the plant material, it has the effect of shifting the radiocarbon dates very early, by hundreds of years. The effect depends on the strength of CO_2 emission from the vent, the direction of the prevailing wind, and the distance of the plants from the vent. The absorption of volcanic CO_2 falls off fairly quickly with distance, so that past 100m (330 ft), the effect of volcanic CO_2 on the radiocarbon date is negligible (Weninger 1990:218).

At El Chichón, the calibrated dates are spread over hundreds of years in some of the eruptions. We have seen reasons why older charcoal samples may be present, but there appear to be only two reasons which might explain why an eruption would happen earlier than the date of the youngest sample contained in its deposits: the contamination of the sample with younger carbon, most likely in situ, or laboratory error, either in preparing the sample or in measuring the ^{14}C itself. The key dates for determining an eruption, therefore, should be the youngest dates, and any estimates should be compatible with the youngest samples. If we assume the calibrated dates are fairly accurate, then the youngest of those dates should be the key date. In table 6, I have dated the past eruptions of El Chichón based on this principle.

Unfortunately, the real world does not always respect reasonable theoretical principles. At Popocatépetl Volcano, Claus Siebe, José Luis Macías,
and their colleagues have recovered thirty radiocarbon samples from one
deposit, the apparent ninth-century eruption. The calibrated dates for this
eruption range over a period of 425 years, from AD 675–1095 (figure 70 on
page 220). It is clear, then, that there is much left to understand about the
vagaries of radiocarbon dating volcanic deposits. Siebe, Macías, and their
colleagues are engaged in a study of the thirty samples they have recovered to try to understand the range of dates. Because most of the dates fall
before AD 850, however, they have tentatively chosen AD 822–823 as the
year of the eruption, a year which corresponds to an acid peak in the
Greenland ice cores. This is not a problem confined to Popocatépetl or El
Chichón, but one which many volcanologists must wrestle with.

One might argue that eruptions can be dated to a time span represented by the overlap of the calibrated 1σ dates. This is a possible argument
which assumes that each tree or plant was alive at the time of the eruption
and that the spread of dates represents the caprices of radiocarbon dating.
Combining dates in this fashion would yield eruption times at El Chichón
earlier than those I have proposed.

In order to test the validity of radiocarbon dating of volcanic eruptions, an experiment was carried out at Pompeii using the sample best associated with the well known eruption of Vesuvius. From the very graphic
description written by Pliny the Younger, who at age seventeen experienced the eruption from nearby Misenum, we know that the exact year
was AD 79. The radiocarbon age of the dated charcoal was 1940 ±80 BP,
which calibrated to AD 66 with a 1σ range of 36 BC to AD 129, a fairly accurate result (Nelson, Vogel, and Southton 1990:202; Sigurdsson 1999:61–64).

In an earlier work, I analyzed the eleven radiocarbon dates available
from El Chichón at that time and found a surprising correlation between
the dates and demographic disaster in the Maya Lowlands. There are now
thirty dates available, and the neat correlation suggested by the eleven earlier dates is not as clear. If, however, we take the youngest dates available
for each deposit, then we can show the dating scheme presented in table
6. What is interesting about this outline is that for four of the six eruptions
during the last two millennia, a demographic disaster in the Maya Lowlands occurs during the 1σ range of dates, and for a fifth, just twenty years
later. For one eruption, there does not seem to be a corresponding, known
demographic disaster (Gill 1994:293–296).

On the other hand, the 1σ ranges of the six eruptions cover almost all
of the last two millennia, so one could argue that there is no correlation between eruptions and demographic disasters. Yet, no two demographic disasters occur within one eruption date range. Given what we will learn
later in this chapter about the lethal effects of tropical volcanoes in induc-
ing death and devastation in Mesoamerica, there remains a tantalizing
possibility that El Chichón's eruptions might be correlated with Maya de-

UNIT	ID	TYPE	^{14}C YR BP	CAL YR -1σ	CAL YR $+1\sigma$	DISASTERS
B	EC-220	Charcoal	550 ±60	1310	1430	1450
B1	CHI9304	Charcoal	845 ±75	1050	1260	1150–1200
C	CHI9203	Charcoal	1225 ±105	687	890	800–910
C1	CHI9318	Charcoal	1465 ±95	450	660	535–595
D1	CHI9373	Charcoal	1695 ±65	250	420	—
D2	CHI9403	Charcoal	1780 ±95	120	370	150–200
D3	CHI9603	Charcoal	2260 ±45	400 BC	350 BC	—
D4	CHI9512	Charcoal	3045 ±105	1430 BC	1130 BC	—
D5	CHI9612	Charcoal	3675 -75/ +80	2200 BC	1950 BC	—
	12WR	Rock	209,000	±19,000		
	DT-9	Rock	276,000	± 6,000		

RB GILL 2000

EL CHICHÓN ERUPTION HISTORY

Table 6. The eruption history of El Chichón as indicated by the youngest radiocarbon dates recovered from each erupted deposit. The dates of demographic disasters in the Maya Lowlands are shown. ^{14}C YR BP indicates the radiocarbon measurement and CAL YR ±1σ indicates the upper and lower 1σ range of the calibrated dates, the most likely range of calendar dates (*Source of radiocarbon dates:* Macías et al 1997:15, Tilling et al 1984:747–749, Rubin 1993; calibration by OxCal 2.18, Ramsey 1995).

mographic disasters—at least some of the demographic disasters—but there is as yet no conclusive proof.

POPOCATÉPETL

Popocatépetl is located about 70 km (45 mi) southeast of Mexico City. Its history can be divided into two distinct periods: the formation of the primitive volcano, some 30 km (18 mi) wide, on which is superimposed the modern cone, 6 to 8 km (3.5 to 5 mi) in diameter and 1,700 m (5,500 ft) high. A major, explosive event, emitting 28 to 30 km^3 of material, marked the transition between the two periods, some 30,000 to 50,000 years ago. It removed the summit of the primitive volcano and opened an elliptical amphitheater 11 km (7 mi) long and 6.5 km (4 mi) wide. Towards the north, its formations join those of Iztaccíhuatl at the Paso de Cortés. The overall height of the volcano from the Puebla plains is about 4,000 m (13,000 ft), its summit reaching 5,465 m (17,929 ft) (Robin and Boudal 1987:115–116).

The terminal cone is composed of two edifices, the older El Fraile and the younger summit Popo. The growth of the terminal cone is characterized by alternating effusive and pyroclastic phases. Explosive phases generally culminate in cataclysmic eruptions. Three periods of intense pyroclastic activity, each marked by violent eruptions, occurred during El Fraile's history. The first occurred more than 10,000 years ago, the second, between 9500 and 8000 years ago, and the third, between 5,000 and 3,800 years ago. Before the destruction of its summit cone, El Fraile reached about 5,700 m (18,700 ft) in height. The summit Popo grew during the second constructional stage of the terminal cone. It dates from about 1800 BC. Activity during the period 1800 BC to AD 790 was probably effusive, depositing about 150 m (500 ft) of lava flows in the crater (Robin and Boudal 1987:128–129; Siebe et al 1996:401).

From AD 790 until today, the activity was dominated by an explosive, violent eruption and regular, ongoing venting of gas and dust. A significant eruption exploded early in the ninth century and may actually have occurred during the winter of AD 822 or the spring of 823, which is dated by evidence from the Greenland Ice Sheet of a major eruption of unknown origin at AD 822–823. (See figure 70 for calibrated dates from carbon samples found in deposits from this eruption.) The eruption column reached at least 25 km (82,000 ft) in height, injecting sulfate aerosols well into the stratosphere. According to Claus Siebe and his colleagues, this eruption was significant enough and sulfurous enough to have affected climate around the world. It was followed by a period of extraordinary eruptive activity. Over the last 900 years, ten or so lava flows with a total thickness of 100 m (330 ft) alternated with plinian deposits. A comparison of the last 1,200 years with the destructive episodes of El Fraile also suggests that cataclysmic events, such as occurred around 1,200 years ago, could occur in

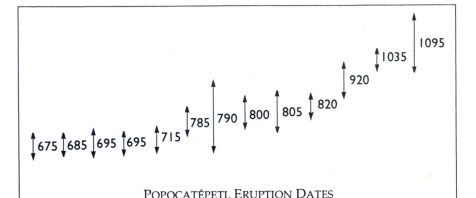

POPOCATÉPETL ERUPTION DATES

Figure 70. Calibrated radiocarbon dates from the apparent ninth-century eruption of Popocatépetl. The dates shown above are thirteen of thirty radiocarbon samples taken from the same volcanic deposit. Note that the dates (more specifically, the calibrated intercept dates) range over a period of 420 years. Claus Siebe, José Luis Macías, and their colleagues have chosen AD 822–823 as the year of the eruption, which corresponds to an acid peak in a Greenland ice core (*Source*: Siebe et al 1997:21; Claus Siebe, April 1999, personal communication).

the near future (Castro 1997; Palacios 1996:320; Robin and Boudal 1987:128–129; Siebe et al 1996:401).

Climatically effective eruptions, then, may have occurred at both El Chichón and Popocatépetl at the beginning of or during the early stages of the Classic Collapse. As can be seen from their respective tables, for those particular deposits, both have radiocarbon samples with 1σ ranges from approximately AD 680 to 890, certainly consistent with Terminal Classic eruptions. In other words, pieces of charcoal were found within deposits at each volcano which came from plants which were alive within the range of years given and which subsequently burned during the eruption. Unfortunately, at the present, it is not possible to pinpoint the dates of the eruptions any more precisely. Such eruptions may have either triggered or exacerbated the cold period of the ninth century and caused severe droughts.

As we will see in chapter 10 when we look at palaeoclimatic records and in chapter 12 when we discuss the archaeological record, there were three periods of particular cold during the Terminal Classic, around AD 800, 860, and 910, time periods which seem to coincide with the three phases of collapse that I will propose in chapter 12. Although the available evidence doesn't allow us to pick the date so closely, I am left wondering whether these two volcanoes, or others around the world, might have played a role in those downward spikes of temperature during the final years of Classic Maya civilization.

ATITLÁN CALDERA

Since we are discussing Mesoamerican volcanism, we might digress for a brief look at a massive eruption that occurred in Guatemala 85,000 years ago and created one of the world's most beautiful lakes. The present Atitlán Caldera is the largest of the silicic volcanic centers in the volcanic front of Guatemala. Although its major eruption predated the Maya by 80,000 years, it was so colossal that it deserves a brief digression.

The caldera's volume is about 260 km³ covering approximately 300 km² (115 mi²). Repeated eruptions over 13 million years have formed three overlapping calderas, Atitlán I to III, roughly similar in size (figure 71). W. W. Atwood concluded in 1933 that the Atitlán basin was formed by the collapse of a great stratovolcano, a volcano composed of both lava flows and pyroclastic material. Only after the enormous size of the great Los Chocoyos eruption became known, however, was it evident that the caldera collapse was associated with a major eruption. The Atitlán III Caldera is now partially filled by three newer stratovolcanoes and contains Lake Atitlán (Rose et al 1980:151; Rose et al 1987:57–58; Williams 1960:29–32).

Quaternary volcanic activity began about 500,000 years ago, with silicic volcanism beginning about 150,000 to 100,000 years ago. The first Quaternary eruptions were small in size. About 85,000 years ago, however, Los Chocoyos, the most massive eruption known in the Mesoamerican region, blasted through the Atitlán II Caldera. The explosive eruptions lasted 20 to 27 days and spewed approximately 275 km³ of rhyolite, some as far away as the African continent. (The largest eruption in historical times, for comparison, was Tambora's 50 km³ eruption in 1815.) At first, the eruption produced 100 km³ of tephra, then it shifted to erupting ash flows. The known areal extent of the deposits covers about 6 million km² (2.3 million mi²). Most western Guatemalan valleys have substantial ash fall deposits from the event, some as thick as 200 m (650 ft).Typical thicknesses of some pumice deposits near the lake is 5 to 10 m (16.5 to 33 ft), the maximum being 60 m (200 ft). Near the end of Los Chocoyos eruption, the volcano collapsed to form the present caldera, Atitlán III. In the years since the great eruption, three andesitic stratovolcanoes have grown within the caldera, San Pedro, Tolimán, and Atitlán, the latter the only one to have had historic activity (Hahn, Rose, and Meyers 1979:101, 111; Newhall et al 1987:81; Rose et al 1987:57–58, 66, 77).

The lake itself is over 300 m (1,000 ft) deep and the collapsed floor of the Atitlán III Caldera lies about 300 m (1,000 ft) below the current lake floor. It has gradually deepened as the outflow of the caldera to the Pacific has been shut off by the growth of Atitlán Volcano. At present the saddle

ATITLÁN CALDERAS

Figure 71. Atitlán I caldera, 11 million years, Atitlán II, 8 million years, and Atitlán III, 85,000 years old. Lake Atitlán lies within Atitlán III. Volcán Atitlán has grown over the southern rim of the caldera, while Tolimán and San Pedro have grown within the caldera. The volcanic activity is moving to the south (adapted from Newhall et al 1987:82).

which blocks drainage to the south of San Lucas Tolimán is only about 30m (100ft) above lake level. Since the great eruption, occasional small eruptions of andesite to rhyolite have erupted through Lake Atitlán (Rose et al 1980:133; Rose et al 1987:77).

The lake level has fluctuated more than 10m (30ft) over periods of several decades (figure 72). Trunks of mature coffee shade trees are now found below lake level, and titles exist to land that is now hundreds of meters out from the shoreline. Most changes in level reflect fluctuations in rainfall and streamflow. During an unusually wet year, the level has risen 3.3m (10ft). Major earthquakes have also affected the lake. Within a month after the great 1976 Guatemala earthquake, the lake level dropped about 2m (6ft), presumably due to quake induced changes in the permeability of the surrounding rock. On the other hand, some changes seem to be independent of rainfall and earthquakes. The magma reservoirs and floors of large calderas are known to inflate episodically, probably in response to the injection of magma into the lower portions of a large magma reservoir. Such inflation may occur every few decades or centuries, last for decades or longer, and be accompanied by increased temperature, gas emission, and

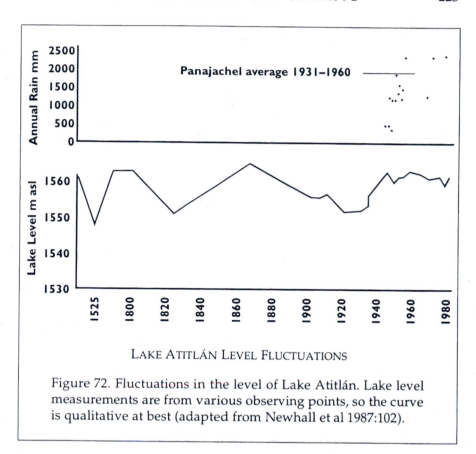

LAKE ATITLÁN LEVEL FLUCTUATIONS

Figure 72. Fluctuations in the level of Lake Atitlán. Lake level measurements are from various observing points, so the curve is qualitative at best (adapted from Newhall et al 1987:102).

hot spring discharge within the caldera. The level of Lake Atitlán rose from 1820 to about 1865, coinciding with Atitlán's only recent historical activity (Newhall et al 1987:102).

Current high lake levels suggest that the magma reservoir may again be inflated. Heat flow measurements inside and just outside the caldera have been high, suggesting hydrothermal convection and a shallow heat source. High heat flow, a geologic record of repeated eruptions since Los Chocoyos, and unexplained lake level fluctuations, perhaps due to a rise of the lake floor, suggest that magma remains beneath Lake Atitlán, and future eruptions are possible (Newhall et al 1987:81, 102).

SANTA MARÍA

1902 was a bad year. A very bad year. On January 16, a major earthquake struck Chilpancingo, Guerrero. On January 18, another shook southwestern Guatemala, with its epicenter 13km (8mi) south of Santa María Volcano. On February 26, a Pacific tidal wave hit the coast of El Salvador, drowning one hundred fifty people. On April 19, a great earthquake, lasting fifty-seven seconds, struck along the western Guatemala segment, with its epicenter at Santa María. C. F. Richter assigned it a value of 8.3 on his scale of earthquake magnitude. The cities of Quetzaltenango, San Marcos, Retalhuleu, and Mazatenango were destroyed and over 1,000 people were killed. On May 7, La Soufrière-St. Vincent exploded to life with a violent eruption on St. Vincent which killed over 1,500 people. In Martinique the following day, at 7:50 AM, in a series of great explosions at Mt. Pelée, red hot gas and volcanic debris shot out of the mountain. Some of it went straight up in a billowing black cloud. Some of it was blasted out sideways, clinging to the mountain and guided by a notch in the crater wall, a deadly glowing avalanche, or *nuée ardente*, a great torrent of black fog followed by a sheet of flame raced downhill at 200 kph (125 mph), reaching St. Pierre in about two minutes. Within minutes, over 30,000 people lay dead and St. Pierre was left totally destroyed. On May 15, Izalco Volcano, in El Salvador, awoke after a fifteen-month repose, one of the longest in Izalco's history. On May 18, La Soufrière erupted again. In July, Masaya, in Nicaragua, came back to life after a forty-three-year period of inactivity. On September 1 and September 3, La Soufrière exploded yet again with eruptions as violent as the first. On September 23, another great earthquake devastated western Guatemala, its epicenter 210 km (130 mi) northwest of Santa María. It was felt in Mexico City, Mérida, and San Salvador. Richter also assigned it 8.3 on his scale, the second 8.3 earthquake in Guatemala in less than one year. After the first major earthquake at Santa María in January, the number of earthquakes per month jumped to forty-five. By October, they had become essentially continuous (Bullard 1976:145; Rose 1972:30–31; Williams and Self 1983:35; Wood 1987:11).

In the afternoon of October 24, local residents observed steam rising from the southwestern flank of Santa María, a volcano with no historical record of eruptions. Earthquakes had been felt throughout the day. At 5:00 PM, loud *retumbos*, subterranean rumblings, were heard in the area around the volcano. By 6:15, fine ash was falling at Finca Helvetia, 14 km (9 mi) west of the volcano. At 8:00 PM, a large cloud was visible over the volcano and lightning began to flash. At 1:00 AM, October 25, the plinian phase of the eruption exploded, large stones began to fall around the southern side of the volcano, and detonations were heard as far away as Costa Rica, some 850 km (530 mi) to the southeast. By 3:00 AM lapilli sized ash was falling in Quetzaltenango. As the intensity of the eruption steadily grew, the debris raining down at Finca Helvetia changed from small cold rocks and pumice to large rocks and pumice. By 6:00 AM, hot rocks and pumice were falling (Rose 1972:31; Williams and Self 1983:36).

Earthquake activity peaked at 3:00 AM, again at 7:00 AM, and finally at 11 AM. The detonations at the height of the eruption could be heard in Oaxaca and Belize. Sulfurous odors reached Guatemala City and Cobán, 160 km (100 mi) to the northeast, and the explosions' shock waves rattled windows there until noon. Off the Pacific coast of Guatemala, Captain

Saunders, on the mailboat SS *Newport*, measured the eruption column height at 27 to 29 km (16.8 to 18 mi or 88,500 to 95,000 ft), using the ship's sextant. Another ship's captain measured the column height at 48 km (30 mi or 157,000 ft), but his method of calculation is not known. Ash fell in Mexico City and Mérida (Williams and Self 1983:36).

By nightfall, the plinian phase of the eruption had ended after eighteen to twenty-four hours. Early on the morning of October 26, renewed activity sent up dark black and brown ash clouds interspersed with pure white steam eruptions. Fine muddy ash fell around the volcano. Finally, on October 29, five days after the start of the eruption, the sky began to clear, although the volcano continued to smoke, rumble, and erupt for several weeks, steam eruptions alternating with ash falls (Rose 1972:31; Williams and Self 1983:35–36).

The *New York Times* reported on October 31, 1902:

> The entire coffee zone of Guatemala has been destroyed by flames and ashes from the volcano Santa María. Eruptions threaten the destruction of every living thing within reach of the fumes and fire that pour from the burning mountain....
>
> Coffee plantations on the coast are buried under seven feet of sand and ashes from the volcano. (p 1)

On November 2, 1902, the *New York Times* reported:

> Thousands of Indians were buried or asphyxiated in the sand. Miles of plantations are under ashes....
>
> Bands of robbers are now swarming the desolated sections, robbing and murdering refugees on the road and looting the abandoned and desolate plantations.
>
> The people left behind on the plantations, it is said, are in danger of death from starvation, for the food supply has been cut off, and there is no way to send in supplies to the affected districts.... (p 1)

In the same issue, Ferdinand Bardwell told his story of the experiences he and his relatives had during the eruptions of the burning mountain:

> Ashes like coarse sand fell in a heavy shower that continued for several hours, and the ashes became lighter and drifted about in clouds of light dust. Breathing was difficult, but the atmosphere was so hot that it seemed as though the skin would be peeled from a person's body. (p 1)

By early 1903, only weak steam eruptions, at intervals of days and then weeks, were noticed at Santa María. Explosive and fumarolic activity continued to diminish until 1911 when it ceased completely. In 1922, a new eruptive phase was heralded by a brief series of explosions, followed by the slow protrusion of lava through the floor of the crater. This marked the birth of the steep sided Peléan dome known as Santiaguito, one of the largest of its kind in the world and still growing decades later. Santa María remained relatively quiet until 1928 when hundreds of people were killed in a Peléan glowing avalanche eruption (Williams 1960:37).

For the people living in northern Yucatán, 1902 was a year of bad drought, as we saw in chapter 6. Rainfall at Mérida was below one standard deviation. Thirty-seven percent of the rain for the year fell in the month of October, after the eruption of Santa María. However, 1903 was even worse, a brutal year. The summer rains failed. Rainfall at Mérida was only 43 percent of normal, the result of climatic disturbances caused or exacerbated by the eruptions. Rainfall for 1904 was also below the standard deviation, another year of severe drought.

Santa María was an almost perfect, sharp pointed, craterless cone until the eruption blasted a large vent through its southwestern flank. The total erupted volume of material was estimated by Williams and Self as $8.6 km^3$ of dense rock equivalent ($2.6 g/cm^3$) or $20.3 km^3$ using a density of $1.1 g/cm^3$. William Rose estimated the volume erupted in one day as $10 km^3$ of dense rock equivalent. According to Stanley Williams and Stephen Self, Santa María is therefore a large volume plinian deposit to be added to the list of at least ten other plinian deposits with a bulk volume of 10 to $25 km^3$. In fact, this deposit ranks in the top few of those deposits, both historic and prehistoric, on magnitude considerations. According to Rose, the eruption ranks among the ten largest historic eruptions. The eruption rate was not only very high at Santa María, it was maintained for at least twenty hours. The eruption column has been calculated, on theoretical grounds, to have been 35 km (22 mi or 115,000 ft), between the reported heights of 28 and 48 km. The lava was silicic, a hornblende dacite, with a silica percentage of 65 percent to 69 percent. The pumice ash fall blanket covered more than 1 million km^2 (300,000 mi^2). The eruption occurred after an apparent repose of 500 to 1,000 years, during which a thick forest cover developed over the mountain. Although there were no historic accounts of eruptions, Cakchiquel legends tell of spectacular eruptions of Gagxanul, the naked volcano—quite a contrast to its forested appearance prior to 1902 (Rose 1972:30–31; 1987:119; Williams 1960: 36; Williams and Self 1983:49).

On January 14, 1903, a final great earthquake struck, its epicenter 700 km (420 mi) west of Santa María, followed by a lesser but still significant earthquake on February 1. Thirteen months of disaster and tragedy were finally at an end, but, as we have seen, severe drought in Yucatán was just beginning (Rose 1972:31; Williams and Self 1983:35–36).

Mystery of AD 536

At the beginning of the Hiatus in Mesoamerica, in AD 536, the densest, most persistent dry fog in recorded history affected Europe, the Middle East, China, and probably the whole world. The summer was cool and hunger, famine, and war were everywhere. The unusually large harvest of 534 had been consumed trying to feed the people. A large percentage of Europe's population died, and the number of Europeans fell to the lowest level between Classical and modern times (Gunn forthcoming).

Magnus Aurelius Cassiodorus Senator was the praetorian prefect, what we might call today the prime minister, of the sixth-century Visigothic kingdom, which had its capital at Ravenna but included Rome. He was also a prolific scholar of the time. Senator, by the way, was his last name and the name by which he was known to his contemporaries. Today, he is generally known as Cassiodorus. In the fall of 536, he wrote a letter from his estate in the country to his deputy, Ambrosius. In it, he described what it was like to live in Italy during that year (Gunn forthcoming):

> People frequently become anxious when they see a change in ordinary happenings since such often presage events which turn out contrary to those which are customary. For nothing happens without a cause, nor is the world entangled in chance happenings. Whatever we see taking place is part of a divine plan. Subjects are anxious when the king changes their constitutions, or goes about in unaccustomed garb. Who is not moved by great curiosity if, contrary to all expectations, something obscure seems to come from the stars? Just as there is a certain security in noting seasons recurring at their proper times, so likewise we are filled with great curiosity when such events seem to be altered. What sort of experience is it, I ask you, to look upon the principal star and not to perceive its usual light? To look upon the moon—the decoration of the night—in all its fullness but without its natural splendor? We all perceive a blue colored sun. We wonder that at noon bodies do not have shadows, that the strongest heat has reached the inertia of extreme tepidity, because—not by the momentary failure of an eclipse, but for the space of an entire year—it has failed to be fixed in its course. What sort of fear is engendered when one has to endure for a rather long time a situation which, even when it occurs with the greatest of speed, is wont to terrify? Thus we had winter without storms, spring without moderate temperature, summer without heat. How can we hope for a temperate climate when the months which could have ripened the fruits froze them instead by its northern blasts? How can the earth provide fertility if it is not warmed by the summer months? How can the grain sprout if the soil has had no rain? We judge these two conditions

as being adverse to all the elements: harsh cold and destructive dryness. The seasons alternate but not by changing themselves, and what is usually produced by mixed showers cannot be gleaned from arid soil. (Senator 536, *Variae* 12.25, translated by Sister Patrice Nugent; see also Barnish 1992:179–181 for an alternate translation of Cassiodorus's letter of AD 536)

Procopius of Caesarea, a Byzantine historian, accompanied the Byzantine general, Belisarius, as his advisor and secretary and spent part of the year AD 536 in Carthage. He described the year in North Africa as follows:

For it has not seemed to me out of order first to record all the events which happened in Libya and after that to turn to the portion of the history touching Italy and the Goths.

During this winter Belisarius remained in Syracuse and Solomon in Carthage. And it came about during this year that a most dread portent took place. For the sun gave forth its light without brightness, like the moon, during this whole year, and it seemed exceedingly like the sun in eclipse, for the beams it shed were not clear nor such as it is accustomed to shed. And from the time when this thing happened men were free neither from war nor pestilence nor any other thing leading to death. And it was the time when Justinian was in the tenth year of his reign. (Procopius 1914, *History of the Wars* IV.xiv.36, 39–42)

In Mesopotamia, John, Bishop of Ephesus, wrote, "The sun was dark and its darkness lasted for eighteen months; each day it shone for about four hours; and still this light was only a feeble shadow…the fruits did not ripen and the wine tasted like sour grapes." The winter, in Mesopotamia, was exceptionally severe, with freak snowfalls and much hardship. The cold and drought finally succeeded in killing off the crops in Mesopotamia and in Italy. A terrible famine ensued in the following years (John quoted in Rampino, Self, and Stothers 1988:87).

In Constantinople, John of Lydus observed, "The Sun became dim in the course of the recently passed fourteenth interdiction, for nearly a whole year, when Belisarius had the highest honor, so that the fruits were killed at an unseasonable time." An anonymous chronicler, usually associated by tradition with the name of Zacharius of Mytilene, referred to observations made in Constantinople, "in the year fourteen…the Sun began to be darkened by day and the Moon by night…from the 24th of March in this year until the 24th of June in the following year" (Lydus quoted in Stothers 1984b:344).

Writing in the thirteenth century, Bar Hebraeus recounted, "And in the year eight hundred and forty-eight [AD 537] there was a sign in the sun the like of which had never before appeared. The sun became dark and his darkness lasted for eighteen months. Each day the middle of the heaven shone faintly with a shadowy light, and every man decided that [the sun] would never recover its full light. That year the fruits did not ripen and the wine tasted like urine" (Bar Hebraeus 1932:7475).

According to Michael Rampino, Stephen Self, and Richard Stothers, "Cold and drought finally succeeded in killing off the crops in Italy and Mesopotamia and led to a terrible famine in the immediately following years." In Ireland, the *Annals of the Four Masters* record references in AD 536 and 539 to a "failure of bread." In the British *Annales Cambriae*, there is a reference in 537 to "*mortalitas in Britannia et Hibernia*," death in Britain and Ireland. The period of widespread famine was followed by the reported outbreak of the Justinian plague in 542 in the Mediterranean region (although Michael Baillie believes it started a few years earlier). It reached as far as Ireland by 545 (Baillie 1991:234; Rampino, Self, and Stothers 1988).

In China, during the spring and fall equinoxes every year, the ancient Chinese looked for Canopus—the brightest star in the constellation of Alpha Carina—to assure themselves of good times ahead and to mark the seasons. In AD 536, however, Canopus was not seen. Records from the state of Ching in southern China report frost and snow in July and August that killed the seedling crop, causing a major famine the following autumn. The accounts also show that the climatic effects were noted until 538. Other kingdoms reported similar disasters. One record indicated the weather was so severe that 70 to 80 percent of the people in one region starved to death (Pang quoted in Weisburd 1985:93).

Records from the Quelccaya ice cap in the Andes of southern Peru indicate a period of serious drought about AD 540–560 and 570–610. One study has suggested that a cold era may have begun around 500. The droughts were coincident with the abandonment of Moche cities and the relocation of the culture to areas closer to water. In the Maya Lowlands, droughts occurred at the same time that cities like Río Azul were being abandoned and others went into a period when no buildings were built or monuments erected—the period known as the Hiatus (Shimada et al 1991:255, 261; Thompson et al 1985). (See chapter 12 for a full description of the Hiatus in the Maya Lowlands.)

> We now know that if we define the period of downturn as AD 536-545, in that period European oaks register their 3rd worst conditions in 1500 years; Fennoscandian temperatures reconstruct their second coldest summer in 1500 years; Foxtail pines from the Sierra Nevada reconstruct their 2nd, 3rd and 4th coldest years in 2000 years; Fitzroya from Chile show their coldest year in 1500 years, etc. (none of the other extreme years match up). Put bluntly, the episode around AD 540 is totally anomalous; no volcano in the last 1500 years has shown anything equivalent, so, what caused the event? [figure 73] (Baillie 1999b)

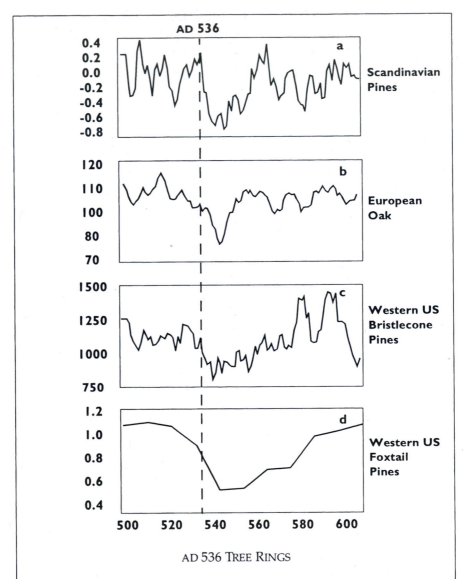

AD 536 TREE RINGS

Figure 73. Tree rings chronologies from Europe and North America. All show notable growth reduction associated with the AD 536 event, *dashed lined.* (*a*) Five point smoothed Fennoscandian temperatures reconstructed from pine ring width and density measurements; (*b*) five point smoothed mean of fifteen European oak chronologies; (*c*) five point smoothed mean of western United States bristlecone pines; (*d*) decadal means of western United States foxtail pines (adapted from Baillie 1994:213).

Using the reported four hours of sunlight at 33°N, as a guide, Stothers calculated that the optical depth would have been approximately 2.5. At maximum altitude, both the sun and the moon would have shone with only 10 percent of their usual brightness. Scattered sunlight would have illuminated the rest of sky, which would not have appeared as dark. The dry fog appeared in the Mediterranean in late March of AD 536 and lasted until June 537, or fifteen months, at 41°N to 42°N, about the latitude of Naples to Rome. Along the North African coast at 30°N, however, it was reported to have lasted eighteen months, which argues for a tropical source of the aerosols. If so, the source's location would have been between 23°N and 23°S because aerosols from south of 23°S do not penetrate the Northern Hemisphere.

WHAT CAUSED THE AD 536 EVENT?

A major tropical eruption can be expected to have left its signature in the Greenland ice cores in the form of sulfuric acid aerosols deposited on the polar ice cap. A very high sulfuric acid signal was believed to have been detected in a Greenland ice core by C. U. Hammer and his colleagues, who assigned a date of AD 540 ±10 but later revised it to AD 516 ±4, and in another Greenland ice core by Herron who estimated AD 535. A computation of the optical depth carried out by Stothers using the strength of the ice core signal gives an optical depth of 2.2, very close to the optical depth calculated from the historical reports. The ice core evidence, however, has been complicated by a recent American Greenland Ice Sheet Project Two (GISP2) core from Greenland, which does not show a strong acid layer at 536–540. The nearest acid layer is at 530 ±2, but it is not believed to be strong enough to account for the 536 event. On the other hand, 14 m (46 ft) of the core is missing between 545–614 ±15. Thus, the signal may conceivably be missing from the American Greenland Ice Sheet Project 2 (GISP2) core or it might be represented by the 530 peak (Baillie 1994:216; Hammer, Clausen, and Dansgaard 1980; Rampino, Self, and Stothers 1988:88; Stothers 1984b:344; Zielinski 1995:20,939).

Since the 530 peak occurs below the gap, one could question whether its dating is as precise as the ±2 years assigned to it. Secondly, El Chichón's 1982 eruption did not leave a signal in snow pits near the location of the GISP2 core, although it has been found in other snow pits around Greenland. Thirdly, individual volcanic signals can be missing from ice cores that are in close proximity to other cores where the signal is present. A tropical volcano, therefore, might leave a much weaker signal than might otherwise be expected. Furthermore, the joint European Greenland Ice-core Project (GRIP) has a peak at 532 and the Dye 3 core (named for a US Air Force radar base in Greenland) has 534. One can build a case that these signals represent the 535/536 event. Given the severity of the worldwide AD 536 event, however, Baillie believes it may be the result of multiple ef-

UNIT	ID	TYPE	^{14}C YR BP	CAL YR -1σ	CAL YR +1σ
C1	CHI9318	Charcoal	1465 ±95	450	660
	CHI9515	Charcoal	1490 ±45	535	635
	CHI9602	Charcoal	1520 ±75	440	600
	EC-189	Charcoal	1580 ±70	400	560
	EC-199	Charcoal	1600 ±200	230	650

RB GILL 2000

EL CHICHÓN CALIBRATED DATES C1 DEPOSIT

Table 7. Calibrated radiocarbon dates from the C1 deposit at El Chichón. Note that all of the 1σ date ranges include AD 536, thus indicating that El Chichón could have erupted at 536 (*Source of radiocarbon dates:* Macías et al 1997:15; Rubin 1993; Tilling et al 1984:747–749; calibration by OxCal 2.18, Ramsey 1995).

fects which are not yet understood (Michael Baillie, October 1998, e-mail to author; Zielinski 1995:20,945).

Wibjörn Karlén examined tree ring records from arctic Sweden. Tree ring widths there indicate summer growing temperatures, a cold year producing narrow rings, a warm year wide rings. In looking for conditions which would favor the advance of glaciers in the region, he selected periods with several years or more of cold temperatures. The tree rings indicate such a multiyear period occurred around AD 550, evidence of a period of severe cold during the middle of the sixth century (Karlén 1984:265).

Rabaul Caldera, in Papua New Guinea, has been proposed as the volcano responsible for the AD 536 mystery aerosol cloud. R. F. Heming identified two collapse episodes at Rabaul, which he dated as 3500 BP and 1400 BP. He estimated that the size of the second eruption was about 24 km^3 of primarily dacitic pumiceous ash flows. Based on the radiocarbon measurements, he favored an age between AD 520 and 560 for Rabaul's eruption. Unfortunately, Heming did not use calibrated dates in estimating the eruption dates of Rabaul. When the youngest calibrated date is considered, the 1σ range of dates for the sample is 660 to 820 and 840 to 860. The 2σ range is 610 to 950. Clearly, the Rabaul eruption is much too late for the 536 event. In addition, the chemical composition of Rabaul's eruption

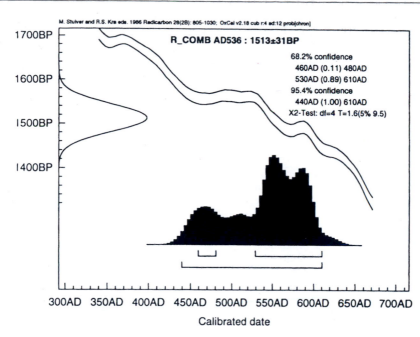

EL CHICHÓN COMBINED CALIBRATED SIXTH-CENTURY DATES

Figure 74. The combined calibrated dates for five radiocarbon samples from ash deposit C1 at El Chichón, as listed in table 7 on the opposite page. The combined 1σ date ranges for the samples are AD 460–480 and AD 530–610, which includes AD 535/ 536. To date (1999), no calculation has been made of the size of the C1 eruption. If the AD 536 event proves to be the result of a volcanic eruption, El Chichón remains a viable candidate (*Sources of radiocarbon measurements:* Macías et al 1997:15; Rubin 1993; Tilling et al 1984:747–749; calibration, combination, and plotting using OxCal 2.18, Ramsey 1995).

products would have required an eruption of 466 km³ compared to the 24 km³ that Heming estimated to have actually erupted (Gill 1994:316–318; Heming 1974:1253, 1259).

In another work, I pointed out that the one available ^{14}C date (as of 1993), a charcoal sample from an ash deposit at El Chichón Volcano, gave a calibrated date with a 1σ range of 407–545, making El Chichón a candidate for a possible AD 536 eruption. Since then additional charcoal samples have been recovered, and all five of the calibrated dates from deposit C1 are consistent with an AD 536 eruption (table 7). Furthermore, a mathematical combination of the dates is plotted in figure 74. It yields a 1σ date range of AD 460–480 and AD 530–610 which, of course, includes AD 536, thus leaving open the possibility that an eruption could have occurred at El Chichón in AD 536. The eruption could have occurred earlier or later as well (Gill 1994:294, 407–545; *Source of radiocarbon dates*: Macías et al 1997:15; Rubin 1993; Tilling et al 1984:747–749; calibration by OxCal ver 2.18, Ramsey 1995 and by CALIB, Stuiver and Reimer 1993, decadal calibration table).

WAS IT AN EXTRATERRESTRIAL IMPACT EVENT?

Baillie and others have raised the possibility that the AD 536 dry fog was not the result of a volcanic eruption, but rather the effect of either an asteroid or a comet striking one of the world's oceans or a cloud of interstellar dust through which the Earth passed. Since there is no undisputed candidate (as of 1999) for the volcano responsible, and the acid signal in the ice is so much less than would be expected from an eruption of sufficient size to cause the observed worldwide effects, the possibility of an impact or a cosmic dust cloud must be considered.

Baillie summarizes the situation as follows. Irish tree-ring chronologies show a widespread growth downturn in the window AD 536-545. The event appears to have been global as there were crop failures and famines from China to North Africa to Ireland followed by plague in the 530s and 540s. There was clearly an environmental downturn across the Northern Hemisphere which was originally thought to be due to a volcanic dust veil, but now may not be—because of the lack of clear cut evidence in the recent ice cores. A lot of mythology, located traditionally just at the time of the 536–545 event, suggests that there were things going on in the sky, including dragons, fireballs, and fiery lances. Cassiodorus, writing at the time, says "something mysterious and unusual seems to be coming on us from the stars." So, Baillie believes a possible working hypothesis is that the Earth suffered a bombardment event in the window AD 536-545 in the style of one of Victor Clube's and Bill Napier's "cosmic swarms" where the Earth is struck by a large number of Tunguska class objects in a short space of time (days to years). Now that the question of an impact has been raised, it clearly deserves further research (Michael Baillie, October 1998, e-mail to author; Baillie 1994:216; 1995; 1999a; Clube and Napier 1990; Stothers 1984a; Zielinski 1995:20,939).

Baillie adds that he cannot rule out that the real vector for the environmental downturn was a change in ocean circulation. We would still have to ask, however, what caused the change in circulation. Overall, we have an event whose cause needs to be resolved. At least, he says, we know where to look in time for the evidence (Michael Baillie, October 1998, e-mail to author).

The one incontrovertible fact to emerge from this discussion of the AD 536 mystery is that the Hiatus occurred at a time of global climatic aberrations which resulted in worldwide cold. It was not a localized Maya phenomenon. Our meteorological model suggests that periods of severe cold are propitious for drought in the Maya Lowlands and, in fact, as we will see in chapter 10, a lake sediment core taken from Punta Laguna in the Mexican state of Quintana Roo indicates a severe drought occurred there during the Hiatus. Once again, Maya demographic disaster is tied to worldwide events.

VOLCANOES AND THE MAYA

Our purpose in this book is to explore how the physical world and, in particular, the weather may have affected the Maya. Having established a climatic role for volcanoes, we can now ask whether volcanoes are known to have affected Mesoamerican weather and whether they have delivered death and destruction to the Maya.

Let's start by looking at historical reports of drought and famine in Mesoamerica between 1440 and 1840 found in Spanish governmental records written during the Colonial period, native chronicles written shortly after the Spanish conquest, and other historical sources.

In Yucatán, there are fairly complete reports which list the tribulations of the Yucatecan people during those years. We find that twenty-four famines were recorded and in thirteen cases, drought was reported to be the precipitating cause. Of those drought/famines eleven, or 85 percent, occurred within two years of a major, tropical volcanic eruption, one which occurred between 20°S and 20°N (table 8).

The most serious problem facing us in trying to analyze this discovery is how to classify a major tropical eruption. About the best we can do is to use the Volcanic Explosivity Index (VEI) which measures the volume of material erupted. Unfortunately, it does not tell us anything about how the material was erupted, whether the eruption was explosive or effusive, what the chemical composition was, how much sulfur was injected into the stratosphere, or how high the eruption column reached. In terms of trying to assess a volcano's climatic impact, therefore, it leaves much to be desired. But it's all we have.

I have chosen to relate Mesoamerican droughts with the VEI magnitude, which, although not perfect, provides a rough indication of the potential climatic effectiveness of an eruption. We will look at tropical eruptions with a magnitude of 4 or larger, although we should recognize that some very sulfurous magnitude 3 or even magnitude 2 eruptions could affect the global climate. By the same token, some magnitude 4 eruptions will have no climatic impact at all (Handler 1989:234).

Using this imperfect guide, we can match 85 percent of the drought/famines reported in Yucatán between 1440 and 1840 to large, tropical eruptions—a surprisingly high correlation.

In addition, a twelfth can be perhaps attributed to a Mediterranean magnitude 4 and three tropical magnitude 3 eruptions which occurred in the same year. (There is a complete list of Colonial Yucatecan famines with sources found in table 11 on pages 306 and 307.)

But maybe, one might argue, the correlation found is an artifact of the way the analysis is set up. Maybe we could take any set of thirteen random numbers, allow a two-year leeway, and match them up to the same volcanic eruptions with similar results. A statistical analysis, however, indicates a 1 in 1,000,000 probability that the matches are due to random chance.

Furthermore, not all Yucatecan famines were credited to drought in the historical records. In the remaining eleven cases, either a different cause was listed or the cause was not stated (table 9). Some famines were attributed to excess rainfall, or hurricanes, or insects, or social and political processes, or combinations of these factors. It is enlightening to note, therefore, that of the remaining eleven famines—those which are not tied to drought in the records—none followed a large, tropical eruption within two years. The nondrought famines produced a correlation of 0 percent, well below random chance.

We would expect years of normal to high rainfall to occur during very different climatic conditions than years of low rainfall, and the zero correlation confirms our expectation. Famine years without drought are not years of volcano weather.

We next turn our attention to the Valley of Mexico, for which there are excellent historical records. In a study prepared for the *Secretaría de Agricultura y Recursos Hidraúlicos* (Department of Agriculture and Water Resources), we find approximately thirty drought episodes reported between 1440 and 1840 which lasted three or more months—some, of course, lasted for years. Of the droughts reported, at least eighteen, or 60 percent, occurred within two years of known, large, tropical eruptions. If we include two eruptions dated by radiocarbon measurements, the correlation is 67 percent. It might be possible to match an additional three droughts with clusters of known magnitude 3 eruptions or with eruptions of unknown magnitude for a total of twenty-three, or 77 percent. Again, a statistical analysis indicates a 1 in 1,000,000 probability that the matches are due to random chance (Castorena et al 1980:76–87).

These are pretty surprising numbers. Clearly, there is a real tie between large tropical eruptions and drought in Mesoamerica.

New data regarding the eruptive history of volcanoes around the world are being added regularly to the record. We might be able to match up more Mesoamerican droughts and famines to volcanic eruptions in the future. The 1994 edition of *Volcanoes of the World*, a compilation of the eruption records gathered by the Smithsonian Global Volcanism Program, points out that 689 volcanoes thought to have erupted during the Holocene, the last 12,000 years, have not been dated (Simkin and Siebert 1994:3).

Next, let's look at the relationship from the perspective of volcanoes. *Volcanoes of the World* lists forty-seven magnitude 4 or greater tropical eruptions between 1440 and 1840. Of those, thirty, or 64 percent, are followed within two years by drought in Mesoamerica known from historical records, and a thirty-first, 66 percent, with a drought in the northern state of Coahuila—once again a really surprising number (Simkin and Siebert 1994:189–208).

One might ask: why did I choose two years? The easy answer is: that is how the data worked out. A more complex answer would have to examine the month in which the eruption occurred; how volcanoes affect the atmosphere; the time period over which sulfuric aerosol precursors are converted to H_2SO_4 and settle into the Junge layer; how drought develops on the ground; whether it turns into famine; and how soon it is recognized and reported by government officials. Sometimes the drought/famine was reported in the same year as the eruption, sometimes one or two years later when full-blown famine had developed.

Brian Goodman has researched the effects of volcanoes on climate and found that an important factor in the response of the atmosphere to an eruption is the thermal inertia of the atmosphere. An eruption which occurs during a cool period will have a much faster effect than an eruption which occurs during a warm period. The atmosphere tends to set into a particular regime of circulation and it stays there until there is a catastrophic shift to a new regime. The shift to the new regime is dependent on how close to the shift point the atmosphere is prior to the eruption. In fact, after the 1982 eruption of El Chichón during an otherwise warm period, three years of reduced rainfall did not begin until 1985, about two and a half years after the eruption. The year 1985 almost qualified as a drought year under our definition of drought as a year with 734 mm (28.9 in) or less of rainfall. The precipitation for 1985 fell to 750 mm (29.5 in). Goodman has developed computer simulations of the interplay between volcanic eruptions and thermal inertia which predict the observed results in the atmosphere (Brian Goodman, October 1999, personal communication).

What makes the difference, then, between a volcanic eruption that causes drought and one that doesn't? It is likely that a whole constellation of factors must line up right for a volcanic eruption to result in drought in Yucatán. In the first place, the volcanoes located within the Tropics between 20°N and 20°S seem to have the most effect. Volcanoes farther to the north and south seem to have less effect on Yucatecan weather. Occasionally, particular, extratropical volcanoes do seem to match with Mesoamerican drought, but the correlation percentage is much less.

Secondly, the mechanics of the eruption, the direction of the blast, whether vertical or lateral, the explosivity, the height of the eruption column, and the quantity and type of ejected material all affect the end result. Thirdly, the chemical composition of the erupted material must be rich in sulfur. Some of the magnitude 4+ eruptions known may not have pro-

HISTORICAL ERUPTIONS AND DROUGHT/FAMINES IN YUCATÁN

Table 8. (*Opposite*) A listing of large, tropical eruptions (magnitude 4+ on the Volcanic Explosivity Index) followed within two years by drought and famine in Yucatán, as reported in historical records. The famines listed are those in which drought was reported to be the precipitating cause. The *superscript* beside the volcano's name indicates the magnitude on the Volcanic Explosivity Index: 3 is moderately large, 4 large, 5 very large, 6 huge, 7 colossal. *f* indicates an explosive eruption. *?* indicates uncertainty in the original magnitude attribution (*Sources for famines*: given in Table 11 on page 307; *Sources for volcanic eruptions*: Bradley and Jones 1992:612–613; Dai, Mosley-Thompson, and Thompson 1991:17,361; Simkin and Siebert 1994:184–210).

[a] Listed as magnitude 4 by Bradley and Jones 1992 and magnitude 3 by Simkin and Siebert 1994. Included here as magnitude 4.

[b] The combination of a Mediterranean magnitude 4 eruption and three tropical magnitude 3 eruptions appears to have had the same climatic effect as one tropical magnitude 4 eruption.

[c] Many eruptions during fifteen years beginning in 1759, including a magnitude 4 in 1764.

[d] Farriss does not list this famine as caused by drought. A reading of the original documents in the Archivo General de la Nación in Mexico City, however, indicates the famine was attributed to a lack of rain (*falta de llubias*) and much sun (*los muchos soles*) during 1794 which caused a crop failure.

[e] A large, unidentified, near-equatorial eruption in 1809 ±2 left its mark in ice cores in Greenland and Antarctica.

[f] The drought/famine of 1834–1836 is reported to have intensified drastically (*desarrollóse duramente*) in 1835.

ERUPTIONS		YUCATECAN FAMINES	
Kuwae,[6] Indonesia	1452	~1453–1454	Drought, Famine, Cold
Cotopaxi,[4] Ecuador	1534	1535–1541	Drought, Famine, Locusts
San Salvador,[4a] El Salvador	1572 ±2	1575–1576	Drought, Famine, Epidemic
Makian,[4?] Indonesia	1646	1648–1650	Drought, Famine, Epidemic
Santorini[4], Greece[b] Cameroon[3†], W Afr Paluweh[3], Indonesia Sumaco[3?], Ecuador	1650 1650 ±6 1650 ±6 1650 ±6	1650–1654	Drought, Famine, Epidemic
Jorullo,[4] Mexico	1764[c]	1765–1768	Drought, Famine, Locusts, Hurricane
Cotopaxi,[4] Ecuador	1768	1769–1774	Drought, Famine, Locusts, Hurricane
San Martín,[4] Mexico	1793	1794–1795	Drought[d], Famine
		1800–1807	Drought, Famine, Locusts
Unknown[4+]	1809[e] ±2	1809–1810	Drought, Famine
Tambora,[7] Indonesia Raung,[4?] Indonesia	1815 1817	1817	Drought, Famine
Galunggung,[5] Indonesia	1822	1822–1823	Drought, Famine
Cosegüina,[5] Nicaragua	1835	1834–1836[f]	Drought, Famine

RB GILL 2000

ERUPTIONS	YUCATECAN FAMINES	
	1551–1552	Famine
	1571–1572	Famine
	1604	Famine
	1618	Famine, Locusts
	1627–1631	Famine, Storm, Locusts
None	1692–1693	Famine, Epidemic, Hurricane, Locusts
	1700	Famine
	1725–1727	Famine, Epidemic
	1730	Famine
	1742	Famine
	1842	Famine

RB GILL 2000

ERUPTIONS AND FAMINES WITHOUT DROUGHT IN YUCATÁN

Table 9. The famines reported in historical sources for Yucatán which are not specifically attributed to droughts. None occurred within two years of a known, large, tropical eruption of magnitude 4 or greater in the Volcanic Explosivity Index. Comparing tables 8 and 9 shows that drought/famines can be correlated with large, tropical volcanic eruptions whereas famines without drought cannot similarly be tied to volcanoes (*Sources for famines:* given in Table 11 on page 307; *Sources for volcanic eruptions:* Simkin and Siebert 1994:184–210).

duced sufficient sulfur to be climatically effective on a global scale. On the other hand, some magnitude 3 eruptions may have been sulfurous enough to have climatic repercussions.

The meteorological conditions of the Tropics at the time of the eruption play an important role. An eruption occurring during a period of worldwide warmth would have a very different effect on Yucatán from one that occurs during a period of cold, the thermal inertia effect. The season of the year matters as well. Although volcanic eruptions that affect the Lowlands seem well distributed throughout the year, certain times of year may be more propitious than others. A volcanic effect on weather which reaches its peak during the October to May dry season could, of course, go almost unnoticed, while one that reaches its peak during the May to October wet season could be devastating.

Atmospheric dynamics play a role in how the aerosol cloud is spread around the world. After the 1982 eruption at El Chichón, for example, the cloud did not move beyond the Tropics for six months after the eruption, an unexpected occurrence. The length of time the aerosol cloud remains concentrated in the Tropics is likely to play a role in how it affects tropical weather. While the aerosol cloud is restricted to the Tropics, its primary effect will be on the Hadley cell circulation. By absorbing and backscattering incoming solar energy, the energy that drives the Hadley circulation, the dynamics of the cell will change, and it will most likely contract, thus shifting the North Atlantic High to the southwest. The fact that mainly tropical volcanoes drive drought in Mesoamerica leads me to suspect that the primary mechanism at work is the effect on Hadley cell circulation.

The position of the high pressure cell in the North Atlantic at the time of the eruption may well determine the effect of the eruption on Yucatecan weather. If it is already located far to the southwest, an eruption may be sufficient to cause drought by moving the high over Yucatán as was the case in 1902. On the other hand, if it is located far to the northeast at the time of the eruption, during a period of global warmth, the cooling experienced after a volcanic blast may not be sufficient to move the high far enough to the southwest to cause significant drought in Mesoamerica, as was the case after El Chichón's 1982 eruption.

Certainly, the length of the effect, how rapidly the sulfuric aerosols clear from the atmosphere, can determine whether a famine develops from a drought. Did the drought start and end soon enough to avoid famine and result in dearth, or did it continue long enough for famine to develop?

Most importantly, however, the effects of drought are not uniform over a broad area, as we saw in the map of drought in Texas during 1955–1956 (figure 43 on page 168). Some eruptions may have affected Yucatán more at one time, while eruptions at other times may have affected different areas of Mesoamerica, like the Valley of Mexico or the Bajío in the central Highlands. In fact, only half of the Yucatecan famines overlap with droughts in the Valley of Mexico. The two droughts reported for the Bajío were not recorded in either the Valley of Mexico or in Yucatán. It does indeed appear that volcano induced drought does not always beset Mesoamerica evenly.

A pattern now begins to emerge from the reports. It would seem that magnitude 4+ tropical volcanic eruptions are often followed by drought in Mesoamerica, but not always in the same part of Mesoamerica. One time the hardest hit area is Yucatán, the next time the Valley of Mexico, the next time the Bajío. It is, of course, possible that droughts occurred during the Colonial period in areas for which reports were either not filed or which I have not yet found, areas like Tabasco, or parts of the Caribbean. It is also possible that magnitude 4 tropical eruptions occurred which have not yet been identified and were not listed in the 1994 edition of *Volcanoes of the World*. The eruptions of El Chichón and Popocatépetl that we have examined, for example, are not listed. The frequency with which droughts follow large, tropical eruptions is far greater than could be expected from random chance.

Mesoamerican drought, however, may also be caused by other climatic regimes. The multiyear droughts of 1616–1627 and 1701–1708 in the Highlands and 1800–1808 throughout Mexico cannot be tied to presently known, tropical volcanic activity and may well be due to climatic regimes whose origins lie elsewhere. The years 1800–1820, for example, marked a very cold period in Northern Hemispheric temperatures. Large, tropical volcanic eruptions are not known for the beginning of the period, although Mt. St. Helens did erupt in a magnitude 5 eruption in 1800. In some records, the decade of the 1810s is the coldest seen (Briffa et al 1998:452; Thompson et al 1986:363).

Finally, in analyzing the serious effects of volcano weather on people, one cannot ignore the vulnerability of the affected society. The position that I have taken in this book is that the Collapse droughts of the ninth and tenth centuries were so devastating that there was nothing the Maya could do to avoid their fate. Other droughts, however, may be more borderline. In those cases, the condition of the society may be a key factor. Was the prior year's harvest bountiful, and are all the granaries and storage facilities full? Are the water reservoirs full? Do the people start out in good health, or have they been run down by prior scanty harvests, or by war, or by social turbulence?

We cannot attribute 100 percent of the Colonial historical drought/ famines to volcanic causes. Surely other factors can cause drought as well. A surprisingly large percentage of the drought/famines in Yucatán and throughout Mesoamerica, however, are seen to follow large, tropical eruptions. Clearly, the interplay between volcanoes and weather can be fatal. We have seen that lethal volcanoes have provoked repeated episodes of massive death and suffering among the Maya.

Discussion

The prior pages have laid the foundation for us to discuss the main question of this chapter: Did volcanoes cause the Classic Collapse?

Like so much in archaeology, there is not enough evidence currently available to answer with a simple yes or no. There are, however, some very intriguing clues which suggest, but do not prove, that volcanoes may have played a role.

The climatic effectiveness of a volcano depends on the quantities of sulfur which it introduces into the stratosphere. The production of ash and other gaseous constituents has little climatic effect. Therefore, a smaller eruption producing large quantities of sulfur will have a greater climatic effect than a larger, more explosive eruption producing less sulfur. Large quantities of sulfur in the atmosphere over Greenland show up as acid peaks in the annual layers of ice—although it must be noted that not all tropical eruptions show up in the Greenland or Antarctic ice cores. The GISP2 Greenland ice core shows two acid peaks in consecutive years at AD 822 and 823 from unknown sources. The acid peaks could be the result of one continuing eruption episode or might indicate two eruptions in consecutive years from different volcanoes.

El Chichón and Popocatépetl emit large quantities of sulfur as a percentage of their erupted magmatic products. Their climatic effectiveness, therefore, is greater than is currently known at most other volcanoes, for the particular eruption size. The radiocarbon evidence from both volcanoes is consistent with eruptions in the early ninth century.

The ninth-century eruption at Popocatépetl has been estimated to be quite large, probably magnitude 5 or 6, with an eruption column estimated at over 25 km (15 mi or 82,000 ft), which would certainly have injected sulfuric aerosols into the stratosphere and would have been climatically effective on a global scale (Claus Siebe, October 1999, e-mail to author; Siebe et al 1996:401).

Prior eruptions at El Chichón are estimated to have been many times greater than the 1982 episode, perhaps an order of magnitude greater, and would also have had significant worldwide impacts. The magnitude of the ninth-century eruption and the height of its eruption column have not been calculated, but eyeball assessments of the depth of the deposits would indicate a much larger eruption than 1982's magnitude 5 eruption. We should remember that the smaller 1982 eruption produced measurable global climatic effects, which were followed by three years of reduced rainfall, although not drought according to our definition.

In fact, radiocarbon dates from El Chichón are consistent with eruptions around the time of the Hiatus, the Classic Collapse, and other Maya demographic disasters. Further research at El Chichón is still needed, however, to definitively establish the prehistoric eruption dates and estimate their magnitudes, the height of their eruption columns, the quantity of sulfur injected into the stratosphere, and to permit us to estimate their climatic effect.

Kelly and Sear produced evidence suggesting that major Northern Hemispheric eruptions may have been followed by an equatorward shift in the position of the North Atlantic High, as would be expected by the meteorological model. In 1902, the eruptions of La Soufrière-St. Vincent, Mt. Pelée, and Santa María were accompanied by a southwestward shift in the location of the North Atlantic High, by significant cooling in Europe and North America, and by severe drought in northern Yucatán. We are thus furnished an actual example of the hypothesis from known weather and volcanic records.

Large quantities of sulfur aerosols in the stratosphere block incoming solar radiation, which results in a cooling of the lower atmosphere. The years following a large eruption, then, are likely to be periods of global cooling, which would indicate conditions propitious for drought in the Maya Lowlands.

If the ninth-century eruptions of both El Chichón and Popocatépetl were large enough to induce or exacerbate periods of cold, these climatic perturbations may have been accompanied by drought in the Lowlands, as were so many volcanic eruptions during Colonial times.

Besides the unknown peaks at AD 822 and 823, the GISP2 core has Classic acid peaks at AD 853, 875, 900, 902, and 915. These have all been assigned to extratropical volcanoes, although some of the attributions appear to be quite tentative. Additional tropical eruptions, therefore, may yet be identified which would coincide with one or more of these peaks. Furthermore, *Volcanoes of the World* lists an unknown eruption at AD 860 which is indicated by tree ring data.

At two West Indian volcanoes, radiocarbon evidence suggests possible Terminal Classic eruptions during the tenth century, although the magnitudes of the eruptions have not been estimated. Mt. Pelée had one eruption which is dated to between cal AD 899 and 960 and another to between cal AD 900 and 1032. La Soufrière-St. Vincent appears to have erupted between cal AD 889 and 1029.

From Arctic Sweden, tree rings show three pulses of extreme cold, around 800, 860, and 910, during a generally cold period in the ninth and early tenth centuries. There were three phases of collapse in the Lowlands, around 810, 860, and 910. It is intriguing to consider that these pulses of cold and demographic disaster may have been driven by volcanic eruptions. To date, palaeoclimatologists have identified a ninth- to tenth-century period of severe drought in two different Yucatecan lakes that peaked at 860 in one and at 922 in the other. We will examine each of these topics in greater detail in the following chapters.

There is at this point, then, a body of tentative evidence which suggests that volcanoes may have played a major role in the destruction of the Collapse. As of yet, however, there is no smoking gun.

Before we leave this topic, what about other Precolumbian demographic disasters in Mesoamerica? There are at least three such events in the Maya Lowlands and one in the Highlands at Tula. The Preclassic Abandonment took place between AD 150 and 200. In one of the most powerful eruptions of the last 2,000 years, Taupo in New Zealand exploded in a huge magnitude 6+ eruption around AD 180. It shot an eruption column a phenomenal 50 km (30 mi or 160,000 ft) into the air. Over 80 percent of the erupted pumice fell at distances greater than 220 km (136 mi). Although it is an extratropical volcano, the sheer power of the eruption would have had global climatic effects (Simkin and Siebert 1994:185; Walker 1980).

The Hiatus occurred between AD 536 and 596. To date it cannot be attributed to any particular volcano, though we saw that El Chichón has radiocarbon dates consistent with a sixth-century eruption. So far, we don't know the size or the exact date of El Chichón's sixth-century eruption and whether it would be large enough to explain the observed dry fog. Mike Baillie has advanced a hypothesis that the worldwide climatic aberrations of the Hiatus may have been caused by extraterrestrial impacts or cometary atmospheric explosions, rather than a volcano. One thing is clear, however, the Hiatus occurred during a period of worldwide atmospheric disruption. It was definitely not a localized Maya phenomenon.

The earliest Mesoamerican drought for which there exists a historical description was reported to have occurred in Tula in the year 1052. One of the millennium's largest eruptions occurred in China in cal AD 1050 ±10 at Baitoushan. At magnitude 7 and erupting around 150 km^3 of pumice, it was one of the four largest known in the last 10,000 years. Although it lies at 42° N, along the Chinese-Korean border and therefore outside of our zone of tropical volcanoes, the AD 1050 eruption was so massive, its sheer size undoubtedly affected weather around the world and resulted in drought in Mesoamerica (Castorena et al 1980:15; Simkin and Siebert 1994:188; VolcanoWorld 1999).

Ice cores from the Antarctic show an acid peak around the year AD 1168. The increased acidity lasted for 7.6 years, the longest period of acidity in the Antarctic ice record in the last 16,000 years. This acid peak coincides with the fall of Tula, as we will discuss later. To date, the guilty volcano remains at large (Hammer, Clausen, and Langway 1997:6).

Finally, Kuwae exploded in a magnitude 6 eruption around 1452, the time of the Postclassic Abandonment, the fall of Mayapán, and the devastating famine of 1 Rabbit in the Mexican Highlands.

There is no evidence that volcanic eruptions alone caused the droughts which occurred during the ninth century and at the time of other demographic disasters. It may well be that the role of the volcanoes was to exacerbate cold spells already underway. Nonetheless, the coincidence is intriguing and bears further investigation. Not all large tropical eruptions result in drought in Mesoamerica, and not all Mesoamerican drought is caused by volcanoes, but a surprisingly large percentage of each is associated with the other.

What the evidence of Colonial drought, famine, and eruptions so clearly demonstrates is that volcanoes and weather have participated in a perverse partnership which repeatedly brought drought, devastation, and death to the Maya and to Mesoamerica.

9. GEOLOGY, HYDROLOGY, AND WATER

P aradoxically, it appears that purely cultural insights often
   may be gained from the study of ecologic context and especially of ancient water management.
                              —Richard E. W. Adams (1991:632)

Water is critical for human survival. A human being can exist for
weeks without food, but only a short few days without water. Water was
a precarious resource in most of the Maya Lowlands. Most Classic Maya
cities relied on surface water reservoirs, which had to be replenished by
rainfall, for their drinking water. In this chapter, we look at the geology
and hydrology of the Lowlands and how they affect water supplies. We
will see how the Maya, who relied on ample annual rainfall to replenish
their surface reservoirs, supplied their cities with water and why water
may have been their Achilles' heel.

The Maya area lies between 14°N and 22°N, entirely within the Tropics, and between 87°W and 93°W (figure 75). It is roughly 900km (560mi)
from north to south and some 550km (340mi) from east to west along the
continental divide, close to the Pacific coast, and about 400km (250mi)
across the Peninsula of Yucatán. About half of the Classic Maya area lies in
modern Mexico, including most of Chiapas and Tabasco and all of
Campeche, Yucatán, and Quintana Roo. The balance covers Belize, the Department of the Petén in Guatemala, and the northern parts of Honduras

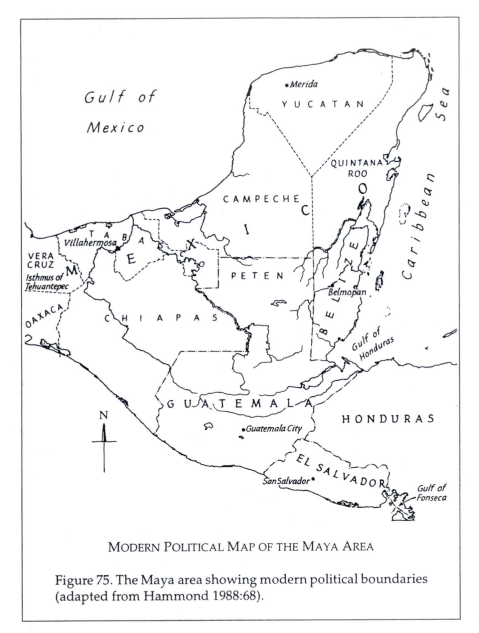

MODERN POLITICAL MAP OF THE MAYA AREA

Figure 75. The Maya area showing modern political boundaries (adapted from Hammond 1988:68).

and El Salvador. It lies within the boundaries of Mesoamerica as originally defined by Paul Kirchoff (Hammond 1988:67–69; Kirchoff 1943).

Tectonically, most of the Classic Maya area lies on the Maya Block of the North American Plate, north of the Motagua Valley (figure 76). To the south of the Motagua Valley lies the Chortis Block of the Caribbean Plate. To the southwest, off the Pacific coast, lies the Cocos Plate which is being

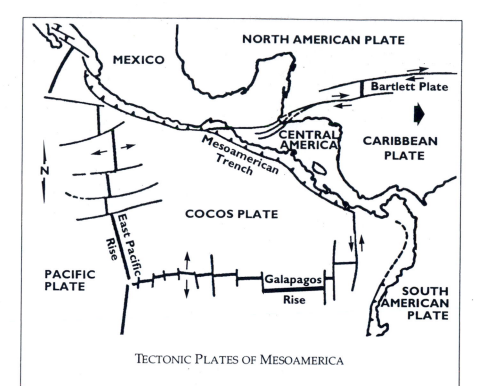

TECTONIC PLATES OF MESOAMERICA

Figure 76. The tectonic plates of Mexico and Central America. At the Mesoamerican trench, off the Pacific coast, the Cocos Plate is being subducted under the North American and Caribbean plates. The boundary between the North American and Caribbean plates runs through the Motagua Valley in Guatemala (adapted from Dengo 1990:67).

subducted under the North American and Caribbean plates, along the Mesoamerican trench (Dengo 1990:66). (See figure 77 for a sketch of the tectonic history of the area.)

GEOLOGY

Tabasco, the Pacific lowlands, the Caribbean coast of northern Yucatán, Quintana Roo, and Belize are strips of geologically recent alluvial deposits (figure 78). The northern third of the Yucatán Peninsula is Tertiary limestone and marl (*sascab*), while the southern part and the areas of Chiapas, Petén, and Belize are comprised of older limestones, with greater elevation and relief and more developed drainage. Older and more elevated Cretaceous and Jurassic limestones, Triassic shales, and older sedimentary rocks lie still further south, forming the hills of southern Petén, the Alta

Verapaz, and the foothills of the Maya Mountains in southern Belize. The Maya Mountains, themselves, are a northern isolated block of much older rocks, separated from the Guatemalan Highlands, and are comprised of sedimentary and metamorphic deposits and Palaeozoic granites (Dengo 1983:G-11; Hammond 1988:71).

Three areas of limestone, becoming successively younger in age and lower in elevation from south to north, form the land mass known as the Yucatán Platform. During most of its history, it has remained a rigid mass, emerging from and being submerged by the surrounding seas as a stable tectonic unit. The result is a widespread area of low topography which makes up the Yucatán Peninsula, including the Petén. The southern end of the Yucatán Platform has been thrust against the Guatemalan Highlands, buckling slowly into high ridges, which have eroded into steep, forested hills, resembling a Chinese landscape. The northern end is the site of the Cretaceous extraterrestrial impact, the Chicxulub crater, believed to be responsible for the terrible ecological catastrophe which resulted in the extinction of the dinosaurs and so many other forms of life about 65 million years ago (Dengo 1983:G-11-A; Hammond 1988:71).

RIVER DRAINAGE

Water drains from the continental divide in five major drainage zones: the Pacific, Caribbean, Gulf, Karstic, and lacustrine zones (figure 79). On the eastern, Caribbean littoral, the Río Hondo, forming the border between Mexico and Belize, is a sluggish river with a fairly constant water level, navigable far upstream by canoe. It undoubtedly served as a major transportation corridor between the Petén and the Caribbean coast in Classic times. Farther to the south, the Belize River and the Sarstoon River also drain out of the Petén and doubtless served as corridors to the coast. These rivers become intermittent or seasonal farther inland (Hammond 1988:77).

TECTONIC HISTORY OF MESOAMERICA

Figure 77. (*Opposite*) The relative movements and positions of the various blocks constituting Mesoamerica and Central America during the area's tectonic history (adapted from Dengo 1990:88).

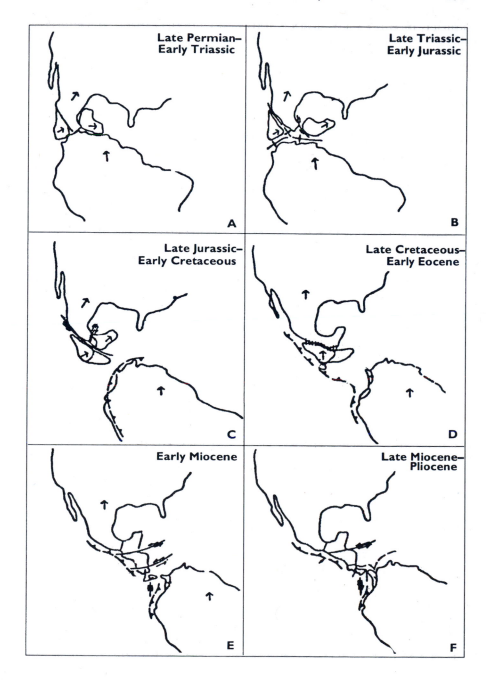

Late Permian–Early Triassic **A**

Late Triassic–Early Jurassic **B**

Late Jurassic–Early Cretaceous **C**

Late Cretaceous–Early Eocene **D**

Early Miocene **E**

Late Miocene–Pliocene **F**

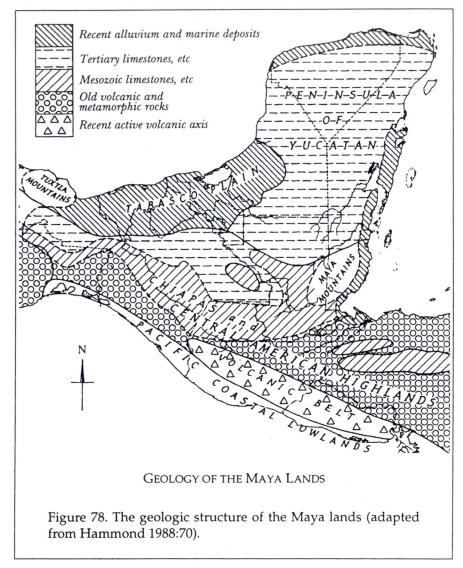

GEOLOGY OF THE MAYA LANDS

Figure 78. The geologic structure of the Maya lands (adapted from Hammond 1988:70).

On the western side of the Maya area, the rivers drain into the Gulf of Mexico. The largest, with a basin that includes most of the Petén and a major part of the Quiché-Verapaz highlands, is the Usumacinta. The first of its tributaries, the Río de la Pasión rises near the Maya Mountains and drains southern Petén. The second, the Río Negro or Chixoy, originates in the continental divide near the headwaters of the Motagua and the Grijalva and zigzags north through the mountain ranges of western Guatemala, forming part of the border between Guatemala and Mexico. The Usumacinta is joined by the waters of the Lacantún and Jatat. To the north, the

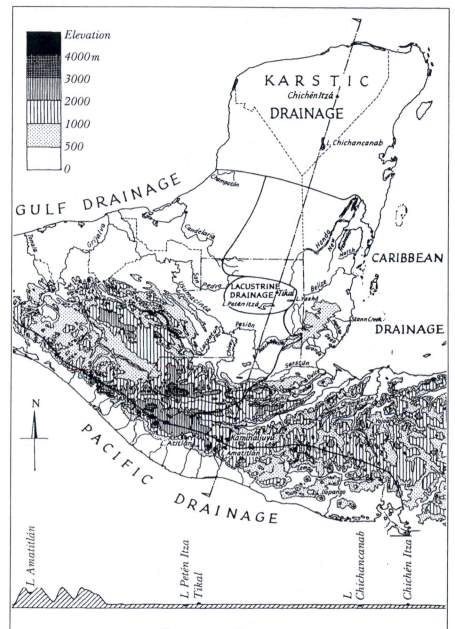

RELIEF AND DRAINAGE

Figure 79. Relief and drainage of the Maya lands showing the major drainage basins. The cross section along the transect indicated on the map shows the relative flatness of the Yucatán Platform in the Lowlands (adapted from Hammond 1988:73).

Candelaria and Champotón drain the southwestern sector of the Yucatán Peninsula (Hammond 1988:78).

The Usumacinta River, one of the major rivers in Mexico, forms part of the border between Mexico and Guatemala, flowing through a region of impervious sedimentary rocks. Unlike the semikarstic drainage basins of rivers like the Hondo, Candelaria, and San Pedro, the Usumacinta cannot rely on a reservoir effect from sediments it dissects. Its flow, therefore, is highly dependent on runoff. Discharge data for the Usumacinta for the years 1949 to 1969 indicate that the average monthly flow for the lowest month of the dry season represents 15 percent of the average monthly flow for the high month of the rainy season. In other words, after a six-month drought, the flow normally drops 85 percent from the end of the rainy season, and often over 90 percent. In some years, the low flow represents only 10 percent of the high flow. According to Alfred Siemens, the arithmetic mean of variations between annual extreme high and extreme low water levels along the Usumacinta is around 10 meters, while the variations on the Hondo, Candelaria, and San Pedro Rivers are of the order of 1 meter. Clearly, during an annual cycle, when the rain stops, the flow drops—dramatically. According to the staff at the Instituto Nacional de Electrificación (INDE), in Guatemala City, no studies have ever been done to determine under what conditions the Usumacinta might go dry. Given the early collapse in the ninth century of the cities along its banks, its apparent dependence on runoff, the evidence of the rapid drop in its flow rate during the dry season, and the severe reduction in flow during the drought of 1998, however, one must wonder whether the Usumacinta might indeed go dry during a prolonged, multiyear drought (INDE staff, Guatemala City, 1986, personal communication; *Reforma* 1998:1; Secretaría de Recursos Hidráulicos nd:207–209; Siemens 1978:121–123).

As we saw in chapter 6, Joel Gunn, William Folan, and Hubert Robichaux have analyzed the river discharge data for the Candelaria River system in the state of Campeche in southern Mexico. As can be seen in figure 79, the Candelaria drains the southwestern portion of the Yucatán Peninsula, emptying into the Laguna de Términos on the Gulf coast. It is the principal river draining the central semikarst. The river is fed from a combination of surface runoff, marshes, and underground reservoirs formed by karstic processes. In spite of the reservoir effect, the volume of water flowing in the Candelaria system is related to the precipitation in the catchment basin. It may be a better record, in fact, than individual weather station data because it is not affected by exceptional local events (Gunn, Folan, and Robichaux 1991:1–8; 1995:9).

For the period 1958 to 1984, they compared the discharge data to the Global Energy Balance, the average annual temperature of the atmosphere. The highest levels of precipitation occurred during hot global conditions, while warm and cool conditions resulted in less rainfall, and cold conditions provoked the lowest level of regional discharge. During their study period, cold conditions yielded less than half the discharge in winter, and resulted in a late onset and early termination of the rainy period with dry summers. Warm periods, on the other hand, produced an early onset of the rainy season and high river discharges. River flows, then, are lower during periods of global cold indicating that precipitation was lower as well. It should be noted that during the study period, there was not an episode of severe Northern Hemispheric cold. By applying our meteorological model to the results obtained in Gunn's, Folan's, and Robichaux's study, severe cold during the ninth century might have resulted in severely reduced precipitation and severely reduced river flow (Gunn, Folan, and Robichaux 1991:1–8; 1995:9).

KARSTIC DRAINAGE

North of the Champotón, lies an area characterized by an entirely different pattern of karstic drainage. The limestone formations in this region are riddled with solution channels that make the rock look like a sponge. The permeability of the formations is extremely high and water flows quite readily through them. Cavern complexes are quite common. When a cavern roof collapses, it leaves a sinkhole, known locally as a *cenote*, particularly in eastern Yucatán. They are generally cylindrical in shape, with steep vertical sides, as much as 30 m (100 ft) deep, as seen in figure 80. If the surface of the land is low enough and the cenote deep enough to reach the water table, then year round water is available, as, for example, in the famous cenotes at Chichén Itza. In western Yucatán, cenotes are large caverns, with imposing openings and huge vaulted chambers with pools of water at the bottom. Water levels in the cenotes rise and fall with the rainy and dry seasons. The karstic region is characterized by a lack of surface streams or lakes. Diego de Landa, Bishop of Yucatán during 1566, wrote, "Nature worked so differently in this country in the matter of rivers and springs, which in all the rest of the world run on top of the land, that here in this country all run and flow through secret passages under it" (Casares 1905:220; Landa 1566:139).

Although rainfall is high, it is seasonal and requires storage for use during the extended dry season. The type of storage usually provided in non-karstified areas by rivers and aquifers to maintain the base flow of streams does not exist in Yucatán. The extreme permeability of the limestone causes rapid infiltration of rainfall and nearly simultaneous discharge of groundwater to the ocean. The limestone is so permeable and movement through the system so rapid that not enough head is developed in the groundwater to provide adequate storage in the aquifer. Salt water encroachment from the ocean which surrounds the peninsula on three sides is also a problem. The large hydraulic conductivity, along with the lack of high hydraulic heads, permits an extensive body of sea water to underlie at least the entire northern third of the peninsula and perhaps all of it (Back and Lesser 1981:121).

The fresh water lens which underlies most of the peninsula is signifi-cant. The Ghyben-Herzberg principle states that for every foot of fresh water above mean sea level, the thickness of the fresh water lens floating on salt water of ocean water density is about 40 feet, in other words, a 40 to 1 ratio. Donald Doehring and Joseph Butler have estimated the fresh water lens, shown in figure 81, to be about 52 m (172 ft) thick at Chichén It-za, with its surface about 1.3 m (4.3 ft) above mean sea level. William Back and Bruce Hanshaw estimated the lens's maximum thickness at 70 m (230 ft), thinning to near zero at the coasts. Its thickness pales in compari-son with Florida's 700 m (2,300 ft) layer, but it is adequate to survive years of drought and provide fresh drinking water to those relying on it, provid-ed the cenote or well penetrates the fresh water lens to a sufficient depth. Some wells and cenotes with shallow depth of water in them will go dry during droughts and, in fact, some go dry during the winter dry season (Back and Hanshaw 1970:330, 364; Back and Lesser 1981:121; Doehring and Butler 1974:593).

Karstic geology is the product of perhaps two separate geologic pro-cesses, one at work at the surface, the other at work in the subsurface. The surface process relies on the following factors:

1.   the existence of soluble rock (limestone, dolomite, chalk),
2.   the presence of carbonic acid (common in humid, tropical forests),
3.   abundant rainfall,
4.   the permeability of the formation,
5.   a favorable topographic and structural situation.
     (Dengo 1983:G-15)

In the subsurface, the Yucatán Platform is underlain by salt water throughout the north and possibly the south as well. At the interface be-tween the salt water and fresh water lies a zone of brackish water, proba-

---

YUCATECAN HYDROLOGY

Figure 80. (*Opposite*) Schematic pattern of the subsurface hy-drology of the Yucatán Peninsula, showing the subsurface flow, cenotes, caverns, freshwater lagoons, and offshore springs. *Black* indicates fresh water (adapted from Siemens 1978:118).

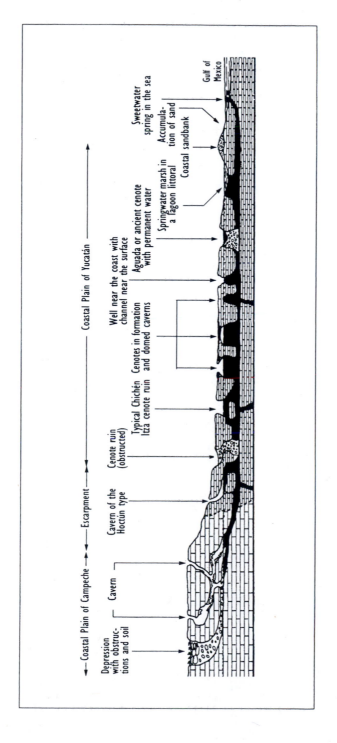

bly much thicker than the fresh water lens. The brackish water is extremely corrosive to limestone, specifically by enhancing the dissolution of aragonite and calcite. As the underlying sea level has risen and fallen repeatedly since the original deposition of the limestones, the layer of brackish water has risen and fallen through the depth of the platform, dissolving solution channels and creating subterranean caverns and cenotes (Back and Hanshaw 1970:364; Back et al 1986:137–140).

The presence of karst and semikarstic geology has very important consequences for Classic Maya civilization. For much of the Maya Lowlands, there is no underground phreatic water level near the surface within reach of water wells. The Maya were known to have dug wells only to about 23 m (75 ft). The rain that falls at the surface travels rapidly through karstic solution channels to the fresh water lens near sea level, or in localized areas, may drain underground to lakes or rivers. In the north, where the surface elevation is relatively low, the fresh water lens is accessible, either through wells, in the far north, or through cenotes, in the cenote zone. Well depths in Yucatán have been estimated to increase at the rate of 18 cm / km (11.8 in / mi) as one moved farther inland. At Chichén Itza, for example, the cenote is approximately 28 m (92 ft) deep, giving access to the fresh water lens which measures about 1.2 m (4 ft) in the cenote. In the east, in low areas along the Caribbean coast, the fresh water lens comes to the surface to form fresh water lakes and lagoons. Farther to the south, however, the surface elevation rises. At Tikal, for example, the first water well to find fresh water was drilled to a depth of 130 m (425 ft). It is clear that the Classic Maya, being a lithic society, could not possibly have drilled a well to 130 m; their limit was about 23 m (75 ft). Wells are also known in the area around Quiriguá, in the Chenes region, and in isolated areas where they tapped small, perched water tables. Water management in the Maya Lowlands, therefore, emphasized collection over diversion, source over allocation. Creating sources of drinking water where none existed was the critical technology which allowed the population of the Petén (Ashmore 1984:151; Casares 1905:215; Matheny 1976:639; Scarborough 1993:78; Scarborough and Gallopin 1991:658).

WATER SUPPLIES

Any city anywhere in the world is necessarily located near sources of fresh drinking water. In the Lowlands, however, such sources were not always naturally available. The Maya had to create them.

Water can be controlled for human consumption, transportation, defense, and ritual use. The examples we will see in this chapter reveal the difference between state controlled community water systems, characteristic of Karl Wittfogel's concept of a hydraulic society, and decentralized, family managed systems. We will also see the difference between more arid areas in the north and more humid areas in the south. The Maya con-

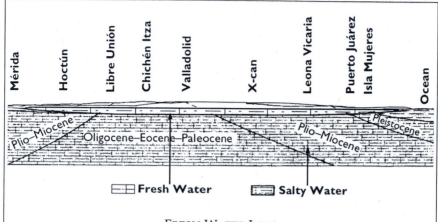

FRESH WATER LENS

Figure 81. An idealized cross section of the Yucatán Peninsula showing the relative distribution of fresh water, thickest in the interior, estimated between 50 and 70m (165 and 230 ft) deep, and thinning towards the coasts. In the center of the diagram, one can see the dry land, shown by the uppermost band of *white*, then the fresh water, a narrow band between the two *bold lines*, and the salt water below (adapted from Back and Hanshaw 1970:366).

trolled water in at least three ways: by draining excess water from inundated lands, by conserving soil moisture, and by collecting and storing water. Reservoir storage and canal diversion systems drew from small perennial drainages and seasonal runoff catchments. To a large extent, in the Maya Lowlands, the water systems define the community (Matheny 1978:186; Scarborough 1991:125, 138; Wittfogel 1957:3).

Large-scale water systems first emerged at the Olmec site of San Lorenzo and in the Maya area at least by the Middle Preclassic. According to Vernon Scarborough, early in the first millennium BC, the Maya were already landscaping their environs. By 1000 BC, they had initiated runoff modifications. The two main components of water management, channelizing or ditching and basin construction, appeared before monumental architecture, as one might expect if water management is critical to the growth of population (Matheny 1982:163; Scarborough 1993:28, 61).

As we have seen, for most of the Maya Lowlands, the phreatic or underground water table was out of reach. For their source of drinking water, therefore, the Classic Maya relied largely on surface water reservoirs, known today as *aguadas*, on subsurface cisterns known as *chultunes*, on sinkholes, known as *cenotes*, and on lakes and fresh water lagoons.

AGUADA AT RANCHO NOYAXCHÉ

Figure 82. The aguada at Rancho Noyaxché in Yucatán. Surface reservoirs provided the only source of drinking water for most Classic Maya cities (illustration by Catherwood in John L. Stephens 1843, 2:139).

NORTHERN YUCATÁN

Northern Yucatán is the region of cenotes—sinkholes or collapsed underground caverns. Because of their depth, the cenotes give access to the underground water table. The water level in different cenotes ranges from 2 m (7 ft) below the surface at Cenote Xlacah at Dzibilchaltún, Yucatán, to 75 m (250 ft) below the surface at Santa Rosa Xtampak. The largest range up to 60 m (200 ft) in diameter. In the north, the locations of communities and their water supplies depend on the cenotes. According to Sylvanus Morley, "They were the most important single factor governing the distribution of the ancient population in northern Yucatán." It should be noted that not all cenotes contain fresh water. Some are saline, others contain stagnant water. Some have small fish and shrimp in them (Matheny 1978:186; 1982:160; Sylvanus Morley 1956:16).

At times, the northern Maya resorted to extreme efforts to utilize cenotes and caverns as their water supply. John Lloyd Stephens wrote that during his visit in February of 1842 to Bolonchen, the water level in the wells was 10–12 ft (3–4 m) from the surface. The wells were actually open-

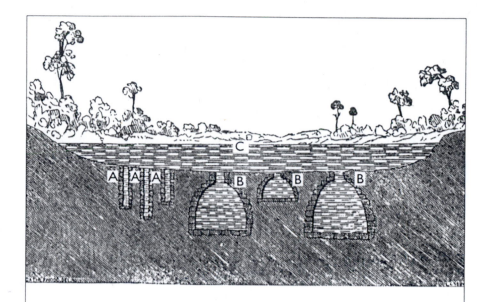

AGUADA AT RANCHO JALAL

Figure 83. The aguada at Rancho Jalal, showing (A) the wells and (B) the chultunes which hold water when the aguada (C) goes dry (adapted from an illustration by Catherwood in John L. Stephens 1843, 2:150).

ings to an underground cavern. Water was present in the wells for eight months of the year. When the wells failed, the residents of the town had to resort to a cave known as Xtacumbi Xunan. A complicated system of ladders provided access to a depth estimated by Stephens to have been 450 ft (140 m) and approximately 1,400 ft (425 m) from the mouth of the cave (Matheny 1978:188; John L. Stephens 1843:2:96–103).

Like most of the Maya region, northern Yucatán has many aguadas, most of which do not hold water for the entire year but dry up during the dry season. Stephens reported finding, during his travels in Yucatán in 1842, an aguada at Rancho Noyaxché, seen in figure 82, whose bottom was lined with large flat stones many layers deep, laid in masonry style, the interstices between filled in with red and brown clay. In the center were four ancient wells, 7 m (24 ft) deep, faced with smooth stone. Along the margin were four hundred *casimbas*, or pits, into which the water filtered and was available when the aguada had gone dry. This was discovered in 1836 by a local *hacendado* who had undertaken an effort to clean out the aguada employing, according to Stephens, fifteen hundred workers and eighty superintendents. The year 1837, according to Stephens, was one of drought.

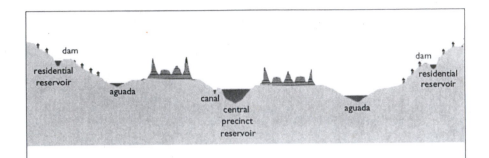

CONCAVE MICROWATERSHED

Figure 84. Late Preclassic hydraulic technology emphasized developing low lying depressions, or *bajos*, as water reservoirs. Scarborough has called these convex microwatersheds. *Dark areas* represent water (adapted from Scarborough 1994:188).

More than a thousand horses and mules watered at the aguada. Some came from Santa Rosa, 30 km (18 mi) away, with barrels on their backs and carried away water. "Families established themselves along the banks; small shops for the sale of necessaries were opened, and the butcher had his shambles with meat." The aguada supplied ample quantities of water and when it went dry, the wells and pits held out until the rains came (John L. Stephens 1843:2:138–141).

At Rancho Jalal, he was shown another aguada, seen in figure 83, which had approximately forty wells and chultunes in its center. When the aguada dried up during the dry season, the wells and chultunes would continue to provide water until the rains returned.

Large-scale water management, a hydraulic society in Wittfogel's terms, began developing in northern Yucatán as early as the Middle Preclassic. Santa Rosa Xtampak, for example had sixty-seven chultunes in operation at least by the Late Preclassic and possibly earlier (Matheny 1978:207).

TIKAL

The earliest landscape engineering was conducted at the margins of low lying depressions, or *bajos*, direct developments of the earliest villages associated with ponded water. As early as the Late Preclassic, the Maya had begun to take advantage of the lower areas of gently sloping landscapes to catch and divert water into man-made channels and reservoirs. Such modifications created what Scarborough has called concave microwatersheds, figure 84, which channeled and retained the natural runoff from the surrounding higher elevations and which held the collected

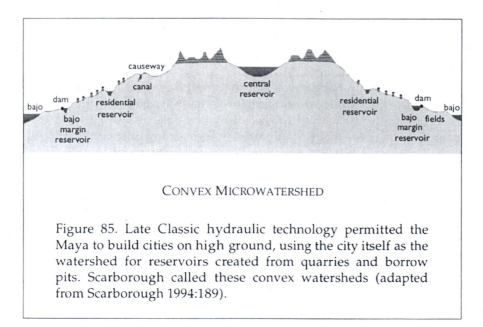

CONVEX MICROWATERSHED

Figure 85. Late Classic hydraulic technology permitted the Maya to build cities on high ground, using the city itself as the watershed for reservoirs created from quarries and borrow pits. Scarborough called these convex watersheds (adapted from Scarborough 1994:189).

water for extended periods of time through the dry seasons. By the end of the Late Preclassic, Cerros, Edzná, and El Mirador, for example, indicate major modifications to their immediate environment with the excavation of canal and reservoir systems and the construction of causeways, used to dam or divert water through depressed zones (Scarborough 1994:187–188).

During the Classic period, according to Scarborough, most large Maya cities occupied elevated natural ridges and hills. In addition to whatever military advantage there might be for such sites, there are definite hydraulic advantages as well. Through a series of accretionary adjustments to the natural terrain, expanding over centuries on the earlier techniques and initially modified land surfaces, hilltop locations were transformed into convex microwatersheds, figure 85, that were specifically engineered to collect and store water during the wet season and distribute it during the dry season. The Maya paved plazas and courtyards and canted these catchment surfaces toward the elevated reservoirs where water was collected and held for extended periods. In short, the city planners designed their cities to be watersheds. As they removed stone and fill to build their structures, they converted the resulting quarries and borrow pits into reservoirs. The elevated sites of the reservoirs permitted water to be released by way of gravity flow to residential zones on the flanks of the hillocks and then on to the lower bajo margin reservoirs and agricultural fields. The absence of household groups around the bajo margin reservoirs suggests that the arriving water may have been polluted by its passage through the residential areas upslope. The lessons learned from Preclassic experimentation were incorporated into these structures. Causeways functioned as dams and clean water for domestic consumption was spatially separated from water for agricultural use (Scarborough 1992:42; 1993:20; 1994:189; Scarborough and Gallopin 1991:661).

Peter Harrison has pointed out that the plazas and other catchment zones are always free of trash middens containing food or human waste, as, for example, the whole of the Central Acropolis at Tikal. It would appear that any waste that was produced in the catchment areas was carefully collected so that it did not enter the water system and foul the water (Harrison 1993:83–84).

Water is needed on a daily basis for human subsistence. It is critical to surviving the dry season. The reservoirs at Tikal were part of a complex water management system that allowed the Maya to collect and hold water during the rainy season and distribute it during the dry season. Control of the water system would have been a source of power in Tikal. Reservoirs are discrete and controllable, especially where they have been designed as part of a city's layout. Access to the reservoirs and to their water could be monitored and restricted. According to Anabel Ford, "The centralized drinking water resources could thus have solidified ties among members of the elite and served to integrate their constituent populations." The discretion to release water to the surrounding population would certainly promote the authority of those responsible for planning, constructing, maintaining, and controlling the water management system (Richard E. W. Adams 1991:632; Ford 1996:301; Scarborough 1992:39, 42; 1996:313).

Ford goes on to note that some Maya nobles of the Classic period referred to themselves as *Ah Nab* or Waterlily People, from the plants which grew in all of the reservoirs, thus indicating how closely their own self-identity was tied to their control of the critical resource, water. (See figure 86.) Interestingly, while water lilies and other floating aquatic plants do lower the temperature of the water and thus lower the rate of evaporation somewhat, they are major consumers of water and need copious quantities for their survival. Nevertheless, their life cycle requirements act to purify standing water by removing pollutants, like nitrogen, phosphorus, sludge particles, organic chemicals, and heavy metals from sewage waters. Aquatic plants, therefore, significantly lower contaminants from effluent, creating potable water. Some modern water treatment facilities have been designed in which water flows through a series of tanks containing aquatic plants not unlike the process described by Scarborough at Tikal (Ford 1996:302).

Gary Gallopin, who carried out an extensive study of the water supply system at Tikal, has characterized the water situation in the Tikal region as similar to that of a desert during much of the year. Given the scarcity of natural surface sources of potable water, he said, Tikal was effectively a seasonal desert, even though rainfall levels were above those of a desert.

Nab

Winik

K'in Ma

Na

WATER LILY LORD GLYPH

Figure 86. *Nab Winik Makina*, Water Lily Lord, in Maya hiero-glyphs, redrawn on the basis of Tikal Temple IV, Lintel 3 (adapted from Ford 1996:303).

As a result, the inhabitants of Tikal built large paved plazas which were engineered to capture rainfall and channel it into reservoirs, thereby creating an oasis in that desert (Gallopin 1990:6).

The reservoirs in Tikal consisted of five principal types, as defined by Robert Carr and James Hazard:

1. Deep dug or constructed reservoirs are very large reservoirs lined with plaster or clay and located in the city center, which was entirely covered with plaster surfaces on the buildings and plazas.
2. Modified aguadas are even larger than deep dug reservoirs, located away from the city center and away from residential areas, with very large catchment basins, but less reliable runoff. Once natural aguadas in a deep bed of impermeable clay near bajos, they were expanded using earthenwork or clay dikes.
3. Natural aguadas were much smaller, located in or next to bajos away from residential areas.
4. Quarry pits were used to hold water after their limestone had been removed.
5. Pozas are small depressions about one meter deep, usually associated with residential structures, perhaps intended for private use (Carr and Hazard quoted in Gallopin 1990:19–22).

Nearly all sites in the Maya area have reservoirs of one or more of the above types, an indication that water storage and water planning was not limited to Tikal but was a pan-Maya problem (Scarborough and Gallopin 1991:660).

The engineering technology demonstrated in the construction of the reservoirs includes apparent desilting tanks, floodgates, dams, weirs, water control earthenworks, and dikes in various locations and combinations, indicative of a complex system of water gathering and storage. Some catchment surfaces were treated with various materials to improve the capture of rainfall, including plaster and clay. Gallopin estimates, however, that portable ceramic containers, like pots and jars, would not have provided significant storage capacity (Gallopin 1990:23–45).

Given the desiccation of the bajos during the dry season, water in reservoirs at the margins of bajos may have been intended for agricultural use and may have been polluted in passing through the residential areas. These reservoirs may have been used to keep the bajos productive through the year, even through the dry season. Excess water was handled by preventing water from entering the reservoir, or by releasing it at the bottom through a spillway or sluice. Water that did not enter the reservoirs directly would flow to the fields. The ability to direct water either to the fields or the reservoir allowed the reservoirs to act as buffers, permitting better control of soil moisture in the fields (Gallopin 1990:54; Scarborough 1983:741; Scarborough and Gallopin 1991:660–661).

Water supply is determined by the volume of storage available, the volume of rainwater captured, and the loss due to withdrawal, evaporation, and seepage. Taking the central $9\,km^2$ ($3.5\,mi^2$) of Tikal as an example, Gallopin calculated that the known tanks would have been large enough to provide a surplus of water under ordinary conditions. In case the rains failed, however, the tanks held enough emergency drought water for 9,800 residents for about six months. The projected tanks would have provided emergency water for another twelve months. The total capacity, then, of the known reservoirs and those projected to exist is eighteen months of water. Given these results, it is very clear that a protracted multiyear drought would have had devastating consequences for the residents of Tikal. They would have run out of water. Their main problem would not have been famine, although famine would certainly accompany a protracted drought. Human beings can last without food for weeks. They can last only a short few days without water. Their most serious problem would have been a lack of water to drink (Gallopin 1990:85–87).

EDZNÁ

During the Late Preclassic a huge hydraulic system, consisting of more than 20km (12mi) of canals and an extensive array of reservoirs, was constructed at Edzná. This system was probably operational by AD 1. The longest canal was over 12km (6mi) long and was as wide as 50m (165ft) at its widest point. At least twelve canals were constructed which converge on the city center something like spokes on a wheel. Other lines visible from aerial photographs may also prove to be ancient canals as well as roads and trails (Matheny 1976:640–642; 1978:198–206).

On the southern end of the city lies a fortress which is surrounded by a moat connected to the main canal. Ray Matheny calls the construction a fortress because of the presence of the moat, a restricted entry causeway, and strategically located mounds that appear to be in defensible positions. The moat was probably dug for defensive purposes and the main canal was dug to provide it with water (Matheny 1976:640–642; 1978:198–206).

The construction of this system was a major undertaking that required a highly organized labor force over a considerable period of time. More soil was moved in building the system than was moved in constructing the Pyramid of the Sun at Teotihuacan. The canal-moat system was clearly part of a grand scheme of city planning designed to collect and store rainwater (Matheny 1976:640–642; 1978:198–206).

The locations of the fortress, main canal, and radiating canals are not the result of haphazard planning, according to Matheny. A hydraulic system designed to bring water into the populated areas of the city was laid out symmetrically, with the city center as the focus. There is also evidence of deliberate water control. Reservoirs in the northwest sector are at a higher elevation than connecting canals. As the water ran from these reservoirs to the south end of the canals near the city center, small feeder canals directed it to other reservoirs closer to public buildings and residences. This, of course, is the reverse of the distribution process seen at Tikal. There is evidence of tanks that were probably used to clean the water collected in the northern canals. From the holding and cleaning tanks, water was directed to other holding tanks, presumably for consumption (Matheny 1976:642; 1978:203; Scarborough 1993:34).

Matheny reported in 1978, after 80 percent of Edzná had been surveyed, that it was comprised of four hundred seventy-one known house mounds, approximately one hundred public buildings and platforms, thirty-one canals, eighty-four reservoirs, a moated fortress, and eighteen rock quarries. The peak population appears to have occurred during the Late Preclassic (Matheny 1978:204).

PUUC

The western side of the Yucatán Peninsula is drier than the east. Its vegetation is tropophytic—adapted to a moist summer and dry winter—and it is classified in the Dry Evergreen Formation Series. The rainfall is roughly half that of the central Petén and subject to large variation. For six months of the year, the Puuc undergoes desertlike conditions. There is no surface water anywhere in the Puuc, except for occasional small, shallow basins known as *sartenejas*. The phreatic water table lies 40 to 90 m (130 to 300 ft) below the surface, well beyond the ability of the Maya to dig wells (McAnany 1990:264–265).

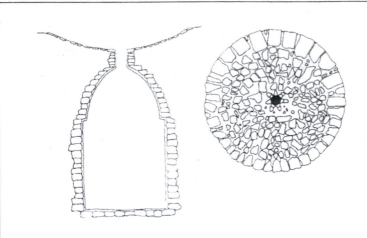

TYPICAL CHULTUN AND CATCHMENT AT LABNA

Figure 87. A chultun and catchment pavement from Labna, Yucatán (Matheny 1982:165).

The challenge for the residents of the Puuc was not only how to buffer themselves against the dry season, but also how to deal with periods of extremely low or no rainfall. Lacking access to any water sources at all, the residents of the Puuc constructed bell shaped water storage facilities known as *chultunes* in order to store water for the dry season. The chultunes of the Puuc are different from those of other regions of the Lowlands with regard to where they were located, how they were constructed, and their function. Chultunes for water storage are bell shaped hemispheroids with flat bottoms and openings in the tops about 45 cm (18 in) wide. Their necks open onto rainfall catchments constructed by contouring the platform surface to channel runoff into the chultunes (figures 87 and 88.) Then openings were punched through a limestone caprock and the storage area was dug into soft, white *sascab* or caliche. The neck was lined with a circular wall of stones behind which a layer of platform fill was deposited and contoured to slope towards the opening. They were plastered on the inside with several thick coats, sometimes painted red, and were served by a paved, plastered, or fill catchment area. When filled, they were sealed by a stone plug to keep out children, animals, and dirt. They are found in major numbers under plazas in ceremonial centers and in small residential settings under habitation platforms (Matheny 1978:207–208; 1982:163; McAnany 1990:265–267, 276–277; John L. Stephens 1843, 2:138, 2:148–150).

Using a storage volume of 30,000 liters (8,000 gal), Back and J. M. Lesser estimated that a chultun could have comfortably supplied drinking

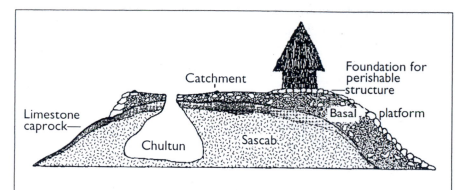

Figure 88. Cross section of a chultun and catchment pavement from Sayil (adapted from McAnany 1990:281).

cooking water for about twenty-five people for one year. The number of chultunes in the larger centers could have supplied up to 6,000 people. Patricia McAnany, on the other hand, estimated that chultunes in the Puuc could support thirty people each, yielding populations for Classical cities of the Puuc Hills ranging between 6,000 and 12,000 inhabitants. Chultunes are believed to have been in use since the Late Preclassic period in northern Yucatán. In contrast to other Maya regions, most water storage in the Puuc was accomplished at the level of the family rather than at the level of the community (Back and Lesser 1981:124; Matheny 1978:207–208; 1982:163; McAnany 1990:265–267, 276–277; John l. Stephens 1843, 2:138, 2:148–150).

In addition to chultunes, some cities in the Puuc utilized other methods of water collection and storage. An 1865 map of Uxmal, for example, indicates the presence of six reservoirs, feeder and collection canals, and a moated fortress, as well as many chultunes (Matheny 1978:209; 1982:168).

Canals

Canals have been identified along many lowland rivers in the Tabasco Plain, along the Grijalva and Candelaria Rivers, and into Veracruz. The primary purpose of these canals was to provide drainage for the adjoining fields. In addition, several canals along the Candelaria bypass regions of sharp bends and connect the main channel in a straight course. These were believed by Matheny to have been constructed to shorten the travel distance by canoe, but may have been designed for flood control. The canals usually occur on the floodplains where the rivers are sluggish. Hundreds of small, narrow canals are known to exist along the Candelaria. In addition to drainage during the wet season, the canals were probably used for fish culture. Rich riverbank soil was collected and used to build up the raised fields reported near the riverbanks. Splash irrigation could be employed during the dry season, and the canals provided a means for transportation of products and people by canoe. Alfred Siemens and Dennis Puleston reported over 180km (110mi) of canals near the site of El Tigre along the San Pedro and Candelaria Rivers. Richard E. W. Adams, W. E. Brown, and Patrick Culbert studied synthetic aperture radar data from the Lowlands and found evidence of widespread canal systems associated with agriculture in the southern and intermediate areas, near Seibal, Tikal, and El Mirador, along the Candelaria River, the Río Hondo, the New River, and at Cerros in northern Belize. Ground confirmation in northern Belize confirmed the presence of canals and raised fields as indicated by the radar data (Adams, Brown, and Culbert 1981:1457–1460; Matheny 1978:192–198).

DISCUSSION

The phreatic water level under most of the Yucatán Peninsula lies just above sea level. For most of the Lowlands, that effectively means that there are no underground water resources. The water table was accessible in the north only in the cenote zone, where the collapse of the cenotes allowed access to the water table, in the far north and east where the elevation approaches sea level and the Maya could dig wells, and along the east coast where the water table comes to the surface in the form of fresh water lagoons. In addition, large quantities of fresh water are available in Lake Petén Itzá. These are the only areas where populations were living at the time of Spanish contact.

The Maya lived in what Gallopin has called a seasonal desert. In order to inhabit most of the Lowlands, they had to design and build their own water resources. For the most part, they had no underground water or lakes. Scarborough's accretionary model describes the gradual modification of the landscape to provide water, thereby making it habitable. Maya hydraulic engineers began by modifying low lying bajos to improve their ability to store water. In other areas, chultunes, canals, and aguadas were used to store water.

At many sites, they developed an extremely clever engineering concept to design the cities themselves to catch the water they needed from rainfall and to store it for later use. The design concept was brilliant. They excavated the quarries and borrow pits for construction material so that they could be converted to reservoirs. By building on high elevations, the water could be distributed by gravity flow through the city winding up finally in the fields to irrigate the crops.

The entire system, however, regardless of the water storage techniques employed, depended on rainfall. Gallopin estimated that the known reservoirs plus those presumed to have existed in Tikal held only an eighteen month supply of water for the residents. Unless the reservoirs were replenished by regular rainfall, the Maya were in trouble. The Maya produced a brilliant engineering solution to the problem of living in a seasonal desert with no natural water resources. But it was their Achilles' heel. The civilization, the cultural tradition including the engineering, built up over millennia, had a fatal vulnerability: its total dependence on consistent rainfall to replenish its reservoirs. When the rains failed, the reservoirs dried up, and the people had no water to drink.

The only areas where Maya culture survived the devastation of the Collapse, as noted above, are those areas that had water. The only common thread linking the surviving communities is the availability of long-term, stable sources of drinking water. Certainly in a severe drought, as we have seen, crop failures, famine, epidemics, rebellion, and war are part of the normal response. The surviving cities undoubtedly suffered the same crop failures, famine, epidemics, and war as those that were abandoned. The difference, it appears, between life and death for the Classic Maya was water.

10. Palaeoclimatology

A among the more persistent notions in Maya archaeology, as Bruce Dahlin has pointed out, is that the climate of the Yucatán Peninsula was stable throughout the Preclassic and Classic periods and that the climate today is an accurate reflection of the climates of prehistoric times. The notion originated with Ellsworth Huntington and was reiterated by Page in 1933 who stated, "The theory that marked changes of climate have had pronounced effects upon the Maya civilization in Yucatán...[has been]...completely discarded by many climatologists because of the absence of direct information and it is doubtful whether there is any satisfactory evidence indicating that important climatic changes have taken place in the Yucatán Peninsula subsequent to the Fifth Century AD...." (Ellsworth Huntington 1915; Page quoted in Dahlin 1983:245).

The Yucatecan climate has not been static over the Holocene, the 12,000-year period since the end of the last ice age. Estimated precipitation rates for hundreds of years at a time have ranged from 50 percent of the twentieth century's average to 125 percent. In other words, the Holocene climate has ranged from severe, sustained drought to prolonged, copious rainfall.

In this chapter, we will look at worldwide palaeoclimatic records in order to identify periods of clear hemispheric climatic anomalies which would have implications for Yucatecan weather. The Maya Lowlands are not isolated from the rest of our planet. When hemispheric climatic changes occur, the Lowlands are also affected.

We will see that periods of widespread, severe cold were coincident with the Preclassic Abandonment, the Hiatus, the Collapse, and the Postclassic Abandonment. According to the hypothesis presented in this book, these would be periods conducive to drought in the Lowlands.

But did drought really occur, especially at the time of the Collapse? We will look at palaeoclimatic evidence for drought at the time of the Preclassic Abandonment, the Hiatus, the Collapse, and the Postclassic Abandonment. In particular, we will see evidence from Yucatecan lake sediment cores, from Lake Chichancanab, which provide unambiguous evidence for a severe 200-year drought from AD 800 to 1000. This drought, in fact, was the most severe in the last 7,000 years. Another core from Punta Laguna shows the most serious drought of the 3,500-year record. Both occurred precisely at the time of the Maya Collapse.

ICE AGE ARIDITY

During the last episode of worldwide cold, the Wisconsin Glacial Stage, the Yucatán Peninsula was an arid area of marsh, savanna, and juniper scrub, looking much more like areas of West Texas than like today's tropical seasonal forests. Abundant postdepositional gypsum in the clays and the presence of kaolinite in cores from Lakes Quexil and Salpetén indicate the lakes, during the last glacial period, were shallow and moderately saline and that lake levels were 30 to 40 m (100 to 130 ft) lower than at present. The lakes themselves may well have been ephemeral pools and halophytic or salty marshes. Temperatures at Lake Quexil were 6.5° to 8°C (12° to 14.5°F) cooler than today. The climate was extremely arid, lasting through the end of the Younger Dryas—about 8000 BC. Pleistocene aridity in Yucatán and the Petén is not unique in tropical America. It is coincident with widespread aridity throughout lowland Central America, montane Costa Rica, and lowland northern South America, and perhaps all of the Tropics. In all the Yucatecan records, tree pollen is rare prior to 8000 BC (Deevey, Brenner, and Binford 1983:211–212; Islebe and Hooghiemstra 1997:589; Leyden 1984:4856; 1985:1289; 1987:407, 410; Leyden et al 1993:165; Markgraf 1989:1).

Records from lowland Central and South America indicate with sufficient detail a widespread, rapid, stepwise Holocene succession of vegetation types, replacing the late Pleistocene grasslands between 8000 BC and 6500 BC. The early Holocene forest pollen in the Petén included pine, oak, and elm along with certain rainforest elements. These early Holocene pollen assemblages were replaced after 7000 BC by semievergreen tropical forest elements. Lakes began to rise, except in northern Yucatán, where Lake Chichancanab continued dry. Succeeding the late Pleistocene dry lakes were marshes or ponds, then ephemeral or shallow saline lakes, and finally large, deep, fresh lakes. This succession is credited to a stepwise increase in precipitation. Rising sea levels during the period would have influenced lake levels in low elevations. From 6500 BC onwards, semievergreen forests and savanna woodlands were replaced by deciduous forests. Lake Chichancanab began to rise rapidly about 5750 BC. Lake levels in northern Yucatán, however, remained low until 3500 BC, after which moister conditions ensued. From 1000 BC to 500 BC, records show declining forest cover, coupled with an increase in savanna woodlands. The simultaneous decrease in water levels suggests that effective moisture decreased as well (Dahlin 1983:249; Hodell, Curtis, and Brenner 1995:392; Markgraf 1989:8).

Because of the absence of pollen prior to 11,000 BC, no decisions can be made with regard to the full glacial climate of the region. With regard to the late Pleistocene and early Holocene, around 10,000 BC, conditions were cool and dry throughout the lowlands, a continuation of the glacial mode. Central American temperatures have been estimated to have been 4°C (7°F) colder in Costa Rica, for example. In the Yucatán and Petén, the climate was arid and supported sparse vegetation. Vera Markgraf has estimated general precipitation decreases of 50 percent for the tropical lowlands during the full glacial. By 7500 BC, precipitation levels had reached or even exceeded modern levels by as much as 25 percent, and temperatures were comparable to today. After 6500 BC, reports from some sites indicate moisture levels decreased to a period of mid-Holocene aridity, appearing to span 1,000 years centered around 4000 BC, as reflected in records from Mexico and the tropical lowlands. At Lake Chichancanab, however, it would appear that distinctly drier conditions did not occur until after 1000 BC (Covich and Stuiver 1974:688; Deevey, Brenner, and Binford 1983:215; Leyden 1985:1289–1293; 1987:412; Markgraf 1989:9, 20–21).

The Petén forest, which dates from about 8000 BC, is not a rainforest, but rather a tropical seasonal forest, characterized by wet and dry seasons. The present Petén forest is the most mesic (moderate moisture) yet shown to have replaced xeric (arid) Pleistocene vegetation. Post-Maya forests regenerated rapidly, but even after four hundred years are not identical to pre-Maya forests. Post-Maya forests are more open, possibly due to a drier climate as well as some continued habitation of parts of the area (Leyden 1984:4856; 1987:412).

LAKE SEDIMENTS

In areas that have been heavily populated and where intensive agriculture has been practiced, like most of the Maya Lowlands, the soils have been so disturbed that they are not reliable indicators of palaeoclimates. Sediments in the lakes, however, have not been disturbed and, therefore, contain a reliable record of the debris which fell to the bottom over the course of history, including pollen, shells, carbon fragments, plant fragments, and so on, which can be studied to determine the nature of past climates and their timing.

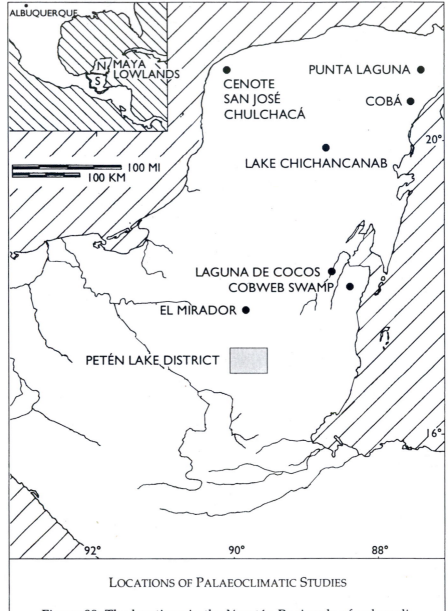

LOCATIONS OF PALAEOCLIMATIC STUDIES

Figure 89. The locations in the Yucatán Peninsula of palaeoclimatological studies mentioned in the text (underlying geographical map adapted from Lowe 1985:2).

Pedological and archaeological evidence recovered by Dahlin and M. E. Chambers from El Mirador indicate a severely dry period that is co-incident with a savanna encroachment, a drop in lake levels, and the aban-donment of the site in AD 150, the time of the Preclassic Abandonment. According to Dahlin, its collapse represents what must have been a terrible moment in lowland Maya prehistory. The evidence in the lake region to the south and Lakes Chichancanab, Cobá, and Macanxoc to the north in-dicate that the dry interval affected most of the Yucatán Peninsula (Dahlin 1983:248–251, 253, 257).

Population levels in the Late Preclassic rivalled Late Classic popula-tions in terms of size and perhaps even number of sites, according to Dah-lin. The archaeological records of many sites can be interpreted as both attempts and failures in coping responses to the onset of prolonged and se-vere drought conditions, particularly in the north. In the southern Lake District, the Early Classic saw an expansion of grasslands, a drop in lake levels, and a reduction of human populations. Hence, climate and, in par-ticular, aridity rather than human disturbance seems to be implicated (Dahlin 1983:257; 1988:19).

Particle size studies of lake sediment cores taken from Lake Quexil and Lake Macanché show two major population declines, the first at the end of the Preclassic into the Early Classic, the second at the end of the Classic (Michael Binford 1983:201; Brenner 1983:206).

Ursula Cowgill and G. E. Hutchinson observed evidence in a core tak-en from Lake Petenxil which indicated that water levels during the Classic were higher, which they attributed to local natural factors plus human dis-turbance. Another possible cause is increased rainfall during the Classic, which resulted in higher lake levels, increased crops, and greater food pro-duction, which supported heavier populations (Cowgill and Hutchinson 1966:121–126).

At Lake Eckixil, the quantity of maize pollen in the record comes to an abrupt halt around AD 900. It does not dwindle down, as one might expect if soil impoverishment were a major factor in the Collapse. Frederick Wise-man concluded, "The collapse was not only a hierarchical phenomenon but also a general catastrophe that affected the bottom of the social pyra-mid, the Maya farmer. The change from an agricultural regime dominated by Zea [maize] and weeds to a forest dominated landscape occurred rap-idly....Rapid depopulation of the Peten [occurred] over less than a centu-ry....If this change coincided with the cessation of temple construction, as I suspect, the event was truly an all encompassing catastrophe, not a slow degeneration" (Wiseman 1978:114).

According to J. Platt Bradbury and his colleagues, the limnological changes seen in a core from Laguna de Cocos, Albion Island, northern Be-lize, may be due to the impact of Maya agriculture, but they cannot ignore the possibility of climatic change. They believe the intense agricultural ac-tivity at the end of the Classic occurred during a time of somewhat drier climate. Furthermore, lower water levels in the lakes at that time may be due to climate rather than agriculture. "These data are interpreted to reflect falling lake levels and perhaps increasing salinity coincident with a decline in agricultural activity. A climatic change to drier conditions is likely to be ultimately responsible" (Bradbury et al 1990:138, 149).

At Lake Chichancanab, Yucatán, near the Yucatán-Quintana Roo border roughly 100km (60mi) south-southwest of Chichén Itza, Alan Covich and Minze Stuiver reported that a lake sediment core indicated a stable, deep lake from about 3500 BC to around AD 450, although, since the resolution of their core was not very good, the ending date of the phase is approximate. Since then, lake levels have been in a "shallow-water phase" (Bradbury et al 1990:149; Covich and Stuiver1974:688).

David Hodell, Jason Curtis, and Mark Brenner have reported more precise evidence in a sediment core from Lake Chichancanab. They have determined that an arid period occurred between AD 800 and 1000, with the peak aridity occurring at AD 922. According to them, "results from Lake Chichancanab provide the first unambiguous evidence for climate drying between AD 800 and 1000." This period of aridity represents the driest episode of the past 7,000 years, a period of severe aridity compared to the rest of the Holocene. According to Hodell, studies are ongoing to quantify the degree of aridity, but "climatic conditions were certainly anomalously dry relative to the remainder of the mid to late Holocene." In fact, he said, "it was pretty seriously dry." Today, for example, the lake is not precipitating gypsum at the coring site. At the time of the Terminal Classic, it was precipitating significant quantities at the coring site, an indication that evaporation was causing the lake waters to become saturated with calcium sulfate, resulting in the precipitation of gypsum. The findings are confirmed by analyses of oxygen isotopes in the sediments. In fact, multiple lines of evidence point to increased aridity between AD 800 and 1000 at Lake Chichancanab (David Hodell, June 19, 1995, personal communication; June 21, 1995, letter to author; Hodell, Curtis, and Brenner 1995:391-394).

Curtis, Hodell, and Brenner examined a core, taken from a second lowland lake, Punta Laguna in Quintana Roo, which extends back 3,500 years. They report a persistently dry period during the Late Classic and Early Postclassic, the period of maximum aridity for the 3,500 years represented by the core. Within this time span, there were three exceptionally arid events centered at AD 862 ±50 cal yr, 986, and 1019, and a dry episode centered around 1391. In addition, they identified a major dry event at AD 585 ±50 cal yr, coincident with the Hiatus. The next exceptional dry period occurred at 1368 to 1429 ±50 cal yr, roughly coincident with the Postclassic Abandonment of the northern Yucatecan cities. Evidence from this lake, then, identifies droughts at the time of the Hiatus, the Collapse, and the Postclassic Abandonment (Curtis, Hodell, and Brenner 1996:37, 45–46).

Evidence of a drying phase after AD 900 was reported by Barbara Leyden and her colleagues from Cenote San José Chulchacá in northern Yucatán. Their short core indicates higher water levels and less salinity in the cenote before AD 900 and more salinity afterwards. The short core indicates a wetter period from about AD 130 to 900, followed by drier conditions. The last thousand years have shown gradually increasing freshness. For the last ninety years, conditions have been fresher than most other periods since the Terminal Preclassic (Leyden et al 1996:41–45; Leyden, Brenner, and Dahlin 1998:119).

CARBON FRAGMENTS

Carbon fragments are the product of fire. Given their association with periodically lowered lake levels, they may be indicative of fires that swept the countryside during periods of drought consistent with ethnographic reports from *The Books of Chilam Balam* that the forests and the countryside burn during drought. According to Hague Vaughan, the total influx of carbonized fragments, both large and small, declines in both the Petenxil and Quexil lake basins during the Classic, although in Quexil at least, the influx of large fragments increases (because of mechanical abrasion in the Petenxil cores, the size of the fragments could not be determined). The fragments may be agricultural in origin or natural and related to climate. Vaughan points out that the size of fragments in the sediments decreases as the distance of the fires from the lake increases. The increasing size would indicate that the fires were closer to the lakes. Shortly before the Collapse, carbonized fragments had practically disappeared from the record, but an increase in carbon fragments occurred at the time of the Collapse itself. Once population reached its lowest level, the influx of large carbonized fragments returns. Vaughan indicates that there were three episodes of reduced rainfall and lowered lake levels during the Postclassic and Early Post-Maya periods indicated by increased carbon fragments. In the Petexbatun area, Nicholas Dunning has also indicated the presence of charcoal fragments in lake cores from Lake Tamarindito during the Late Classic (Dunning et al 1998; Vaughan 1979:73, 128–129, 137).

It is interesting that research conducted by Sally Horn and Robert Sanford has determined that fires raged through the tropical rainforests of the La Selva Biological Station in the northern Caribbean lowlands of Costa Rica and in the *páramo* surrounding Cerro Chirripó in the Cordillera de Talamanca at the same time. Carbonized plant fragments from those fires have been carbon dated to cal AD 880–900 ±70yr. Soil analyses done in the mountains of Costa Rica, at La Chonta in the Cordillera de Talamanca, suggest increased aridity in the century leading up to the fires. The presence of unusual, contemporaneous episodes of fire over so great a distance in the Maya Lowlands and Costa Rica and the evidence of increased aridity in both areas may indicate that the droughts were of a wide regional nature (Horn and Sanford 1992:354; Islebe and Hooghiemstra 1997:600).

MESOAMERICAN DROUGHTS

Detailed studies of twenty-one lake cores from Lake Pátzcuaro in the Mexican state of Michoacán indicate that a period of heavy soil erosion from the surrounding watershed, presumably due to agriculture during the Classic period, came to an end about AD 750. Soil erosion rates then dropped sharply, indicating a sharp drop in agricultural activity lasting until 1100. Sr/Ca ratios in the core indicate a severe, prolonged drought which occurred between roughly AD 750 and 850. Populations, in fact, may have disappeared from the basin during this drought. The droughts affecting Mesoamerica at the end of the Classic may have been quite widespread (Metcalfe et al 1994:141; Street-Perrott 1994:42; O'Hara, Street-Perrott, and Burt 1993:49).

In the Zacapu Basin, also in Michoacán, diatoms record a very rapid drop in lake level about AD 850. Sarah Metcalfe concluded that the drying record at Zacapu a millennium ago "seems to reflect a drying of the climate across the region as a whole, the most pronounced of the whole of the Holocene" (Metcalfe 1995:205–206).

A lake sediment core from La Piscina de Yuriría, Guanajuato, in central Mexico, shows farming activity in the region between approximately AD 300 and 950 from the presence of *Zea mays* pollen in the sediments. The pollen drops sharply after approximately 950, indicating a decrease in agricultural activity. During this period, pine pollen decreases and juniper increases, indicating dryness. In fact, the lake itself probably dried up sometime during the most intense period of desiccation (Metcalfe et al 1994:138).

Reconstructions of lake levels for three basins in the central Mexican Highlands indicate that the most severe climatic episode was a period of marked aridity occurring between AD 550 and 1100 in Lakes Pátzcuaro, Hoya San Nicolás de Parangueo, La Piscina de Yuriría, and Zacapú. La Piscina de Yuriría probably went dry and Lake Pátzcuaro was significantly reduced in both depth and area. Many of the highland lake basins were abandoned. According to Sarah O'Hara and her colleagues, new centers that appeared during this period were built in defensive positions, indicating the need for protection against attack. They believe that repeated periods of severe drought in Mexico have been associated with civil unrest and military conflict (O'Hara, Metcalfe, and Street-Perrott 1994:967–968, 976–977).

In the Mexican Highlands, water level records from Lake Chalco indicate a period of desiccation that began approximately AD 950 (Street-Perrott and Perrott 1990:610).

NEW WORLD DROUGHTS

Charles Ortloff and Alan Kolata have suggested that the decline of the Tiwanaku state in the south central Andes occurred as a result of severe drought which hit the region. Agricultural systems in the region began failing as early as AD 850 due to receding water tables. There followed sequential collapses of different agricultural systems according to their vulnerability to intensifying drought conditions. The state itself finally collapsed between 1000 and 1100 following a dramatic decline in mean annual precipitation which began in 950. According to Ortloff and Kolata, "Despite centuries of sophisticated manipulation of the hydrologic regime for the benefit of agricultural production, Tiwanaku agro-engineers were incapable of responding to a drought of unprecedented duration and severity" (Ortloff and Kolata 1993:195, 212, 218).

At nearby Quelcayya ice cap, whose modern annual accumulation records correlate well with Lake Titicaca water levels and with La Paz, Bolivia, rainfall, the evidence indicates that two periods of severe drought occurred during the last 1,500 years. The first was at AD 535–665, during the Hiatus, with particularly dry periods around AD 540–560 and 570–610, ±20 years and the second at AD 855–985, during the Collapse and coincident with the drought around Lake Chichancanab in Yucatán and other Yucatecan lakes. Each of the Quelcayya droughts lasted about one hundred thirty years (L. G. Thompson et al 1988:763).

An increase in the microparticle concentration in the Quelcayya ice cap was seen between AD 535 and 665. During the sixth century, the Moche, or Mochica, culture abandoned its largest cities, lost its dominion over other cultures, and relocated to other areas There was an interval of peak microparticle concentration between AD 855 and 985, indicative of drought conditions in the Southern Hemisphere, at least around Quelcayya. More recent work has provided evidence of a drought centered on 900 in the form of increased dust particles and decreased precipitation. (Shimada et al 1991:261; Thompson et al 1985).(Curtis, Hodell, and Brenner 1996:37, 45–46; Lonnie Thompson, 22 December 1998, e-mail to author; Thompson et al 1985:973).

At nearby Sajama ice cap in Bolivia, an ice core shows an increase in dust particles around AD 900, as well. Thus, ice cores from two Andean glaciers demonstrate that the central Andes region was also in the throes of drought at the time of the Maya Collapse. It seems that the climatic anomaly affecting Mesoamerica was also felt in the Andes (Lonnie Thompson 1998; Lonnie Thompson et al 1998:1862).

AMERICAN TREE RINGS

Tree ring records from Mesoamerica go back only some two hundred years. Wood rots quickly in the tropical climate. A search of all available sources for the existence of tree ring records south of 23°N in Mexico and

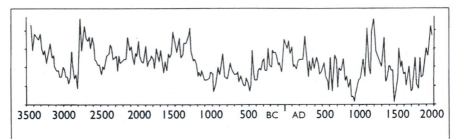

3500 3000 2500 2000 1500 1000 500 BC AD 500 1000 1500 2000

WHITE MOUNTAIN TREE RINGS

Figure 90. Ring widths, twenty-year averages, in the growth of bristlecone pines near the upper tree line in the White Mountains, California, measured in hundredths of a millimeter. The variations in height indicate summer warmth, or its duration. Note the very deep lows about AD 890–930 and 1450–1500 (adapted from Lamb 1982: 133).

Central America found none suitable for climatic interpretation. Some data have been collected in Mexico as far south as Oaxaca and some in El Salvador, but those records that do exist are typically short and not suited for dendroclimatological work (Stockton, Boggess, and Meko 1985:95).

Tree rings from the Southwest of the United States go far back in time. The Southwest, however, participates in the Pacific weather system. The winds which bring storms and the storm systems themselves blow in from the west, from the Pacific. As a result, except for occasional short lived winter cold fronts, *nortes* or northers, there is not a regular relationship between weather in the Southwest and weather in Yucatán. There may well, however, be a relationship between severe cold in North America and drought in the Maya Lowlands. The rings from bristlecone pines in the White Mountains of California (figure 90) show a period of warmth lasting from 500 BC to about AD 550, followed by cold. The lows reached during the sixth century are comparable to the lows seen during the Little Ice Age. There followed a sharp drop from about AD 790 to about 950 and a sharp drop in about 1450. The two coldest points reached in the entire 5,500-year record occur in about AD 910 and 1450, with a severe frost event being recorded in 1453–1454 (Bradley 1985:350; LaMarche and Hirschboeck 1984:125; Lamb 1982:133).

PROXY CLIMATE RECORDS

Climatologist Hubert Lamb noticed a relationship between Maya demographic processes and European weather:

On the other side of the Atlantic the Mayan civilization, whose temple-pyramids are now lost in the dense tropical rain-forest and warm, moist, enervating climate in the southern low-lands of the Yucatan peninsula, had its high period from about AD 300 to 800. Its realm spread from latitude 14 or 15 to 25°N in Central America. Is it just a coincidence that the time of its fullest flowering coincides so precisely with the period of droughts in the zone from the Mediterranean to central Asia or was the climate in those latitudes in Central America drier than before or since? (Lamb 1982:160)

The answer to Lamb's question lies in the meteorological model proposed earlier. As we saw, a period of drought in the Mediterranean would indicate the North Atlantic High had moved to the northeast bringing warm, dry weather to the Mediterranean region, warmer weather to Europe as a whole, and ample rainfall to the Maya Lowlands. The answer to Lamb's question, then, is not that Yucatán's climate was drier, but rather that it was wetter, yielding larger maize crops, increasing the flow of energy through the system, thus supporting more levels of hierarchical organization and more complex social organization. By the same reasoning, when the North Atlantic High moved far to the southwest, cold, wet weather covered Europe and drought visited the Maya Lowlands, restricting the flow of energy through the system.

A general relationship between cold weather in northern Europe and drought in Yucatán can be postulated because Yucatán lies at the southwestern corner of the area affected by the North Atlantic High, and Sweden lies at the northeastern corner. If the North Atlantic High moves to the northeast, it brings warm summers to northern Europe and warm moist conditions prevail in Yucatán. If it moves to the southwest, it brings drought to Yucatán and cold weather pours into Arctic Europe. With both Yucatán and Arctic Sweden participating in the Atlantic weather system, significant changes in Atlantic weather, including both the air masses and the ocean currents, are likely to be reflected in weather in the two areas. Tree ring records from northern Sweden, then, can act as a possible proxy weather record for the movement of the North Atlantic High and, thus, for Yucatecan drought.

SWEDISH TREE RINGS

A long, reliable palaeoclimatic record, which goes back to AD 432, is available from Arctic Sweden, together with associated lake varves—annual layers laid down in lake sediments in freezing climates (figure 91). Swedish tree ring widths are largely the result of summer temperatures. When the weather is warm, the tree rings are wider, when cold, narrower. The warmer the temperature, the thicker the growth. They are therefore an

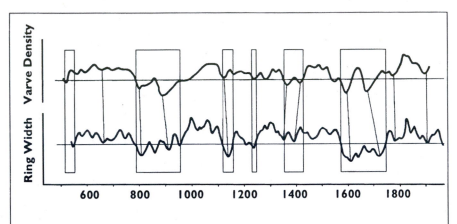

SWEDISH LAKE VARVES AND TREE RINGS

Figure 91. The *upper curve* shows the relative density of fluctuations in the organic content of lacustrine sediments from Vuollep Allakasjaure, a lake in northern Sweden. The *lower curve* shows variations in tree ring widths in northern Sweden, plotted as a thirty-one-year running mean. Periods of multiyear consecutive cool summers occurred around AD 550, 800, 860, 910, 1140, 1240, and during 1570–1750. Cool summers also occurred periodically between 1770 and 1915. The lake varve record indicates a period of cool summers in the fourteenth and fifteenth centuries. Cool periods are indicated by *rectangles* (adapted from Karlén 1984:268).

excellent record of past summer temperatures. Similarly, the annual layers, or varves, laid down in a lake in a freezing climate are wider during warm summers. By using the two series together, one can estimate cold periods and warm periods.

In a study of glacier front fluctuations in northern Sweden at Storglaciären, the tree ring record was searched to find periods of mass balance favorable for glacier advances. Such periods depend on cold summer temperatures. Several consecutive years of positive mass balance will result in a glacier front advance. During the period of the Storglaciären mass balance series, years in which the tree rings' widths measured less than 0.6 mm (0.02 in) were correlated with positive mass balance and subsequently advancing glacier fronts. According to Wibjörn Karlén, the tree ring record would indicate that "periods of cool summers...occurred around AD 550, 800, 860, 910, 1140, 1240, and during 1570–1750...and between 1770 and 1915." The dates chosen by Karlén correlate closely with the Hiatus, with the first drought phase I propose for the Collapse around

810–820, with the second drought phase around 860, and with the third drought phase around 910–920. The three pulses can be seen in the thirty-one-year running mean depicted in figure 91. The three phases of collapse are discussed in greater detail from an archaeological perspective in chapter 12 (Karlén 1984:264–269).

Radiocarbon dates from buried soils and sheared off tree rings indicate that glacier advances probably occurred around AD 800–900; the dendrochronology demonstrates that the climate at that time was approximately as cold for as long a time as during the Little Ice Age in the 1600s and the early 1700s. Additional support for glacier advances around AD 800 exists from lacustrine sediments. The 800s were a time of severe cold in Arctic Sweden (Karlén 1984:264–269).

Karlén conducted primarily ^{14}C dating, but also carried out lichenometric and lacustrine sediment studies to determine glacier advances in Scandinavian mountains. Based on the studies, he determined periods of advance during the last 2,000 years dated to about AD 50, 550, 900, 1350, and 1530, ±100 years (Karlén 1982:26).

A more recent study of the same tree ring record was published by Keith Briffa and his colleagues in 1990. Based on twenty-year running means, they have concluded that periods of cool summers occurred in AD 780–830, 850–870, 1110–1160, 1330–1360, 1570–1620, and 1800–1820. They note that although the second half of the twelfth century was quite warm, the first half was quite cold. Periods of *very cold* summers occurred during the late eighth to early ninth centuries, coincident with the start of the Collapse, during the first half of the twelfth century, and during the second half of the fourteenth and the second half of the fifteenth centuries (Briffa et al 1990:437–438).

Two periods of cold weather deviations can be identified in the twentieth century from the tree ring record, the first right after 1900 and the second a brief dip in the 1980s. In Yucatán, the first period was the severe drought of 1902–1904. The second was a period of diminished rainfall from about 1981 to 1987. In particular, the three years from 1985 to 1987 averaged 785 mm (31 in), off 17 percent from the normal 945.5 mm (37 in). They were part of the only three year period of diminished rainfall since 1902–1904. They followed the downturn in global temperatures in the period after the eruption of El Chichón in 1982 (Briffa et al 1990:434–439).

Fritz Hans Schweingruber and his colleagues have carried out radiodensitometric analyses of pines from near the polar timberline in Scandinavia. In their studies, they measured the density of the latewood cell growth in individual tree rings. They concluded that years with especially cold Arctic summers occurred in the ninth and tenth centuries. During those centuries, they mention in particular the summers of AD 800, 853, 877, 881, 911, 940, and 961 (Schweingruber et al 1988:563).

At least one record from Greenland indicates a significant δ^{18}O shift to the most negative values during the last 8,000 years, indicating cold temperatures around AD 850. In addition, minor glacial advances in Norway occur about the same time (Dahl and Nesje 1994:276; Leemann and Niessen 1994:266).

There is ample evidence, then, from multiple sources that the ninth century was a period of severe cold in the Northern Hemisphere.

NEW WORLD EVIDENCE

Mexico, of course, has glaciers on the high volcanoes. Unfortunately, periods of extratropical glacier advances, in other words periods of Northern Hemispheric cold, correspond in Mexico to periods of cold and dry climate without significant glacier formation. Mexican glaciers need a special combination, then, of cool but not too cold temperature and high precipitation. The two most recent periods of glacial advance in Mexico occurred about AD 1 and around AD 1800 (Heine 1973:162).

George Denton and Wibjörn Karlén examined the evidence of glacier advances in the St. Elias Mountains of southern Yukon Territory and Alaska. They radiocarbon dated fourteen terminal moraines in the mountains identifying two major periods of glacier advance and one minor period. The two major periods occurred 1350 to 450 BC and spanning the Little Ice Age AD 1490–1920. The minor advance (minor because it was shorter in duration, not in terms of cold temperatures) occurred between AD 700 and 900. In addition, they cite evidence from the high Sierra Nevada of a period of glacier advance, intense cold, and high snowfall, between AD 850 and 1050, dated by lichenometry (Denton and Karlén 1973:155, 201).

The ninth-century cold is also seen in tree rings from Almagre Mountain, Colorado, and from trees growing in terminal moraines in the Sierra Nevada of California. Louis Scuderi has found evidence of it in upper tree line tree rings from the Sierra Nevada which show a sharp drop to a minimum shortly after AD 800. A July temperature reconstruction from Windy Lake, Baffin Island, in the Canadian Arctic, shows an irregular decrease from the sixth to the tenth centuries. In fact, L. D. Williams and T. M. L. Wigley believe evidence for the eighth- to tenth-century cold period can be found throughout the Northern Hemisphere and that it may be composed of more than one episode of cooling. Both the Colorado and California tree ring records also reach lows in the fifteenth century at the beginning of the Little Ice Age I, coincident with the Postclassic Abandonment (Scuderi 1990:83; Williams and Wigley 1983:290–291).

Scuderi has identified intervals of increased volcanic activity which coincide with the greatest concentration of dated glacial deposits in the Sierra Nevada. These periods include 500 BC to AD 50, AD 150 to 250, AD 540 to 600, AD 800 to 950, and 1600 to 1890. Intervals of decreased volcanic activity are 950 to 500 BC, AD 50 to 150, AD 300 to 450, AD 600 to 750, 1000 to 1250, and 1890 to 1980. These latter periods are associated with few or no dated glacial moraines in the southern Sierra Nevada and a minimal number of severe ring width decreases at the Cirque Peak site. They are, however, associated with periods of cultural florescence in the Maya Lowlands (Scuderi 1990:84).

SUMMARY

Early Holocene: Evidence from Yucatán through lowland Central America to northern South America indicates a period of extreme aridity associated with the last Pleistocene glacial stage. Yucatán was an area of juniper scrub savanna, much like today's West Texas. The forests of Petén began to grow after the end of the Younger Dryas period, after 8000 BC. After 6500 BC, semievergreen forests and savannas were replaced by deciduous forests. General precipitation levels during the late glacial stage were 50 percent less than today's levels and subsequently increased to 25 percent more than today during the early Holocene.

AD *150–200:* Water levels at Lake Quexil dropped to their lowest levels around AD 200 and population levels in the area declined substantially. Low levels were also seen in the lake region to the south and from Lakes Chichancanab, Cobá, and Macanxoc, indicating a peninsula-wide event. A period of severe drought occurred at El Mirador at the time of its collapse. Scuderi identified the period AD 150 to 250 as a period of increased volcanic activity, coincident with dated glacial advances in the Sierra Nevada. In the Maya Lowlands, this was the period of the Preclassic Abandonment which devastated the Maya area. El Mirador was abandoned and not reoccupied until the Late Classic.

AD *530–590:* Reports of worldwide climatic anomalies during the sixth century are coupled with drought in the Lowlands. In chapter 8, we saw worldwide reports, following the AD 536 mystery event, of serious climatic disturbances characterized by summer frosts and abnormally cold winters reported from Italy, North Africa, Mesopotamia, and China. Bristlecone pine tree rings from the White Mountains in California show a sharp cold period during the sixth century. Swedish tree rings indicate cool summers around AD 550, as well. Scuderi identified the period AD 540 to 600 as a period of increased volcanic activity, coincident with dated glacial deposits in the Sierra Nevada. In South America, the Peruvian Quelccaya Ice Cap indicates a dry period AD 540–560 and 570–610. In the Maya Lowlands, this was the period of social turbulence and war known as the Hiatus. A lake sediment core from Punta Laguna establishes evidence for a serious drought during the Hiatus.

AD *790–950:* The ninth and tenth centuries were a period of widespread cold throughout the Northern Hemisphere and drought in the

Maya Lowlands. California tree rings from the White Mountains show a sharp drop in temperatures from AD 790 to 950. Glacial advances in the Sierra Nevada were dated by Denton and Karlén to AD 850–1050. Glacier advances in Alaska were dated by Denton and Karlén to AD 700–900. Williams and T. M. L. Wigley found evidence from Almagre Mountain, Colorado, of the ninth-century cold, as well. In fact, Williams and Wigley believe evidence for the eighth- to tenth-century cold can be found throughout the Northern Hemisphere. Scuderi has identified the period AD 800–950 as a period of increased volcanic activity, associated with dated glacial deposits in the Sierra Nevada.

From Arctic Sweden, Karlén identified multiyear periods of particularly cool summers, conducive to glacial advances, around AD 800, 860, and 910. Radiocarbon dates from buried soils and sheared off trees indicate that glacial advances occurred from AD 800–900. The climate was as cold for as long a time as during the Little Ice Age. Briffa and his colleagues identified periods of cool summers in Arctic Sweden from AD 780–830 and 850–870, with very cold summers occurring in the late eighth/early ninth centuries. Schweingruber and his colleagues carried out radiodensitometric analyses of pines from the near polar timberline in Arctic Sweden. They identified a major cold phase from AD 790–820 and particularly cold summers in AD 800, 853, 877, 881, 911, 940, and 961. The temperatures in Greenland shifted significantly colder around 850. Farther to the south, the Nile froze in 829.

From the Maya Lowlands, Hodell, Curtis, and Brenner have reported evidence from lake sediment studies conducted at Lake Chichancanab which indicate a period of severe aridity between AD 800 and 1000, peaking about 922. This is the driest episode in the last 7,000 years. They have reported on a second core taken from Punta Laguna in Quintana Roo which shows evidence of exceptionally arid events centered at AD 862 ±50 cal yr and 986 ±50 cal yr. The evidence indicates the period from 800 to 1050 was the driest at Punta Laguna during the last 3,500 years. Barbara Leyden and her colleagues reported evidence of a drying phase at Cenote San José Chulchacá after AD 900. Platt Bradbury and his colleagues report falling lake levels and increasing salinity at the end of the Classic from Laguna de Cocos, Albion Island, Belize. They believe that a climatic change to drier conditions is likely to be responsible. El Chichón appears to have erupted in the late eighth century or early ninth century. Popocatépetl staged a major eruption in 822 or 823. The period dated to between 770 and 890 was one of worldwide high volcanic activity. All lowland Maya cities were either abandoned or severely depopulated during the Classic Collapse.

AD *1110–1160:* An additional period of severe cold in Arctic Sweden has been identified by Karlén, Briffa et al, and Schweingruber et al between AD 1110 and 1160. This is approximately coincident, as we will see in chapter 11, with the fall of Tula during a period of cold and drought in the Mexican Highlands, a period of population decline in Yucatán identified by Dahlin, and the abandonment of the Early Postclassic ports on the northwest coast of Yucatán. An episode of population decline also appears to have occurred in Copán beginning in 1150. The demographic disaster may well have encompassed all of Mesoamerica.

AD *1240 and 1330–1360:* Records of severe cold exist in northern Sweden for periods around 1240 and 1330–1360. A historical record of severe drought in the Mexican Highlands exists for 1332–1335, as we will read in the next chapter.

AD *1450–1500:* Both the Colorado and California tree rings show evidence of a fifteenth-century cold period. The sharpest drop in the White Mountain record occurs in 1450. In northern Europe the period is known as the Little Ice Age I. It appears as well in the Swedish tree rings. Historical records from central Mexico indicate severe cold, heavy snowfall, and severe drought around 1451–1454. Mayapán, Chichén Itza, and Uxmal were abandoned in 1451 during the Postclassic Abandonment—a period of cold, drought, and famine.

11. Drought and Famine

F amine, war, and disease are pictured in the Book of Revelation as the three deadly enemies of the human race. Drought of itself can bring on a famine. Drought can be a cause of war, which in turn contributes to famine. Drought and crop failure bring undernourishment and starvation, which in turn contribute to disease. The three go together—famine, war, and disease—and in seeking the facts about the results of drought, we find the three so intertwined that they cannot be clearly separated.

—Ivan Ray Tannehill (1947:23)

Unlike floods, droughts do not telegraph their arrival. Heavy rain over a short period of time almost always foretells a consequent flood if prior rainfall has conditioned the basin for a high rate of runoff. But a few weeks or months of limited rainfall can only suggest the possibility of the onset of a drought, but possibility does not easily translate into probability, a substitute of uncertainty....Drought duration, however, is broad, spanning months or years, not hours or days as does the flood crest.

—N. C. Matalas (1991:256)

The tales of suffering and hurt and pain as people died without food and water fill the histories of the Maya and other Mesoamericans. The stories are not easy to read. Moreover, they are difficult for us to understand from the perspective of our modern global civilization.

It is clear that drought has struck Mesoamerica repeatedly throughout its history. We will see the reports of drought in the Aztec chronicles, in the Maya *Books of Chilam Balam*, and in the histories of drought compiled from Colonial reports. There are two especially important lessons to learn from the accounts that follow, not only that drought and famine occurred in the Maya Lowlands and in Mesoamerica in general, but also how often they are reported.

In a study of worldwide natural hazards and catastrophes, geographer Edward Bryant concluded that droughts are responsible for the greatest total loss of life and the greatest overall impact of any natural hazard. According to meteorologist Ivan Tannehill, history shows that drought lies at the bottom of most famines, a topic we examined in detail in chapter 4. Although, in Yucatán, famines were also caused by plagues of locusts and hurricanes which destroyed crops, the most severe famines were those which lasted for several years and which generally had drought as their cause. (See table 11 on page 307.) Famine took a heavy toll in Yucatán during the Colonial era. In addition to famine, war, and disease, however, the lowland Maya of Yucatán and the Petén were afflicted by thirst. When the rains failed, they ran out of water and thirst became a greater problem than hunger (Edward Bryant 1991:9, 105; 1984:60–62; Tannehill 1947:23).

Is devastating drought an unusual occurrence in Mesoamerica or has it been seen before? We will see that drought has been associated by others with the fall of Teotihuacan, Tula, and Mayapán. We will see from historical reports of the Colonial era that drought repeatedly ravaged Yucatán causing severe die-offs among the Maya and unimaginable suffering and human pain. The scourge of the late Colonial era was not plague but famine. For example, according to Colonial Spanish historian Diego López de Cogolludo, approximately half the population died from famine between 1648 and 1656 and, according to official records, the number of *encomienda* tributaries declined 40 percent during the famine between 1765 and 1773. Clearly severe drought is not an unusual occurrence. It's a recurring cycle with deadly demographic consequences, and it has happened over and over again (Patch 1993:43, 138, 160).

In this chapter, we look first at the Mexican Highlands and then at the Maya Lowlands.

TEOTIHUACAN

Early in the first millennium, Teotihuacan, a city in the Mexican Highlands just north of today's Mexico City, consolidated its position as the premier city of its time with trade and political links throughout Mesoamerica, including the Maya Lowlands, becoming the only Preco-

SECONDS	MINUTES	HOURS	DAYS	YEARS
Lightning	Tornadoes	Blizzards	Heat waves	Drought
Earthquakes	Hailstorms	River floods	Cold waves	Epidemic
Landslides	Tsunamis	Volcanic eruptions	River floods	War
Avalanches			Cyclones	
Meteorites			Insect population explosions	
Atmospheric fireballs				

TIME SCALE OF DISASTERS

Table 10. The time scale over which different disasters usually cause their effects (adapted from Hidore 1996:7).

lumbian superpower. It withdrew from regional power during a period of worldwide cold around AD 530 to 590. Teotihuacan's retreat coincides with the period of social and political turbulence, conflict, and drought known as the Hiatus in much of the Maya Lowlands. The turbulence in the Maya region is often attributed to Teotihuacan's withdrawal. It could be, however, that the Teotihuacanos and the Maya were being buffeted by drought and famine at the same time. Although I am not aware of any specific evidence from the Mexican Highlands of drought at the time of Teotihuacan's retrenchment, it was certainly a period of global climatic aberrations, as we have seen. There is, of course, evidence of drought from the Maya Lowlands.

After its retrenchment during the Hiatus, Teotihuacan continued to be populated, but it had lost its position of supremacy and was merely one city among others. It was finally abandoned in the period AD 750–800, although Joyce Marcus believed that Teotihuacan's population fell after AD 800 to below 30,000 from its peak of over 200,000, but continued to be inhabited for some time (Marcus 1992:395).

The widely accepted view of Teotihuacan's fall is championed by René Millon, who believed that the city collapsed around AD 750, after the deliberate, fiery destruction of the Ciudadela, the center of the city, in an internal revolt. The timing is intriguing because we saw evidence in the last chapter of drought in the Mexican Highlands beginning around AD 750. It would appear, then, that severe drought was coincident with the final abandonment of Teotihuacan and, as we have seen, conflict, famine, and drought often go hand in hand. A severe drought, then, does not rule out the possibility that conflict may also have occurred as part of the complex of effects driven by drought (Millon 1993:32–33).

In fact, Enriqueta García proposed that the final fall of Teotihuacan was due in part to an intense drought, part of a worldwide weather pattern which started in the eighth century. AD 800–1200 coincides with a low-stand in lake levels in the Basin of Mexico, which would suggest a period of depressed annual rainfall. Even more importantly, as Richard E. W. Adams pointed out, the phases of florescence and decline in the Basin of Mexico seem to follow the rise and fall of the basin's lake levels and, thus, the fluctuating cycles of rainfall (Richard E. W. Adams 1977:318; García 1974:35; Sanders 1970:88).

D. E. Dumond and Florencia Muller argued that Teotihuacan and Cholula, a city in the nearby Valley of Puebla, lasted until AD 800 when they collapsed or declined together. Nigel Davies also saw Cholula as having suffered a fate similar to that of Teotihuacan, which he dated to AD 750. Teotihuacan did not fall alone, he proposed, Cholula fell at the same time. It may be that they were both subjected to external, climatic pressures which would explain their simultaneous collapse (Davies 1977:120; Dumond and Muller 1972:1208.

Their final collapse came around AD 750–800, at the beginning of another period of worldwide cold, highland and lowland drought, and the beginning of the period of widespread Mesoamerican demographic disaster. Teotihuacan's misfortunes may well be attributed to drought, famine, and internal revolt working together and may be part of a regional climatic disturbance affecting most of Mesoamerica.

TULA

By the twelfth century, the Toltecs had consolidated the Highlands into a state with Tula as their capital. Colonization movements had established new frontiers of agriculture in the north central Highlands of Mexico and in a band of the northern Highlands along the western Sierra Madre to the extreme north of the State of Durango. The northward surge of civilization occurred during a time of warm, humid weather for the region which made the area suitable for farming. The rise of Tula as an imperial capital, located far north of the normal seats of power in central Mexico, halfway between the Valley of Mexico and the new agricultural lands of the north, is evidence that the population center had shifted to the north. The northern advance of this civilization, however, ended in complete collapse. Beginning in the twelfth century, a mass exodus of sedentary people, instigated by a southward shift of the northern zone of aridity, produced a permanent retreat of the agricultural frontier, at the same time as there was an apparent exodus of Toltecs to the south, perhaps to Culhuacán. By 1179 it was all over (Armillas 1964:76; Diehl 1983).

Tula fell, then, during the latter part of the twelfth century. Unlike Teotihuacan and the Classic Maya cities, there are native histories compiled shortly after the Spanish conquest that relate the circumstances of its fall. Its destruction has been tied to drought, cold, and war by the native chronicles.

Fernando de Alva Ixtlilxóchitl was the great grandson of the last ruler of Texcoco. As a historian, he appears to have had access to sources unavailable to other writers. His histories were written after the Spanish Conquest, about AD 1600. In them, he tells the story of the Toltec dispersal, which he attributes to the reign of Topiltzin:

> In the tenth year of his reign, the famine and barrenness of the land began. Most of the people were dying and the weevils ate the supplies stored in the granaries. Many other persecutions and calamities came from heaven, which seemed to rain fire, and the drought [which lasted twenty-six years] was so great that the rivers and springs dried up. In the twenty-third year of his reign, they were so lacking in strength and sustenance that the three kings mentioned came with a powerful army and easily took the city of Tula, the capital of the empire. Even though King Topiltzin fled the city, a few days later they caught up with him and killed his people...and the few Toltecs that were left escaped into the mountains of the lake at Culhuacán. This was the end of the Toltec empire, which lasted 572 years; and the kings who had come to subjugate it, seeing it so ruined, returned to their provinces. Although they were victorious, even they were very damaged and had lost most of their armies, most of whom had died from the famine. The same calamity befell their lands, because the land was everywhere dry and barren.... (Alva Ixtlilxóchitl 1891:472–473, my translation)

Davies discounted the tales of hunger and pestilence, frosts and drought, because, he said, such phrases were part and parcel of the standard Mesoamerican formula for describing periods of disaster! Of course they were part and parcel of the standard formula. They described recurring phenomena which repeatedly devastated Mesoamerica (Davies 1977: 400).

Pedro Armillas believed a cooling process began in the twelfth century that culminated in the Little Ice Age between the fifteenth and nineteenth centuries. The cooling resulted in increased aridity in northern Mexico. The Mexican steppes were displaced southward, forcing the sedentary people of the region to migrate towards the south, towards more humid conditions. The advance and retreat of the frontier of Mesoamerican civilization in northern Mexico, then, can be explained by the environmental changes produced by changes in the general circulation of the atmosphere and particularly in rainfall in northern Mesoamerica similar to the advance and retreat of ecotones we have seen in western Europe and the Sahel. The result was a southward retreat of the northern border of

Mesoamerica and the northern zone of aridity, an ecotonal shift of at least 250 km (155 mi). The Fennoscandian tree rings, by the way, indicate a period of cold in northern Europe at the same time (Armillas 1964:78–79).

Drought, cold, famine, and war appear to have played important roles in the fall of the Toltec Empire.

COLONIAL DROUGHTS IN THE HIGHLANDS

Severe cold, summer frosts, drought, and famine have been reported in the Colonial era as well. Historical records from the Bajío in central Mexico, for example, indicate that a severe drought accompanied by frosts in August occurred at elevations as low as 1800 m (5940 ft) between 1785 and 1789. Geographer Alexander von Humboldt described the situation during his visit to Mexico. "A very remarkable meteorological phenomenon contributed to the scarcity; the maize, after an extraordinary drought, was nipped by frost on the night of 28th, August, and what is more singular, at an elevation of 1,800 meters. The number of inhabitants carried off by this union of famine and disease throughout the whole surface of the kingdom was estimated at more than 300,000." It seems that after another unusually early frost in 1789, the ecclesiastical cabildo of Guanajuato decided to change their patron saint (Humboldt quoted in Swann 1980:101).

In reviewing a table of eighteenth-century droughts in Mexico, Ernesto Jáuregui Ostos commented, "It is curious to observe in the table that, in general, the lack of rain (above all in the early months of planting: April, May, June) occurred in the eighteenth century associated with invasions of polar air which were evidence of the prevalence of a regime of meridional circulation and which produced early frosts in August or September in the Mexican Highlands." Clearly, the ethnographic reports of cold, drought, and famine at the time of Tula's collapse are quite plausible (Jáuregui Ostos 1979:41).

ANNALS OF THE AZTECS

The chronicles of Aztec history written shortly after the Conquest contain numerous references to climatological disasters. Particular periods of severe drought and famine are reported: four years from 1332 to 1335 and the years from 1447 to 1454. Anton Kovar prepared a chronological compilation of climatological references to the three droughts from the following Aztec annals (Kovar 1970:28–31):

1332   Then began the years during which it did not rain.
          Relations of Chalco Amaquemecan–third relation

1333   It was then that it did not rain in any part of Chalco during this year.
          Relations of Chalco Amaquemecan–fifth relation

1335 It was the fourth year that it did not rain in the country of the Chalcas; however, in the plantings of the Tlacochalcas, the rain fell though their fields were in the middle of the Chalcas.

Relations of Chalco Amaquemecan–seventh relation

1347 For the first time the mountain now called Popocatépetl was seen to smoke....It was twelve years that *Tlazolyaoltl*, "fraternal war" (fictitious war), was held but it was ended after four years of drought, four years during which not a drop fell.

Relations of Chalco Amaquemecan–sixth relation

Although drought and cold weather began as early as 1447, a devastating drought lasted from 1450 to 1454 which culminated in the famine of 1 Rabbit, the Aztec name of the year 1454 (Kovar 1970:28–31):

1447 There was so much snow that many people died.

Codex Telleriano-Remensis

1449 Also in this year so much snow fell that it covered everything.

Relations of Chalco Amaquemecan–seventh relation

1450 ...the snow that fell over the entire land was so high that it reached in most parts a stadium and a half, which caused the destruction and collapse of many houses as well as the destruction of all trees and plants and the country was so cold that many people died and especially older people; and during the three following years all plantings and products of the earth were lost so that most people died.

Alva Ixtlilxóchitl

This year there were heavy frosts which froze everything. There was hunger and need. Thus began the five years during which there was nothing to eat.

Relations of Chalco Amaquemecan–third relation

In this year there was again a heavy frost which caused hunger for five years and which did not leave anything to eat during the entire year.

Relations of Chalco Amaquemecan–seventh relation

1451   Crops lost.

Alva Ixtlilxóchitl

In this year knee deep snow fell; it fell during five days.

Códice Chimalpopoca–Anales de Cuauhtitlán

...a deep freeze fell which froze maize when it was germinating.

Anales de Tlatelolco and Códice de Tlatelolco

Third year of hunger. All the way to Chalco came the ferocious beasts and buzzards and birds of prey, the same as to all other villages. Everywhere, in the forest and grasslands died even young men and women. Their flesh was so wrinkled and dry as if they were old persons. Hunger was very great.

Relations of Chalco Amaquemecan–seventh relation

1452   Crops fail again.

Alva Ixtlilxóchitl

Another frost came and maize froze at the very moment of germination.

Anales de Tlatelolco and Códice de Tlatelolco

Second year of hunger, need, and suffering for lack of food in Chalco. The buzzards were searching everywhere for corpses to eat in the hills, lowlands, and forests. The young men looked like old people because their flesh was so full of folds and wrinkles. The boys and girls became so because of hunger.

Relations of Chalco Amaquemecan–third relation

The hunger continued.

Relations of Chalco Amaquemecan–seventh relation

1453   Crops fail once more.

Alva Ixtlilxóchitl

...another frost fell during the *Tecuilhuitl* [the Feast of the Lords, June 12–July 1]. Then the ears froze. In this year there was also an earthquake and fissures appeared in the ground and chinampas collapsed; and people were selling themselves to others because of hunger.

Anales de Tlatelolco and Códice de Tlatelolco

In the year 128 [after the foundation of Tenochtitlán], hail fell in Mexico to such a degree that houses collapsed and the lake froze over.

Historia de los Mexicanos por sus pinturas

This was already the fourth year during which there was nothing to eat.

Relations of Chalco Amaquemecan–third relation

There was still nothing to eat. The deadly hunger continued.

Relations of Chalco Amaquemecan–seventh relation

1454   At the beginning there was a very large eclipse of the sun, and then illness grew and so many people were dying that it appeared as if nobody was going to survive, such was the calamity that afflicted this land and hunger was so great that many sold their children in exchange for maize in the province of Totonicapán where no such calamity occurred.

Alva Ixtlilxóchitl

There was such a famine that many people died.

Codex Telleriano-Remensis

...It stopped raining. The Mexicans became much disturbed because of hunger and the Mexicans did not go to their fields anymore.

Anales de Tlatelolco and Códice de Tlatelolco

In this year, everything became bad. There was then the war of the Chalcas in the margins of the mountains and it ended for this reason, there was no more war. There were three years of hunger; there were no provisions....

Códice de Chimalpopoca–Anales de Cuauhtitlán

It is said that this year, 1 Rabbit, was an extremely unfortunate one; there were many deaths. The people died of thirst. From Chalco came foxes, ferocious beasts, lizards, etc. and they devoured the people. The famine was so great that the old Mexicans sold themselves; they took refuge in the woods where they lived unhappy and feeble. For four years there was nothing to eat in the country, so that the older Mexicans sold themselves and two divisions, it is said, delivered themselves into servitude. It is for this reason that the Totonacs came to buy Mexicans with maize, it was to Cuextlán that they brought maize to the Mexicans. Up to that time they had not as yet had the custom of using maize bread. They put themselves into holes and died in any place they found and the lizards devoured them for there was no one to bury them.

Annals of Chimalpahin

This is the year in which it was said that people became scared for reason of a great mortality, pestilences, and hunger. Coyotes, ferocious beasts and birds of prey came all the way to Chalco in search of people to attack. Such was the hunger that the ancient Mexicans sold themselves as slaves to obtain something to eat. Others went into the hills trying to escape the aridity and dryness which affected the vegetation and there they tried to plant something with their hoes. Certainly, there was nothing to eat and because of this the old Mexicans sold themselves as slaves in exchange for food. Thus another kind of people arose with those who became Totonacs because a great number of said Totonacs bought Mexicans in exchange for dry maize, shelled, both in Cuextlán where Mexicans went to sell themselves and in Tenochtitlán where dry shelled maize was brought to buy them, but even with tortillas folded and dipped into something, there was not enough to go around and for this reason some people simply made holes in the ground and crawled into them to await death and when it came they were devoured by buzzards because there was no one to bury them. There was some relief in only those parts of the country where some rain fell.

Relations of Chalco Amaquemecan–seventh relation

People sold themselves into slavery for food while buzzards and lizards ate the corpses of the dead. It was a terrible time. These pictures of drought ravaged Mexicans are awful scenes of suffering, pain, hurt, and loss.

DROUGHT IN YUCATÁN

The Maya suffered as much as the Mexica. Let us turn our attention now to the Maya Lowlands. In the north, the Maya developed a particular cultural and historical tradition, possibly different from the south. Each community compiled and kept its own version of history in chronicles known as *The Books of Chilam Balam*. After the Conquest, some of these books were transcribed from the original hieroglyphic format into an alphabetic system using Roman letters to record Maya words and, in some cases, ongoing events continued to be recorded. Because the Maya believed that time was cyclical and that past events would recur in the future during the same calendrical cycle, much of the history is cast as prophecy.

According to Ralph Roys, the prophecies contained in *The Books of Chilam Balam* are replete with references to swarming insects, scanty rains, hunger, and thirst. Among the katuns, 10 Ahau was particularly noted for drought and severe heat and such mortality that the vultures would enter the houses to eat the corpses of the dead (Roys 1949:166–178).

The drought of 1450–1454 also devastated Yucatán. A written record of drought in Yucatán is from *The Book of Chilam Balam of Maní* and can be dated, by its reference to the fall of Mayapán about 1451, which falls in katun 8 Ahau (Craine and Reindorp 1979). (The date of Mayapán's fall will be discussed further in chapter 12.)

> The city of Mayapán was destroyed on a day of a Katún 8 Ahau. Lahun Chablé will establish, to the south, a Katún 8 Ahau. With his eyes on the heavens, the ruler will implore food and drink. The warrior will thank him who will give him food and drink. The fields, having been impoverished, shall be searched for food and water which will not be found anywhere in the Petén or in the entire land, wherever there are Bacabs. (Craine and Reindorp 1979:83)

> The destruction of Mayapán, which is in the south, took place in the Katún 8 Ahau. Lahun Chan established the Katún 8 Ahau and directed his powerful gaze toward heaven, imploring hard bread and water. No one entertained the soldier with bread or water. The people, on the plain and in the forest, were chilled. Everything was searched, but nothing [neither food nor water] could be found on the plains, or in the forest, or in the whole world, or in all of Petén. (Craine and Reindorp 1979:156)

The same drought is described in *The Book of Chilam Balam of Chumayel*:

> Katun 8 Ahau came. 8 Ahau was the name of the katun when their government occurred. There was a change of the katun, then there was a change of rulers…[missing fragment]…when our rulers increased in numbers, according to the words of their priest to them. Then they introduced the drought. That which came was a drought, according to their words, when the hoofs [of the animals] burned, when the seashore burned, a sea of misery. So it was said on high, so it was said. Then the face of the sun was eaten; then the face of the sun was darkened; then its face was extinguished. They

were terrified on high, when it burned at the word of their priest to them, when the word of our ruler was fulfilled at the word of their priest to them. (Roys 1933:77)

As we saw earlier, Alva Ixtlilxóchitl reported an eclipse at the time of the famine of 1 Rabbit, 1454, which falls in katun 8 Ahau. The above passage most likely describes the drought at the fall of Mayapán as well.

The physical destruction of Mayapán was the result of an internal revolt of its vassals during a time of cold and drought. Once again, we see the pattern of drought, cold, famine, and conflict. The drought beginning around 1450 was part of a global pattern of weather changes, including the onset of the Little Ice Age I in Europe, 1450–1500, one of the two severest periods of cold in the Sierra Nevada in the last 2,000 years, and the brutal drought and famine of 1 Rabbit in the Mexican Highlands.

The fall of Mayapán is not the sole story of drought in the Lowlands. *The Book of Chilam Balam of Maní* goes on to list other droughts, which unfortunately cannot be accurately dated because there is no datable event to tie them to, but which emphasize the repetitive nature of drought driven death in the Lowlands:

In Katún 6 Ahau they shall eat trees and rocks as they shall be dying of starvation. Seated on their beds, on their mats, the dying governors, with their relatives beside them, shall speak of food and they will talk incessantly, wishing the trees would fructify. Three times it has happened this way and three times it has been necessary to make bread with the cup root because of the famine. (Craine and Reindorp 1979:84–85)

Uucil Abnal will establish a Katún 4 Ahau. Throughout this Katún there will be misfortunes for Chichén Itza. There will be a scarcity of squash and ears of corn. The field workers will awaken at dawn, facing the south, sad faced and with death in their eyes, weeping because of the lack of bread and water and conversing about the plague of ants that threaten the beehives in their care. (Craine and Reindorp 1979:85)

On the day 12 *Kan*, 1 *Pop*, the twelfth year was being counted [of Katún 5 Ahau]. There was fighting day and night with uncertain fortune. In the twelfth year the sky burned and envy came to an end. There was much praying in Hunab Ku, for this was the beginning of seven years of drought. Many solid rocks were cracked [Cracking rocks: in order to bring an end to the drought, many people were sacrificed] and bird nests burned. This was the Katún when the Itzas, desiring to obtain their stored provisions, returned to their wells and their caves, where they again became contented on their mats and on the dais. Here, in their caves, their discord and struggles ended, they lived, prayed, and died. (Craine and Reindorp 1979:108–109)

In the fourteenth Tun [1 *Ix* falls on] 1 *Pop* [of Katún 5 Ahau]. The fourteenth Tun was the time of the great count. It was the time when the fire which was set in the Petén broke out among the clouds in the sky and was seen everywhere. It was the time when the face of the sun and the face of the moon were covered. In the fourteenth Tun, vegetation disappeared and the people prayed to the gods. It was a time of few children and few young people, a time when governors and the count of the years were lost, a time of great calamities, general death, and misfortune. (Craine and Reindorp 1979:110)

After the sixteenth year came the seventeenth on 4 Muluc. It was a time of the gathering of food and other secret preparations for war. It was a year of tigers, and there was much death. The Petén was swept by a great drought; there was no water in the wells, the hayfields dried up, and there was great hunger and thirst throughout the land. The bul cum [misfortune associated with flies, death, and mourning] roared at the gates of the villages. Everyone mourned and had a sad face. It was the time that the fathers and mothers were remembered. For three folds of the Katún the Itzás died and were lost, and they went into the forest to live. (Craine and Reindorp 1979:112)

When Max Canul left the government it was the thirteenth year of his birth: a year of tigers, a year of plague of ants and of great misery because of the scarcity of bread and water, slaughter of the Mayas, and the flocks of vultures in the houses because of the great drought. It was a time of hardships for the Itzás. (Craine and Reindorp 1979:122)

Beginning with and during Kan, vultures will enter the houses in your villages because of the great numbers of dead Mayas and dead animals. (Craine and Reindorp 1979:67)

From *The Book of Chilam Balam of Chumayel*, we read the following descriptions:

It was the year of '81 when it began [an epidemic in 1781]. After that there was a great drought also. There was scarcely any rain. The entire forest was burned, and the forest died. (Roys 1933: 143–144)

Sudden death with hunger; the vultures enter the houses of the pestilence. There is sad havoc [bul cum] with flies [swarming] at the crossroads. (Roys 1933:157)

Other books of Chilam Balam contain similar references. As can be seen from the excerpts quoted, drought and famine repeatedly visited the Yucatán Peninsula, driving the people from their homes and into the forests to survive on famine foods. One drought and famine, in fact, is clearly tied to the abandonment of Mayapán. What is important, however, is not the exact dates of famines, but rather their frequency in the annals.

POSTCONTACT FAMINES

Following the Conquest, colonial Spanish historians recorded histories of repeated drought and famine (table 11). The suffering and death they described is hard to imagine from a modern perspective, as we are about to see.

Diego de Landa, the first Bishop of Yucatán, reported the first Postcontact famine which was brought on by a five-year period of drought and locusts from 1535 to 1540, between the first and second Spanish *entradas*. The famine was so severe, he said, that people fell dead by the roadside (Landa 1566:54–56).

Historian Juan Francisco Molina Solís, writing early in the twentieth century, reported numerous accounts of Yucatecan famines in his histories. We will follow below Molina Solís's accounts as presented in Ricardo Molina Hübbe's *Las Hambres de Yucatán* (*The Famines of Yucatán*) (1941). The translations are my own.

Within ten years of the founding of Mérida, there occurred a famine which lasted six months. The Visitor, Tomás López, promulgated ordinances at the time citing: "To remedy the daily hunger which this land is accustomed to having...so many hardships as are seen in this land in the sterility of one year alone. We all feel it when it happens, but no one remembers it, except when hardships are being felt." The Spanish learned very quickly that drought and famine were recurring phenomena in Yucatán (Molina Hübbe 1941:14).

In 1571, the rains again failed and an ensuing epidemic devastated Yucatán. According to Molina Solís, "the inhabitants suffered starvation, especially the Indians, who, in search of food, abandoned their homes and wandered through the forests....The Franciscans report that the villages were depopulated, that the Indians fled and that all, without fail would go to the emptiness of the Petén, if they were not rescued" (Molina Hübbe 1941:15).

The drought of 1648 was exceptionally hard, so much so that Molina Solís said it "sterilized the earth...and produced intense heat." The lack of water continued until the month of August, putting the inhabitants in great distress. As a result, a terrible epidemic "sunk its claws in," and almost all of the population laid infected with disease. Entire families died abandoned in Mérida. The dead included many of high rank, most of the canons of the Cathedral, *encomenderos*, priests, and the governor, don Estéban de Azcárraga (Molina Hübbe 1941:19).

The droughts continued until 1656. The year 1651 left very painful memories in Yucatán, perhaps because of the mistakes and abuses of the governor, the Count of Peñalva. As Molina Solís recounts:

> The starvation as it developed was terrible and desolating, because there was neither corn nor wheat, nor any other grain for ordinary sustenance: at first the lack of cereals was supplemented with meat, which also became scarce; hens ran out; there were no pigs; cattle were rare. The poor, wasted and gaunt, desperately left for the countryside in search of sustenance, and pulling up grass and roots, ate them to avoid starvation; the streets, roads, parks, plazas, and other public places were sown with corpses; the inhabitants of the towns looked more like specters than living men, and many abandoned their homes, driven by hunger: entire places were abandoned, because their inhabitants went to the forests of the south in search of food, the best populated sites of Yucatán were threatened with being left deserted and barren. (Molina Hübbe 1941:20–21)

In 1725, the rains again failed and caused a famine which lasted until 1727, during the administration of the conqueror of Belize, Marshall don Antonio de Figueroa y Silva:

> A terrifying and alarming aspect revisited the land which made many Spanish families think of uprooting themselves completely from the country, moving their residence to New Spain, Cuba, or Puerto Rico. Such was the scarcity that corn came to be sold at the unusual price of twenty pesos the load, and giving only sixty-three poorly counted grains for one real; roots were being eaten, and the bones of any animal found in the streets and fields were converted into powder to be eaten as flour, and everywhere squalid specters wandered in search of necessary food; although in vain, because there was nothing with which to provide the most urgent necessities of life; the starving fell of dissipation and hunger, the number of corpses was so high, that they were collected in wagons to be taken to the cemetery, and according to statistics from the Secretariat of Government, the number of deaths in the province from this pitiful scourge reached 16,000, leaving the population decimated. (Molina Hübbe 1941:24–25)

YEAR	OCCURRENCE	SOURCE
~1454	Drought, Famine, Cold	*Chilam Balam of Maní*, Craine and Reindorp 1979:156
1535–1541	**Drought, Famine, Locusts**	Landa 1566:54–56
1551–1552	Famine	Molina Hübbe 1941:13
1564	Drought	Cook and Borah 1974 2:115
1571–1572	Famine	Cogolludo Lib. 6, cap. 9
1575–1576	Drought, Famine, Epidemic	Molina Solís 1:166
1604	Famine	Cook and Borah 1974 2:115
1618	Famine, Locusts	Cárdenas Valencia, *Relación historial*, 68
1627–1631	**Famine, Storm, Locusts**	Cogolludo, Lib. 10, caps. 7, 17
1648–1650	Drought, Famine, Epidemic	Cogolludo, Lib. 12, caps. 12–14; Molina Hübbe 194:19
1650–1654	**Drought, Famine, Epidemic**	Cogolludo Lib. 12, caps. 12–14, 17, 21; Farriss 1984:426; *Chilam Balam of Chumayel*, Roys 1933:120
1669	Drought	*Chilam Balam of Chumayel*, Roys 1933:120
1692–1693	Famine, Epidemic, Hurricane, Locusts	AGI, Mexico 369, Bishop to crown, 18 April, 1693
1700	Famine	AGI, México 1035, Definitorio franciscano, 16 June 1700
1725–1727	**Famine, Epidemic**	Molina Solís 3:178–181, Molina Hübbe 1941:23
1730	Famine	AGI, México 898, Oficiales reales to Crown, 20 October 1745

YEAR	OCCURRENCE	SOURCE
1742	Famine	AGI, México 898, Oficiales reales to Crown, 20 October 1745
1765–1768	Drought, Famine, Locusts, Hurricane	AGI, México 3054, Governor to Julián de Arriaga, México 3057, Encomenderos to oficiales reales, 11 Sep 1775
1769–1774	**Drought, Famine, Locusts, Hurricane**	AGI, México 3057, Governor to Audiencia, 1 March 1774; Informe Ayuntamiento Mérida, 1775
1795	Drought, Famine	AGN, Intendentes 75, Necesidad de maíz en Yucatán, January 13 and March 13, 1795
1800–1804	**Drought, Famine, Locusts**	AGN, Intendentes 75, Governor to Viceroy, 10 August 1800, AA, Oficios y decretos 5, Cabildo Mérida to Bishop, 31 July 1804
1805, 1807	Drought, Famine	Molina Hübbe 1941:27
1809–1810	Famine, Epidemic	AA, Oficios y decretos 7, Governor to Bishop, 20 July 1810
1817	Drought, Famine	Molina Hübbe 1941:27
1822–1823	Drought, Famine	Molina Hübbe 1941:28–29
1834–1836	Drought, Famine	Molina Hübbe 1941:29, John L. Stephens 1843 (2):187
1842	Famine	Stephens 1843 (2):187

R B GILL 2000

HISTORICAL FAMINES IN YUCATÁN

Table 11. Record of droughts and famines in Yucatán. **Bold italic years** indicate a severe famine. *AA*: Archivo del Arzobispado, Mérida; *AGI*: Archivo General de Indias, Sevilla; *AGN*: Archivo General de la Nación, Mexico (*Sources*: AGI (1795); Cook & Borah 1974; Craine & Reindorp 1979; Landa 1566; Molina Hübbe 1941, John L. Stephens 1843; Farriss 1984:61–62 for all others).

Between 1769 and 1770, drought again precipitated a famine. The first documented case of grain imports is for 1770, the year of the worst famine in the peninsula's history (Patch 1993:222).

> The most painful and harmful that can be conceived, because the scarcity was so great that people were obliged to seek sustenance in tree roots, birds, and animals in the countryside. So great was the interior population that wandered through the streets, plazas, roads, and parks, wasted from starvation, that thousands of persons fell emaciated and lifeless, to never again rise; families of comfortable means found themselves reduced to poverty, consuming their resources, and entire towns are deserted because their inhabitants emigrated en masse, begging bread which would free them from death....At the gates of Campeche, throngs of people from more than sixty leagues came in search of alms and help to sustain life. (Molina Hübbe 1941:25–26)

Famines, driven by the lack of rain, occurred from 1805 to 1810 and in 1817, following the eruption of Tambora. We won't repeat the prior descriptions of hunger, starvation, and death that we have already seen. Maya migrated en masse to the principal towns and from there into the forests in a desperate struggle for survival (Molina Hübbe 1941:27).

Between 1822 and 1823, the rains failed, provoking further drought and famine. Newly independent from Spain, the suffering this time did not reach the levels experienced during the Colonial times. However, civil disorder was recorded with this famine. Bands of beggars overran towns, gripped by hunger and desperation. They were converted into gangs which employed very violent means to obtain anything to eat. Groups of hungry natives wandered through the cities in search of food, while in the countryside gangs attacked the *haciendas* and villages. For the first time, the Mexican government imported grain from abroad (Molina Hübbe 1941:28–29).

The last of the great famines of Yucatán began in 1834 and worsened in 1835 and 1836. The climatic aberrations, however, were not restricted to Yucatán alone. Severe cold and unusual snowfall in Northern Mexico beset General Antonio López de Santa Anna in February of 1836 as he and his troops marched to San Antonio and the Battle of the Alamo (Padillo Ríos and Rodríguez Viqueira 1980:40; Florescano 1980:16–17; Sancho y Cervera and Pérez-Gavilán Arias 1981:46–47).

The diary kept by Baron de Waldek, a traveler who was visiting the peninsula, reads:

> I cannot find enough corn for my subsistence in the interior of the country. The shortage is extreme: the people are hungry and are exposed to atrocious suffering. A few days ago an Indian

killed a young child twelve years old with machete blows in order to steal two and a half reales of corn that he was carrying. Another Indian snuck into a house, passed through the dining room without stopping where pieces of silverware lay on the table, went into the kitchen, and stole the pot where corn was cooking. The roads are not safe for the mule drivers who are carrying corn: they run the risk of being attacked by starving Indians and they themselves steal the grain that is entrusted to them....Every day at the gates of the warehouses, scenes of tumult occur which remind me of the worst days of the French Revolution. The people, urged on by hunger, gather near the stores to obtain at double the price the bread which is their only food. The women get into arguments and come to blows. The crowd grows, the door opens, the front rows are swept away by the rear of those storming the warehouse and it frequently happens that poor women are trampled and lose their lives in these skirmishes. And this is nothing compared to what happens in the interior. It is impossible to walk a league with bread under your arm, while one could travel alone with a treasure in total safety. When I leave, my greatest concern will be to hide from the Indians the load of corn and other provisions which I must take. (Molina Hübbe 1941:30–31)

Effects of Drought

Single crop failures were a common occurrence in Yucatán. True famines were produced by successive years of poor or failed crops. They caused exceedingly heavy losses among the Maya with estimates of the dead running up to one-half or more of the population per episode. Cogolludo, for example, estimated that almost half of the Maya inhabitants died during the series of droughts, famines, and epidemics which scourged the peninsula from 1648 to 1656. Documents in the Archivo General de Indias, in Seville, list 58,879 tributaries (Maya men between the ages of fourteen and sixty) in 1765 and 34,776 in 1773, a loss of 41 percent, and the total may have reached over 50 percent by the time of the final tally. Nancy Farriss pointed out that some of the loss of population was possibly the result of flight rather than death. Nonetheless, the mortality was enormous. Prolonged famine generally resulted in widespread epidemics which the weakened population could not resist (Farriss 1984:60, 426, 471; 1986:94).

The five-year drought and famine of 1769–1774, although not the most severe of Yucatán's famines, is the best historically documented. When colonial authorities surveyed the effects, town after town reported that the only people left were the *batabob* and the *principales*, the elite of their communities, who were forced to sell off their property to buy grain from the

Spanish when their own stores ran out. At least they survived (Farriss 1984:186, 367).

> Not all of the macehuales perished, obviously, but a simple comparison of population figures before and after the famines conveys a strong enough picture of devastation even without the ghastly details supplied in the Spanish accounts. These speak of corpses strewn along the roads and left to the vultures to dispose of, or gathered up to be dumped, unrecorded, in large pits. Some reported that starving mothers killed and ate their infants, but none of these reports was firsthand. (Farriss 1984:186)

OTHER MEXICAN DROUGHTS

Jaime Sancho y Cervera and David Pérez-Gavilán, in their study of droughts in Mexico, quote the following description of epidemics associated with drought from the native chronicles, "The people began to awaken and to become withered and thin from the hunger they suffered and others became sick, eating things that were bad for their health" (Sancho y Cervera and Pérez-Gavilán Arias 1981:44).

In Mexico, as a whole, Enrique Florescano investigated historical droughts and found eighty-eight droughts between the sixteenth and nineteenth centuries. The droughts varied in duration, some lasting three, four, five, up to nine years. The Colonial droughts were often accompanied by social turbulence. The drought of 1693 and the manipulation of grain reserves by *hacendados*, for example, sparked a mutiny in the capital during which crowds stoned the corn exchange and the municipal palace and attacked and sacked the viceroy's palace. The rioters later burned the municipal palace, the viceroy's palace, the corn exchange, the corregidor's house, the prison, and the gallows (Florescano 1980:14–16).

Following the droughts of 1805, 1806, and 1807 in Yucatán, the successive droughts of 1808, 1809, and 1810 in Yucatán and throughout Mexico preceded the *grito* of Father Hidalgo and the Mexican War for Independence. The rebels of 1810 were desperate, hungry peasants. The droughts of 1808–1810 coincided with a very sharp drop in ring widths between 1808 and 1812 from Sierra Nevada trees indicating a severe cold spell in North America (Florescano 1980:14–16; Legrand and Delmas 1987:673).

In the first decade of the twentieth century leading up to the Mexican Revolution, during the last ten years of the Porfiriato, the rule of Porfirio Díaz, there was an intensification of drought, especially in northern and central Mexico, in the states of Querétaro, Hidalgo, Chihuahua, and Nuevo León, and in Yucatán, with loss of crops and cattle, resulting in high prices for grains and meat. In every year of the decade from 1900 to 1910, moderate to severe droughts were recorded. As in the case of the War for Independence, the Mexican Revolution followed years of drought, agricultural disasters, scarcity, hunger, and widespread discontent. As we have seen, the first decade of the twentieth century was a time of severe cold in the northern latitudes, accompanied by cold North Atlantic water temperatures, and severe drought in Mérida (Florescano 1980:16–17; Padillo Ríos and Rodríguez Viqueira 1980:40; Sancho y Cervera and Pérez-Gavilán Arias 1981:46–47).

These events, drought, famine, and social conflict, are not something buried in our forgotten past. In recent years, disturbances very similar to those recorded in Mexico's history have recurred. Between 1990 and 1996, for example, a severe drought hit the northern part of Mexico, especially Chihuahua and surrounding states. Rainfall levels in some years dropped as low as 10 percent of normal. Cattle herds in Chihuahua were reduced by over 50 percent, more than 1.1 million head, and dead animals lined the highways. The countryside was largely depopulated as *campesinos* left their homes. On May 30, 1996, about three hundred impoverished Mexicans held up a corn train in northern Nuevo León, making off with about forty tons of maize, while in mid-June Durango residents sacked another corn train. On June 23, hundreds of residents of Durango held up yet another train, carrying off tons of wheat (Institute for Agriculture and Trade Policy 1996:1).

Were it not for the free and easy flow of food from one part of the world to another in today's global economy, it is clear that the drought in the north would have caused a serious famine accompanied by social conflict and heavy mortality.

DISCUSSION

The Mesoamerican pattern of drought, famine, disease, and war occurred repeatedly from the fall of Teotihuacan, to the fall of Tula and Mayapán, to the Mexican War of Independence and the Mexican Revolution. The same pattern, as we will see, played a role in the disappearance of Classic Maya civilization.

It is difficult for us to imagine, from a modern perspective, the suffering and death, babies dying in their mothers' arms, bodies lying in the streets and plazas where the emaciated, gaunt specters could move no further, small animals eating the bodies, and buzzards entering the houses to feed on the shriveled corpses inside. Yet it happened repeatedly in the Maya Lowlands. The historical records are there to read. It happened so often in the past and it happened during the Terminal Classic. If, as we have seen, the droughts were the most severe of the Holocene, then the famine and death surely would have been the most severe of the Holocene as well.

12. Abandonment and Collapse

Expansion and severe contraction, periods of boom followed by periods of bust and cyclical collapse characterize the history of the Maya Lowlands during the last two millennia.

The first great florescence of Maya culture burst forth during the Preclassic when the first, true, Maya urbanism developed. Then catastrophe set in. Between AD 150 and 200, major cities from the Gulf coast in the north to the Pacific coast in the south were staggered or emptied during a drought at the time of the Preclassic Abandonment. Populations recovered, most of the cities rebuilt and boomed in the ensuing three hundred years. During the Hiatus, lasting from about AD 536 to about 590, social turbulence erupted, with rebellion, war, and demographic collapse halting construction in large areas of the Lowlands. Río Azul, for example, was abandoned and population in the surrounding countryside dropped 70 percent during a drought. The rains returned, and during the next two hundred years, the Lowlands boomed in a way never seen before or since. Then, devastation on a scale rarely suffered in world history destroyed Classic Maya civilization beginning around AD 810 as a brutal drought struck the Yucatán Peninsula. The Southern Lowlands were largely wiped out, but small populations hung on in the north, the east, and central Petén, around stable sources of drinking water, and slowly began to rebuild a new Maya culture. By about 1200, population levels in the north had recovered to the point that political integration and centralization could occur. The political hegemony of Mayapán lasted until 1451–1454, when disaster again befell the Maya and their major northern cities were abandoned during another drought. When the Spaniards arrived in AD 1528, they found petty, warring states with little political cohesion.

As we have seen in prior chapters, each of these four periods of drought and social turbulence coincides with episodes of widespread cold in the Northern Hemisphere and evidence for drought in the Lowlands.

PRECLASSIC ABANDONMENT

The growth and development of Maya culture and civilization can be traced in the Lowlands from the earliest agricultural beginnings around 2500 BC. By the second century AD, a Maya cultural tradition of considerable complexity had developed. Large-scale urbanism distinguished the dominant center of the time, El Mirador, which boasted truncated buildings between 33 and 70 m (110 to 230 ft) high with base areas as large as city blocks, an acropolis 330 m (1100 ft) long, a central plaza nearly 0.5 km (0.3 mi) long, a sacred precinct wall 3 km (2 mi) long, and several reservoirs. In fact, the largest temple complex ever constructed in the Maya Lowlands may have been built there. Before AD 150, El Mirador was clearly a vibrant, dynamic Preclassic city (Matheny 1986:332).

> At some point between AD 150 and AD 200, however, the massive architecture around the Tigre Plaza appears to have been abandoned. Buildings fell into disrepair, and roofs collapsed, smashing the intact vessels on the floors....The discovery of three intact Chicanel vessels, a biface, and waste flakes on the floor of 4D2–1 suggests the abandonment may have been rather rapid, although this assumption may be incorrect. At any rate, it appears reasonable to state that there is no evidence to suggest that any construction or ritual/occupational function of the large monumental architecture occurred after AD 150, since the structural decay was evident then....Toward the latter part of the Late Preclassic period, a major disruption seems to have taken place with a near total abandonment of the major architecture in the Tigre area. (Hansen 1990:211–213)

The abandonment of chultunes, important ideological iconography, and large buildings, as well as the presence of intact Preclassic vessels on the floors of structures, indicate not only that the Tigre area was abandoned, but also that later inhabitants or visitors did little to molest, modify, or maintain the existing structures (Hansen 1990:216).

Bruce Dahlin recovered pedological and archaeological evidence which indicated a severely dry period that was coincident with savanna encroachment, a drop in lake levels, and the abandonment of El Mirador around AD 150. The evidence included the salinization of topsoils, the desiccation of reservoirs and swamps, and the habitation of seasonally inundated swamps. Similar evidence was found at Nakbe in the Calakmul region. In addition, Lake Quexil in the Lake District dropped to its lowest level around AD 200, and savanna pollen reached its maximum at Quexil and Yaxhá/Sacnab. The period AD 150–200 was a time of increased volcanic activity worldwide, and in the Sierra Nevada, it was a time of major glacier advances. Unfortunately, the Scandinavian tree ring records do not go back this far (Richard E. W. Adams 1998:5; Dahlin 1983:248–251, 257).

Richard Hansen compiled a very impressive review of the literature dealing with the Preclassic Abandonment. At some sites, the end of the Preclassic was marked by the actual desertion of the site. At others, there was a reduction in population or a hiatus in construction. For the Late Preclassic Lowlands, Hansen compiled reports of abandonment, population contraction, or hiatus from Dzibilchaltún in the north, to Tikal, Uaxactún, and Seibal in the core, possibly all the way to Quiriguá in the south. His list includes twenty-four other sites spanning the Maya area (Hansen 1990:216–221).

Richard E. W. Adams's and Fred Valdez's work at Río Azul and across the border in Belize indicated growing Late Preclassic populations and a severe retrenchment during the Early Classic (figure 92). Early Classic population levels in the Petén Lake District were truncated, although lakeside populations in the Tayasal-Paxcamam region around Lake Petén Itza, where ample supplies of water were available, seem to have developed smoothly from the Preclassic to the Early Classic. Evidence from the Usumacinta, Candelaria, and Champotón watersheds of the southwestern Lowlands indicate population declines as well (Richard E. W. Adams, 1992, personal communication; Chase 1990:158; Rice and Rice 1990:126).

In the Highlands, the large site of Kaminaljuyú saw the abandonment of its major ceremonial complexes and the degeneration of its subsistence and production systems. The turmoil extended into the Central Depression in Chiapas, as well as sites in the Central Highlands. Along the Pacific Coast, most of the major sites were totally vacated, especially near the Guatemalan-Mexican border and, in the south, near Puerto de San José, including a partial abandonment at Izapa. As Hansen understates, "A review of the archaeological literature indicates that this observation...is pan-Maya in its manifestation" (Dahlin 1983:248–251, 253, 257; Hansen 1990:218–220).

The Preclassic Abandonment was clearly a major catastrophe throughout the Maya region from the northernmost parts of the Yucatán Peninsula to the Pacific coast in the south. The devastation and suffering were widespread and were not to be seen again over such a large area for six hundred years. As we saw, it was a time of peninsula-wide drought in the Lowlands.

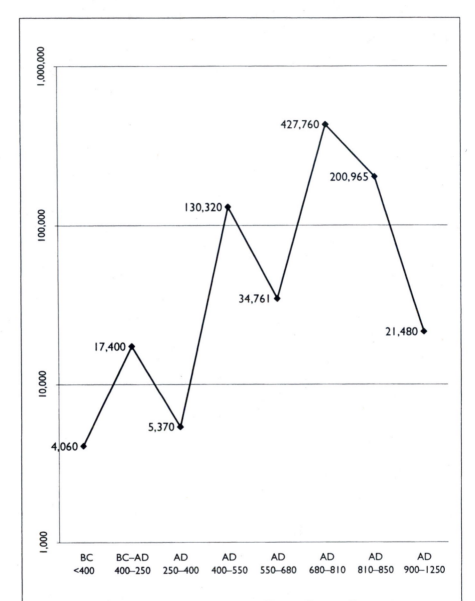

POPULATION HISTORY OF THE THREE RIVERS REGION

Figure 92. Population history of the Three Rivers region—Río Azul, Río Bravo, and Booth's River along the Belizean-Guatemalan border. Note the demographic disasters at the time of the Preclassic Abandonment, the Hiatus, and the Classic Collapse.

Continued on next page

Figure 92—*Continued*

On three occasions, the area lost 70 percent or more of its population. Clearly, demographic disasters were recurring, devastating phenomena, and each coincides with known periods of drought in the Maya Lowlands. The chart is plotted on a logarithmic scale (*Source:* Richard E. W. Adams et al 1999:196).

HIATUS

El Mirador never recovered from the Preclassic Abandonment, although a small population inhabited the site during the Late Classic. Other sites, like Komchen didn't recover until the Late Classic. Most of the sites affected by the Preclassic Abandonment passed through a period of retrenchment before resuming a course of growth and development. The fourth and fifth centuries, in fact, saw what may have been the artistic zenith of Maya civilization. Between AD 535 and 593, however, as dated by Gordon Willey, a sharp reduction occurred in dedicating stelae and monuments in the Petén, a period known as the Hiatus, which serves as the dividing line between Early and Late Classic. The effects of the Hiatus were pronounced in the Three Rivers region (along the Guatemalan-Mexican-Belizean border) and, according to Willey, there is a marked drop in stela carving and dedication for an interval of about sixty years in the central core, in the southwest along the Río de la Pasión and upper Río Usumacinta, from Piedras Negras, in the west, to Copán, in the east. The event is obviously quite widespread. On the other hand, the eastern Lowlands may have been less affected, and Willey believes that for the north, the Hiatus is a time of cultural vigor (Richard E. W. Adams, 1993, personal communication; Mathews 1985:26; Willey 1977:72–73).

Tikal, in the central core, appears to have been hard hit. During the Hiatus, it lost its preeminent position among Petén cities. On a Mesoamerican scale, Teotihuacan withdrew from its role as the Mesoamerican world power, and Tikal lost its principal ally. Tikal was attacked and seemingly defeated on the battlefield by Caracol, a comparatively smaller city in southern Belize. It appears to have been a time of revolts and civil wars. In Tikal, the dynasty which had ruled throughout the Early Classic was overthrown. In the end, as Richard E. W. Adams put it, "It was not until AD 650 that Maya civilization began to function again, and then it was somewhat different than before" (Richard E. W. Adams 1991b:196–197; Mathews 1985:31).

Linda Schele and Peter Mathews, among others, questioned whether the Hiatus actually occurred, or whether it is the result of seeing Maya history from the perspective of Tikal. They argued that the Hiatus is only really visible at Tikal. In other words, it is a Tikal event and not a Maya event (see Culbert 1991:316).

Data from Río Azul, however, provide conclusive evidence linking the Hiatus to a demographic collapse. Adams concluded that the city itself fell and was destroyed about AD 540. In addition, populations in the countryside contracted sharply, not to recover until the eighth century. He is convinced that the Hiatus was not a political perturbation among the elite classes alone, but a more far reaching upheaval affecting all levels of Maya society near Río Azul. Settlement studies performed along the Guatemalan-Belizean-Mexican border, in the Three Rivers region which includes Río Azul, have demonstrated a 73 percent reduction in the population of the area as a whole (figure 92) (Richard E. W. Adams 1992; Richard E. W. Adams et al 1999:196).

The reality of the Hiatus as a genuine demographic disaster is well established. As we saw in the drought map of Texas in 1955–1956 (figure 43 on page 168), the impact of drought can appear to be almost random, with areas of moderate drought surrounded by areas of severe drought. The Hiatus may well have been a period when certain areas were more affected by drought than others, and the random pattern of drought may explain why some cities were able to mount attacks while others were reeling and vulnerable.

On a worldwide basis, AD 536 was the year of a great climatic aberration which brought drought, cold, famine, and death throughout the Northern Hemisphere. It was a time of severe cold in both the Sierra Nevada and Arctic Scandinavia. Scuderi identified AD 540–600 as a period of increased volcanic activity coincident with a concentration of dated glacial deposits. The meteorological model would indicate that a time of worldwide cold was propitious for drought in the Lowlands, and in fact, Curtis, Hodell, and Brenner have reported a severe drought at Punta Laguna, in Quintana Roo, centered around AD 585 ±50 yr. This second episode of demographic disaster for the Maya, then, was also coincident with hemispheric cold and lowland drought.

CLASSIC COLLAPSE

During the eighth century AD, the Maya Lowlands were divided into a number of independent polities. Simon Martin and Nikolai Grube suggested, based on their interpretation of epigraphic evidence, that there were two superstates, Tikal in the Early Classic and Calakmul in the Late Classic. Joyce Marcus proposed that there were six polities, Richard E. W. Adams proposed eight, and Peter Mathews sixty to seventy. Regardless of which estimate is used, the Maya Lowlands were not organized as one hierarchical political structure, but rather as independent, self-governing city-states. Any explanation of the Classic Collapse, therefore, must ex-

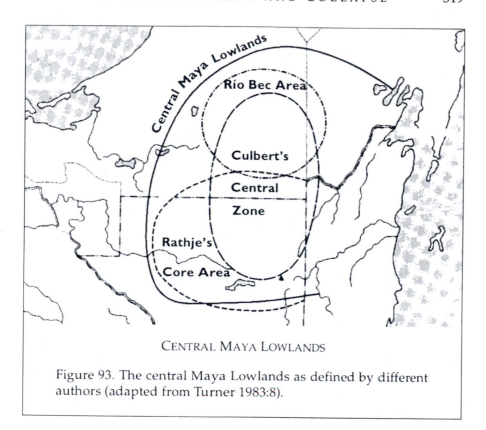

CENTRAL MAYA LOWLANDS

Figure 93. The central Maya Lowlands as defined by different authors (adapted from Turner 1983:8).

plain why many independent states all collapsed at roughly the same time. A solution to the mystery of the Maya Collapse must also be a solution to the question of the simultaneity of the collapse of multiple states (Richard E .W. Adams 1986:437; Marcus 1983:478; Martin and Grube 1994; Mathews 1991:28–29).

The centuries following the Hiatus saw a surge in population levels to their all time highs. Estimates for the Classic population levels range from J. Eric Thompson's estimate of 2–3 million and B. L. Turner II's estimate of 2.6–3.4 million, to T. Patrick Culbert's estimate of 5–6 million, to Herbert Spinden's 1929 estimate of 8 million, to Richard E. W. Adams's 9–14 million, and Sylvanus Morley's estimate of 13 million. The specific areas covered by the preceding estimates differ in their geographical details. (See figure 93 for examples of the differing definitions of the central Maya Lowlands.) However, the numbers give us an idea of the breadth of estimates proposed. Clearly, the population of the Lowlands numbered in the millions of people. The population density was one of the greatest known in the preindustrial world, comparable to that of Java and China, and to the Basin of Mexico at the time of the Spanish Conquest (Richard E. W. Adams 1981:250–251; Cook and Borah 1974:22; Culbert 1988:86; Rice and Culbert 1990:25–26).

Norman Hammond estimated the areal extent of the average Maya state at about 2,000km² (770mi²), which, using Culbert's estimate of 200 people/km², would yield a population of 400,000 per polity, with an urban population of 80,000. Culbert and his colleagues have estimated the size of the Tikal state at 1,963 km² (757 mi²), with a population of 425,000 during the Late Classic. They calculated an urban population of 62,000 for the city of Tikal, with a suburban population of 30,000, and a dependent rural population of 30,000 to 60,000 depending on the size of the surrounding rural area used. For comparison, Classical Athens had a population of 275,000 in 2,600km² (1,000 mi²). We can see, therefore, that Maya polities were relatively large, heavily populated city states (Culbert et al 1990:117; Hammond 1991:259, 278).

The Maya Lowlands, around the year AD 750, were clearly densely populated with well developed urban nuclei, and as we have seen, estimates of the overall population of the Lowlands range from 3 million to 14 million. Between AD 790 and 910, a demographic catastrophe, unparalleled in known human history, devastated the Maya and destroyed their Classic civilization. Millions of people died, major urban centers were abandoned forever, and the richest, most densely populated rural areas of the Petén were never repopulated. Recolonization only began in the mid-twentieth century. Assuming the surviving population numbered no more than 1,000,000 people, the die-off that occurred during the ninth century was between 67 and 93 percent. Either figure describes a period of cultural disintegration and human suffering that is difficult to comprehend (Richard E. W. Adams 1981:251).

It is clear that the Collapse was a severe demographic disaster. But an equally important question remains. Why didn't the Maya recover in the ensuing thousand years? They populated the Petén and built beautiful cities once, why didn't they do it again? One argument has been that their population levels fell too low to allow a comeback in a thousand years. The evidence from other regions, however, would contradict that idea. Early historic depopulation was great in the Americas. In fact, a well documented instance of recovery following depopulation from 50 to 1 (the loss of 98 percent of the population) was reported by Henry Dobyns. We will return to this question in greater detail (Dobyns 1966:416).

SOUTHERN LOWLANDS

First, we need to make some sense of how the Collapse proceeded. The best method to track the progress of the Collapse may well be by analyzing the last inscribed date on monuments at each site. Monuments, for our purposes, include stelae, columns, wall panels, lintels, and staircases, in or on pyramids, temples, palaces, and residences which have hieroglyphic texts inscribed on them. Although the traditional view held that the Collapse occurred more or less randomly over the course of a century, John

Lowe, in his tour de force, *The Dynamics of Apocalypse*, demonstrated that the Collapse was not entirely random, but, in fact, showed a slight linear trend from southwest to northeast, according to his analysis. In fact, there was even more pattern to the Collapse than Lowe saw (Lowe 1985:15, 27).

The La Mojarra text from Veracruz demonstrates that the practice of erecting hieroglyphic texts predates the Classic period. Among the Maya, however, the stela cult appears to have developed originally in the Tikal-Uaxactún area and to have spread directly from there to the rest of the Maya Lowlands. According to Lowe, "In terms of the dissemination of the monument cult, the Southern Maya Lowlands formed a single interacting population." During the Terminal Classic, however, "the increase in the death rate in sites brings the dated monument process to a halt, and apparently that increase is related to a spatial collapse of the area encompassed by centers erecting monuments...a generally implosive geographic patterning of site collapse is apparent" (Justeson and Kaufman 1993:1703; Lowe 1985:15, 27).

SIGNOR-LIPPS EFFECT

If we can, in fact, correlate the cessation of monument building, as indicated by the last dates at each site, with the death of the site, then we can examine the pattern of collapse. In order to do that, it is necessary to turn, for a moment, to palaeontology where researchers have long wrestled with the problem of trying to tie the evidence of the fossil record to a chronological sequence of events.

Walter Alvarez, Luis Alvarez, Frank Asaro, and Helen Michel proposed in 1980 that the extinction of the dinosaurs, and over half of the rest of life on Earth at the end of the Cretaceous era, was due to the impact of a huge asteroid which caused a massive climatic catastrophe, first dropping then raising temperatures around the globe. They proposed that the extinction was catastrophically sudden, not gradual (Alvarez et al 1980:1095–1108).

Interestingly enough for Mayanists, the asteroid's or comet's impact point is the northern coast of Yucatán, centered on the village of Chicxulub, 17 km (10.5 mi) east of the port of Progreso. The buried crater measures 100–200 km (60–120 mi) in diameter, and a portion of the circumference of its floor can be detected from a semicircular ring of cenotes at the surface. When the impact occurred, the Gulf of Mexico was first emptied, then a huge tsunami sloshed back and forth like waves in a bathtub while a fireball carbonized everything between Yucatán and Idaho. The resulting blackout of the sun and extreme climatic disturbances killed most of the Earth's life forms, including the dinosaurs (Monastersky 1992a:56–58; 1992b:100; Morgan et al 1997:472; Pope, Ocampo, and Duller 1991:105; Swisher et al 1992:954–958).

Although the impact theory has now achieved a consensus status, it had to overcome fierce opposition along the way. The most vocal critics were other palaeontologists who believed they saw in the fossil record evidence of a gradual extinction of numerous taxa, the best known being the dinosaurs, ammonites, and certain bivalves. The criticism lodged against the Alvarezes' theory was: given the gradual extinction apparent in the fossil record, how could an impact, or any catastrophe, cause extinctions prior to the actual event (Gould 1992:2–12)?

Philip Signor and Jere Lipps decided to analyze the evidence for gradual declines to determine whether the data actually supported a gradual decline, in contrast to a catastrophic extinction, or whether they might be consistent with an abrupt event. Their analysis provides the mathematical foundation necessary for understanding the data of the fossil record. Their conclusions are known as the Signor-Lipps effect (figures 94 and 95).

Catastrophic hypotheses for mass extinctions are commonly criticized because many taxa gradually disappear from the fossil record prior to the extinction. Presumably, a geologically instantaneous catastrophe would not cause a reduction in diversity or a series of minor extinctions before the actual mass extinction. Two types of sampling effects, however, could cause taxa to appear to decline before their actual biotic extinction. The first of these is reduced sample size provided in the sedimentary record and the second, which we examine in greater detail, is artificial range truncation. The fossil record is discontinuous in time and the recorded ranges of species or of higher taxa can only extend to their last known occurrence in the fossil record. If the distribution of last occurrences is random with respect to actual biotic extinction, then apparent extinctions will begin well before a mass extinction and will gradually increase in frequency until the mass extinction event, thus giving the appearance of a gradual extinction. Other factors, such as regressions, can exacerbate the bias toward gradual disappearance of taxa from the fossil record. Hence, gradual extinction patterns prior to a mass extinction do not necessarily eliminate catastrophic extinction hypotheses....

The apparent decline of taxa prior to a mass extinction may simply reflect sampling effects and not actual diversity trends. Therefore, the apparent record of decline in diversity of various taxa prior to the Cretaceous-Tertiary extinction need not be considered evidence for a gradual extinction mechanism. (Signor and Lipps 1982:291)

In other words, animals die randomly, their remains are preserved randomly, and palaeontologists dig randomly. The result is an apparent gradual die-off, even though the actual extinction could have been totally abrupt.

The concept can be applied to archaeology as well, in particular to the last dates of monuments in the Lowlands. Many sites have badly eroded, illegible stelae and inscriptions, some of which may well have been erected as katun ending markers, maybe even in the final years of the Classic. Other stelae and inscriptions have been defaced, reused, looted, lost, or not yet discovered—reasons which are random in nature. A site may have failed to erect a marker for reasons unrelated to its demise. The presence of dated monuments and their discovery in legible condition represent the random sampling effects described by Signor and Lipps. An apparent gradual cessation of monument building, therefore, is not necessarily evidence of a gradual collapse. An abrupt end could also produce a record of apparent gradual decline.

One can approach the possibility of abrupt disasters in the Lowlands from two perspectives. The first is to assume that all the sites collapsed together at one time. This approach requires one to accept that at sites that have a large number of known, legible stelae, erected over hundreds of years, as many as five katun ending markers are missing, which is probably unlikely.

The second approach is to assume that there was more than one episode of collapse and to try to break down the last dates into groups, so that no more than two katun ending markers are missing at any particular site—with the exception of Naachtun. If one uses dates from all known sites, however, there is a further problem. Some small sites erected only one or two stelae during their lifetimes. It is difficult in those cases to claim that the absence of stelae during a particular period is indicative of anything meaningful. By limiting the analysis to those cities with a courtyard count—a way of measuring the size of a city—greater than 10 in Richard E. W. Adams's and Richard C. Jones's rank ordering scheme, most of which erected a number of stelae during their lifetimes, then the absence of any further monuments may well be indicative of the death of the site. By limiting the missing katun markers to no more than one, the last dates can be grouped into three fifty-year periods: AD 760–810, 811–860, and 861–910. I initially chose the ending dates of these three periods based on the Swedish tree ring records which indicated particularly severe cold spells that might be indicative of drought in Mesoamerica. Applying the Signor-Lipps concept, I reasoned that perhaps one or two katun ending markers might be missing from various sites for the reasons discussed earlier. I counted backwards allowing for two missing katun markers, or forty to fifty years and drew a line across the table I had prepared, as shown in table 12. I then located the cities on a map and drew lines around each cohort, as shown on the map in figure 96. I was quite surprised to find a certain geographical unity to the resulting groupings. Only Nakum, La

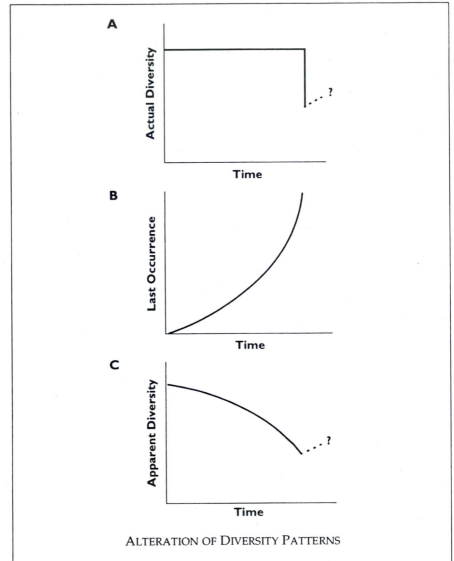

ALTERATION OF DIVERSITY PATTERNS

Figure 94. The alteration of diversity patterns by artificial range truncation. In *A*, the diversity is suddenly reduced by a catastrophic extinction event. *B* presents a cumulative probability curve, showing the probability of artificial range truncation. Imposing the artificial range truncation of *B* on the hypothetical diversity pattern of *A* results in an apparent gradual decline, as shown in *C*. An abrupt event, then, will appear in the record to be a gradual decline (adapted from Signor and Lipps 1982:293).

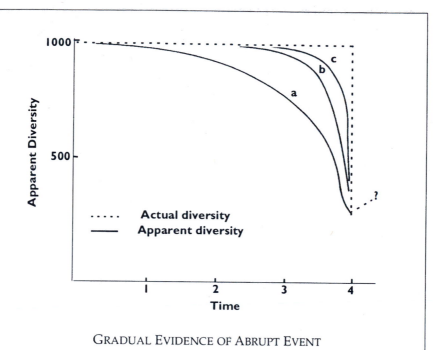

GRADUAL EVIDENCE OF ABRUPT EVENT

Figure 95. As sampling techniques improve, the data improve and the apparent gradualness diminishes. The data approach the abrupt event but never replicate it. According to Signor and Lipps, an abrupt event will always appear to have started before it actually did (adapted from Signor and Lipps 1982:294).

Honradez, and Oxpemul, out of twenty-two cities, are not contained within the rest of their cohort (Richard E. W. Adams 1981:240).

In figure 96, the groups of cities are encircled by a dotted line for AD 760–810, a dashed line for AD 811–860, and a solid line for AD 861–910. The results are quite surprising. Most of the 760–810 sites are grouped together in the west and southwest. The 811–860 sites are in the southeast and the 861–910 sites are concentrated in the core and in the north. Furthermore, attempts to shift the cutoff dates earlier or later result in meaningless groups. Applying the Signor-Lipps effect to last dates, it is apparent from the map that there were three periods of collapse. The first occurred about AD 810 and struck primarily the west and southwest. The second occurred about AD 860 and devastated the southeast. The third is more difficult to estimate. There appears to have been a major cessation of activity in 10.3.0.0.0, AD 890. Only two sites survived to produce monuments later, until AD 906, 10.3.17.12.1, at Uxmal and AD 909, 10.4.0.0.0, at Toniná, none in the Southern Lowlands. (Although a jade gorget with an

SITE	RANK	STARTING DATE	LAST DATE AND SOURCE		1ST YRS	NO.	LAST
Naachtun	21	9.04.10.00.00	9.16.10.00.00	L	524	237	761
Nakum	16	9.17.00.00.00	9.17.10.00.00	L	771	9	780
La Honradez	16	9.17.00.00.00	9.18.00.00.00	L	771	19	790
Polol	10	9.17.07.00.04	9.18.00.00.00	L	777	13	790
Yaxhá	20	8.16.00.00.00	9.18.03.00.00	L	357	436	793
Palenque	11	9.08.16.15.13	9.18.09.04.04	L	610	189	799
Yaxchilán	15	9.00.00.00.00	9.18.17.13.14	SF	435	373	808
Calakmul	42	9.04.00.00.00	9.19.00.00.00	L	514	296	810
Piedras Negras	11	9.00.00.00.00	9.19.00.00.00	L	435	375	810
Copán	14	9.01.10.00.00	9.19.10.00.00	SF	465	355	820
Naranjo	42	9.09.02.00.04	9.19.10.00.00	L	615	205	820
Oxpemul	11	9.12.15.00.00	10.00.00.00.00	L	687	143	830
Machaquilá	10	9.14.00.00.00	10.00.10.17.15	SF	711	130	841
Ucanal	11	10.01.00.00.00	10.01.00.00.00	L	849	0	849
Caracol	17	9.04.00.00.00	10.01.10.00.00	SF	514	345	859
Tayasal	10	9.18.15.00.00	10.02.00.00.00	L	805	64	869
Tikal	85	8.12.14.08.15	10.02.00.00.00	L	292	577	869
La Muñeca	11	9.17.10.10.00	10.03.00.00.00	L	781	108	889
Seibal	23	9.15.15.00.00	10.03.00.00.00	L	746	143	889
Uaxactún	23	8.14.10.13.15	10.03.00.00.00	L	328	561	889
Chichén Itza		10.01.17.05.13	10.03.00.15.01	L	866	24	890
Uxmal		10.03.06.00.00	10.03.17.12.01	L	895	11	906

RB GILL 2000

STARTING/ENDING HIEROGLYPHIC DATES IN MAYA LOWLANDS

Table 12. Last dates on Maya monuments for sites of rank order 10 or greater, grouped by years. Except for the case of Naachtun in the first group, there are no more than two missing katun markers at each site within each group. This leads to the conclusion, applying the Signor-Lipps effect, that three successive abrupt events may have occurred about AD 810, 860, and 890–910 (*Sources*: Adams and Jones 1981; Lowe 1985:213–216; Schele and Freidel 1990:381).

inscribed date of 10.4.0.0.0, January 18, 909, was found at Tzibanché, it does not constitute a monument. It does, of course, represent the last date found on anything in the Southern Lowlands.) These dates may be indicative of two episodes of collapse, one in 890, the other in 909. On the other hand, it might indicate one last, devastating catastrophe in 909 or, of course, shortly thereafter. A third possibility would be a serious, deepening drought which was underway by 890 and peaked after 910. There are no dates recorded anywhere on Maya monuments after 10.4.0.0.0, January 18, AD 909 (GMT), including Chichén Itza, as we will see later in this chapter, until Mayapán emerges around 1200.

Wibjörn Karlén identified multiyear periods of severe cold from Swedish tree rings around AD 800, 860, and 910, although the entire century was cold. Throughout the Northern Hemisphere, as evidenced by palaeoclimatic records from California, Colorado, Alaska, Canada, and northern Europe, it was as cold as during the Little Ice Age. A period of severe cold in the Northern Hemisphere would indicate climatic conditions conducive to a southwestward displacement of the North Atlantic High, bringing drought to Yucatán. The three surges of cold in Arctic Sweden occur around the time of the three proposed phases of collapse in the Lowlands. As evidence for two of the three phases, Curtis, Hodell, and Brenner have reported lake sediment studies indicating a severe drought at Punta Laguna with its peak in 863 and a severe drought at Lake Chichancanab with its peak at 922. Other studies from Laguna de Cocos on Albion Island in Belize and Cenote San José Chulchacá in northern Yucatán have indicated increased aridity in the Terminal Classic.

The evidence from settlement data at Tikal indicates that even those cities in the central zone which survived into the late ninth century may have been battered earlier in the century. Culbert estimated that the population during Tepeu 3 or Eznab time, AD 830–909, was only one-tenth the size of Tikal's pre-AD 800 maximum. In addition, Culbert suggested that the latest major construction at Tikal dates to AD 810, although the last date present is 10.2.0.0.0, AD 869. Whatever later construction occurred tends to be small and of shoddy workmanship. Culbert emphasized, however, that many buildings remain to be dated. Tikal appears to have barely stayed alive through the ninth century until it finally fell, probably in AD 890–910. Robert Fry examined the surrounding agricultural zone to determine whether Tikal's urban inhabitants had fled to the country. His surveys indicated that the depopulation in the rural areas was as great as in the urban core. Tikal appears to have lost 90 percent of its urban and rural population around AD 810. The implication, then, is that even though cities in the central core survived until 890–910, they may have only barely survived (Culbert 1973:67–73; see also Fry 1969).

ANCIENT FAMINE

One sign of possible ancient famine is found at Tikal. According to Peter Harrison, human remains from a Terminal Late Classic midden showed signs of burning and chewing that point to cannibalism. One of the widely accepted circumstances of cannibalism in human societies is survival cannibalism, practiced when people have absolutely nothing left to eat and are on the verge of death from starvation. Cannibalism which shows up so late in the history of Tikal in the midst of severe environmental stress could, in fact, be evidence of desperate people in a life or death situation (Harrison quoted in Pohl 1985).

Otherwise, specific archaeological evidence for ancient famine is not available. There is, however, evidence of the general nutritional status of the Maya. Frank Saul studied the skeletal remains of ninety individuals representing time periods from 800 BC to AD 1000. The skeletons show evidence of nutritional stress and disease, specifically, growth arrest at weaning, scurvy, and treponemal infection. Saul concluded that the general level of health and energy was so depressed among a significantly large portion of the population that it may have contributed to the collapse of Maya culture (Massey 1989:7).

THE GULF COAST PEOPLE

As the Collapse unfolded, most of the inhabitants of the Lowlands died where they lived—or at least nearby. Although there is no evidence of massive migrations of millions of people, the migration of some tens or hundreds of thousands from the Petén to the Puuc and Chichén Itza is likely. The Gulf Coast People began to move as well. Their homeland lay along the Gulf coast from eastern Veracruz through Tabasco to Campeche, in a region known as the Chontalpa or Nonoalco. It included the area of the Usumacinta-Grijalva delta, a low semi-swamp which Eric Thompson de-

---

THREE PHASES OF COLLAPSE

Figure 96. (*Opposite*) A map of last monument dates at sites of rank order 10 or greater in Richard E. W. Adams's and Chris Jones's scheme, shown with *solid circles*. The lines have been drawn to include some sites whose last dates are known but which have a rank order of less than 10, *open circles*. ❶, ①, ▪▪▪▪ indicate last dates between AD 760 and 810, ❷, ②, ▪ ▪ ▪ between AD 811 and 860, and ❸, ③, ▬▬▬ between AD 861 and 910 (*Sources*: Adams and Jones 1981; Lowe 1985:213–216; Schele and Freidel 1990:381; underlying geographical map adapted from Lowe 1985:2).

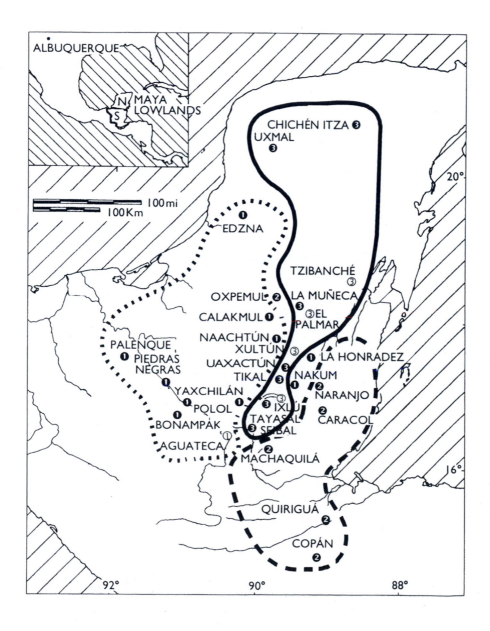

scribed as "a vast green desolation broken by innumerable ponds, swamps, and sinuous, muddy streams which the almost imperceptible gradient does little to speed." The natural transport was by water. Both Nahuat and Maya speaking villages were, and still are, interspersed in the region, and many of the inhabitants were bilingual. Hernán Cortés's mistress and interpreter, Marina, who spoke both Putún and Nahuat, came from the region (J. E. S. Thompson 1970:5–7).

In the west, groups of Gulf Coast People, variously known as Nonoalca, Chontal, Putún, Itza, Xíu, Dzul, Acalán, and others, moved to the southeast up the Usumacinta and the Río de la Pasión to Altar de Sacrificios and Seibal. At Seibal, there is a clear distinction between the original inhabitants and the new arrivals, not only in iconography and hieroglyphs, but also in the physical characteristics of the people portrayed on stelae, although not in the population as a whole. In the east, they settled at Ucanal on the Belize River and they may have moved up the Río Azul to the city of Río Azul, although Adams believes that Puuc or Yucatec invaders are more likely. They established themselves in the north at Uxmal, at Chichén Itza, and at Dzibilchaltún, although the time of their arrival is not clear (Richard E. W. Adams 1993, personal communication; Danforth 1994; J. Graham 1990:43; Tourtellot 1990:139).

They were seagoing traders who circled the peninsula in canoes from the Chontalpa to the Sula Plain in Honduras, establishing trading ports at Xicalango, Isla Cerritos, Cozumel, Nito, and as far south as Quiriguá. This migration does not appear to have been organized, but rather a series of independent movements of separate groups who may have been hostile to one another. Murals at Chichén Itza depict both Maya and Gulf Coast People as victorious warriors and submissive captives at the same battle. Gulf Coast Peoples appear to have fought each other as fiercely as they fought the indigenous Maya (A. Andrews and Robles C. 1985:67; Sharer 1985:250–252; J. E. S. Thompson 1970:7–8; Wren and Schmidt 1991:212).

Other groups of Gulf Coast People moved east to the Mexican Highlands to establish Tula and perhaps other cities. A great diaspora of Gulf Coast Peoples appears to have occurred in the mid-ninth century, a period of serious environmental stress in Mesoamerica, although there may have been earlier migrations as well (Davies 1977:150–160).

The Terminal Classic probably saw the migration of tens or hundreds of thousands of southern refugees north to the Puuc and to Chichén Itza. A genuine explosion of building activity resulted at Chichén Itza and in the Puuc during the waning years of the Classic period. At both Chichén Itza and Uxmal, the known dates span relatively short periods. (See table 13 on page 332 for Uxmal and table 14 on page 341 for Chichén Itza.) There was probably a movement of people into the Southern Highlands around Toniná as well (Schele and Freidel 1990:392).

In the end, however, the migrations involved relatively small numbers of people, and we are left with the conclusion that millions of Classic Maya died near where they lived.

WEST COAST

Along the western coast, the data are very sparse. Joseph Ball, however, identified a 150 to 250 year Postclassic gap in the ceramic sequence at Laguna de Términos and along the Campeche-Tabasco coastal plain to the west, which would indicate a contraction of population in the region beginning with the onset of the Collapse (Ball 1985:239).

THE NORTHERN LOWLANDS

In the Northern Lowlands, in the cenote zone, a larger population survived the effects of the Classic catastrophe. During the Terminal Classic, Maya states flourished in the northwestern plains and in the modified northeastern forests. It was a time of vigorous activity for cities like Uxmal, Sayil, Chichén Itza, Yaxuná, and Cobá. By AD 910, however, most of these cities had been abandoned, and those in which populations survived no longer engaged in the full complexity of Classic Maya culture (Schele and Freidel 1990:346).

The chronology in the north is more difficult to sort out than for the south. Clearly, some populations survived the Collapse and continued to inhabit the area until the arrival of the Spanish in the sixteenth century. How the various populations survived, how many survived, and where they survived is more problematic.

In the Puuc, the ninth century saw an explosive rate of population increase, perhaps due to refugee migrations fleeing the deteriorating conditions in the south. For the region as a whole, H. E. D. Pollock concluded that Classic Puuc civilization ended suddenly and at its peak, sometime in the tenth century, possibly for climatic reasons.

> Building activity seems simply to have ceased rather than to have continued in the old style or to have taken on new directions. The existence of several partly completed buildings, each employing an advanced and apparently late masonry technique, suggests a climatic termination to what had been a thriving architectural tradition. (Pollock 1980:589–590)

At Uxmal, according to Jeff Kowalski, "combined architectural, ceramic, epigraphic, and sculptural evidence from Uxmal and elsewhere certainly suggests that Pure Florescent buildings were not built long after AD 907." A painted capstone in the East Structure bears a date of AD 906, the last date at Uxmal. Structures were started but never completed, not only at Uxmal, but also at other sites as well. The three corrected radiocar-

LOCATION	TYPE	AD	LONG COUNT	SOURCE
Nunnery, Stela 17	Carved	895	10.03.06.00.00	Kowalski 1987:36
		900	10.03.11.00.00	
Nunnery, Building Y Capstone	Painted	897	10.03.08.07.12	Thompson 1973:
		907	10.03.18.09.12	Fig 4
House of the Governor Altar 4	Carved	898	10.03.09.00.00	Kowalski 1987:37
		911	10.04.02.00.00	
Ball Court Rings	Carved	905	10.03.15.16.14	Kelley 1982:15
		905	10.03.15.16.15	
Nunnery, E Structure, Capstone	Painted	906	10.03.17.12.01	Thompson 1973:62

LOCATION	TYPE	CAL AD 1σ RANGE	SOURCE
Casa del Adivino	14C	±619–667	Andrews IV, V 1980:283
Las Monjas Addition	14C	±715–889	Andrews IV, V
	14C	±870–1040	1980:283

RB GILL 2000

HIEROGLYPHIC AND RADIOCARBON DATES AT UXMAL

Table 13. Known dates from Uxmal. Where alternative readings are possible, both dates have been given. The radiocarbon dates have been calibrated and the 1σ range is indicated. The House of the Governor dates are considered tenuous (calibration by CALIB, Stuiver and Reimer 1993).

bon dates associated with architecture at Uxmal range from cal AD 619–667 to 870–1040, the latter from a lintel in the North Structure of the Nunnery which appears to be a Late Classic date. All the known hieroglyphic dates from Uxmal fall in katun 12 Ahau ending 10.4.0.0.0, between AD 890 and 909 (table 13). These are the only known lowland monument dates occurring after AD 890 (including Chichén Itza, as we will see further on) until Mayapán emerges in the late twelfth century. Uxmal seems to have continued building buildings—or at least leaving legible dates—twenty years longer than any other lowland site. Kowalski estimates the final abandonment of Uxmal between AD 925 and 975 (Kowalski 1987:39, 51, 245).

In the northwestern zone as a whole, all known important Terminal Classic sites collapsed. At Dzibilchaltún, Andrews IV and Andrews V identified the period after AD 1000 as a period of severe depopulation, with no major architecture reported. What few buildings were constructed appear to involve the reuse of earlier veneer (Andrews IV and V 1980:311; Andrews V and Sabloff 1986:444).

Turning to the northeastern zone, William Folan describes the maximum period of development at Cobá as occurring during the Machukaani period between AD 600–800. "Following these periods of considerable activity and political importance, Cobá entered into apparent decline, manifested by a reduction in its political and economic importance around AD 900–1000. Cobá probably functioned at this time as a chiefdom rather than as the state-level society it had been during its Machukaani period." A lake sediment core taken from Lake Cobá shows an absence of maize pollen during the Collapse, indicating a cessation of agricultural activity in the area. *Zea* shows up again later. Cobá, which is located at the site of a fresh water lagoon, appears to have survived the Collapse—but to have survived badly battered. Based on the pollen evidence, it may have been briefly abandoned during the Collapse (Folan 1983b:213; Leyden, Brenner, and Dahlin 1998:111).

CHICHÉN ITZA: TRADITIONAL HISTORY

The history of Chichén Itza is the most enigmatic of all the major Maya cities. Yet it is an enigma which must be addressed. Its history, according to the orthodox consensus, represents a serious anomaly. As all the rest of the great Maya cities lay empty, deserted, and silent, the traditional history says that Chichén Itza boomed, apparently unaffected by the devastation, suffering, and death that surrounded it. How can that be? How can Chichén Itza, alone among all the great Maya cities, have escaped the effects of the drought and famine which ravaged the rest? These are important questions which deserve a lengthy digression to address.

Over the past century, its history has been repeatedly reinterpreted, moving its period of florescence earlier and earlier. The current orthodox theory of Chichén Itza's history is more or less as proposed by Alfred Tozzer in 1957. He identified five major periods. Chichén Itza I ran from AD 600 to 900 and was identified as the Yucatán-Maya phase, as distinguished from the southern Classic, a style developed in the north and similar to the style developed in the Puuc. A number of buildings at Chichén were assigned by Tozzer to this period.

The next period is Chichén II which ran from AD 948 to 1145, the Toltec-Maya phase. Tozzer believed there was an *entrada* of Toltec warriors between AD 950 and 1000 who conquered the local population and began an extended occupation of the city and surrounding areas. This would have been the time for the arrival of K'uk'ulkan I, although Tozzer believed the evidence for such an actual person is weak (Tozzer 1957:30–32).

> The position of the city in connection with its neighbors, starting just before or about the beginning of the second millennium, is pre-eminent as proved by archaeology....
>
> In this second epoch of Chichén history, no other contemporaneous site anywhere in the Maya area shows such activity or such amazing results from the infusion of new ideas which came from the Toltec and the Territory later to be called Mexico. (Tozzer 1957:31)

Gordon Willey observed that following the establishment of the Toltec related presence, "there can be little doubt but that Chichén Itza then became the power center of the northern Maya Lowlands for approximately the next 200 years." Ralph Roys believed that "the previous hegemony of Chichén Itza, before Mayapán became a ruling city, probably covered pretty well the entire peninsula." Chichén was believed to have achieved a level of statehood and organizational development rarely achieved by other Maya states. This was believed to be a period of substantial construction activity and cultural vigor. Many of the major buildings at the site were believed to date from this period. Chichén II came to an end with the supposed abandonment of the city by the Itza around 1150 (Roys quoted in Tozzer 1957:31; Tozzer 1957:32; Willey 1986:174).

Tozzer identified a second Mexican related period as Chichén III which ran from 1150 to 1260, from the abandonment by the Itza to the founding of Mayapán. He suggested that the Itza and K'uk'ulkan II may have arrived during this period (Tozzer 1957:35).

Chichén IV, 1280–1450, follows, an archaeologically uninteresting period during which the Itza are beset with difficulties. Tozzer marked the end of this period with the Hunac Ceel episode, which he believed occurred in 1451, after which the Itza again abandoned Chichén and migrated to Tayasal in Lake Petén Itza (Tozzer 1957:47).

The last phase is Chichén V, 1460–1542. The Itza were gone and the Spanish arrived to conquer the Northern Lowlands (Tozzer 1957:58).

It is important to emphasize that the traditional view of Chichén Itza's history holds that its period of greatest political, cultural, and artistic accomplishment occurred after AD 950. Furthermore, there was a clear distinction drawn between the periods of Maya dominance and Toltec or Mexican dominance at the site. In fact, the city itself was seen as consisting of two separate centers, one Maya, the other Toltec, which were built during distinct, temporally separated periods.

Willey, however, while supporting much of the traditional history of Chichén Itza, has pointed out a serious shortcoming:

> One of the problems and complexities of the Early Postclassic Period in the Northern Lowlands is what appears to be a lack of other large sites in the Chichén Maya-Toltec tradition. That is, Chichén Itza is not only a paramount city of the period; it is the only great city. (Willey 1986:172)

A great city, however, cannot develop in a vacuum. As we saw in chapter 3, a certain minimum critical mass is necessary for complexity to develop in any organized system. A major capital must be supported by a large sustaining area of surrounding agricultural zones, populated by peasants producing food surpluses, and a network of regional centers, supplying the agricultural zones with trade goods and receiving and redistributing their agricultural surpluses. There must be sufficient food available within one day's transportation distance or about 30 km (18 mi). An advanced, complex, hierarchical society requires a strong flow of energy through it to support the levels of complexity. But none of the support system existed for the supposed imperial Chichén Itza. It was meant to be the capital of an empire, but an empire of what? The surrounding country was devastated by the Collapse and appears to have been largely abandoned.

If we assume, for the sake of argument, that Chichén had an urban population of roughly 30,000 people—a number which could be either high or low—and we assume that the agricultural surplus available to support it was 10 to 20 percent, then the surrounding area would have had a population of 150,000 to 300,000. Yet there is no evidence currently available to suggest that such large populations existed in the countryside during the Postclassic.

Chichén Itza itself, however, does appear to have been inhabited during the Postclassic. The question, then, is not whether people were living there, but what was the size of the population. Was the Postclassic population the largest Chichén had ever seen, or was it severely reduced from its Classic peak? In other words, did it boom before the Collapse or after?

TOLTECS

Before we can suggest a possible answer to that question, we have to look at the question of whether or not there was a Postclassic Toltec invasion and conquest. It is reasonable to surmise that the non-Maya artistic influences found at Chichén were brought by the arriving immigrants who are pictured on stelae and in murals. But who were these people? They have been variously described as Itza, Putún, Chontal, Gulf Coast People, Mexicans, or Toltecs. Their homeland has been identified as either the

Chontalpa or Nonoalco, along the Veracruz-Tabasco-Campeche coast or Tula in the Mexican Highlands (J. E. S. Thompson 1970:11; Tozzer 1957:36).

One of the arguments made for dating the zenith of Chichén Itza in the Postclassic is that the art and architecture show clear associations with that of Tula, Hidalgo. Chichén Itza, therefore, was believed to have been invaded by Toltecs who brought their art and architecture with them. Since Tula was a Postclassic city, so Chichén Itza must have been a Postclassic city.

But who were the Toltecs? Nigel Davies identifies the Toltecs as the merger of two distinct migrations, the Nonoalca migration from the east and the Tolteca-Chichimeca migration from the west. It was the merger of these two peoples that resulted in changing Tula from a sleepy city to the dominant city of its time, AD 850–1179, in the Mexican Highlands (Davies 1977:149–160).

Who, then, were the Nonoalcas? According to Davies, "the Nonoalcas' place of origin, the Tabasco region, is relatively easy to identify." He believes that they were a Gulf Coast People, with their legendary homeland, Huehuetlapallan Nonoalco, lying just south of Coatzacoalcos, along the Tabasco-Veracruz border, adjacent to the Chontalpa, a possible homeland of Chichén Itza's immigrant settlers. In the merger of the two ethnic groups at Tula, the Nonoalcas were the more learned ethnic group. "They stand out as par excellence the *Kulturvolk*, the bearers of the most prized arts and skills of Mesoamerica and guardians of the ancient lore." In fact, he believes that the first Topiltzin Quetzalcóatl was a Nonoalca (Davies 1977:149–160, 167–168).

> It is not altogether surprising that one should possess more archaeological evidence of these people [the Tolteca-Chichimeca] than of the westward moving Nonoalcas; the latter probably constituted a less numerous elite, whereas the Tolteca-Chichimecas formed the bulk of the combined population. It is natural that the written sources refer more to the Nonoalcas, who, if fewer in number, were certainly more literate; they were thus likely to keep written records, even if these were later destroyed, to survive mainly as oral sagas. The Nonoalcas surely provided the intellectual leadership of Tollan's population, as Torquemada and others imply. In Tollan, they presumably contributed the brains, and the Tolteca-Chichimecas the brawn. (Davies 1977:176–177)

We are left to ask when this migration may have happened. Davies emphasizes that the founding of Tula cannot be conclusively established, but he suggests that the Tula-Mazapan horizon begins in the mid-ninth century (Davies 1977:127, 175).

Some of the buildings at Chichén are very Maya in their appearance while others seem to be more Mexicanized in style. When the traditional history was being developed, each major building was assigned to the

Classic or Postclassic periods depending on whether the architectural style was determined to be Maya or Toltec. As can be seen in table 14 on page 341, however, the first so-called Toltec architecture in Chichén has been dated to the mid-ninth century as well. The founding of Tula and the introduction of so-called Toltec influences to Chichén Itza appear to be contemporaneous events and may both be the result of a mid-ninth century diaspora of Gulf Coast Peoples from their ancestral homeland in the region of Tabasco.

In other words, the art and architectural forms seen at Chichén Itza and at Tula, rather than having been brought to Chichén Itza from Tula, may have been taken to each place by migrating Gulf Coast People from adjacent homelands along the Tabasco-Veracruz border. The similarity of style may indicate neighboring homelands for both groups of newly arrived immigrants, rather than a direct colonial tie between the two cities, as the similarity of artistic styles and religious traditions in both Lima and Mexico City is the result of a common homeland for their new immigrants, rather than the result of either Lima or Mexico City being a colony of the other.

K'UK'ULKAN

What about the clear presence of Quetzalcóatl-K'uk'ulkan, a deity known to be associated with Tula, at Chichén Itza? As we have seen, the first Topiltzin Quetzalcóatl at Tula was a Nonoalco. In fact, according to Davies, K'uk'ulkan was associated with the Gulf Coast even in the days of Teotihuacan.

> The new Quetzalcóatl may have emanated from Teotihuacan, but the development of his worship seems to have germinated outside that center, in Tabasco or in the Huaxteca. It subsequently spread to Xochicalco and the Mixteca and later to Tollan Xicoctitlan [Tula]. (Davies 1977:122)

The concept of K'uk'ulkan may, in fact, have a Maya origin. In modern Yucatec, Quetzalcóatl, generally translated as the feathered snake, is known as K'uk'ulkan. I have long been troubled by the idea that people would worship a feathered snake, although I am certainly aware of similar religious traditions throughout the world. Nevertheless, it is more reasonable, in my opinion, to accept that the supreme deity would be humanlike and would have a name or title like God of Gods, or the King of Gods, or the Lord of Heaven.

Let us suppose, then, that the supreme god, or possibly even a monotheistic god, would be called God, the Lord of Heaven. What would he be called in modern Yucatec Maya? *K'u* is God, *k'ul* is used to mean either a divinity or a secular administrative officer, just as Lord in English and

THE HEAD-LEAF GLYPH

Figure 97. The standard form, according to Beyer, of a glyph frequently seen at Chichén Itza, which can be read as *k'uk'um kan*, feather snake, representing *K'u u k'ul ka'an*, God, the Lord of Heaven. The feather is self-evident, although it was previously read as a leaf. The snake head has two fangs, the upper half of the body has a snakeskin pattern and the lower half represents the locomotion scales, which is the way snakes are depicted artistically throughout Mesoamerica. It is clearly a drawing of a snake (Beyer 1937:158).

Señor in Spanish are used both religiously and secularly. *Ka'an* means heaven. In modern Yucatec, then, God, the Lord of Heaven would be called *K'u u k'ul ka'an*, a virtual homophone for K'uk'ulkan.

There is no readily available pictorial representation of either God or heaven. However, there are near homonyms available. The Maya were known for their tendency to design glyphs based on rebus writing and to pun, or choose near homonyms to represent an idea. Feather is *k'uk'um* and *kan* is snake (see Barrera Vásquez 1980). *K'uk'um kan*, feather snake, is a near homonym for *K'u u k'ul ka'an* and would serve as a rebus representation for the supreme deity. K'uk'ulkan, or Quetzalcóatl, would derive his feather snake name from the rebus representation, *k'uk'um kan*, for God, the Lord of Heaven, *K'u u k'ul ka'an*. If it is true that the so-called head-leaf glyph (figure 97) represents K'uk'ulkan, and let me emphasize that my proposed reading is at this time very speculative and could be wrong, the implications would be dramatic. K'uk'ulkan would be mentioned in Classic texts, before the rise of Tula as a Mesoamerican power.

The Gulf Coast People who arrived at Chichén Itza may have been Maya speakers and may well have brought the concept of K'uk'ulkan from their Gulf Coast homeland. One might conclude that the Nonoalcas were also Maya speakers who migrated to the Mexican Highlands. As Davies puts it,

> The possibility should not be overlooked that at least part of
> such a composite group of migrants might have been speakers of

a Mayoid language....Not only did Chontal prevail in the Tabasco area at the time of the Conquest, interspersed with Nahuatl, but Mayan cultural influences had been actively present there during the Late Maya Classic period, that is to say, in the era preceding the Nonoalca departure. (Davies 1977:167-168)

The Toltecs, the Chichén Itza migrants, and K'uk'ulkan, the deity, then, may well have been Gulf Coast People from the Tabasco-Veracruz border. If the same artistic, architectural, and religious forms were carried to both Chichén Itza and Tula by related peoples, it is not necessary to postulate a direct colonial tie between Tula and Chichén Itza in order to explain the art and the religious similarities at the two sites any more than it is necessary to postulate a colonization of Lima by Mexico in order to explain the similarity of architectural, artistic, and religious traditions in the two cities. We must look to the archaeology of the Tabasco-Veracruz region for confirmation.

CHICHÉN ITZA: DATES

Attempts to date structures based on stylistic arguments can be highly subjective. Different investigators have used stylistic arguments to place the same structures at Chichén Itza in time periods hundreds of years apart.

The most important dates are those furnished us by the city itself, dates from carved inscriptions and dates from radiocarbon samples from within various structures. Table 14 presents the inscribed dates as originally interpreted together with recent reinterpretations of certain key dates. It also includes the available ^{14}C dates. One critical, salient fact is that the reinterpreted hieroglyphic dates are in line with available ^{14}C dates. Two independent sources of dates, then, coincide with each other.

Thompson's proposed readings of two dates, AD 968 and 998, were anomalous with regard to the other available dates, falling after AD 900. The supposed Postclassic dates were then relied on as proof of major Postclassic construction at Chichén. Both dates, however, have now been reinterpreted. The first, his proposed date for the Caracol frieze, AD 968, has been reinterpreted by David Kelley as 10.3.0.15.1, which converts to AD 890 based on the Goodman-Martínez-Thompson correlation (Kelley 1982:13).

The second, the date on a column in front of the High Priest's Grave, which Thompson gave as AD 998, I reinterpret as AD 880. The column has a portrait carved on the front with a text inscribed horizontally across the top and vertically down the right side (figure 98). The critical date runs vertically from F1 or F2 to F6 and it reads 10 *Ix*, [*K'in*] (perhaps with *ti'*), 2 *Xul*, 11 *tun*, (perhaps *ti'*) 1 *Ahau*, which gives 10.2.10.14.14: April 22, 880, using the GMT correlation between the Maya calendar and our own Gregorian calendar. This follows the normal format for dates at Chichén Itza,

LOCATION	STYLE	LONG COUNT	AD	SOURCE
Water Trough Lintel 1	Maya	10.01.17.05.13	866	Thompson 1937:186 See Kelley 1982:13–14
Water Trough Lintel 2	Maya	10.01.18.06.06	867	Thompson 1937:186
Casa Colorada Band	Maya	10.02.00.01.09 10.02.00.15.03	869 870	Kelley 1982:14
Halakal	Maya	10.02.00.07.09	870	Thompson 1937:186
Akab ts'ib	Maya	10.02.01.00.00	870	Thompson 1937:186
Yula, Lintel 1		10.02.04.08.04	874	Thompson 1937:186
Yula, Lintel 2		10.02.04.02.01 10.02.04.08.12	873 874	Krochok 1988:152 Thompson 1937:186
Great Ball Court	Toltec	10.01.15.03.06 10.02.08.06.11 10.03.01.09.06	864 877 890	Wren Schmidt 1991:208 Gill 1994:422 Gill 1994:422
Initial Series	Toltec	10.02.09.01.09	878	Thompson 1937:186
Temple of Three Lintels	Maya	10.02.10.00.00	879	Thompson 1937:186
Las Monjas	Toltec	10.02.10.11.17	880	Thompson 1937:186
High Priest's Grave	Toltec	10.00.12.12.08 10.02.10.14.14 10.08.10.11.00	842 880 998	Schele Freidel 1990:356 Gill 1994:422 Thompson 1937:186
Temple of Four Lintels	Maya	10.02.12.01.08	881	Thompson 1937:186
Temple of Four Lintels	Maya	10.02.12.02.04 10.02.13.00.09 10.03.05.05.09	881 883 894	Thompson 1937:186 Krochok 1988:153 Krochok 1988:153
Temple of One Lintel	Maya	10.02.15.00.00	884	Thompson 1937:186

LOCATION	STYLE	LONG COUNT	AD	SOURCE
Temple of the Hieroglyphic Jambs, Str 6E3	Maya	10.02.15.02.13	884	Ruppert 1952: Fig 151 Kelley 1982:12–13
Structure 6E1	Toltec	10.02.15.00.00	884	After Str 6E3, Gill 1994
		10.01.00.00.00	849	Style, Proskrkff 1970:465
Caracol stela	M/T	10.02.17.00.00	886	Thompson 1937:186
		10.03.07.00.00	907	Kelley 1982:12
Caracol frieze	M/T	10.03.00.15.01	890	Kelley 1982:13
		10.07.00.05.01	968	Thompson 1937:186
Temple of the Warriors	Toltec	Style	850–950	Schele and Freidel 1990: Photo

LOCATION	STYLE	1σ RANGE	CAL AD	SOURCE
Casa Colorada– beam	Maya	±650–770	670	Andrews IV, V 1980:283
La Iglesia 1–beam	Maya	±650–770	670	Andrews IV, V 1980:283
La Iglesia 2–beam	Maya	±780–970	890	Andrews IV, V 1980:283
El Castillo–lintel	Toltec	±790–980	890	Andrews IV, V 1980:283
El Castillo (rerun)	Toltec	±780–1010	890	Andrews IV, V 1980:283
Las Monjas– East Patio		±670–1120	890	Andrews IV, V 1980:283

RB GILL 2000

HIEROGLYPHIC AND RADIOCARBON DATES AT CHICHÉN ITZA

Table 14. Hieroglyphic and radiocarbon dates from major buildings and stelae at Chichén Itza. Some hieroglyphic dates have possible alternative readings, all of which are listed. Note that the only dates with proposed interpretations past AD 900 also have alternative readings prior to 900. The long count dates were all correlated using the GMT correlation, regardless of the correlation originally used when proposed. Radiocarbon dates were calibrated using CALIB (Stuiver and Reimer 1993).

as deciphered by Eric Thompson, a way of inscribing dates which is unique to the North and is characterized by four consecutive numbers with a *k'in* glyph occasionally introducing the date sequence and occasionally following the first number, exactly the pattern of glyphs and numbers present in the right-hand column, F1 to F6. It is important to emphasize that the glyphs themselves, as opposed to the numbers, were unreadable at the time the stela was discovered, except for F6 which was clearly an *Ahau*. The numbers, however, are quite clear in Edward Thompson's original photographs. Unfortunately, today, the entire text on the actual stela is totally illegible, so we must rely on the photographs. The interpretation presented here, then, is based on the numbers and the position of the glyphs in the Yucatecan format. From the numbers alone, it is possible to calculate the date without having to read the glyphs. In another work, I analyze the date in greater detail (Beyer 1937:127–145; Gill 1994:423–434; Edward H. Thompson 1938:23, 61; J. Eric S. Thompson 1937:1).

The two anomalous dates, which had been relied on as proof of Chichén's Postclassic vigor, are no longer Postclassic. They are both Classic dates. There are no hieroglyphic dates at Chichén past AD 890, as can be seen in table 14 on page 341. All the monumental and radiocarbon dates are no longer anomalous at all. They fall within the same pattern seen at other great Maya cities in the Lowlands and, on their face, they suggest that Chichén Itza was a great Classic city whose period of florescence ended along with its dates by AD 900.

If this is true, Chichén Itza is no longer an anomaly in Maya archaeology and it is no longer necessary to explain why it alone was spared the scourges of the Collapse.

THE HIGH PRIEST'S STELA

Figure 98. (*Opposite*) A drawing of the column in front of the High Priest's Grave at Chichén Itza. The glyphs across the top of the portrait are numbered A–F1. The glyphs along the right side are F1–F6. Glyphs F2–F6 follow the Yucatecan method of dating exactly, giving the date 10 *Ix*, 2 *Xul*, 11 *tun*, 1 *Ahau* or April 22, 880. Although not indicated in the drawing, the *Ahau* glyph at F6 may well have been proceeded by a *ti'* sign, as seen at other sites in the Chichén Itza area (modified from a drawing by Peter Mathews in Lincoln 1986:162).

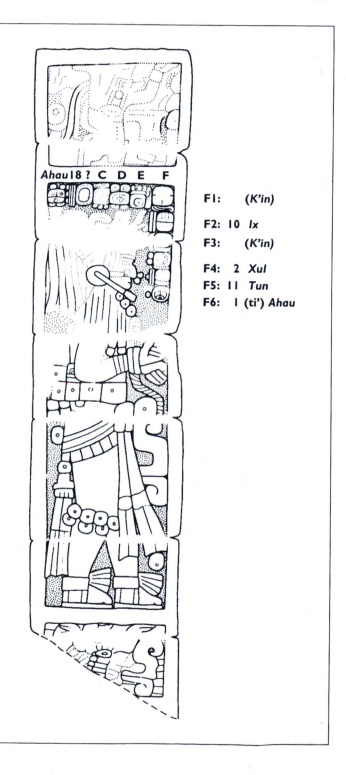

Ahau 18 ? C D E F

F1:   (*K'in*)

F2: 10 *Ix*

F3:   (*K'in*)

F4: 2 *Xul*

F5: 11 *Tun*

F6: 1 (*ti'*) *Ahau*

POSTCLASSIC CAVE RITUALS

Some have pointed to radiocarbon dating of charcoal from a cave near Chichén Itza as evidence of Postclassic habitation of the site. Radiocarbon dates associated with religious rites in a cave at Balankanché, near Chichén Itza, however, parallel similar finds reported from Belize (table 15). The Balankanché materials support the idea that the ceremonial center of Chichén Itza had been abandoned by AD 970 and religious activities were shifted to the cavern at Balankanché, as happened at other sites.

> A series of caves in southern and central Belize—Actun Balam, Río Frío Cave E, Actun Polbilché, and the Eduardo Quiroz Cave—were all used by the Maya at the end of the Classic. Ceramics correlating with Tepeu 3 [AD 800–900] were found in the first two while the latter two showed both Tepeu 3 horizon and Early Postclassic [AD 900–1100] materials. These finds suggest, perhaps, that religious and ritual activities may have been shifted to caves at a time when the old Classic ceremonial centers were being abandoned.... (Willey 1986:162, citing various reports by Pendergast)

In the mythology that exists throughout the Maya area, caves are home to the gods of rain, wind, thunder, lightning, rainbows, clouds, and corn. When hot, humid, tropical air comes in contact with the cool air of the caves, condensation occurs and sometimes even forms mist. The cool cave walls are normally damp from condensation. Subterranean rivers run through many caves. As water percolates from the surface of the ground, it drips from walls and stalactites. In addition, when incense is burned in cave ceremonies, the smoke billows out of the caves like clouds. In modern times, the Kekchi of Alta Verapaz perform rituals at the cave of the rain and thunder deities. Karen Bassie-Sweet concluded that the fact that modern Maya believe that clouds are created in caves suggests that the ancient Maya cave ceremony might have been an attempt to create rain. It is particularly interesting to note that the period of greatest activity in caves was, as noted above by Willey, when the old Classic ceremonial centers were being abandoned, a period of intense drought. Bassie-Sweet may well be correct that the ancient Maya were trying to create rain. According to *The Book of Chilam Balam of Maní* (see page 302 of this book), the Maya retreated to their caves in times of drought, where they lived, prayed, and died (Bassie-Sweet 1991:79, 82, 138; Craine and Reindorp 1979:108–109).

CONSTRUCTION

Richard E. W. Adams has argued that the presence of and number of acropoles and courtyards serve as an indicator of the size and complexity of Maya cities. By relying on principles of self-organization and extending

SITE	ITEM	LAB ID	[14]C	-1σ	CAL AD	+1σ
Cave shrine	Twig charcoal	LJ-272	1090 ±20	690	968	1160
Cave shrine	Twig charcoal	LJ-273	1090 ±20	690	968	1160
Cave shrine	Rerun LJ-272	P-1132	1072 ±51	896	979	1012
Cave shrine	Rerun LJ-273	P-1133	1028 ±42	979	1009	1023

RB GILL 2000

RADIOCARBON DATES AT BALANKANCHÉ CAVE

Table 15. Reported ^{14}C dates from Balankanché Cave near Chichén Itza (*Source*: Andrews IV and Andrews V 1980:283; calibration by CALIB, Stuiver and Reimer 1993).

Adams's argument, the construction of major formal buildings, or the lack thereof, can be an indicator of the vitality of a city and, by implication, of the population levels present. As Robert Carneiro put it, "A civilized state generates monumental architecture the way a colony of polyps generates a reef." Grand public architectural projects require large populations, not only for workers but also for the social complexity necessary to accomplish their conceptualization, design, organization, construction, and subsequent maintenance. They require a large agricultural surplus and an agricultural distribution system to support the workers, managers, and designers. A sudden cessation of construction, extending over centuries, can indicate a precipitous drop in population levels (Richard E.W. Adams 1981:216–220; Carneiro 1974:180).

The hard dates at Chichén Itza, the written dates and the ^{14}C dates, indicate that the major construction at the site was completed prior to AD 900. If that is true, the only later construction may be residential units which Charles Lincoln has identified as being architecturally similar to Mayapán (Charles Lincoln, May 1992, personal communication). In the aftermath of the Collapse, no major public construction appears to have been carried out by the severely reduced population that may have continued to inhabit the site. One can surmise that only after a period of time did the population levels rebuild to a point where residential construction was undertaken.

CHICHÉN ITZA: NEW INTERPRETATIONS

During the 1980s, various archaeologists, epigraphers, and art historians took new looks at the buildings and inscriptions of Chichén Itza. One by one the so-called Toltec buildings, inscriptions, and dates were reinter-preted and generally placed much earlier. Marvin Cohodas, for example, believed all the Toltec buildings at Chichén Itza were constructed before AD 900 (Cohodas quoted in Weaver 1981:398–399).

Along the same lines, Charles Lincoln made a most interesting obser-vation about the architecture at Chichén Itza:

> Nowhere do we see a veneer-vaulted structure with Pure Flo-rescent [Maya] or Puuc style buried beneath a similarly vaulted structure with Modified Florescent [Toltec] sculpture....More con-cretely, where a succession of super-imposed buildings has been encountered at Chichén Itza, the sequence documented is one of replacement and enlargement of the same architectural type.
>
> In the realm of settlement pattern analysis, a pattern of inte-gration rather than segregation characterizes the distribution of Maya and Toltec-type structures at Chichén Itza. This interpreta-tion does not seem to support the idea of a two-phase sequence and ethnic replacement. (Lincoln 1986:183, 188)

He points to five well documented examples showing a direct associ-ation between Maya hieroglyphs and Toltec figural or iconographical sculpture in Toltec buildings: the Temple of the High Priest's Grave, the Caracol, the Great Ball Court, Structure 6E1, and the Castillo. Lincoln ar-gues that Chichén Itza was one cosmopolitan, multiethnic, integrated city that functioned together as a major urban center (Lincoln 1986:187–188).

Linnea Wren and Peter Schmidt have pointed out that the reliefs at Chichén celebrate both Maya and Toltec warriors as conquerors and pa-rade both Maya and Toltec as humiliated captives. Toltec sculpture also portrays individuals whose costumes and weapons combine both Maya and Toltec elements. According to Wren and Schmidt, the Mayas and Toltecs were contemporaneous, they lived and fought side by side (Wren and Schmidt 1991:212).

THE BOOK OF CHILAM BALAM OF TIZIMÍN

Although it is dangerous to rely solely on ethnohistorical evidence to try to elucidate the past history of the Lowlands, ethnohistory is an addi-tional branch of evidence that can be added to the growing body of evi-dence. Along those lines, then, Munro Edmonson's translation of *The Book of Chilam Balam of Tizimín* starts off with a remarkable passage. Edmonson counted back through the recitation of katuns from the known starting point of the Spanish arrival and assigned dates to the katuns mentioned. His translation of the beginning of *The Book of Tizimín* is as follows:

8 Ahau (692),
   6 Ahau (711),
4 Ahau (731),
   Second Ahau (751),
Forty years,
   And then followed
One year,
   Which was the first *tun*
Of 13 Ahau (771).
   It was 13 Ahau.

8 Ahau (692),
   6 Ahau (711),
4 Ahau (731),
   2 Ahau (751).

Then arrived
   The East priest Bi Ton,
The chief
   Of the Tutul Xiu,
One year
   Before it was one
   hundred years.

8 Ahau (692)
   Had been revealed;
Chichen Itza
   Had been manifested:
The grove
   Born of Heaven there.

6 Ahau (711),
   4 Ahau (731),
2 Ahau (751),
   13 Ahau (771).
That was the counting
   Of the mats.
11 Ahau (790),
   9 Ahau (810),
7 Ahau (830),
   5 Ahau (849),
3 Ahau (869),
   1 Ahau (889),
Two hundred years
   Chichen Itza ruled.
Then it was destroyed.
   Then they went
To the settlement
   Of Champoton,
Where there were then
   The homes
Of the Itza
   The gods who own men.
6 Ahau (968)
   Completed the seating
Of the lands
   Of Champoton.
4 Ahau (987),
   Second Ahau (1007).
(Edmonson 1982:3–7)

Edmonson provided the following paraphrase to his translation:

From the end of the Xiu cycle in 692 to 751, and then came the end of the Itza cycle in 771.

From 692 to 751, then East priest Bi Ton arrived, the chief of the Toltec Xiu. It was 710. From 692 when Chichen Itza was the seat of the cycle to 731 to 771, the end of the Itza cycle to 810 to 849 to 889, Chichen Itza ruled two hundred years. Then it was destroyed and they went to Champoton, the home of the Imperial Itza. By 968, they finished subjugating the territory of Champoton. (Edmonson 1982:3–7)

It would seem, then, according to Edmonson's translation, that the Itza arrived at Chichén around AD 690 and inhabited the city for two hundred years until about 890. This is certainly consistent with the radiocarbon dates and the epigraphic evidence. The Tutul or Toltec Xiu are said to have arrived between 750 and 790. According to this interpretation, during the time of the supposed Toltec *entrada* around 950, as the traditional history would have it, the Itza had abandoned the site and were involved in subjugating Champotón. Three lines of evidence, epigraphic, radiocarbon, and ethnohistorical, converge to suggest that the period of Chichén Itza's florescence was between 690 and 890. A similar chronology of events is recounted in *The Book of Chilam Balam of Chumayel* (Edmonson 1986:51–52).

The idea of the Postclassic imperial glory of Chichén Itza is so embedded in the thoughts of most researchers that Edmonson, himself, dismisses the pre-AD 948 histories recounted in the Tizimín and the Chumayel as "essentially mythological as they relate to the Classic period" but he finds "no reason to mistrust the account from the tenth century on" (Edmonson 1982:xvi; 1986:51).

CAPITAL CITY

Finally, a city cannot exist by itself. As we have seen, a city depends on a network of other cities and towns to supply it with food and craft goods. As Fernand Braudel put it, a capital city requires its retinue of assistants and subordinates. It requires peasant surpluses in the fields, which are gathered and redistributed through a network of rural centers. It requires other prosperous cities with which it can trade. Yet those other cities in the Lowlands that survived the Collapse, like Cobá, were in a process of decline in the Postclassic from which they never recovered. Yaxuná, a secondary center some 20km (12mi) from Chichén, was abandoned around AD 900 (Braudel 1984:27, 30; Shaw 1998:300–301).

IMPLICATIONS

The result of the corrected readings is that all the known dates at Chichén Itza, both hieroglyphic and radiocarbon, now fall before AD 900. The radiocarbon evidence from Chichén Itza itself ranges from cal AD 670 to 890, ± a few years at either end. Two independent sources of dates, hieroglyphic and radiocarbon, coincide; both fall before AD 900. Further, they fall within the stated dates for the arrival of the Itza at Chichén Itza in katun 8 Ahau, ending AD 692, and their abandonment of the city for Champotón in katun 1 Ahau, ending 889, in *The Book of Chilam Balam of Tizimín* and slightly different but similar dates in *The Book of Chilam Balam of Chumayel*, as interpreted by Edmonson. There appears, from the dates on buildings, to have been no major construction after 900. If one accepts the recent reinterpretations of the hieroglyphic dates, the radiocarbon dates, Edmonson's interpretation of Itza chronology, and the recent stylistic arguments, the implications are profound. Chichén Itza would appear to have been a Classic Maya city and to have suffered the same fate as other Classic Maya cities. It would appear to have fallen victim to the devastation of the Collapse. If so, this implies that there never was a Postclassic Toltec Empire at Chichén, that Chichén never was the dominant imperial city of the north during the Postclassic, that its history is similar to the other cities of the Maya Lowlands, and that it suffered a fate similar to all the rest.

The anomaly of a city booming while all else lay in ruin, a city existing without visible means of support, with no source of energy, would be closed. Chichén Itza would have been destroyed by the same fundamental processes that destroyed all the other great Maya cities throughout the Lowlands.

This question cannot be answered definitively at this time. Only further careful archaeological stratigraphy and ceramic and stylistic studies can confirm this new interpretation.

What About the Art and Architecture?

Although artistic and stylistic arguments are not definitive for dating the boom period of Chichén Itza, we cannot ignore the clear similarities between many iconographic elements and artistic styles at Chichén and Tula. As Karl Taube put it, "I recognize that many traits found in the Toltec or Modified Florescent art of Chichén Itza are of Maya origin, I also believe that there is a profound and special relationship between Chichén Itza and Tula." He goes on to say, however, that ethnic identity in the past has been confused with political affiliation, and I would add, political affiliation has been further confused with specific time periods (Taube 1994:213, 244).

I, myself, do not try to deny a special relationship of some sort between Tula and Chichén Itza. What I call into question is the traditional chronology which calls for an invasion of Toltec troops and a conquest of Chichén after AD 910, during the Postclassic. The hard dates at the site suggest that Chichén boomed during the Classic. Whatever the tie was with Tula, it appears more likely to have existed during the Classic. Thus, whether through immigration from a common motherland, or through invasion and conquest, or through extensive trading links, or through yet another relationship, in order to fit the hard data, it appears the chronology needs to be shifted to the Classic from the Postclassic. The tie with Tula, then, can be incorporated into a new chronology which recognizes the hard dates from the city itself.

Postclassic

Classic civilization throughout the Maya Lowlands appears to have collapsed by at least AD 910. The immediate aftermath, however, is very difficult to determine. There are indications from some lines of evidence that the collapse was abrupt. Other lines of evidence indicate a more grad-ual decline over the course of a century or so. Most of the Classic Maya area was abandoned abruptly. Copán shows evidence of a stepped aban-donment over four hundred years, and Lamanai, on the East Coast, cities around the Petén lakes, and Chichén Itza show evidence of continued oc-cupation, albeit with severely reduced populations.

The two events of significance during the Postclassic were the found-ing and rise of Mayapán into the capital city of the north and the growth of a line of coastal trading communities, with their associated ports, stretching from the Chontalpa around the peninsula to Honduras. Chich-én Itza was probably not an imperial capital but instead probably lay bat-tered and devastated like Cobá and Lamanai, with reduced populations continuing to inhabit the site.

SOUTHERN AND CENTRAL LOWLANDS

Most sites in the southern and central Lowlands were abandoned after the Collapse. Those few sites not abandoned had reduced populations. Surviving inhabitants in the Petén Lake District were concentrated on is-lands or along the shores, where long-term stable sources of drinking water were available. In the basins of Lakes Yaxhá and Sacnab, population was confined to the Topoxte Islands and a landlocked peninsula in the southwestern portion of Lake Yaxhá. In Lake Macanché, population was restricted to Macanché Island. In addition, on the isthmuses of Muralla de León and Ixlú, and on the Zacpetén peninsula, the Postclassic population is not broadly distributed across the landscape, but rather situated in densely settled nucleated communities on naturally defensible landforms, largely surrounded by water and broken terrain (Rice and Rice 1985:168,173; D. Rice 1986:309–310).

Culbert has described the Postclassic population level for the southern Maya Lowlands as follows:

> We do, in fact, have solid archaeological evidence indicating where Postclassic populations lived and some idea of their mag-nitude....Postclassic occupation was island oriented; eight islands and an isolated peninsula have dense Postclassic settlement....
>
> The total area of all the sites, however, is quite small, and it seems unlikely that more than a few thousand structures were represented by all the Postclassic sites of the lake district....
>
> There have not been enough rural surveys to rule out the pos-sibility that large Postclassic populations lurked in the hinterlands in areas yet to be discovered by archaeologists. But the few sur-veys in rural areas have found them as barren of Postclassic pop-ulations as the centers of sites. To posit large populations hidden

"somewhere out there" requires an act of faith of which I am incapable.

The present evidence, then, suggests that the southern lowlands...was very sparsely populated in Postclassic times....The Maya Collapse was a demographic disaster in which a population loss that must have numbered in the millions occurred during the ninth and tenth centuries. (Culbert 1988:88–89)

The problem of trying to determine absolute population levels is particularly difficult. B. L. Turner II has estimated that the depopulation rates for the central Maya Lowlands between AD 800 and 1000 were between 53 and 65 percent. From a maximum population approaching 3 million, he estimates that it had dropped to less than 1 million by 1000 and continued to drop to around 75,000 at the arrival of the Spanish. Richard E. W. Adams has estimated the peak population for the southern and central Lowlands at 12 to 14 million, with a decline to 1.8 million in the Postclassic, a depopulation rate of 85 to 90 percent. Both Turner's and Adams's rates are staggering and depict a level of human suffering seen in world history in only one other recorded event, sixteenth- to seventeenth-century Mesoamerica after the Spanish Contact (Richard E. W. Adams 1991b:268–269; 1993, personal communication; Turner 1990:310; Whittington 1991:167).

NORTHERN YUCATÁN

Most of the area of greatest cultural achievement during the Classic period, the Southern Lowlands, lay empty and abandoned during the Postclassic with remnant populations trying to scratch out their existence among the ruins or in small communities. The two zones with the most active Postclassic populations were northern Yucatán and the eastern Caribbean coast.

The northern hills, the area known as the Puuc where the beautiful Classic city of Uxmal is located, showed only the barest traces of culture during the Postclassic, and the area was largely deserted. It was abandoned by the early tenth century (Kowalski 1987:51; Pollock 1962:12).

I would suggest a date of around AD 900 to 915 for the House of the Governor [at Uxmal], after which several structures at Uxmal and other Puuc sites were begun but never completed. This strongly suggests a short lapse of time, following which the Puuc centers undoubtedly were abandoned by about AD 925–975. (Kowalski 1987:51)

Uxmal, according to Kowalski, Roys, and Tozzer, remained uninhabited until the Xíu, under Ah Suytok Tutul Xíu, established themselves there in 1441, only to abandon it for Maní during the following katun around

1451. Edmonson, it should be noted, believes the Xíu arrived at Uxmal in 1264 (Edmonson 1986:37; Kowalski 1987:59).

The principal urban activity of the Postclassic in the north seems to be centered on the walled city of Mayapán. People lived in or at least camped at Mayapán from Formative times through the present. However, because of only a trifling amount of Early Postclassic pottery, G. W. Brainerd postulated the virtual abandonment of the site following the Collapse (Pollock 1962:6).

What would become the capital of Mayab, as the Maya called the Yucatán Peninsula, had its Postclassic revival as a small ceremonial center devoted to the worship of K'uk'ulkan. Its principal pyramid appears to be a small-scale copy of the Castillo at Chichén Itza.

> A matter worth recording is that our recent work in Yucatán has made it amply clear that a major break in cultural tradition, as witnessed by a sharp degeneration of the quality of the remains came about....
>
> Civic and religious buildings were smaller in scale, less massive in design, and the lofty stone vaults and the great structures at Chichén Itza were all but forgotten, being replaced by flat-ceilinged beam-and-mortar roofs. There was no fine cutting and shaping of stone for building or for sculpture. Indeed, the stone itself was selected with little care, most of it being of inferior quality. Poor masonry was hidden by quantities of plaster, and there was the tendency to resort to modeling in stucco in place of carving in stone. Such stone sculpture as there was seems for the most part to have relied on stucco and paint for the final effect, and, even allowing for the present eroded condition, there appears to have been little of artistic merit. Pottery and products of the lesser arts and industries were almost without exception of poor quality. Mayapán was born when civilization was in eclipse, and...culture never again approached the excellence of earlier centuries. (Pollock 1962:16)

Morley read three stela dates at the site as AD 1185, 1244, and 1283. According to Brainerd, the beginning of Mayapán as a center of importance, indicated by the construction of buildings, dates from around 1200. Edmonson credits the founding of Mayapán to a compromise reached between the Xíu of Uxmal and the Itza of Chichén Itza who agreed in 2 Ahau (1244–1263) to seat the cycle at a centrally located place which was to be ruled jointly. About 150 to 200 years after the construction of the small ceremonial center, Mayapán had grown to a city of 12,000 inhabitants. It was a walled city in which the leaders of its vassal communities from across its territory were required to live. It is located at the site of a number of cenotes, which assured the city of a supply of water (Edmonson 1982:xvi; Pollock 1962:3–7, 15).

Because some noted archaeologists like Daniel Brinton, Alfredo Barrera Vásquez, and Sylvanus Morley believed that Mayapán dominated a Postclassic confederacy made up of equal partners, Chichén Itza, Uxmal, and Mayapán, it should be noted that Kowalski, Roys, and Tozzer all agree that the League of Mayapán, lasting from AD 1000 to 1200, never existed as envisioned. Uxmal was abandoned during this period, and Mayapán had not yet achieved its prominent position, if it had achieved any position at all. If a league of sorts existed, it was probably only in the decade before the abandonment of Mayapán, after the arrival of Ah Suytok Tutul Xíu and his followers at Uxmal, and before their departure for Maní. Roys wrote (Kowalski 1987: 63; Tozzer 1957:51):

> It is very difficult, if not impossible, to reconcile [this historical material] with an oft-published belief that there was a league of Mayapán, Uxmal and Chichén Itza in the 11th and 12th centuries. I do not doubt that such a league really did exist at a much later time. Also, it could have included the three cities in question. But, if so, I would suggest that it consisted of the walled city of Mayapán as the dominant member, along with a small but important and aggressive group of Xíu, camping out among the magnificent ruins of Uxmal, and another warlike aggressive group living in posthegemonic Chichén Itza, which continued to be an important center of pilgrimage, in spite of its loss of military supremacy. (Roys quoted in Tozzer 1957:51)

The end came in 1451–1454. According to Landa, it was the result of political dissension caused by oppression on the part of the ruling group. The ethnohistoric accounts tell of fighting, seizure, and depopulation. There is ample evidence of burned buildings and widespread looting. *The Book of Chilam Balam of Maní*, however, speaks of cold, drought, and famine during the same katun as the devastating cold, drought, and famine of 1 Rabbit in the Mexican Highlands (Craine and Reindorp 1979:156; Landa 1566:44, 46, 48–49).

At about the same time, Mayapán, Uxmal, Chichén Itza, and Cobá appear to have been abandoned by their populations in what could be called the Postclassic Abandonment. By the time of the arrival of the Spaniards, the capital of Mayab lay empty and deserted (Pollock 1962:15).

The period 1450–1500 was a period of widespread cold in the Northern Hemisphere. Tree rings from the Sierra Nevada indicate the most severe cold in the last 2,000 years in that region. In Europe, 1450 marked the beginning of the Little Ice Age I. Severe drought, cold, and famine battered the Mexican Highlands during the famine of 1 Rabbit. Drought, cold, famine, and war were all part of the collapse of Mayapán, a pattern which has repeated itself so often in Mesoamerican history.

Turning our attention to Chichén Itza, *The Books of Chilam Balam* indicate that its Postclassic history is a series of abandonments followed by reoccupations of the site. Throughout, however, it remained a venerated religious center, an object of pilgrimages. Its role and its importance were most likely similar to that shortly before the Conquest: a politically important city, of enormous religious prestige, but not in a position to dominate the North, and certainly not the greatest Maya city ever developed. Later in the Postclassic, most of the city was uninhabited, and the populations present were unable to even maintain the existing structures.

> At Chichén Itza, a considerable amount of pottery typical of the major period at Mayapán has been found under conditions suggesting that the great civic and religious buildings of the old Maya-Toltec city were no longer in use and may even have been falling into ruin. (Pollock 1962:12)

Its final abandonment, according to Roys, Tozzer, Kowalski, and Edmonson, was by the Itza in 1451, at the time of the Hunac Ceel episode, which is concurrent with the abandonment of Uxmal, Mayapán, and Cobá. A group of Itza, calling themselves the remnant of the Itza, moved to Lake Petén Itza in Guatemala and settled at Tayasal. Remnant populations continued to live in and near the ruins. In fact, Edmonson interprets *The Book of Chilam Balam of Tizimín* as indicating that tribute was still being paid to Chichén Itza in the eighteenth century, an indication of its continuing religious prestige (Edmonson 1982:xvi, xx; Kowalski 1987:59, 62–63; Tozzer 1957:49–50).

PORTS

A gradual deployment of Gulf Coast People occurred along the west and north coasts of Yucatán during the Early Postclassic. Skilled canoeists in their homeland, they seem to have developed sea going canoes and the skill to use them about this time. The canoe, or boat, seen by Christopher Columbus on one of his travels was as long as a galley, eight feet wide, with a cabin amidships, and carried upwards of twenty-five men with additional women and children as passengers. The emergence of sea going canoes or boats greatly facilitated the transport of merchandise, and the Gulf Coast People dominated the trade (Andrews and Robles C. 1985:64–65; Jeremiah Epstein, January 31 1988, letter to author; J. E. S. Thompson 1970:127).

The ports were developed at strategically important locations, at the mouths of rivers or estuaries, on islands, or near saltmaking facilities, key positions for trade and military purposes. Around AD 1200, according to

Anthony Andrews, the northwest and north coast was abruptly abandoned and seagoing trade in the Late Postclassic was concentrated on the east coast (A. Andrews 1983:32–33).

It should be noted that Richard Diehl chose the year 1179 as the year of Tula's abandonment during a period of drought, cold, famine, and war in the Mexican Highlands. The drought may have been very widespread in Mesoamerica and may have played a role in the abandonment of these ports as well, although specific evidence of drought in the Lowlands has not yet emerged (Diehl 1983:160–163).

EAST COAST

Along or near the East Coast, an interesting pattern of contraction appears in the archaeological record from Cobá in the north to Copán in the south. In this region, cities were either abandoned or severely reduced in population, while the rural areas continued to be inhabited. The region as a whole suffered a terrible demographic disaster with significant overall reductions in population until the number of people fell to a level that could be supported by the flow of energy from agriculture. If subsistence agriculture were to have survived anywhere in the drought ravaged Maya Lowlands it would have been along the East Coast where the sea breeze effect is responsible for the heaviest rainfall and where enough rainfall may have occurred to support subsistence agriculture. Nonetheless, the area was hard hit by the Collapse, but not wiped out. We will look at the histories of a few representative sites to get a clearer picture of this pattern.

Cobá. Following a period of vibrant political and economic activity, Cobá entered into apparent decline, manifested by a reduction in its political and economic importance around AD 900–1000. William Folan concluded that it was reduced from a state to a chiefdom, but did manage to survive the Collapse. As noted earlier, the absence of *Zea* pollen in lake cores at the time of the Collapse might indicate that Cobá was abandoned and then reoccupied—a pattern seen at Colha. Certainly local maize cultivation ground to a halt, which suggests abandonment. It should be noted that Cobá is located at a fresh water lagoon fed by the underground water table. According to David Freidel, populations continued to inhabit the rural areas near Cobá. There is little evidence of large-scale population during the Early Postclassic at Cobá, however. After AD 1100, all construction ceased at Cobá. The satellite communities and sites at the end of the *sak be,* or highway, between Cobá and Yaxuná were abandoned, and a further serious decline in population occurred. Yaxuná, itself, was sacked and abandoned around AD 900. Leyden, Brenner, and Dahlin have identified the period leading up to Cobá's final demise as a dry period (A. Andrews and Robles C. 1985:71; Folan 1983b:213; David Freidel, 1996, personal communication; Leyden, Brenner, and Dahlin 1998:119; Shaw 1998:300–301).

During Manaachi times, AD 1200–1400, construction resumed with the building of numerous temple-shrines. Cobá showed strong ties to Mayapán. At the time of Mayapán's collapse, during the fifteenth century, Cobá also faltered, losing the major part of its power as a political and economic unit, and was virtually abandoned. It did continue thereafter to be a major pilgrimage center, but only a few families were living in its vicinity (Folan 1983b:213–214).

Colha. Colha was abandoned at the time of the Collapse and later reoccupied. The Classic came to a violent conclusion. Colha's abandonment was associated with destruction and human slaughter. Late Classic residences were destroyed by demolition and fire. Two elite mass graves have been discovered, one of which holds twenty-eight decapitated skulls, apparently the result of elite executions. The rural areas near Colha, however, continued to be inhabited, which is the same pattern seen around Cobá. (Hester 1985:6, 12, 16, 18; Tom Hester, March 1994, personal communication; Fred Valdez, 1992, personal communication).

Copán. The history of Copán may reflect a stepped decline into the abyss of oblivion characteristic of several sites, rather than the abrupt finality seen at most Classic cities. Anncorinne Freter defined three phases of population decline during the Postclassic at Copán. Populations peaked in the Copán Valley during the first half of the ninth century at 20,000–26,000 people, with 80 percent, or 16,000–20,000, living in the urban Copán Pocket and the Residential Core, and 4,000–6,000 in the Rural Sustaining Area. During the first phase of decline, between AD 850 and 1000, the population dropped to 13,000–17,000. Just as importantly, however, there was a significant difference between the urban center and the rural areas. The urban population fell to 8,000–10,500, a 50 percent decline, while the rural population actually rose to 5,000–6,500, a 15 percent increase (Freter 1988:166–180).

The second phase dates from 1000 to 1150, during which the population in the whole valley fell to 7,000–9,000 people, another 50 percent decline. The third phase lasts from 1150 to approximately 1250. During this phase, the population is very sparse, no more than 2,000–3,000 people for the valley as a whole, a 70 percent decline. This third period is contemporaneous with the abandonment of Tula and the ports on the northwest and north coasts of Yucatán. After 1250, the Valley of Copán was virtually depopulated. During the sixteenth century, in fact, Spanish landowners in the valley had to import workers from other areas to cultivate their tobacco fields, since the Valley of Copán was uninhabited (Freter 1988:166–180).

We can see, then, a similar pattern from Cobá in the northeast to as far south as Copán. The agricultural productivity of the East Coast was sufficient to support agrarian life and small scattered urban populations, but was insufficient to support the previous highly developed urban life. In other words, the flow of energy was severely reduced, but not shut off. Farther inland, however, the rainfall was insufficient for even subsistence levels of agriculture and the countryside was abandoned. The example of the East Coast demonstrates the principle proposed early in the book that as the flow of energy is reduced, the hierarchical levels of organization collapse to the level which can be supported by the available energy.

Altun Ha/Lamanai. Let's look at the contrast between available sources of drinking water. Altun Ha was abandoned at the end of the Classic, its temples deserted. All of its readily accessible tombs were desecrated. Remnant populations may have continued to occupy some outlying sites for a short while after the final collapse of the center before a total abandonment of the site. The site enjoyed a brief, weak renaissance in the fifteenth and sixteenth centuries. Altun Ha relied on surface reservoirs for its water (Pendergast 1986:224).

Lamanai, on the other hand, just 40 km (25 mi) away, avoided complete abandonment. It did not escape unscathed, however, and never recovered its Classic vitality. Withdrawal from the northern and central parts of the Lamanai zone began in the ninth and early tenth centuries, reflected mainly by a cessation of major temple renewal. Some small residential groups were established on the periphery of these two zones. Commoners then established residences in formerly sacrosanct temple compounds. The more northerly residential groups in the Northern Zone were abandoned by mid-Terminal Classic times as part of a general shrinkage in the physical extent of the community that affected the northern and central parts of the Central Precinct as well. There is no evidence of construction at any large central and northern buildings in the heart of Lamanai past the Late Classic. Clearly, life continued at Lamanai, but nothing approaching the vitality of the Classic period was seen after the Collapse. No further grand public architecture was undertaken, only one wattle and daub structure which served as a temple and a residential platform. The construction of major public buildings ceased. Much of the site lay abandoned and uninhabited. Lamanai did survive the Classic Collapse, but it survived badly wounded (Pendergast 1986:227–231).

The contrasting destinies of Altun Ha and Lamanai, which were located just 40 km (25 mi) apart, are very instructive. Certainly both cities were engulfed in the turmoil of the Terminal Classic, and one can presume, both were afflicted by similar climatic conditions. Lamanai was located near a stable source of fresh water and survived. Altun Ha relied on reservoirs and died.

Ports. The Late Postclassic saw the development of coastal trading communities along the East Coast, while the economic importance of the west and north coasts waned. A population buildup occurred along the East Coast, as well as the reoccupation of a number of interior sites. The growth of Tulum, for example, dates from AD 1100–1200. Coastal trade was important as far south as Honduras (Barrera Rubio 1985:51; A. Andrews 1983:33).

POSTCLASSIC POPULATION LEVELS

North. Populations did survive in the north, in the cenote zone, as well as in the east, in Belize and Quintana Roo, where long-term stable sources of drinking water were available. But what was their size? One possible way to estimate their size is to consider the population size at the time of Spanish contact, around 1528. The archaeological data would seem to indicate larger populations in the north at the time of the Conquest than after the Collapse. The population would have had time to rebuild in the ensuing six hundred years since the Classic catastrophe. Contact period estimates have ranged from Roys's low estimate of 300,000 to Sanders's estimate of 532,000 to 592,000, to Jakeman's 1,375,000, to Lange's 2,285,800, to Wagner's estimate of 8,000,000. After reviewing the applicable evidence, Sherburne Cook and Woodrow Borah concluded that the probable population in 1528 was about 800,000. They note, however, that *The Books of Chilam Balam* speak of drought, hurricane, plague, and pestilence over the course of the prior eighty years and that the population in 1450 may well have been higher. Peter Gerhard has also analyzed the data and estimates the total population of Yucatán in 1511 slightly higher at 1,028,000. The lower estimates noted above are based on the first colonial census of 1549, while the higher ones, particularly Lange's and Wagner's, are derived from the region's maximum carrying capacity based on an analysis of agricultural systems and the subsistence base. The higher estimates may give an indication of how much greater the population could have been at the time of the Collapse (Cook and Borah 1974:23, 38; Farriss 1984:424; Gerhard 1979:62).

GUATEMALAN HIGHLANDS

So far, we have concentrated on the Lowlands, but before leaving the subject, it is worth taking a look at the Guatemalan Highlands as well. Work in the Highlands by William Sanders and Carson Murdy has demonstrated that the Valley of Guatemala did not escape the effects of the Collapse either. After reaching a peak of 120,000 people, Postclassic population levels rapidly declined to less than 20 percent of their Classic peak, probably not exceeding 19,000, a devastating 84 percent loss. Populations in the Canchón Plateau peaked at about 110,000 people, then plummeted to around 33,000 in the Early Postclassic (figure 99) (Murdy 1996:95–96; Sanders and Murdy 1982:55–56).

RECAPITULATION

Preclassic. The Preclassic witnessed the first florescence of Maya culture. During this period, true urbanism developed on a grand scale. Major cities with huge public temples and residential palaces were built. The Preclassic also suffered the first known episode of collapse and abandonment

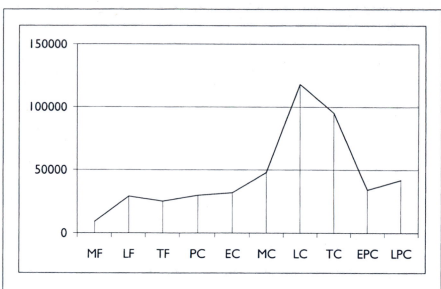

POPULATION VALLEY OF GUATEMALA-CANCHÓN PLATEAU

Figure 99. Population curve of the Valley of Guatemala-Canchón Plateau region in the Guatemalan Highlands. Note the severe demographic disaster at the time of the Classic Collapse, between the Late Classic, *LC*, and the Early Postclassic, *EPC* (*Source*: Murdy 1996:84).

between AD 150 and 200. It appears to have been pan-Maya, cities being abandoned or depopulated from northern Yucatán to the Pacific Coast. El Mirador, the first large Maya urban center, was abandoned at this time. Palaeoclimatic evidence from the El Mirador region indicates a serious drought coincident with its abandonment. Evidence from other areas indicates the drought may have been peninsula-wide.

Hiatus. Populations rebuilt during the Early Classic in many cities hit by the Preclassic Abandonment. Beginning around AD 535, many were again battered. Political chaos and turbulence reigned at some sites for at least sixty years, perhaps more. Dynasties were overthrown and the relatively smaller site of Caracol apparently fought larger Tikal and won. Many sites failed to erect monuments, temples, or dated edifices. At least one site, Río Azul, was abandoned around AD 540 and never recovered. Its rural area was depopulated at the same time. Lake sediments at Lake Quexil also indicate a population contraction during the Hiatus. There are historical reports of severe cold and atmospheric aberrations from Rome, North Africa, Mesopotamia, and China in AD 536. Palaeoclimatological evidence indicates anomalous weather in Scandinavia and Peru as well. A lake sediment core from Punta Laguna shows evidence of a drought at this time.

Classic. The final burst of Classic florescence occurred during the Late Classic. The building boom hit its highest levels during the seventh and eighth centuries and populations peaked in the eighth century. The Collapse appears to have progressed in three phases, as measured by the last known dates on monuments and buildings. The first phase appears to have occurred in or by AD 810 and was most severe in the west. The second phase appears to have occurred in or by AD 860 and was concentrated in the east. The final phase appears to have occurred in or by AD 910, concentrated in the core, in the north, and in the highland communities in the south. In this phase, there appears to have been a coherence of last dates around 10.3.0.0.0, AD 890, with two sites, Uxmal in the north and Toniná in the Highlands to the south, recording dates of 10.3.17.12.1, AD 906 and 10.4.0.0.0, AD 909, respectively.

Palaeoclimatic records from Lake Chichancanab indicate a 200-year period of aridity between AD 800 and 1000, the driest episode in the last 7,000 years, peaking at 922. Additional data from Punta Laguna indicate the most serious period of aridity in the last 3,500 years from 850 to 1050, with peaks centered around 862 and 986. Laguna de Cocos and Cenote San José Chulchacá also show evidence of drought at the end of the Classic. The drought began, then, about 800 and continued until 1000. The Collapse appears to have begun around 810 and to have been complete by about 910. Palaeoclimatic records from highland Mexico and lowland Costa Rica suggest the droughts may have affected a wide area.

Early Postclassic. Unlike the South, which was largely abandoned, severely reduced populations in the North, the East Coast, and the Petén Lake District continued to occupy a number of sites. It would appear that population levels were insufficient for construction of any significance to have occurred between the Collapse and about 1200, with the possible exception of Cobá and perhaps Lamanai, where a residential platform was constructed. During these three hundred years, populations regained sufficient levels for residential construction to resume at certain sites. It is very possible that no Toltec Empire occurred and that Chichén Itza followed the same pattern of collapse, population reduction, and lack of major construction as the other northern cities. Tula, the ports on the northwest and north coasts, and Copán appear to have been abandoned in the period 1150–1200, in what may have been a Mesoamerica-wide demographic disaster.

Late Postclassic. At Mayapán and Cobá, ceremonial construction may have begun during the thirteenth century. From 1200 to 1450, a degree of political integration and centralization appears to have developed with the rise of Mayapán as the capital of the north. In addition, some limited, and very poor quality construction of residential and ceremonial buildings occurred in several sites. In 1451–1454 the region was again hit hard. Mayapán, Chichén Itza, Uxmal, and probably Cobá were all abandoned at the same time. In the Mexican Highlands, a five-year deadly famine lasting from 1450–1454, accompanied by heavy snow, severe cold, and drought, was reported in several annals. At the same time, *The Book of Chilam Balam of Maní* reports cold, drought, and famine coincident with the fall of Mayapán. The Little Ice Age I was just beginning in the Northern Hemisphere.

The Maya north encountered by the Spaniards in 1528 was divided into numerous, petty, warring states, with no visible political integration.

13. Summary and Discussion

A s you know by now, the main theme of this book is that the Collapse and disappearance of Classic Maya civilization was the result of a series of brutal droughts which ravaged the Maya Lowlands between AD 800 and 1000. In order to pose this hypothesis, however, it is often necessary to overcome serious preconceptions held by many archaeologists. First is the idea that the collapse of a complex civilization is the result of an intricate, interacting, complex network of causes and effects, none of which could bring down the civilization on its own. The idea of an engine which drives the train of collapse has not been acceptable. Second, is the idea that a theory which proposes such an engine of collapse does not have philosophical respectability, and anyone who would propose one is not familiar with the philosophical issues involved, nor with the complex, multifactorial theories which have been previously proposed. Third, is the argument that droughts have occurred in the past and Maya society withstood them, so they should have been able to withstand them again when they occurred. Fourth, is the idea that much of the Maya Lowlands is a tropical forest with abundant, always dependable rainfall, and it is therefore unreasonable to expect a devastating drought to have occurred there. Fifth, and perhaps the most difficult one to overcome, is the idea that when human beings suffer a devastating catastrophe, it is really their own fault, and by looking at the society itself, you can eventually uncover the cause within the arena of human volition and action. Civilizations, it is believed, collapse from internal processes and not external shocks.

PHILOSOPHY AND EXPLANATION

This is not the forum to develop a philosophy of archaeology or to delve deeply into the philosophy of science. I would like to mention briefly, however, that a full philosophical theory of explanation, as proposed by Paul Thagard, recognizes six strands of explanation, some of which are appropriate in some instances, others in others, but no one of which is always appropriate in all circumstances.

One of the six strands is causal explanations. It is not necessary to propose a complex, interacting schematic explanation to be philosophically acceptable. In certain circumstances, a complex schematic approach may provide the best explanation, but not in all cases. Science has two aims, prediction and explanation, and in order to explain it is, in fact, not necessary to predict (Salmon 1984; Thagard 1992:118–126).

The debate over the importance of internal processes and external shocks has not been limited to archaeology alone. It has played out within many time dependent, historical disciplines like history, palaeontology, evolutionary biology, and geology. Until recently in these disciplines, there has been no theoretical role for catastrophic, external shocks causing catastrophic changes in the system. The focus has been on internal, uniformitarian processes. In recent years, however, these fields have come to recognize that there are roles for both internal processes and external shocks. It is not a question, therefore, of either one or the other but rather how both approaches can work together to describe the alternating periods of stability and crisis seen in most historical records. Internal processes provide very appropriate descriptions of the long periods of stability in most historical records and may well explain some periods of historical chaos and abrupt change. External shocks, however, have now been implicated in major catastrophic upheavals evident in the other time dependent disciplines.

I would like to repeat here my earlier emphasis that I do not claim in this book that multicausal explanations of cultural change are always invalid. I do claim that multicausal explanations are not necessarily *always* valid. Sometimes, unicausal or monocausal explanations, in fact, fit the available data better than do multicausal ones. There are roles, therefore, for both multicausal and unicausal explanations.

CLIMATE AND HUMAN AFFAIRS

What is the role of climate in human affairs? Climate is clearly external to human society. Is it any more than the pleasure we feel on a pretty day, or the displeasure of gloomy days, or the temporary damage caused by a hurricane?

Most archaeologists today deny a role for climate in the unfolding of human history. Most especially, the catastrophic effects on societies that severe climatic aberrations can wreak is denied. As Joseph Tainter said, "Human societies encounter catastrophes all the time. They are an expectable aspect of life, and are routinely provided for through social, managerial, and economic arrangements" (Tainter 1988:53).

This issue has particularly interested historians and demographers. Using historical demographic records from Europe, several independent studies have determined a very direct relationship between climate and the size of human populations in different areas of Europe. Historians discovered an important link between climate and agricultural prices, with all the subsequent effects which ripple through an economic system. Demographers also found that relatively small changes in climate, temperature increases or decreases on the order of 1°C (1.8°F), can have measurable impacts on population levels. In general, for whatever reasons, when winter temperatures increased in Europe, populations increased. When winter temperatures decreased, populations decreased, and the reverse for summer temperatures.

Surely, the way European societies interacted with the climate was complex, but the controlling variable in these studies was a factor external to the society itself, the climatic temperature. There can be no clearer demonstration of the impact of climate on society than the rise and fall of population levels due to minor temperature variations.

It should also be clear that if relatively small temperature differences can have measurable effects on the health of a society, a genuine climatic disaster, like a severe multiyear drought, can have catastrophic effects. In fact, the historical records of drought and famine in Colonial Yucatán tell a tale of recurring devastation in which large percentages of the population, perhaps up to 50 percent at times, have died from the effects of climatic catastrophes. If climate can cause the death of 4 percent of a population at one time and 50 percent at another time, it is a reasonable step to take to accept that climate can also cause the death of 75 percent or 90 percent of the population at another time under exceptional circumstances. Such devastation appears to have occurred in the Maya Lowlands every 250 to 350 years between AD 1 and 1500.

ENVIRONMENT

Climate is not the only external factor with which a society must interact. Humans live in a physical world, and our most important challenge is to exploit the physical world to extract the maximum amount of energy and raw materials for our societies. The interwoven external factors with which we must interact are climate, geography, geology, and ecology.

Drought, for example, may be less devastating in areas where there are underground reserves of water to be exploited during multiyear droughts than in areas where there are only surface water reservoirs which must be replenished annually.

In coping with the physical environment, human societies develop a suite of traits and practices which include activities like hunting and gathering on the one hand or agriculture on the other. Farmers develop a suite of cultivars best adapted to a certain range of climate, geology, and geography and evolve agricultural practices which maximize the harvests from those crops. These suites of traits and practices are designed for certain climatic and physical regions and do not serve their societies well in areas for which they were not designed. Thus the expansion of Bantu farmers in Africa was stopped at the boundary between summer rainfall and winter rainfall regions because their culture could not effectively exploit the areas further south. Austronesian culture expanded across the Pacific to areas where they could thrive and not to areas where the indigenous hunting and gathering cultures more effectively exploited the environment.

The exploitation of the environment can also lead to distinct social organization, as Carole Crumley showed in Western Europe, where not only Roman military might, but also Roman agricultural techniques and social organization, followed the ecotonal shift to the north around the beginning of the Roman Climatic Optimum and collapsed to the south when the ecotone retreated to the south and the Roman Climatic Optimum ended.

COMPLEXITY AND SELF-ORGANIZATION

A human organization functions as a dissipative structure at the edge of chaos. The reaction of an organization to an external shock cannot be predicted. As Per Bak and Kan Chen demonstrated in a laboratory system, the same perturbation repeated over and over can have a wide range of effects, from none at all to collapse. The reaction of a system far from equilibrium, as Ilya Prigogine showed, is stochastic. Small causes can have dramatic effects. The argument, then, that droughts occurred before and Maya society withstood them is inconclusive because it is impossible to predict with certainty the reaction of a system to an external perturbation. In addition, some droughts were simply more devastating than others.

Organizations always exist at the edge of chaos. As they evolve, they move through alternating periods of stability and periods of crisis. As an organization proceeds through turbulence and chaos, the outcome cannot be predicted. During these periods, the stable, deterministic processes are not dominant. In fact, the process of resolving periods of chaos gives individual human actors the greatest opportunity to truly affect the outcome, to have the greatest impact on their society, and to create revolutionary changes in the direction of development of their cultures.

During the course of evolution, biological as well as societal, information processing has achieved an increasingly important role. Selection for social organisms is no longer on a biological basis, but rather on an information basis. As Richard Newbold Adams has pointed out, however, information does not become part of human society until it lodges in some human nervous system. It can only self-organize in the minds of human beings. As humans organize into societies, the information grows proportionately to the flow of energy available to the society. The rate of increase of the information is a function of the rate of increase of the per capita energy consumption of the society. Human organizations, like all dissipative structures, rely on a constant flow of energy and raw materials. If the flow is severed, the organization collapses (Richard Newbold Adams 1988:82–83, 86).

As long as free energy is available, human organizations will develop a way to utilize it. In fact, organized structures everywhere maximally utilize the flux of energy passing through them. The process begins with an immature system through which energy is flowing. As it evolves, its trajectory is characterized by an increase in complexity, an initial increase in the energy flow through it, followed by a decrease in the energy flow and entropy as the system approaches a more and more nonequilibrium state, and an increase in its susceptibility to perturbations from the environment.

The complexity of a system like a civilization is limited by the flow of energy and raw materials available to support it. The higher levels will not develop unless the materials and energy are available. Nor will they survive if the flow of energy and materials is severed. As Adams emphasized, life forms that succeed in developing structures that channel great amounts of energy can readily be doomed if the energy sources are cut off.

Complex organizations are built up as simple constituents interact in heterarchical relationships to form new, higher levels of hierarchy. It is extremely important to recognize that one cannot predict the characteristics of the next level by knowing those of the constituents in the lower level. In far from equilibrium structures, an organization's characteristics are a property of the collectivity of its elements and cannot be inferred from a study of the individual elements in isolation. Reductionism is no more useful in understanding higher levels of organization in physical sciences than it is in social sciences. The tendency of higher levels to exhibit innovative, creative, and totally unpredictable characteristics is known as emergence.

Ervin Laszlo emphasized that the flight of the arrow, in the development of human societies, may be interrupted or temporarily halted at any point. It may be made to skip from one stage to the next. But it may not, except under the impact of unusually powerful external factors, like a climatic catastrophe, be fully and steadily reversed.

Along the same lines, Lewis Binford, Prigogine, Allen, Lazslo, Service, Richard Newbold Adams, and others believed that cultures tend to homeostasis unless perturbed by external shocks. The Maya Collapse was the result of external shocks to a complex, multilevel social system which relied on the constant flow of energy and raw materials—food, water, and raw materials for trade goods. When that flow was severed by drought, when the Maya were denied water and food, the system collapsed. And they were not to blame. The Collapse was not the result of bad management, administrative deficiencies, or poor agricultural techniques. It was the result of forces over which they had no control and against which there was no solution that they could implement. The Maya, like all of us, lived in a physical world subject to physical laws and were devastated by physical shocks in the face of which they were totally powerless.

ARCHAEOLOGICAL THOUGHT

The challenge, J.-C. Gallay said, is to practice integral archaeology without falling prey to eclecticism. We have ranged widely through ideas and disciplines in this book, not in a spirit of eclecticism, but in order to discuss the theoretical hypotheses and the physical evidence which support the conceptual focus underlying the theory presented here. The actions and interactions of human societies in and with the physical world are of primary importance in their development (Gallay quoted in Malina and Vašíček 1990:137).

Leslie White proposed that culture undergoes evolutionary processes of change which are irreversible and nonrepetitive. Only systems can evolve. Culture may diffuse piecemeal, but only a systematic organization of cultural elements can evolve. White also postulated the principle that a culture or socioeconomic system is a material and, therefore, thermodynamic system. Culture, he said, is an organization of things in motion, a process of energy transformations. Culture evolves as the amount of energy per capita increases, or as the efficiency of putting energy to work is increased. In other words, Culture = Energy × Technology. In addition, he believed, culture advances as the proportion of nonhuman to human energy is increased—by domesticated animals and machines (Leslie White 1959:45, 47, 56, 144–145).

Because nonhuman sources of energy were largely absent in early societies, Betty Meggers formulated in 1954 an important law of cultural development for archaeological societies: "The level to which a culture can develop is dependent upon the agricultural potential of the environment it occupies." In her formulation, Culture = Environment × Technology. In early societies, then, the agricultural potential is the source of the energy flowing through the system which supports its complexity (Meggers 1955:121, 129; 1960).

The end result of White's and Meggers's laws can be summed up by ecologists Eugene and Howard Odum's maximum power principle: "That system survives which gets most energy and uses energy most effectively in competition with other systems." Those systems that prosper in the competition among alternative choices are those that develop more power inflow and use it best to meet the needs of survival.

COLLAPSE OF CIVILIZATIONS

Robert M. Adams pointed out in 1974 that there were abrupt shifts in the development of early civilizations. Their trajectories were not smooth and gradual. Long periods of relative stability, when few changes occurred, were interrupted by periods of dizzyingly abrupt change. We have seen that the theory of self-organization and dissipative structures, for which Ilya Prigogine won a Nobel Prize in 1977, postulates that the evolution of a system develops through alternating periods of stability and chaos when radical changes can occur, just as Adams described for the evolution of civilizations (Robert M. Adams 1974:249).

What do we mean when we refer to a civilization? Samuel Huntington has proposed what is perhaps the most interesting, certainly the most all encompassing definition of a civilization: the highest cultural grouping of people and the broadest level of cultural identity people have short of that which distinguishes humans from other species (Samuel Huntington 1993:24).

Will and Ariel Durant argued that civilizations never really collapse and die. They live on assimilated into the culture of surviving nations. "Civilizations are the generations of the racial soul," they said. "As life overrides death with reproduction, so an aging culture hands its patrimony down to its heirs across the years and the seas." In their view, Classic Maya civilization never really died, it lives on in the culture of the various modern lowland and highland Maya peoples. Yet something did die. Hundreds of cities and towns lie empty, abandoned, and overgrown to this day. Modern Maya cultures produce pale reflections of the dynamic, vibrant political and artistic accomplishments of the Classic period. George Cowgill hit closer to the mark when he said that "the collapse of a civilization, then, should refer to the end of a great cultural tradition" (Cowgill 1988:256; Durant and Durant 1968:90–94).

Many writers on the subject blame collapses on the victims themselves. As the Durants put it, "a civilization declines through the failure of its political or intellectual leaders to meet the challenges of change." Vilfredo Pareto, writing in 1920, however, recognized the tendency of others to try to affix blame for the declining fortunes of nations. The ancient Hebrews, he said, saw the wrath of God at work. The Romans were convinced that every evil was the result of a violation in the rites of worship. Others have blamed a corruption of morals, or violations of morality, law, and brotherly love, or capitalism, or inequalities of wealth, and so on. He concluded, however, that to believe those explanations is to believe that life is the cause of death, since death always follows life. Instead, Pareto argued that there were natural undulations in the cycles of fortune of nations and the people themselves and their actions were not the cause of their own misfortunes. Pareto's writings are among the first not to blame the victims of cultural disasters for their misfortunes (Pareto 1920:1016–1018, 1022–1023, 1074–1075, 1145).

The perspective of cultural collapse which forms the basis of this book is that cultures tend toward stability and homeostasis. A culture is designed to handle a certain range of external variation. Drastic internal change, however, can be induced by drastic external factors. Such external factors may include, but are certainly not limited to, war, disrupted trade routes, disease, crop losses, climatic catastrophes, and so forth. In the case of the Maya Collapse, the external factors were severe climatic shocks over which the Maya had no control and against which any administrative system, any agricultural technique, any level of agricultural production, and any leaders would have been equally impotent and ineffective.

We should remember the admonition of Jeremy Sabloff and Gordon Willey that we saw earlier:

> Too often, as will be shown below, workers in the Maya area have attempted to explain the collapse in terms of internal processual events alone, a sort of consideration of Maya culture and its environmental setting *in vacuo*. External forces, such as Mexican incursions, were relegated to a secondary role and were used to fill in gaps in the internally focused hypothesis. What we are saying here, in essence, is that in the Maya area processual factors, such as the ecological effects of population increases in a "type X environment," or the long term inviability of a "theocratic state," can be understood only after external historical factors are controlled. (Sabloff and Willey 1967:312)

What is the relationship between external shocks and causes? I have proposed that a cause is that without which a set of circumstances would not occur. Vulnerabilities and predispositions are not causes. They do not come into play until they are acted on by a cause and could exist forever without affecting a society unless stimulated by a cause.

If we look at the external environmental shocks able to damage a system, the one with the highest levels of mortality is drought. No other comes close to being able to eliminate such huge numbers of people in such a short time. The ultimate manifestation of drought on human societies is famine and thirst.

From an archaeological perspective, Ross Hassig determined that the only really useful typology to apply to the study of famine was to break them down into two categories, (1) ecological, those caused by natural events such as floods, insects, droughts, frosts, or epidemics, and (2) social, those caused by government edict, hoarding, profiteering, and the like. Hassig believes that this dichotomy separates those famines caused by factors beyond the immediate control of the society in question and those that could be controlled but are not. It should be noted that the schedule of famines and their causes, prepared by Nancy Farriss for the Colonial period in Yucatán, lists only ecological causes—although some are not attributed to any cause (Farriss 1984:61–62; Hassig 1986b:305–306).

In Mesoamerican society, we saw, there was no well developed, long-distance transportation system for basic food commodities. Most food for a city was drawn from within a 30 km (18 mi) radius. Populations of cities were seriously restricted in their ability to reach out to distant areas for sustenance because all transport was on the backs of human beings. Even in Europe, which had the transportation advantage of draft animals and wagons, the history of European famine records that most famine stricken communities died in isolation until the railroads arrived. In Colonial Mesoamerica, even the importation of grain by ship in 1770 was insufficient to alleviate the highest recorded mortality from famine in Yucatecan history. In Precolumbian Mesoamerica, when the people ran out of food and water, they died.

MAYA COLLAPSE

Elsewhere, I have excerpted eighty-eight theories or variations on theories which attempt to clarify the circumstances under which the Maya civilization or the Classic Maya cultural tradition ceased to exist. Of all the writers, the only one to address the fundamental concept of this work, the role of the flow of energy and raw materials in maintaining an elaborate social structure, was Clive Ponting. He proposed a reduction in the food surplus on which the ruling elite, together with the priestly class and the army, depended for their existence, making it impossible to sustain the elaborate superstructure the Maya had built. Others have discussed reduced food supplies, or even famine, but not in terms which approach the concept of energy flows supporting cultural complexity (Gill 1994:167–207; Ponting 1991:83).

In the case of the Maya, due to the length and severity of the droughts, the flow of food and water was shut off, the people died from hunger and thirst, and the social system collapsed from the bottom up.

THE EFFECT OF DROUGHT

Pretty, sunny days do not by themselves kill anyone. Death is caused by the cascade of events which flow from sunshine that turns angry. The immediate cause of death will always be something other than a sunny day. The engine that drives the train of cascading events, however, is the drought. Were it not for the drought, the chain of events leading to death would not form.

An analogy exists in HIV infection. No one dies from HIV itself. The immediate cause of death is always from an opportunistic infection, an organ failure, or a general system collapse as a result of multiple opportunistic infections. Were it not for HIV, however, the resulting impairment of the immune system and the opportunistic infections would not have killed the organism.

Drought has four intertwined principal effects: starvation and thirst, disease, migration, and conflict. In fact, it is often impossible to determine whether a victim has died of starvation or disease, the two are so interwoven. Mass migration occurs in most famines. As Sorokin described, the mapless migrations of large numbers of people is, in fact, diagnostic of developing famine. Conflict often occurs in the early stages of famine, but not always. It occurs most often when there is a great disparity between the famine's effects on different groups or classes within the population. As a famine progresses, however, the people are too weak to fight. In the end, most famines are resolved, as Sorokin said, "by the scythe of death...and by the catastrophic exhaustion of the famine after it has taken its full toll of suffering and death." The result is a new equilibrium between the population and the food supply.

How Do Millions Disappear?

How do millions of people disappear? They either fail to reproduce, they move, or they die.

In the Maya Lowlands, there is no evidence for a failure to reproduce or for a mass migration of millions of people. Therefore, they must have died.

How, then, do millions die? Of the causes of death that we reviewed, the only two capable of killing millions of people are famines and epidemics. There were no endemic diseases present in the population at the time of Spanish Contact which might have explained the disappearance of millions of Classic Maya. Although epidemics of many diseases played a major role in the death of millions of people after the arrival of the Spanish, those diseases are still present in Mesoamerican native populations. Even though diseases can mutate and become relatively benign, it is unlikely that disease by itself was the cause of the death of millions. Diseases contracted in conjunction with famine by severely weakened victims, although not normally capable of inflicting huge numbers of casualties on a population, can cause, together with starvation, huge numbers of deaths. Death from starvation usually occurs when 33 to 50 percent of body weight has been lost, and intractable diarrhea resulting in dehydration is the most common terminal event. In most famines, it is impossible to tell whether a victim has died of starvation or disease, the two are so intertwined.

The most likely cause of the death of millions of people, therefore, is starvation and thirst coupled with disease.

PEASANTS

Fernand Braudel observed, "The world between the fifteenth and eighteenth centuries consisted of one vast peasantry where between 80 percent and 95 percent of people lived from the land and from nothing else. The rhythm, quality, and deficiency of harvests ordered all material life." Classic Maya life was similarly dependent on agriculture and similarly ordered by the harvests (Braudel 1973:18).

Peasants, the primary agricultural producers responsible for those harvests, are distinguished from primitive producers by the fact that they deliver their agricultural surpluses to an urban center where a dominant group uses them to underwrite its own standard of living and redistributes the excess to groups in society that do not farm but must be fed in return for the specific goods and services which they provide. "There were no peasants before the first cities," wrote Robert Redfield, "and those surviving primitive peoples who do not live in terms of the cities are not peasants." Preindustrial cities, on the other hand, could not exist without the agricultural surpluses of the peasants. In large areas of the world today, peasants furnish the funds of rent and profit which underwrite the entire social structure. The presence of cities in Classic Mesoamerica suggests that the rural population, the food producers, lived as peasants.

Yet peasants always walk a razor-thin line between survival and famine induced death. Ronald Seavoy has proposed that famines are endemic to all peasant societies. Annual periods of hunger and periodic famine affect all peasant societies regardless of their race, religion, climate, population density, subsistence crops grown, or geographic area. Even peasant societies that have low population densities and cultivate fertile soils experience famine.

The reason, according to Seavoy, lies in the subsistence rationality, a way of looking at the world which defines peasants. The concept of the subsistence compromise is the attempt by peasants to grow sufficient crops for their needs with the least expenditure of labor on the assumption that all years will be normal years. Commercial rationality, in contrast, as practiced by commercial farmers, tries to maximize profits by maximizing labor inputs. Peasants, on the other hand, try to maximize their free time by minimizing the amount of hard work done. They measure their well being by the amount of free time they have rather than by their material possessions. This tendency has been reported in modern Mesoamerican peasant societies.

Famine is a phenomenon which recurs often enough that it is well within the memories of many persons in each village. The peasantry know the value of enough food in storage to feed themselves until the next abundant harvest, yet they consistently fail to produce an assured food surplus and regularly endure a hungry gap just before the annual harvest.

SOCIAL DISINTEGRATION

Famine is generally a class affliction. It hits the poor hardest and first. As the crisis deepens, crops and grazing are reduced. Servants and dependents of farmers are evicted and they are the first to move. Herds begin to die and are sold off at low prices. Wives and children of migrating men either stay with relatives, come to town to beg for a living, or seek shelter in relief camps. Those first affected are pastoralists, evicted farm servants, rural laborers, dependents, male laborers in urban areas, women in service occupations, weavers and other craftsmen, and occupational beggars.

The disintegration begins, then, with the lowest levels of the society, including the peasants, and it proceeds from the bottom up. The first reaction of the peasantry is a communitywide response. The second phase is family by family. In the third and terminal phase, it is every man and woman for himself or herself. As the food supply and energy source are reduced, the degree of social integration drops level by level.

The government response to famine is usually scornful disbelief. When the reality of famine is finally accepted, the scornful disbelief turns into an astonishing underestimation of the magnitude and the intensity of the famine. The next phase of government reaction is an expansion of regulation, regimentation, and social and economic control.

There follows an intensification of ritual as people and government leaders seek divine intervention for their tribulations. When nothing has worked, people often begin to move—mass migration is diagnostic of worsening famine. In some cases, famine results in war, rebellion, or other forms of conflict which end up exacerbating the disaster. In the end, the principal cause of death among famine victims is disease, and it is generally impossible to distinguish death from disease and death from starvation, they are so intertwined.

METEOROLOGY

The Maya Lowlands, today, are an area of abundant seasonal rainfall, for the most part. How, then, does one explain the presence of a drought and famine at a site like Tikal, which regularly receives 2,000mm (80in) of rain per year?

The Lowlands lie at the northern margin of the tropical rainfall zone, north of the rainforest zone, in an area of wet/dry seasons. Precipitation diminishes from the south to the north, reaching low levels along the northern coast at Progreso, 440mm (17in), and even lower levels on the offshore *cayos* to the north, 330mm (13in). Clearly, a southward shift in the northern Yucatecan aridity, in the ecotonal boundary between humid and arid, would be devastating to a culture which, for the most part, relied on surface water reservoirs for their *sole* source of water. Under what conditions, then, might this occur?

Atmospheric circulation is characterized by three large convection cells, similar to Bénard cells in laboratory systems: the Hadley cell between the equator and 30°, the Ferrel cell between 30° and 60°, and the Polar cell between 60° and 90°. The primary cell is the Hadley cell which is thermodynamically driven by solar radiation. In the Hadley circulation, air is heated at the equator, rises until it reaches the tropopause where it can rise no farther, then flows poleward to between 25° and 35°, where it descends to the surface and flows back toward the equator. The descending air is very dry, having lost most of its moisture, and the zone between 20° and 40° is the location of most of the world's great deserts. Due to considerations of atmospheric physics, the actual flow in the Northern Hemisphere is toward the northeast aloft and the southwest below.

This circulation pattern is most pronounced over the oceans where local topographic effects do not interfere with the flow. Over the North Atlantic Ocean, the North Atlantic High is the descending branch of the Hadley circulation. It is an area of little rainfall, known to sailors as the Horse Latitudes. As the North Atlantic High moves to the north in the summer, drought occurs in the Mediterranean region. As it moves south in the winter, drought comes to Mesoamerica. The North Atlantic High moves back and forth in a northeast-southwest channel from year to year.

There appears to be an association between cold weather in the Northern Hemisphere and the southwestward displacement of the North Atlantic High. During the last glacial maximum, Yucatán was a juniper-scrub savanna, more like today's West Texas than today's Petén forests. M. A. Perlmutter, M. D. Matthews, Peter Lamb, and others have proposed that the subtropical highs were displaced far to the south during the ice ages, although others would disagree believing the position of the highs is a function of atmospheric physics and not subject to much movement. Nonetheless, Brian Goodman has suggested that when the North Atlantic High is far to the southwest, the Siberian High moves to the west to cover parts of Arctic Europe, bringing deep cold to that area. J. K. Angell and J. Korshover have suggested a possible correlation between the mean surface temperature and the latitude of the subtropical highs in the Northern Hemisphere. Cold temperatures in the European Arctic, then, suggest a southwestward displacement of the North Atlantic High.

In addition, Stefan Hastenrath has associated drought in the Caribbean area with an equatorward extension of the North Atlantic High. C. C. Wallén has suggested that decreases in rainfall in Mexico are associated with a southward regression of the North Atlantic High and a cooling of the northern latitudes. Enriqueta García, Pedro Armillas, and Ernesto Jáuregui Ostos all proposed relationships between the position of the North Atlantic High and rainfall in Mexico. Jáuregui Ostos believed there was a strict relationship between the position of the high and rainfall in the Mexican Highlands. The position that I have taken in this book, however, is that there is a stepwise difference in precipitation once the high retreats south of a certain position. Once it is north of that position, its exact location is not material to the amount of rain that falls in Yucatán.

During the twentieth century, the location of the North Atlantic High's central high pressure averaged about 34°N and 33°W. During the first five years of the century, however, it was displaced far to the southwest at 30.4°N and 36.1°W. The first pentad of the century was a time of severe drought in Yucatán, as indicated by the Mérida rainfall record. Rainfall in Mérida was only 39 percent of average in 1903, a year when the summer rains failed. (1902 would have been even worse had it not been for the heavy rains induced by Santa María's ash cloud in October.) Temperature records for the Northern Hemisphere and, in particular, the Arctic, indicate the coldest temperatures of the century, a time when Arctic temperatures reached their low point in the historical records. Summer sea surface temperatures in the North Atlantic similarly reached their low point for the century. Solar radiation, as measured in Washington, DC, and in Europe, was reduced substantially.

In Yucatán as a result, the first decade was the driest of the century. Since then, the North Atlantic High has moved to the northeast, and severe, multiyear drought has not returned to the Lowlands.

A particular concatenation of clearly documented events occurred, then, early in the twentieth century: cold Northern Hemisphere temperatures, a southwestward displacement of the North Atlantic High, cold sea surface temperatures, reduced solar radiation, and severe drought in Yucatán. There is no evidence that the same coincidence of events will occur again in the future. It did occur once, however, and it could have occurred on a number of occasions. At the very least, it provides a model which demonstrates how drought can come to the Maya Lowlands. 1902 was a year of seemingly unending disasters for Mesoamerica, including three large tropical volcanic eruptions in Guatemala and the West Indies followed by three years of severe drought in Mérida.

VOLCANOES, DROUGHT, AND FAMINE

Another confirmation of the model occurred after Tambora exploded in 1815, the most massive eruption of the last 1,800 years. The year 1816 was known in New England as the "year without a summer," a year with summer snowfall as far south as Pennsylvania and, in the Northern Hemisphere, was the coldest of the nineteenth century. Tambora's volcano weather produced the last great subsistence crisis of the western world, the last widespread famine in North America and Western Europe. In the Maya Lowlands, severe drought and the resulting crop failures developed into famine by 1817. A similar set of cold and dry circumstances occurred after the enormous eruption of Coseguina in Nicaragua in 1835, coincident with drought and famine in Yucatán.

Although historical data become sparser and less reliable as we go far-ther back in time, it appears that a fourth historical confirmation of the model occurred in the early 1450s. The beginning of a severe episode of cold, sometimes known as the Little Ice Age I, which lasted from about 1450 to 1500, coincided with a time of deep snow, frosts, drought, and fam-ine in the Valley of Mexico, culminating in the ferocious famine of 1 Rabbit in 1454, as reported in various Aztec chronicles. In the Maya Lowlands, *The Book of Chilam Balam of Maní* reports that Mayapán was abandoned during a time of cold, drought, and famine at about the same time. A huge eruption occurred at Kuwae in about 1452.

The four confirming examples given above each occurred within two years of large, tropical volcanic eruptions. In fact, most colonial droughts and famines in Mesoamerica followed large, tropical eruptions. Historical sources record twenty-four Yucatecan famines for the years between 1440 and 1840, of which thirteen are linked to drought as the precipitating cause. When we compare those drought/famines to a list of large, tropical eruptions during the same years, we find that eleven of them, 85 percent, followed a large, tropical eruption within two years—a really surprising number. A statistical analysis of the data indicates a 1 in 1,000,000 proba-bility that the matches occurred by random chance.

Furthermore, none of the nondrought famines can be matched to large, tropical eruptions. Obviously, famines which occurred in years without drought did not occur in years of volcano weather.

In the Valley of Mexico, we find that thirty droughts lasting three months or longer were recorded between 1440 and 1840. Of those, twenty-three, or 77 percent, follow large, tropical eruptions within two years—an-other surprising number. (The discussion here assumes that we accept two correlations based on radiocarbon dates, one based on uncertain magni-tudes, and two based on clusters of magnitude 3 and extratropical magni-tude 4 eruptions. If we exclude the five more tentative matches, the correlation is 60 percent.) Again, the statistical probability that these matches occurred by random chance is 1 in 1,000,000.

Turning the perspective around and looking at the relationship from the point of view of the volcanoes, we see that of forty-seven currently known, large, tropical volcanic eruptions between 1440 and 1840, thirty, or 64 percent, were followed within two years by drought in Mesoamerica and a thirty-first by a drought in Coahuila which would yield 66 percent—yet more surprising numbers. (Without the radiocarbon matches, the per-centages would be 61 percent and 64 percent.)

When a tropical volcano explodes in a large, magnitude 4+ eruption, there is a 61 to 64 percent chance that drought will follow in Mesoamerica within two years. These correlations are well above random chance. The matches that we see have seen have a probability of only 1 in 1,000,000 of being due to random chance. There appears to be, then, an undeniable tie between lethal tropical volcanoes and repeated suffering in Mesoamerica.

The fatal effects of volcanoes are not direct but operate through climatic and atmospheric disruptions. Volcanoes and weather through millennia have played a deadly duet which delivered drought and death to the Maya and to Mesoamerica.

VOLCANISM

When highly sulfurous, explosive volcanic eruptions inject sulfuric acid precursors into the stratosphere, they are converted by solar energy to droplets of about 75 percent sulfuric acid, which are very effective at absorbing and reflecting incoming solar radiation, but not at absorbing outgoing infrared radiation from the Earth's surface. The result is a cooling of the atmosphere below the tropopause, in the troposphere where we live. Volcanic eruptions at the time of the Collapse, therefore, may have exacerbated or even triggered the ninth- and tenth-century period of cold.

One of the most sulfurous volcanoes in the world is El Chichón, located in the state of Chiapas, in southern Mexico near the Guatemalan border. During the 1982 eruption, which was the most lethal in recorded Mexican history, sulfur represented about 1 percent of the erupted products. The particularly high percentage of sulfur appears to be the result of a combination of factors, including sulfur deposition on the Cocos Plate, which is being subducted under the North American Plate and forming the source material for the magma body feeding El Chichón, and the presence of large sedimentary deposits of sulfur rich strata through which the magma must rise. Studies of past eruptions have indicated little change in the chemistry of the erupted products. One can reasonably conclude that past eruptions would have also been sulfur rich and climatically effective.

The prehistoric eruption history of El Chichón is not definitively determined. The data that do exist, however, indicate eruptive episodes around the time of the Preclassic Abandonment, the Hiatus, the Collapse, the fall of Tula, and the Postclassic Abandonment, times of hemispheric cold, postulated drought, and political and social turbulence in the Lowlands. The coincidence of hemispheric cold, El Chichón eruptions, and abandonment and collapse in Mesoamerica suggests the possibility that El Chichón may have been involved, although definitive evidence is still lacking. The eruption history of El Chichón clearly needs to be investigated and its possible role in the Collapse decided.

Popocatépetl, near Mexico City, is an enormous volcano, one of the world's twenty largest and highest. Its internal plumbing system is huge. When it explodes, it is capable of erupting enormous quantities of material which are just as sulfurous as El Chichón. Its last major eruption has been dated to between 822 and 823 and, given what we know about Popo, it is sure to have had a major climatic effect (Claus Siebe, April 1999, personal communication; Juan Manuel Espíndola, January 1997, personal communication).

There is no convincing evidence that volcanoes are implicated in the Classic Collapse, but there are some intriguing suggestions. Both El Chichón and Popocatépetl appear to have erupted early in the ninth century, just at the beginning of the Collapse. Mt. Pelée and La Soufrière-St. Vincent appear to have erupted early in the tenth century, when the last remaining remnants of Classic Maya culture disappeared coincident with the worst drought of the last 7,000 years at Lake Chichancanab and an extended period of aridity from 800–1000. Acid peaks in the Greenland GISP2 ice core indicate large eruptions in 822, 823, 853, 875, 900, 902, and 915. Some of these are undoubtedly due to northern volcanoes. However, not all tropical eruptions show up clearly in Arctic and Antarctic ice cores, so there could have been other large eruptions that are not reflected in the ice. Tree ring data suggest an additional major eruption in 860 when the drought at Punta Laguna was the worst. The Terminal Classic was a very volcanically active period and a cold period, conditions which would have set the stage for volcanically induced disaster among the Maya.

At this point, we know that the Popocatépetl eruption was quite large, probably magnitude 5 or 6, but we don't know the magnitude of the other four eruptions one each at El Chichón and Mt. Pelée and two at La Soufrière-St. Vincent. We don't know, therefore, whether they could have served as the triggers of death. In time, the eruption sizes will be calculated and perhaps currently unknown eruptions at other volcanoes will be identified. For now, we must remain intrigued and undecided, but very aware of the devastation that volcanoes have repeatedly visited on the Maya and aware of the very real possibility that volcanoes were the long distance assassins that aimed death and disappearance at the Maya.

PALAEOCLIMATOLOGY

Joel Gunn, William Folan, and Hubert Robichaux have produced another, independent line of research which confirms the relationship between cold temperatures and Yucatecan precipitation. They have determined that periods of global cold, as indicated by the Global Energy Balance, result in reduced precipitation in the Yucatán Peninsula, as measured by Candelaria River discharge data. In other words, they found that cold global temperatures reduce rainfall in the Maya Lowlands.

Palaeoclimatological records for the end of the last glacial maximum, obviously a time of worldwide cold, indicate arid conditions throughout lowland Mesoamerica, Central America, South America, and lowland tropical areas throughout the world. During the last 2,000 years, there have been repeated episodes of severe cold, varying from years to decades to more than a century in length. During Precolumbian times, particularly cold episodes have occurred between AD 150 to 200, 530 to 590, 790 to 950, 1110 to 1160, 1330 to 1360, and 1450 to 1500. The archaeological records from the Maya Lowlands and other areas of Mesoamerica indicate repeated episodes of political and social turmoil which fall during at least five of these six periods of severe cold in the Northern Hemisphere. The first period, AD 150 to 200 coincides with the Preclassic Abandonment and the fall of El Mirador. The second from 530 to 590 corresponds to the Hiatus and the abandonment of Río Azul. The third from 790 to 950 coincides with the Classic Collapse during which the records from Scandinavia indicate three episodes of severe cold, around 800, 860, and 910, although the entire century and a half was generally cold. The fourth lasted from 1110 to 1160. Tula was abandoned in a period of cold and drought, according to the chronicles, during the latter half of the twelfth century along with the ports of the north and northwest Yucatecan coast. The final abandonment episode occurred at Copán sometime between 1150 and 1250. The fifth period, 1330–1360, includes the first known drought from the Aztec chronicles in the Mexican Highlands. Whether that drought extended to the Maya Lowlands is not known at this point. The sixth period of cold was the Little Ice Age I, between 1450 and 1500. The Postclassic Abandonment occurred about 1451, also, according to *The Book of Chilam Balam of Maní*, during a period of cold and drought. According to the chronicles, the Mexican Highlands were devastated at the same time, with deep winter snowfall, summer frost, and punishing drought.

According to the meteorological model proposed here, severe cold in the Northern Hemisphere is associated with a southward displacement of the North Atlantic High, which is associated with drought in the Caribbean region as a whole and in the Maya Lowlands in particular. Palaeoclimatic records of severe cold in the Northern Hemisphere, therefore, indicate periods of time when hemispheric circulation patterns would have been propitious for drought to occur in the Maya Lowlands and, in fact, the demographic disasters and droughts listed in table 16 coincide with periods of cold listed above.

Wibjörn Karlén identified multiyear periods of cool summers, conducive to glacier advances in Arctic Scandinavia, around 800, 860, and 910, although the century as a whole was generally cold. These periods of extreme cold *may* have been associated with severe drought in the Lowlands and the three pulses of collapse that I have proposed.

The effects of drought, however, are rarely uniform over large areas. The effects on neighboring regions can be quite varied. During the late 1980s and early 1990s, for example, San Antonio and South Texas suffered drought, while Houston and southeast Texas endured very heavy rainfall. During the terrible drought year of 1955–1956 in Texas, areas of moderate drought were distributed through areas of severe drought in a very random fashion. Thus, the apparent pattern of drought affecting certain areas of the Lowlands more at one time and less at another, even though the region as a whole was experiencing drought, is to be expected.

David Hodell, Jason Curtis, and Mark Brenner have reported evidence for severe drought in the Yucatán Peninsula during the Terminal Classic.

DEMOGRAPHIC EVENT	CLIMATIC EVENT	SOURCE
Preclassic Abandonment AD 150–200	Drought at El Mirador and throughout Yucatán Peninsula	Dahlin 1983
Hiatus AD 535–590	Drought at Punta Laguna	Curtis, Hodell, Brenner 1996
Classic Collapse AD 800–900	Drought at Punta Laguna	Curtis, Hodell, Brenner 1996
	Drought at Lake Chichancanab	Hodell, Curtis, Brenner 1995
	Drier at Laguna de Cocos	Bradbury et al 1990
	Drying at San José Chulchacá	Leyden et al 1996
Postclassic Abandonment AD 1450	Drought at Punta Laguna	Curtis, Hodell, Brenner 1996
	Dry period at Cobá	Leyden, Brenner, Dahlin 1998
	Drought at Mayapán	Book of Chilam Balam of Maní, Craine and Reindorp 1979
	Drought in Yucatán	Book of Chilam Balam of Chumayel, Roys 1933

RB GILL 2000

COLLAPSE, ABANDONMENT, AND DROUGHT EVIDENCE

Table 16. Events of demographic disaster in the Maya Lowlands and the coincident droughts. Note that every major demographic disaster has been associated by researchers with a drought in the Maya Lowlands.

According to their analysis of a lake sediment core from Lake Chichancanab, a 200-year drought started in AD 800 and lasted until 1000. It was the most serious drought in the last 7,000 years. They propose that the drought reached its peak in 922. As we have seen, there are no dates from the Maya Lowlands past AD 910 until the rise of Mayapán centuries later. The same authors have reported on a second core taken from Punta Laguna in Quintana Roo, which shows evidence of exceptionally arid events centered at AD 862 ±50 cal yr and 986 ±50 cal yr. The evidence indicates the period from AD 800 to 1050 was the driest at Punta Laguna during the last 3,500 years, which is the length of the core's record. Barbara Leyden and her colleagues reported evidence of a drying phase at Cenote San José Chulchacá after AD 900. Platt Bradbury and his colleagues report falling lake levels and increasing salinity at the end of the Classic from Laguna de Cocos, Albion Island, Belize. They believe that a climatic change to drier conditions is likely to be responsible. To date, then, studies at four different sites confirm the existence of a Terminal Classic climatic change which is described as either drought or increasing dryness.

The circumstances of the Collapse are not unique in Maya history. Drought and demographic disaster have been partners in death on other occasions. In fact, all of the major episodes of demographic contraction in the Lowlands appear to have been associated with drought, as can been seen in table 16. There can be little doubt that the principal predator of the Precolumbian Maya was drought.

GEOLOGY AND HYDROLOGY

The Yucatán Peninsula is largely a region of karst geology. It is characterized by Cretaceous limestone deposits which are riddled with solution channels. As a result, the formations hold little to no ground water. The rain that falls on the surface moves quickly to the layer of fresh water just above and below sea level that underlies most of the peninsula. Above the salt water lies a fresh water lens with an estimated thickness of 70 m (230 ft) at its maximum, thinning to zero at the coasts. The depth of the fresh water is such that the Classic Maya lacked the ability to use it for their water needs. A recent well at Tikal, for example, encountered water at a depth of 130 m (425 ft), while a well drilled even deeper in the 1950s failed to encounter fresh water at all.

Most Classic Maya had no access to long-term stable sources of drinking water. The only areas with access to the fresh water lens were the northern cenote zone, where the deep cenotes or sinkholes reached the fresh water, farther north and east where the land elevation approaches sea level and the Maya could dig wells, and along the east coast of the peninsula where the fresh water table was at ground level and formed large fresh water lagoons. In addition, long-term stable sources of drinking water were available in the central Petén Lake District, especially around Lake Petén Itza.

Most Maya cities, however, relied on surface reservoirs, today known as aguadas, for their water supply. The aguadas, and the surrounding urban space, were carefully engineered to capture rainfall and store it for later use. Vernon Scarborough, in his accretionary model of landscape engineering, has described how the Maya first developed concave microwatersheds by expanding the water storage capacity of low lying depressions. They later began creating convex microwatersheds by designing their cities as catchment areas on elevated positions and channeling the resulting runoff to the quarries and borrow pits excavated during construction. At Edzná, on the other hand, long canals were dug to bring water to the reservoirs. In the Puuc and elsewhere, chultunes or underground cisterns were constructed for the storage of water to supply mainly residential areas. In the north, aguadas were augmented with wells, pits, cisterns, and casimbas which continued to hold water after the aguada had dried up.

Vernon Scarborough and Gary Gallopin have analyzed the reservoir capacity for the central Tikal district. Their calculations indicate that the known reservoirs and those projected to have existed, taken together, would have held an eighteen-month supply of water. They have concluded that the amount of water stored in portable containers like ceramic pots was negligible.

For most Maya, rainfall was their *sole* source of water. If the rains failed, the aguadas would run out of water within a short time. By the same token, if a reduced level of rain during a multiyear drought failed to meet the loss of water determined by withdrawal for use, evaporation, and seepage, the aguadas would ultimately go dry. Most Maya had no other source for drinking water.

No society can exist without drinking water. In the end, the reservoirs dried up and they ran out of water to drink. The only cities where human beings survived the Collapse were those located near long-term stable sources of drinking water. The Maya did not survive in the 95 percent of cities that depended on surface reservoirs for their water supply.

YUCATECAN DROUGHT

Historical and ethnohistorical records indicate repeated, severe, fatal droughts during the late Prehispanic, Colonial, and early Independence periods. Drought was a frequent visitor to the Yucatán Peninsula. In at least one recorded drought, between 1648 and 1656, as much as 50 percent of the population may have died. The toll of human suffering during the known severe droughts is difficult to comprehend, from a modern perspective. The streets, parks, plazas, and roads were littered with gaunt, emaciated corpses, people who could move no further and dropped where they were. Many died in their own beds and the buzzards entered the houses to eat their bodies. Dogs, coyotes, foxes, and other small animals gnawed on the bones and flesh of the cadavers. In the early phases, corpses were picked up in wagons and dumped in common graves. In many places, however, there was no one to bury the bodies. In the later phases, the bodies lay where the people died. In some droughts, armed gangs were reported to roam the countryside attacking haciendas and towns looking for food to eat. The same reports of unimaginable suffering and death occur again and again in the 500 years of historical records between 1330 and 1836, as drought and famine returned repeatedly to Mesoamerica.

ABANDONMENT AND COLLAPSE

Preclassic. The archaeological record indicates repetitive periods of political turbulence in the Lowlands and Mesoamerica, including population contractions and the abandonment of cities. The first such episode occurred between AD 150 and 200, the Preclassic Abandonment. Richard Hansen compiled a review of the literature which indicates that it devastated the Maya region all the way from northern Yucatán south to the Pacific coast. Many cities were totally abandoned and large regions show sharp contractions in population levels. During this time, El Mirador, then the largest of all Maya cities, collapsed during a drought and was not reoccupied until the Late Classic. Sierra Nevada glaciers appear to have made a significant advance at this time indicating Northern Hemispheric cold. In AD 180, New Zealand's Taupo exploded in the most intensive eruption of the Holocene.

Hiatus. The next period of upheaval, the Hiatus, occurred in the sixth century between 536 and 590. The most severely affected areas were the central region of the Petén and the southwest, along the Pasión-Usumacinta valleys. Many cities in these regions ceased erecting monuments or constructing major buildings. Río Azul, in northeast Petén, was abandoned and rural populations in the region plummeted over 70 percent. Dynasties appear to have been overthrown. Smaller cities attacked larger cities and won. It was a period of bitter cold in North America and severe cold in Europe. Historical accounts of the dry fog of AD 536 from Rome, North Africa, Mesopotamia, and China indicate a severe worldwide weather anomaly which caused bitter winter cold, summer frost, crop failures, and famine around the world. The Hiatus was clearly a worldwide phenomenon and not a localized Maya event.

Classic. The Classic Collapse may have begun as early as 790, certainly by 810, and was over by 910. It devastated all of the Maya Lowlands and the Highlands as well. There are no hieroglyphic dates anywhere in the Lowlands after AD 910 until the rise of Mayapán in the late twelfth century. In particular, the last hieroglyphic date at Chichén Itza is AD 890, and the radiocarbon dates from major buildings at the site all indicate pre-890 construction phases. Based on the dates from the city itself, Chichén Itza appears to have had its florescence during the Late Classic and to have declined during the Collapse, never to rebuild its Classic grandeur and importance. Further archaeological research is needed to determine the extent of Postclassic occupation at the site. Those few cities which did not lose their entire populations, like Cobá, Lamanai, Copán, and perhaps others, saw severe contractions in their population levels.

In palaeontology, the Signor-Lipps effect demonstrates that abrupt extinction events will leave a palaeontological record indicating an apparent gradual decline, because of the random nature of how animals die, how their remains are preserved, and how palaeontologists dig to find them. Similarly, stelae and monuments are randomly erected, preserved, eroded, defaced, looted, and discovered. The apparent record of random, gradual disintegration during the Collapse does not rule out the possibility of abrupt events. An abrupt event would leave a gradual archaeological record.

When one analyzes the record of last dates at sites of rank order 10 or more in the Lowlands, grouping together sites which have missed no more than two katun ending markers, a pattern of collapse seems to emerge. The Collapse appears to have proceeded in three distinct phases. The first affected region was the west and southwest, which has no dates after 810. The next to succumb was the southeast, which has no dates after 860. The last to fall was the central core, the north, and the late intrusion from the Lowlands into the Highlands, all of which have no dates after 910. There are no dates after 890, in fact, except for Toniná and Uxmal.

The palaeoclimatic records from North America, Europe, and the Arctic, for the ninth and early tenth centuries, all indicate a period of significant cold, as cold as the Little Ice Age. Scuderi has identified the period as one of increased volcanic activity. Popocatépetl, El Chichón, La Soufrière-St. Vincent, and Mt. Pelée appear to have erupted at this time. Ice core and tree ring records indicate repeated eruptions at these and other volcanoes during the Terminal Classic.

To repeat, in a study of lake sediment cores from Lake Chichancanab in Yucatán, Hodell, Curtis, and Brenner identified a period of aridity lasting from AD 800 to 1000. It was, in fact, the driest episode in the last 7,000 years. Their study provides unambiguous evidence of severe drought at the time of the Collapse. The drought, which appears to have begun around AD 800, peaked at about 922. The same authors, Leyden and her colleagues, and Bradbury and his colleagues, as we have seen earlier in this chapter, also reported droughts during the Terminal Classic and Early Postclassic from studies done at other lakes and cenotes.

Tula. Tula collapsed and was abandoned between 1120 and 1180, according to Richard Diehl's synthesis of the evidence. Pedro Armillas believes that this was the result of the southward push of farmers, driven by cold, drought, and famine in the provinces to the north of and around Tula. Rebellions and war broke out at the same time. A period of severe cold in Arctic Sweden has been identified by three research groups, falling between 1110 and 1160.

1250, 1330. A period of severe cold in Scandinavia appears to have occurred around 1240 and between 1330 and 1360. Around 1330, according to the chronicles of Prehispanic history written after the Conquest, one of Mesoamerica's earliest droughts known from historical sources occurred. It appears to have lasted from 1330 to 1334.

Postclassic. The final episode of Prehispanic abandonment occurred in 1451 when Mayapán, Uxmal, Chichén Itza, and Cobá were deserted during the Postclassic Abandonment. According to *The Book of Chilam Balam of Maní*, it was a period of cold, drought, famine, and thirst in the Lowlands. In the Mexican Highlands, the chronicles tell of a drought which rocked the Aztec Empire. No rain fell for four years. Heavy snows and summer frost were reported. People, including two divisions of soldiers, were said to have sold themselves or their children into slavery for enough corn to survive. The sharpest drop in the White Mountain bristlecone pine record in California occurred in 1450. Other records from both California and Colorado also indicate severe cold. In Europe, 1450 to 1500 represents the Little Ice Age I. El Chichón appears to have erupted during the fifteenth century and a huge eruption occurred at Kuwae in Indonesia about 1452.

WHY WAS THE COLLAPSE DIFFERENT?

There is a final question that needs to be considered. Why did the Maya recover from previous collapses, but not after the Classic Collapse? I believe there were two major differences. The results of two palaeoclimatic studies suggest the Classic droughts were the most serious to hit the Yucatán Peninsula during the Holocene. The mortality, therefore, was undoubtedly higher than in other droughts, so high that the surviving populations were relatively small. Secondly, the Postclassic has been shown to have been a period of repeated droughts. Those people trying to live away from long-term stable sources of drinking water would have been subjected to repeated episodes of starvation, thirst, and death.

The Maya succeeded in creating a civilization in a seasonal desert by creating a system of water storage and management which was totally dependent on consistent rainfall. Any attempts to recolonize abandoned areas would have relied on rainfall and would have been cut short by recurring episodes of drought. The cold periods recorded in the Swedish tree rings indicate that conditions would have been propitious for drought about every hundred years during the Postclassic. The failure of Maya populations to rebound after the Collapse, then, could be due to severely reduced levels of population and repeated episodes of adverse climate.

CONCLUSION

Hundreds of archaeological sites, cities, and towns are known in the Maya Lowlands. No single theory can explain uniformly the abandonment of every one. Quite possibly, during the course of the turmoil and anarchy of the Collapse, some were invaded by hostile armies and the entire population of the city massacred, perhaps some saw their populations migrate in search of food and water, some may have had drinking water but lost their crops to drought and their inhabitants slowly died of starvation and disease. Most, however, were overwhelmed by brutal forces of nature over which they had no control and against which there was no defense. Most of the Maya cities ran out of food and water and one by one their inhabitants died slow, painful, pitiful deaths from starvation, thirst, and disease.

The upheavals and disasters of the Collapse were driven by the engine of drought. In the end, the Maya survived only where they could find drinking water. The difference between life and death for the Maya was water.

14. Bibliography

Adams, Richard E. W.

1977   *Prehistoric Mesoamerica*. Little, Brown and Company, Boston.

1981   Settlement patterns of the central Yucatán and southeastern Campeche regions. In *Lowland Maya settlement patterns*, edited by Wendy Ashmore, pp 211–258. University of New Mexico Press, Albuquerque.

1986   Rio Azul. *National Geographic* 169(April):420–451.

1991   Nucleation of population and water storage among the ancient Maya. *Science* 251:632.

1992   *Ixcanrío regional archaeological project 1991 interim report*. The University of Texas at San Antonio.

1997a   *Transformations, periodicity, and urban development in the Rio Azul/La Milpa region*. Paper presented at Complex Societies Group, University of Arizona, Tucson, October 31–November 2, 1997.

1997b   *Ancient civilizations of the New World*. Westview Press, Boulder, CO.

1998   Introduction to a survey of the native prehistoric cultures of Mesoamerica. Unpublished manuscript.

Adams, Richard E. W., W. E. Brown Jr., and T. Patrick Culbert
    1981   Radar mapping, archeology, and ancient Maya land use. *Science* 213:1457–1463.

Adams, Richard E. W., and Richard C. Jones
    1981   Spatial patterns and regional growth among Classic Maya cities. *American antiquity* 46:301–322.

Adams, Richard E. W., Hubert R. Robichaux, Fred Valdez Jr., Brett Houk, and Ruth Mathews
    1999   Transformations, periodicity, and urban development in the Río Azul/La Milpa region. Appendix 2. In *Río Azul, an ancient Maya city*, edited by Richard E. W. Adams, pp 190–207. University of Oklahoma Press, Norman.

Adams, Richard E. W., and Woodruff D. Smith
    1977   The Maya Collapse and mediaeval Europe. *Archaeology* 30:292–301.

Adams, Richard Newbold
    1988   *The eighth day: social evolution as the self-organization of energy.* University of Texas Press, Austin.

Adams, Robert McC.
    1974   Anthropological perspectives on ancient trade. *Current anthropology* 15:239–258.

Ager, Derek
    1993   *The new catastrophism: the importance of the rare event in geological history.* Cambridge University Press, Cambridge.

Ahrens, C. Donald
    1988   *Meteorology today.* West Publishing Company, St. Paul, MN.

Albarède, Francis
    1997   Isotopic tracers of past ocean circulation: turning lead to gold. *Science* 277:908–909.

Albritton, Claude C., Jr.
    1989   *Catastrophic episodes in Earth history.* Chapman and Hall, London and New York.

Allen, Peter M.
    1985   Ecology, thermodynamics, and self-organization: towards a new understanding of complexity. In *Ecosystem theory for bio-*

logical oceanography, edited by Robert Ulanowicz and Trevor Platt, pp 3–26.

Alley, Richard B., and Michael L. Bender
1998   Greenland ice cores: frozen in time. *Scientific American* 277(February):80–85.

Alva Ixtlilxóchitl, Fernando de
1891   Relaciones. In *Obras históricas,* edited by Alfredo Chavero. Oficina Tip. de la Secretaría de Fomento, Mexico, DF.

Alvarez, Luis W., Walter Alvarez, Frank Asaro, and Helen V. Michel
1980   Extraterrestrial cause for the Cretaceous-Tertiary extinction. *Science* 208:1095–1108.

Ambrose, Stanley H.
1998   Late Pleistocene human population bottlenecks, volcanic winter, and differentiation of modern humans. *Journal of human evolution* 34:623–651.

Andrews, Anthony P.
1983   *Maya salt production and trade.* University of Arizona Press, Tucson.

Andrews, Anthony P., and Fernando Robles C.
1985   Chichén Itza and Cobá: an Itza-Maya standoff in Early Postclassic Yucatán. In *The Lowland Maya Postclassic,* edited by Arlen F. Chase and Prudence M. Rice, pp 62–84. University of Texas Press, Austin.

Andrews, E. Wyllys, IV, and E. Wyllys Andrews V
1980   *Excavations at Dzibilchaltun, Yucatán, Mexico.* Middle American Research Institute, Tulane University, New Orleans.

Andrews, E. Wyllys, V and Jeremy A. Sabloff
1986   Classic to Postclassic: a summary discussion. In *Late Lowland Maya civilization: Classic to Postclassic,* edited by Jeremy A. Sabloff and E. Wyllys Andrews V, pp 433–456. University of New Mexico Press, Albuquerque.

Angel, J. Lawrence
1966   Porotic hyperstosis, anemias, malarias, and marshes in the prehistoric eastern Mediterranean. *Science* 153:760–763.

Angell, J. K., and J. Korshover
    1974   Quasi-biennial and long-term fluctuations in the centers of action. *Monthly weather review* 102:669–678.

Appenzeller, Tim
    1994   Clashing Maya superpowers emerge from a new analysis. *Science* 266:733–734.

Armillas, Pedro
    1964   Condiciones ambientales y movimientos de pueblos en la frontera septentrional de Mesoamerica. In *Homenaje a Fernando Márquez-Miranda*, pp 62–82. Universidades de Madrid y Sevilla, by Ediciones Castilla, Madrid.

Arnold, David
    1988   *Famine*. Basil Blackwell, Oxford.

Ashmore, Wendy
    1984   Classic Maya wells at Quiriguá, Guatemala: household facilities in a water-rich setting. *American antiquity* 49:147–153.

Aykroyd, W. R.
    1974   *The conquest of famine*. Chatto & Windus, London.

Back, William, and Bruce B. Hanshaw
    1970   Comparison of chemical hydrogeology of the carbonate peninsulas of Florida and Yucatan. *Journal of hydrology* 10:330–368.

Back, William, Bruce B. Hanshaw, Janet S. Herman, and J. Nicholas Van Driel
    1986   Differential dissolution of a Pleistocene reef in the groundwater mixing zone of coastal Yucatan, Mexico. *Geology* 14:137–140.

Back, William, and J. M. Lesser
    1981   Chemical constraints of groundwater management in the Yucatan Peninsula, Mexico. *Journal of Hydrology* 51:119–130.

Baillie, Michael G. L.
    1991   Marking in marker dates: towards an archaeology with historical precision. *World archaeology* 23(2):233–243.
    1994   Dendrochronology raises question about the nature of the AD 536 dust-veil event. *The Holocene* 3:212–217.
    1995   *A slice through time: dendrochronology and precision dating*. Routledge, London.

1999a   *Exodus to Arthur: catastrophic encounters with comets.* B. T. Batsford Ltd, London.

1999b   Exodus to Arthur: catastrophic encounters with comets. CCNetDIGEST, 5 January 1999, humbpeis@livjm.ac.uk. Original article appeared in *Archaeology Ireland*, no. 46, winter 1998.

Bak, Per

   1996   *How nature works: the science of self-organized criticality.* Springer-Verlag, New York.

Bak, Per, and Kan Chen

   1991   Self-organized criticality. *Scientific American* 264:46–53.

Ball, Joseph W.

   1985   The Postclassic archaeology of the western Gulf Coast: some initial observations. In *The Lowland Maya Postclassic*, edited by Arlen F. Chase and Prudence M. Rice, pp 235–244. University of Texas Press, Austin.

Barber, D. C., A. Dyke, C. Hillaire-Marcel, A. E. Jennings, J. T. Andrews, M. W. Kerwin, G. Bilodeau, R. McNeely, J. Southton, M. D. Morehead, and J.-M. Gagnon

   1999   Forcing the cold event of 8,200 years ago by catastrophic drainage of Laurentide lakes. *Nature* 400(22 July):344–348.

Bar Hebraeus

   1932   *The chronography of Gregory Abû'l Faraj, the son of Aaron, the Hebrew physician, commonly known as Bar Hebraeus, being the first part of his political history of the world.* Oxford University Press, London.

Barnish, S. J. B. (editor and translator)

   1992   *The variae of Magnus Aurelius Cassiodorus Senator.* Liverpool University Press, Liverpool.

Barrera Rubio, Alfredo

   1985   Littoral-marine economy atTulum, Quintana Roo, Mexico. In *The Lowland Maya Postclassic*, edited by Arlen F. Chase and Prudence M. Rice, pp 50–61. University of Texas Press, Austin.

Barry, Roger G., and Richard J. Chorley

   1987   *Atmosphere, weather and climate.* Methuen, London and New York.

Bassie-Sweet, Karen
    1991   *From the mouth of the dark cave: commemorative sculpture of the Late Classic Maya.* University of Oklahoma Press, Norman.

Bateson, Gregory
    1972   *Steps to an ecology of mind: collected essays in anthropology, psychiatry, evolution, and epistemology.* Chandler Publishing Company, San Francisco.

Becker, Jasper
    1996   *Hungry ghosts: Mao's secret famine.* The Free Press, New York.

Beyer, Hermann
    1937   *Studies on the inscriptions of Chichén Itza.* Carnegie Institution of Washington, Washington.

Binford, Lewis R.
    1972   *An archaeological perspective.* Seminar Press, New York.
    1981   *Bones: ancient men and modern myths.* Academic Press, New York.

Binford, Michael W.
    1983   Paleolimnology of the Petén Lake district, Guatemala. I. Erosion and deposition of inorganic sediment as inferred from granulometry. *Hydrobiologia* 103:199–203.

Birkinshaw, Julian M., and Allen J. Morrison
    1995   Configurations of strategy and structure in subsidiaries of multinational corporations. *Journal of international business studies* 26:729–753.

Blanton, Richard E., Stephen A. Kowalewski, Gary Feinman, and Jill Appel
    1981   *Ancient Mesoamerica: a comparison of change in three regions.* Cambridge University Press, Cambridge and New York.

Boserup, Ester
    1965   *The conditions of agricultural growth: the economics of agrarian change under population pressure.* Earthscan Publications, London.

Bowman, Sheridan
    1990   *Radiocarbon dating.* University of California Press/British Museum, Los Angeles.

Bradbury, J. Platt, R. M. Forester, W. Anthony Bryant, and A. P. Covich
    1990   Paleolimnology of Laguna de Cocos, Albion Island, Rio Hon-
            do, Belize. In *Ancient Maya wetland agriculture: excavations on
            Albion Island, northern Belize*, edited by Mary DeLand Pohl, pp
            119–154. Westview Press, Boulder, CO.

Bradley, Raymond S.
    1973   Recent freezing level changes and climatic deterioration in the
            Canadian Arctic Archipelago. *Nature* 243:398–400.
    1985   *Quaternary paleoclimatology: methods of paleoclimatic reconstruc-
            tion*. Allen & Unwin, Boston.

Bradley, Raymond S., and Philip D. Jones
    1992   Records of explosive volcanic eruptions over the last 500
            years. In *Climate since A.D. 1500*, edited by Raymond S.
            Bradley and Philip D. Jones, pp 606–622. Routledge, London.

Braudel, Fernand
    1973   *Capitalism and material life, 1400–1800*. Harper and Row, New
            York.
    1984   *Civilization and capitalism, 15th–18th century: the perspective of
            the world*. Harper & Row, Publishers, New York.

Brenner, Mark
    1983   Paleolimnology of the Petén Lake district, Guatemala. II.
            Mayan population density and sediment and nutrient loading
            of Lake Quexil. *Hydrobiologia* 103:205–210.

Briffa, K. R., P. D. Jones, F. H. Schweingruber, and T. J. Osborn
    1998   Influence of volcanic eruptions on Northern Hemisphere
            summer temperature over the past 600 years. *Nature* 393(4
            June):450–455.

Briffa, K. R., T. S. Bartholin, D. Eckstein, P. D. Jones, W. Karlén, F. H.
Schweingruber, and P. Zetterberg
    1990   A 1,400-year tree-ring record of summer temperatures in Fen-
            noscandia. *Nature* 346:434–439.

Broecker, Wallace S.
    1987   The biggest chill: when ocean currents shifted, Europe sud-
            denly got cold. Could it happen again? *Natural history*
            96(10):74–82.
    1995   Chaotic climate. *Scientific American* 273(November):62–68.

1997   Thermohaline circulation, the Achilles heel of our climate system: will man-made CO_2 upset the current balance? *Science* 278:1582–1588.

1998   Paleocean circulation during the last deglaciation: a bipolar seesaw? *Paleoceanography* 13(2):199–121.

Broecker, Wallace S., and George H. Denton
1989   The role of ocean-atmosphere reorganizations in glacial cycles. *Geochimica et cosmochimica acta* 53:2465–2501.

1990   What drives glacial cycles? *Scientific American* 262(January):49–56.

Broecker, Wallace S., Dorothy M. Peteet, and David Rind
1985   Does the ocean-atmosphere system have more than one stable mode of operation? *Nature* 315:21–26.

Brumfield, Elizabeth M.
1995   Heterarchy and the analysis of complex societies. In *Heterarchy and the analysis of complex societies*, edited by Robert M. Ehrenreich, Carole L. Crumley, and Janet E. Levy, pp 125–131. American Anthropological Association, Arlington, VA.

Bryant, Edward A.
1991   *Natural hazards.* Cambridge University Press, Cambridge.

Bryant, Vaughan M.
1994   The Paleolithic health club. In *1995 yearbook of science and the future,* pp 114–133. Encyclopedia Britannica, Chicago.

Bryson, Reid A.
1973   Drought in Sahelia: who or what is to blame? *Ecologist* 3:366–371.

Budyko, M. I., G. S. Golitsyn, and Y. A. Izrael
1986   *Global climatic catastrophes.* Springer-Verlag, Berlin.

Bullard, Fred M
1976   *Volcanoes of the Earth.* University of Texas Press, Austin.

Butzer, Karl W.
1980   Civilizations: organisms or systems? *American scientist* 68:517–523.

Cahill, Kevin M. (editor)
1982   *Famine.* Orbis Books, Maryknoll, NY.

Caldwell, John C., and Pat Caldwell
  1996   The African AIDS epidemic. *Scientific American* 274:62–68.

Calvin, William H.
  1998   The great climate flip-flop. *The Atlantic monthly* (January). Two parts. http://www.theatlantic.com/issues/98jan/climate.htm

Cantagrel, J. M., A. Gourgaud, and C. Robin
  1984   Repetitive mixing events and Holocene pyroclastic activity at Pico de Orizaba and Popocatépetl (Mexico). *Bulletin volcanologique* 47:735–748.

Carlson, Dennis G.
  1982   Famine in history: with a comparison of two modern disasters. In *Famine*, edited by Kevin M. Cahill, MD, pp 5–16. Orbis Books, Maryknoll, NY.

Carneiro, Robert L.
  1967   On the relationship between size of population and complexity of social organization. *Southwestern journal of anthropology* 23:234–243.
  1974   A reappraisal of the roles of technology and organization in the origin of civilization. *American antiquity* 39:179–186.
  1978   Political expansion as an expression of the principle of competitive exclusion. In *Origins of the state: the anthropology of political evolution*, edited by Ronald Cohen and Elman R. Service, pp 205–223. Institute for the Study of Human Issues, Philadelphia.

Casares, David
  1905   A notice of Yucatan with some remarks on its water supply. *Proceedings of the American Antiquarian Society* 17 (New series):207–230.

Castorena, Guadalupe, Elena Sánchez Mora, Enrique Florescano M., Guillermo Padillo Ríos, and Luis Rodríguez Viqueira
  1980   *Análisis histórico de las sequías de México*. Documentación de la Comisión del Plan Nacional Hidráulico, vol 22. Secretaría de Agricultura y Recursos Hidráulicos, Comisión del Plan Nacional Hidráulico, Mexico, DF.

Castro, Renato
  1997   *Catastrophic prehistoric eruptions at Popocatépetl and Quaternary explosive volcanism in the Serdán-Oriental Basin, East-Central*

Mexico. Instituto de Geofísica, UNAM, Coyoacán 04510, Mexico, DF.

Chaffin, Tom
  1998   Whole Earth mentor: a conversation with Eugene P. Odum. *Natural history* 107:8–12.

Chaisson, Eric
  1987   *The life era: cosmic selection and conscious evolution.* Atlantic Monthly Press, New York.

Charney, J. G.
  1975   Dynamics of deserts and drought in the Sahel. *Quarterly journal of the Royal Meteorological Society* 101:193–202.

Chase, Arlen F.
  1990   Maya archaeology and population estimates in the Tayasal-Paxcamán zone, Petén, Guatemala. In *Precolumbian population history in the Maya Lowlands*, edited by T. Patrick Culbert and Don S. Rice, pp 149–166. University of New Mexico Press, Albuquerque.

Childe, V. Gordon
  1951   *Social evolution.* Meridian Books, The World Publishing Company, Cleveland.
  1956   *Piecing together the past: the interpretation of archæological data.* Frederick A. Praeger, New York.

Ciudad Real, Antonio de
  1984   *Calepino maya de Motul*, edited by René Acuña. 2 vols. Instituto de Investigaciones Filológicas, Universidad Nacional Autónoma de México, Mexico, DF.

Clube, Victor, and Bill Napier
  1990   *The cosmic winter.* B. Blackwell, Oxford.

Colinvaux, Paul A., Kam-biu Liu, Paulo de Oliveira, Mark B. Bush, Michael C. Miller, and Miriam Steinitz Kannan
  1996   Temperature depression in the lowland tropics in glacial times. *Climatic change* 32:19–33.

Cook, Sherburne F., and Woodrow Borah
  1974   *Essays in population history: Mexico and the Caribbean.* University of California Press, Berkeley.

Covich, Alan, and Minze Stuiver
1974 Changes in oxygen 18 as a measure of long-term fluctuations in tropical lake levels and molluscan populations. *Limnology and oceanography* 19:682–691.

Cowgill, George L.
1988 Onward and upward with collapse. In *The collapse of ancient states and civilizations*, edited by Norman Yoffee and George L. Cowgill, pp 244–276. University of Arizona Press, Tucson.

Cowgill, Ursula M., and G. E. Hutchinson
1966 The history of the Petenxil Basin. *Memoirs of the Connecticut Academy of Arts and Sciences* 17:121–126.

Cox, G. W.
1981 The ecology of famine: an overview. In *Famine*, edited by John Robson, pp 5–18. Gordon & Breach, New York.

Craine, Eugene R., and Reginald C. Reindorp (editors)
1979 *The Codex Pérez and the book of Chilam Balam of Maní.* University of Oklahoma Press, Norman.

Crumley, Carole L.
1979 Three locational models: an epistemological assessment for anthropology and archaeology. In *Advances in archaeological method and theory*, vol. 2, edited by Michael B. Schiffer, pp 141–173.
1994a Historical ecology: a multidimensional ecological orientation. In *Historical ecology: cultural knowledge and changing landscapes*, edited by Carole L. Crumley, pp 1–16. School of American Research Press, Santa Fe.
1994b The ecology of conquest: contrasting agropastoral and agricultural societies' adaptation to climatic change. In *Historical ecology: cultural knowledge and changing landscapes*, edited by Carole L. Crumley, pp 183–201. School of American Research Press, Santa Fe.

Crumley, Carole L., and William H. Marquardt
1987 Regional dynamics in Burgundy. In *Regional dynamics: Burgundian landscapes in historical perspective*, edited by Carole L. Crumley and William H. Marquardt, pp 609–623. Academic Press, Inc., San Diego.

Culbert, T. Patrick
     1988   The collapse of Classic Maya civilization. In *The collapse of ancient states and civilizations*, edited by Norman Yoffee and George L. Cowgill, pp 69–101. University of Arizona Press, Tucson.
     1991   Maya political history and elite interaction: a summary view. In *Classic Maya political history: hieroglyphic and archaeological evidence*, edited by T. Patrick Culbert, pp 311–346. Cambridge University Press, Cambridge.

Culbert, T. Patrick (editor)
     1973   *The Classic Maya Collapse*. University of New Mexico Press, Albuquerque.

Culbert, T. Patrick, Laura J. Kosakowsky, Robert E. Fry, and William Haviland
     1990   The population of Tikal, Guatemala. In *Precolumbian population history in the Maya Lowlands*, edited by T. Patrick Culbert and Don S. Rice, pp 103-122. University of New Mexico Press, Albuquerque.

Curtis, Jason H.
     1997   *Climatic variation in the circum-Caribbean during the Holocene.* PhD dissertation, University of Florida, Gainesville.

Curtis, Jason H., and David A. Hodell
     1993   An isotopic and trace element study of ostracods from Lake Miragoane, Haiti: A 10,500 year record of paleosalinity and paleotemperature changes in the Caribbean. In *Climate change in continental isotopic records*, edited by P. K. Swart, K. C. Lohmann, J. McKenzie, and S. Savin, pp 135-152. American Geophysical Union, Washington.

Curtis, Jason H., David A. Hodell, and Mark Brenner
     1996   Climate variability on the Yucatan Peninsula (Mexico) during the past 3500 years, and implications for Maya cultural evolution. *Quaternary research* 46:37–47.

Dahl, Svein Olaf, and Atle Nesje
     1994   Holocene glacier fluctuations at Hardangerjøkulen, central-southern Norway: a high-resolution composite chronology from lacustrine and terrestrial deposits. *The Holocene* 4(3):269–277.

Dahlin, Bruce H.
1983   Climate and prehistory on the Yucatan peninsula. *Climatic change* 5:245–263.

Dai, Jihong, Ellen Mosley-Thompson, and Lonnie G. Thompson
1991   Ice core evidence for an explosive tropical volcanic eruption 6 years preceding Tambora. *Journal of geophysical research* 96(D9):17,361-17,366.

Dando, William A.
1980   *The geography of famine.* V. H. Winston & Sons, New York; John Wiley and Sons, London.

Danforth, Marie Elaine
1994   Stature change in prehistoric Maya of the southern Lowlands. *Latin American antiquity* 5(3):206–211.

Darwin, Charles
1859   *The origin of species: by means of natural selection.* 1952 ed. Encyclopedia Britannica, Inc., Chicago.

Davies, Nigel
1977   *The Toltecs: until the fall of Tula.* University of Oklahoma Press, Norman.

Decker, Robert, and Barbara Decker
1989   *Volcanoes.* W. H. Freeman and Company, New York.

Deevey, Edward S., Jr.
1960   The human population. *Scientific American* 203(3):195–204.

Deevey, Edward S., Jr., Mark Brenner, and Michael W. Binford
1983   Paleolimnology of the Petén Lake district, Guatemala. III. Late Pleistocene and Gamblian environments of the Maya area. *Hydrobiologia* 103:211–216.

Demarest, Arthur A.
1989   Ideology and evolutionism in American archaeology: looking beyond the economic base. In *Archaeological thought in America,* edited by C. C. Lamberg-Karlovsky, pp 89–102. Cambridge University Press, Cambridge.

Dengo, Gabriel
    1983   *Informe preliminar de la geología regional de la cuenca media del Río Usumacinta, Guatemala y México.* Instituto Nacional de Electrificación, Guatemala.
    1990   La posición de Chiapas en relación a las placas litosféricas. In *Geología del Estado de Chiapas,* edited by José Luis de la Rosa Z., Aldemar Eboli M., and Moisés Dávila S., pp 66–81. Departamento de Geología, Comisión Federal de Electricidad, Mexico, DF.

Denton, George H., and Wibjörn Karlén
    1973   Holocene climatic variations—their pattern and possible cause. *Quaternary research* 3:155–205.

de Selincourt, Kate
    1997   Environment: doing bad by doing good. *World press review* 44:34.

Devereux, Stephen
    1993   *Theories of famine.* Harvester Wheatsheaf, New York.

Devine, J. D., H. Sigurdsson, A. N. Davis, and S. Self
    1984   Estimates of the sulfur and chlorine yield to the atmosphere from volcanic eruptions and potential climatic effects. *Journal of geophysical research* 89:6309–6325.

de Vries, Jan
    1981   Measuring the impact of climate on history: the search for appropriate methodologies. In *Climate and history: studies in interdisciplinary history,* edited by Robert I. Rotberg and Theodore K. Rabb, pp 19–50. Princeton University Press, Princeton.

di Castri, Francesco, and Andrew J. Hansen
    1992   The environment and development crises as determinants of landscape dynamics. In *Landscape boundaries: consequences for biotic diversity and ecological flows,* edited by Andrew J. Hansen and Francesco Di Castri, pp 3–18. Springer-Verlag, New York.

Diamond, Jared
    1997   *Guns, germs, and steel.* W. W. Norton & Company, New York.

Diehl, Richard A.
    1983   *Tula: the Toltec capital of ancient Mexico.* Thames and Hudson, London.

Dirks, Robert
  1980   Social responses during severe food shortages and famine. *Current anthropology* 21:21–44.
  1993   Starvation and famine: cross-cultural codes and some hypothesis tests. *Cross-cultural research* 27:28–69.

Dobyns, Henry F.
  1966   An appraisal of techniques with a new hemispheric estimate. *Current anthropology* 7:395–416.

Doehring, Donald O., and Joseph H. Butler
  1974   Hydrogeologic constraints on Yucatán's development. *Science* 186:591–595.

Drennan, Robert D.
  1984   Long-distance movement of goods in the Mesoamerican Formative and Classic. *American antiquity* 49:27–43.

Dumond, E. E., and Florencia Muller
  1972   Classic to Postclassic in highland central Mexico. *Science* 175:1208–1215.

Dunning, Nicholas P., David J. Rue, Timothy Beach, Alan Covich, and Alfred Traverse
  1998   Human - environment interactions in a tropical watershed: the paleoecology of Laguna Tamarindito, El Petén, Guatemala. *Journal of field archaeology* 25:139–151.

Durant, Will, and Ariel Durant
  1968   *The lessons of history.* Simon and Schuster, New York.

Durkheim, Emile
  1895   Emergent properties. In *Selected writings,* edited by Anthony Giddens, pp 69–71. Cambridge University Press, Cambridge.

Duxbury, Alyn C.
  1971   *The Earth and its oceans.* Addison-Wesley, Reading, MA.

Edmonson, Munro S. (editor)
  1982   *The ancient future of the Itza: The Book of Chilam Balam of Tizimín.* University of Texas Press, Austin.
  1986   *Heaven born Mérida and its destiny: The Book of Chilam Balam of Chumayel.* University of Texas Press, Austin.

Eldredge, Niles, and Stephen Jay Gould
    1972   Punctuated equilibria: an alternative to phyletic gradualism.
            In *Models in paleobiology*, edited by Thomas J. M. Schopf, pp
            82–115. Freeman, Cooper & Company, San Francisco.

Ellsaesser, Hugh W.
    1986   Comments on "Surface temperature changes following the six
            major volcanic episodes between 1780 and 1980." *Journal of
            climate and applied meteorology* 25:1184–1185.

Ellsaesser, Hugh W., Michael C. MacCracken, John J. Walton, and Stanley
L. Grotch
    1986   Global climatic trends as revealed by the recorded data. *Re-
            views of geophysics* 24:745-792.

El-Najjar, Mahmoud Y., and Abel L. Robertson Jr.
    1976   Spongy bones in prehistoric America. *Science* 193:141–143.

Encyclopaedia Britannica
    1976   *The new Encyclopaedia Britannica*. 30 vols. Encyclopaedia Bri-
            tannica, Inc, Chicago.

Farriss, Nancy M.
    1984   *Maya society under colonial rule: the collective enterprise of surviv-
            al*. Princeton University Press, Princeton.
    1986   Indians in colonial northern Yucatán. In *Ethnohistory*, supple-
            ment to the *Handbook of Middle Americans Indians*, edited by
            Ronald Spores, pp 88–102. University of Texas Press, Austin.

Finley, Moses I.
    1985   *The ancient economy.* 2nd ed. Hogarth Press, London.

Flannery, Kent V.
    1968   Archaeological systems theory and early Mesoamerica. In
            Contemporary archaeology: a guide to theory and contributions, ed-
            ited by Mark P. Leone, pp 222–234. Southern Illinois Universi-
            ty Press, Carbondale and Edwardsville.
    1972   The cultural evolution of civilizations. *Annual review of ecology
            and systematics* 3:399–426.

Flohn, Hermann, and Roberto Fantechi
    1984   *Climate in Europe: past present and future: natural and man in-
            duced climatic changes, a European perspective*. D. Reidel Pub-
            lishing Company, Dordrecht and Boston.

Florescano, Enrique
    1980   Una historia olvidada: la sequía en México. *Nexos* 32:9–18.

Foege, William H.
    1971   Famine, infections and epidemics. In *Famine: a symposium deal-
            ing with nutrition and relief operations in times of disaster*, edited
            by Gunnar Blix, MD, Yngve Hofvander, MD, and Bo
            Vahlquist, MD, pp 64–73. Almqvist & Wiksells, Uppsala.

Folan, William J.
    1983a   Physical geography of the Yucatan Peninsula. In *Coba: a Clas-
            sic Maya metropolis*, edited by William J. Folan, Ellen R. Kintz,
            and Laraine A. Fletcher, pp 21–48. Academic Press, New York.
    1983b   Summary and conclusions. In *Cobá: a Classic Maya metropolis*,
            edited by William J. Folan, Ellen R. Kintz, and Laraine A.
            Fletcher, pp 211–217. Academic Press, New York.

Folan, William J., Joel Gunn, Jack D. Eaton, and Robert W. Patch
    1983   Paleoclimatological patterning in southern Mesoamerica.
            Journal of field archaeology 10:453-468.

Folan, William J., Joyce Marcus, Sophia Pincemin, María del Rosario
Domínguez Carrasco, Laraine Fletcher, and Abel Morales López
    1995   Calakmul: new data from an ancient Maya capital in
            Campeche, Mexico. *Latin American antiquity* 6(4):310–334.

Ford, Anabel
    1996   Critical resource control and the rise of the Classic period
            Maya. In *The managed mosaic: ancient Maya agriculture and re-
            source use*, edited by Scott L. Fedick, pp 297–303. University of
            Utah Press, Salt Lake City.

Franková, Slávka
    1980   Comment in Social responses during severe food shortages
            and famine, by Robert Dirks. *Current anthropology* 21(Febru-
            ary):21–44.

Freter, AnnCorinne
    1988   *The Classic Maya Collapse at Copán, Honduras: a regional settle-
            ment perspective*. University Microfilms International, Ann Ar-
            bor.

Fritts, Harold C.
    1976   *Tree rings and climate*. Academic Press, New York.

Frost, Robert
    1916   The road not taken. In *The top 500 poems*, edited by William
            Harmon, 1992, p 900. Columbia University Press, New York.

Fry, Robert E.
    1969   *Ceramics and settlement in the periphery of Tikal, Guatemala.* PhD
            dissertation, University of Arizona, Tucson.

Fukuyama, Francis
    1995   *Trust.* Free Press, New York.

Gallopin, Gary G.
    1990   *Water storage technology at Tikal, Guatemala.* University of Cin-
            cinnati, Cincinnati.

Galloway, Patrick R.
    1986   Long-term fluctuations in climate and population in the pre-
            industrial era. *Population and development review* 12(1):1–24.

García, Enriqueta
    1964   *Modificaciones al sistema de clasificación climática de Koppen.* In-
            stituto de Geografía, Universidad Nacional Autónoma de
            México, Mexico, DF.
    1974   Situaciones climáticas durante el auge y la caída de la Cultura
            Teotihuacana. *Boletín del Instituto de Geografía de la UNAM*
            5:35–69.

Garcia, Rolando V., and Pierre Spitz
    1986   *The roots of catastrophe.* Pergamon Press, Oxford.

Garnsey, Peter
    1988   *Famine and food supply in the Graeco-Roman world: responses to
            risks and crises.* Cambridge University Press, Cambridge.

Gates, W. Lawrence
    1976   Modeling the Ice-Age climate. *Science* 191:1138–1144.

Gell-Mann, Murray
    1994   *The quark and the jaguar.* W. H. Freeman and Company, New
            York.

Gerhard, Peter
    1979   *The southeast frontier of New Spain.* Princeton University Press,
            Princeton.

Gibbons, Ann
> 1993   How the Akkadian Empire was hung out to dry. *Science* 261:985.

Gilbert, Geoffrey
> 1993   Introduction. In *An essay on the principles of population*, edited by Thomas R. Malthus, pp vii–xxv. Oxford University Press, Oxford.

Gill, Richardson B.
> 1994   *The great Maya droughts*. PhD dissertation, University of Texas at Austin, Austin.

Glowienka, R.
> 1985   Studies on the variability of Icelandic Low and Azores High between 1881 and 1983. *Beiträge zur Physik der Atmosphäre* 58:160–170.

Goertzel, Ben
> 1998   World wide brain: the emergence of the global web intelligence and how it will transform the human race. http://goertzel.org/ben/webart.html (13 July 1998).

Golkin, Arline
> 1987   *Famine, a heritage of hunger: a guide to issues and references*. Regina Books, Claremont, CA.

Goodman, Brian Merritt
> 1984   *The climatic impact of volcanic activity*. PhD dissertation, University of Wisconsin–Madison, Madison.

Gorczyński, Ladislas
> 1904   Sur la diminution de l'intensité du rayonnement solaire en 1902 et 1903. *Comptes rendus de l'Académie des Sciences* 138:255–258.

Gordon, Arnold L.
> 1986   Interocean exchange of thermocline water. *Journal of geophysical research* 91:5037–5046.

Gould, Stephen Jay
> 1987   *Time's arrow, time's cycle*. Harvard University Press, Cambridge.
> 1992   Life in a punctuation: a visitor to Russia reflects on change in nature and the nature of change. *Natural history* 101:10–21.

Graham, John A.
    1990   Monumental sculpture and hieroglyphic inscriptions. In *Excavations at Seibal, Department of Petén, Guatemala*, edited by Gordon R. Willey, pp 1–79. Peabody Museum, Cambridge.

Graham, N. E., and Tim P. Barnett
    1987   Sea surface temperature, surface wind divergence, and convection over tropical oceans. *Science* 238:657–659.

Gray, William M.
    1990   Strong association between West African rainfall and U.S. landfall of intense hurricanes. *Science* 249:1251–1256.

Gribbing, John R.
    1976   *Forecasts, famines and freezes.* Walker and Company, New York.

Guilderson, Thomas P., Richard G. Fairbanks, and James L. Rubenstone
    1994   Tropical temperature variations since 20,000 years ago: modulating interhemispheric climate change. *Science* 263:663–665.

Gunn, Joel
    Forthcoming Prologue: A. D. 536 and its 300-year aftermath. In *Tracing A. D. 536 and its aftermath: the years without summer*, edited by Joel Gunn.

Gunn, Joel D., and Richard Adams
    1981   Climatic change, culture, and civilization in North America. *World archaeology* 13:87–100.

Gunn, Joel D., and Carole L. Crumley
    1991   Global energy balance and regional hydrology: a Burgundian case study. *Earth surface processes and landforms* 16:579–592.

Gunn, Joel D., William J. Folan, and Hubert R. Robichaux
    1991   An analysis of discharge data from the Candelaria River system in Mexico: insights into paleoclimates affecting the ancient Maya sites of Calakmul and El Mirador. Unpublished manuscript.

    1995   A landscape analysis of the Candelaria watershed in Mexico: insights into paleoclimates affecting upland horticulture in the southern Yucatán Peninsula semi-karst. *Geoarchaeology* 10:3–42.

Gutiérrez Coutiño, Ricardo, Mauro Moreno Corzo, and Cándido Cruz Borraz
  1983   Determinación del volumen del material arrojado y grado de explosividad alcanzado por el Volcán Chichonal, Estado de Chiapas. In *El Volcán Chichonal*, pp 68–80. Instituto de Geología, Universidad Nacional Autónoma de México, Mexico, DF.

Hahn, Gregory A., William I. Rose Jr., and Thomas Meyers
  1979   Geochemical correlation of genetically related rhyolitic ash-flow and air-fall ashes, central and western Guatemala and the equatorial Pacific. In *Ash flow tuffs*, edited by W. Elston and C. Chapin. Geological Society of America, Boulder, CO.

Haigh, Joanna D.
  1996   The impact of solar variability on climate. *Science* 272:981–984.

Hall, Peter
  1966   Introduction. In *Von Thünen's isolated state*, edited by Peter Hall and translated by Carla M. Wartenberg, pp xi–xliv. Pergamon Press, Oxford.

Hallam, A.
  1983   *Great geological controversies*. Oxford University Press, Oxford.

Hammer, C. U., H. B. Clausen, and C. C. Langway Jr.
  1997   50,000 years of recorded global volcanism. *Climatic change* 35:1–15.

Hammer, C. U., H. B. Clausen, and W. Dansgaard
  1980   Greenland ice sheet evidence of post-glacial volcanism and its climatic impact. *Nature* 288:230–235.

Hammond, Norman
  1988   *Ancient Maya civilization*. Rutgers University Press, New Brunswick, NJ.
  1991   Inside the black box: defining Maya polity. In *Classic Maya political history: hieroglyphic and archaeological evidence*, edited by T. Patrick Culbert, pp 253–284. Cambridge University Press, Cambridge.

Handler, Paul
  1984   Possible association of stratospheric aerosols and El Niño type events. *Geophysical research letters* 11:1121–1124.

1989 The effect of volcanic aerosols on global climate. *Journal of volcanology and geothermal research* 37:233–249.

Handler, Paul, and K. Andsager
1989 Volcanic aerosols, El Niño, and the Southern Oscillation. *Journal of climatology* in prep.

Hansen, Richard D.
1990 *Excavations in the Tigre Complex, El Mirador, Petén, Guatemala.* New World Archaeological Foundation, Brigham Young University, Provo, UT.

Harrison, G. A. (editor)
1988 *Famine.* Oxford University Press, Oxford.

Harrison, Peter D.
1993 Aspects of water management in the southern Maya Lowlands. In *Economic aspects of water management in the Prehispanic New World,* edited by Vernon L. Scarborough and Barry L. Isaac, pp 771–119. JAI Press, Greenwich, CT.

Hassig, Ross
1981 The famine of One Rabbit: ecological causes and social consequences of a Pre-Columbian calamity. *Journal of anthropological research* 37:172–182.
1985 *Trade, tribute, and transportation.* University of Oklahoma Press, Norman.
1986a One hundred years of servitude: *tlamemes* in New Spain. In *Ethnohistory,* edited by Ronald Spores, pp 134–152. University of Texas Press, Austin.
1986b Famine and scarcity in the Valley of Mexico. In *Economic aspects of Prehispanic highland Mexico,* edited by Barry L. Isaac, pp 303–318. JAI Press, Greenwich, CT.
1992 *War and society in ancient Mesoamerica.* University of California Press, Berkeley.

Hastenrath, Stefan
1976 Marine climatology of the tropical Americas. *Archiv für Meteorologie, Geophysik und Bioklimatologie* Ser. B 24:1–24.
1978 On modes of tropical circulation and climate anomalies. *Journal of the atmospheric sciences* 35:2222–2231.
1985 *Climate and circulation of the tropics.* D. Reidel Publishing Company, Dordrecht and Boston.

Hatfield, Thomas M.
1964   *The Texas drought of 1950–1956.* Master's thesis, University of Texas, Austin.

Heine, Klaus
1973   Zur Glazialmorphologie und präkeramischen Archäologie des mexicanischen Hochlandes während des Spätglazials (Wisconsin und Holozäns). *Erdkunde* 27:161–180.

Heming, R. F.
1974   Geology and petrology of Rabaul Caldera, Papua New Guinea. *Bulletin of the Geological Society of America* 85:1253–1264.

Hester, Thomas R.
1985   *Late Classic-Early Postclassic transitions: archaeological investigations at Colha, Belize.* Center for Archaeological Research, University of Texas at San Antonio, San Antonio.

Hewitson, Bruce C., and Robert G. Crane
1992   Large-scale atmospheric controls on local precipitation in tropical Mexico. *Geophysical research letters* 19:1835–1838.

Hidore, John J.
1996   *Global environmental change.* Prentice-Hall, Upper Saddle River, NJ.

Hodell, David A., Jason H. Curtis, and Mark Brenner
1995   Possible role of climate in the collapse of Classic Maya civilization. *Nature* 375:391–394.

Hoffman, Paul F., Alan J. Kaufman, Galen P. Halverson, and Daniel P. Schrag
1998   A Neoproterozoic snowball Earth. *Science* 281:1342–1346.

Hofmann, David J.
1987   Perturbations to the global atmosphere associated with the El Chichón volcanic eruption of 1982. *Reviews of geophysics* 25:743–759.

Hofstadter, Douglas R.
1979   *Gödel, Escher, Bach: an eternal golden braid.* Vintage Books, New York.

Holland, Thomas D., and Michael J. O'Brien
    1997   Parasites, porotic hyperstosis, and the implications of chang-
            ing perspectives. *American antiquity* 62(2):183–193.

Hollingsworth, Thomas H.
    1980a   Background paper for first theme: an introduction to popula-
            tion crises. In *The great mortalities: Methodological studies of de-
            mographic crises in the past*, edited by Hubert Charbonneau and
            André LaRose, pp 17–20. Ordina Editions, International
            Union for the Study of Population, Liège.
    1980b   A preliminary suggestion for the measurement of mortality
            crises. In *The great mortalities: methodological studies of demo-
            graphic crises in the past*, edited by Hubert Charbonneau and
            André LaRose, pp 21–28. Ordina Editions, International
            Union for the Scientific Study of Population, Liège.

Horel, John D., Andrea N. Hahmann, and John E. Geisler
    1989   An investigation of the annual cycle of convective activity
            over the tropical Americas. *Journal of climate* 2:1388–1403.

Horn, Sally P., and Robert L. Sanford Jr.
    1992   Holocene fires in Costa Rica. *Biotropica* 24:354–361.

Hosler, Dorothy, Jeremy A. Sabloff, and Dale Runge
    1977   Situation model development: a case study of the Classic
            Maya Collapse. In *Social process in Maya prehistory*, edited by
            Norman Hammond, pp 553–590. Academic Press, London.

Hsü, Kenneth J.
    1990   Actualistic catastrophism and climate change. *Palaeogeogra-
            phy, palaeoclimatology, palaeoecology (global and planetary change
            section)* 89:309–313.

Huggett, Richard
    1990   *Catastrophism: asteroids, comets and other dynamic events in Earth
            history.* Verso, London.

Hugo, Graeme J.
    1984   The demographic impact of famine: a review. In *Famine as a
            geographical phenomenon*, edited by Bruce Currey and Graeme
            J. Hugo, pp 7–32. D. Reidel Publishing Company, Dordrecht.

Huntington, Ellsworth
    1913   Guatemala and the highest native American civilization. *Pro-
            ceedings of the American Philosophical Society* 52:467–487.

1915   Maya civilization and climatic changes. *Proceedings of the 19th International Congress of Americanists* 19:150–164.

Huntington, Samuel P.
1993   The clash of civilizations? *Foreign affairs* 72:22–49.

Ingram, M. J., G. Farmer, and T. M. L. Wigley
1981   Past climates and their impact on Man: a review. In *Climate and history: studies in past climates and their impact on Man*, edited by T. M. L. Wigley, M. J. Ingram, and G. Farmer, pp 3–50. Cambridge University Press, Cambridge.

Institute for Agriculture and Trade Policy
1996   Mexico buys US grain. 13(12):7. http://www.envirolink. org/ pubs/IATP/nafta/vol13no12.html (June 28, 1996).

Islebe, G. A., and H. Hooghiemstra
1997   Vegetation and climate history of montane Costa Rica since the last glacial. *Quaternary science reviews* 16:589–604.

Islebe, Gerald A., Henry Hooghiemstra, Mark Brenner, Jason H. Curtis, and David A. Hodell
1996   A Holocene vegetation history from lowland Guatemala. *The Holocene* 6:265–271.

Jacob, John S., and C. T. Hallmark
1987   Raised fields at Colha, Belize: a pedoarchaeologic assessment. Unpublished manuscript. Department of Soil Science, Texas A & M University, College Station.

Jakosky, Bruce M.
1986   Volcanoes, the stratosphere, and climate. *Journal of volcanology and geothermal research* 28:247–255.

Jantsch, Eric
1980   *The self-organizing universe.* Pergamon Press, Oxford.

Jáuregui Ostos, Ernesto.
1979   Algunos aspectos de las fluctuaciones pluviométricas en México en los últimos cien años. *Boletín del Instituto de Geografía de la UNAM* 9:39–64.

Jelliffe, Derrick B., and E. G. Patrice Jelliffe
1971   The effects of starvation on the function of the family and of society. In *Famine: a symposium dealing with nutrition and relief*

operations in times of disaster, edited by Gunnar Blix, MD, Yngve Hofvander, MD, and Bo Vahlquist, MD, pp 54–63. Almqvist & Wiksells, Uppsala.

1980   Comment in Social responses during severe food shortages and famine, by Robert Dirks. *Current anthropology* 21(1):21–44.

Jones, Glenn A.
1991   A stop-start ocean conveyor. *Nature* 349:364–365.

Jones, E. P., L. G. Anderson, and B. Rudels
1998   *The Arctic Ocean and the global thermohaline circulation.* Paper presented at the 32nd Annual Canadian Meteorological and Oceanographical Society Congress. June 1–4, 1998, Dartmouth, Nova Scotia.

Justeson, John S., and Terrence Kaufman
1993   A decipherment of epi-Olmec hieroglyphic writing. *Science* 259:1703–1711.

Karlén, Wibjörn
1982   Holocene glacier fluctuations in Scandinavia. *Striae* 18:26–34.
1984   Dendrochronology, mass balance and glacier front fluctuations. In *Climatic changes on a yearly to millennia basis: geological, historical and instrumental records*, edited by Nils-Axel Mörner and Wibjörn Karlén, pp 263–271. D. Reidel Publishing Company, Dordrecht.

Kauffman, Stuart A.
1993   *The origins of order: self-organization and selection in evolution.* Oxford University Press, New York.

Kelley, David H.
1976   *Deciphering the Maya script.* University of Texas Press, Austin.
1982   Notes on Puuc inscriptions and history. In *The Puuc: new perspectives*, edited by Lawrence Mills. Central College, Pella, IA.

Kelly, P. M., P. D. Jones, C. B. Sear, B. S. G. Cherry, and R. K. Tavakol
1982   Variations in surface air temperatures: Part 2. Arctic regions, 1881–1980. *Monthly weather review* 110:71–83.

Kelly, P. M., and C. B. Sear
1984   Climatic impact of explosive volcanic eruptions. *Nature* 311:740–743.

Kelly, P. M., T. M. L. Wigley, and P. D. Jones
    1984   European pressure maps for 1815–1816, the time of the eruption of Tambora. *Climate monitor* 13:76–91.

Kerr, Richard A.
    1993   Pinatubo global cooling on target. *Science* 259:594.
    1994   Did Pinatubo send climate-warming gases into a dither? *Science* 263:1562.
    1998   Sea-floor dust shows drought felled Akkadian Empire. *Science* 279:325–326.

Keys, Ancel, Josef Brozek, Austin Henschel, Olaf Mickelson, and Henry Taylor
    1950   *The biology of human starvation.* University of Minnesota Press, Minneapolis.

Kirchoff, Paul
    1943   Mesoamerica: its geographic limits, ethnic composition and cultural composition. In *Ancient Mesoamerica*, edited by John A. Graham, pp 1–10. Peek Publications, Palo Alto, CA.

Kondratyev, Kirill Ya.
    1988   *Climate shocks: natural and anthropogenic.* John Wiley and Sons, New York.

Kondratyev, Kirill Ya., and Ignacio Galindo
    1997   *Volcanic activity and climate.* A. Deepak Publishing, Hampton, VA.

Kontopoulos, Kyriakos M.
    1993   *The logics of social structure.* Cambridge University Press, Cambridge.

Kosko, Bart
    1993   *Fuzzy thinking: the new science of fuzzy logic.* Hyperion, New York.

Kovar, Anton
    1970   The physical and biological environment of the Basin of Mexico. In *The natural environment, contemporary occupation and 16th century population of the valley: The Teotihuacan Valley Project: final report*, edited by William T. Sanders, Anton Kovar, Thomas Charlton, and Richard A. Diehl, pp 13–68. Department of Anthropology, The Pennsylvania State University, University Park, PA.

Kowalski, Jeff
    1987   *The House of the Governor: a Maya palace at Uxmal.* University of
            Oklahoma Press, Norman.

Krochok, Ruth
    1988   *The hieroglyphic inscriptions and iconography of Temple of the Four
            Lintels and related monuments, Chichén Itza, Yucatán, Mexico.*
            Master's thesis, University of Texas at Austin.

Kunzig, Robert
    1996   In deep water. *Discover* 17(December):86–96.

Labeyrie, L. D., J. C. Duplessy, and P. L. Blanc
    1987   Variations in mode of formation and temperature of oceanic
            deep waters over the past 125,000 years. *Nature* 327:477–482.

LaMarche, Valmore C., Jr., and Katherine K. Hirschboeck
    1984   Frost rings in trees as records of major volcanic eruptions. *Na-
            ture* 307:121–126.

Lamb, Hubert H.
    1972a   British Isles weather types and a register of the daily sequence
            of circulation patterns 1861–1971. *Geophysical memoirs* 116:1–
            85.
    1972b   *Climate: present, past and future.* Methuen and Company; New
            York: Barnes and Noble Books, London.
    1982   *Climate, history and the modern world.* Methuen, London.
    1995   *Climate, history and the modern world.* Routledge, London and
            New York.

Lamb, Hubert H., and A. I. Johnson
    1966   Secular variations of the atmospheric circulation since 1750.
            Geophysical memoirs 110:3–125.

Lamb, Peter J.
    1978   Case studies of tropical Atlantic surface circulation patterns
            during recent sub-Saharan weather anomalies: 1967 and 1968.
            Monthly weather review 106:482–491.

Lamberg-Karlovsky, C. C.
    1989   *Archaeological thought in America.* Cambridge University Press,
            Cambridge.

Landa, Diego de
  1566   *The Maya.* 1975 translation of *Relación de las cosas de Yucatán.*
          J. Philip O'Hara, Chicago.

Langley, S. P.
  1903   Variation of atmospheric absorption. *Nature* 69:5.

Larson, Daniel O., Hector Neff, Donald A. Graybill, Joel Michaelsen, and
Elizabeth Ambos
  1996   Risk, climatic variability, and the study of Southwestern pre-
          history: an evolutionary perspective. *American antiquity*
          61:217–241.

Laszlo, Ervin
  1987   *Evolution: the grand synthesis.* Shambala Publications, New Sci-
          ence Library, Boston.

Lee, Ronald D.
  1981   Short-term variation: vital rates, prices, and weather. In *The
          population history of England, 1541–1871: a reconstruction,* edited
          by E. A. Wrigley and R. S. Schofield, pp 356–401. Harvard Uni-
          versity Press, Cambridge.
  1986   Malthus and Boserup: a dynamic synthesis. In *The state of pop-
          ulation theory: forward from Malthus,* edited by David Coleman
          and Roger Schofield, pp 96–130. Basil Blackwell, Oxford.
  1987   Population dynamics of humans and other animals. *Demogra-
          phy* 24(4):443–465.
  1993   Accidental and systematic change in population history: ho-
          meostasis in a stochastic setting. *Explorations in economic histo-
          ry* 30:1–30.

Leemann, Andreas, and Frank Niessen
  1994   Holocene glacial activity and climatic variations in the Swiss
          Alps: reconstructing a continuous record from proglacial lake
          sediments. *The Holocene* 4(3):259–268.

Legrand, M., and R. J. Delmas
  1987   A 220-year continuous record of volcanic H_2SO_4 in the Ant-
          arctic ice sheet. *Nature* 327:671–676.

Lemdahl, Geoffrey
  1991   A rapid climatic change at the end of the Younger Dryas in
          south Sweden-palaeoclimatic and palaeoenvironmental re-
          constructions based on fossil insect assemblages. *Paleogeogra-
          phy, palaeoclimatology, paleoecology* 83:313–331.

Le Roy Ladurie, Emmanuel
    1967   *Times of feast, times of famine.* 1971 translation and revision of *Histoire du climat depuis l'an mil.* Noonday Press, New York.
    1990   Histoire et climat. *Historia* 519:68–75.

Lewin, Roger
    1992   *Complexity: life at the edge of chaos.* Macmillan, New York.

Leyden, Barbara W.
    1984   Guatemalan forest synthesis after Pleistocene aridity. *Proceedings of the National Academy of Science* 81:4856–4859.
    1985   Late Quaternary aridity and Holocene moisture fluctuations in the Lake Valencia Basin, Venezuela. *Ecology* 66:1279–1295.
    1987   Man and climate in the Maya lowlands. *Quaternary research* 28:407–414.

Leyden, Barbara W., Mark Brenner, and Bruce H. Dahlin
    1998   Cultural and climatic history of Cobá, a lowland Maya city in Quintana Roo, Mexico. *Quaternary research* 49:111–122.

Leyden, Barbara W., Mark Brenner, David A. Hodell, and Jason H. Curtis
    1993   Late Pleistocene climate in the Central American Lowlands. In *Climate change in continental isotopic records*, edited by P. K. Swart, K. C. Lohmann, J. McKenzie, and S. Savin, pp 165–178. American Geophysical Union, Washington.

Leyden, Barbara W., Mark Brenner, Tom Whitmore, Jason H. Curtis, Dolores R. Piperno, and Bruce Dahlin
    1996   A record of long- and short-term climatic variation from northwest Yucatán: Cenote San José Chulchacá. In *The managed mosaic: ancient Maya agriculture and resource use*, edited by Scott L. Fedick, pp 30–52. University of Utah Press, Salt Lake City.

Lincoln, Charles E.
    1986   The chronology of Chichén Itza: a review of the literature. In *Late Lowland Maya civilization: Classic to Postclassic*, edited by Jeremy A. Sabloff and E. Wyllys Andrews, V, pp 141–198. University of New Mexico Press, Albuquerque.

Lindzen, Richard S.
    1993   Palaeoclimate sensitivity. *Nature* 363:25–26.

Lorenz, Edward N.
1991   Dimension of weather and climate attractors. *Nature* 353:241–244.

Lough, J. M., and H. C. Fritts
1987   An assessment of the possible effects of volcanic eruptions on North American climate using tree-ring data, 1602 to 1900 AD. *Climatic change* 10:219–239.

Lowe, John W. G.
1985   *The dynamics of Apocalypse: a systems simulation of the Classic Maya collapse.* University of New Mexico Press, Albuquerque.

Luhr, James F.
1991   Mount Pinatubo: volcanic shade causes cooling. *Nature* 354:104–105.

Macdonald, Alison, and Carl Wunsch
1996   An estimate of global ocean circulation and heat fluxes. *Nature* 382:436–439.

Macías, José Luis, Juan Manuel Espíndola, Y. Taran, M. F. Sheridan, and A García
1997   Explosive volcanic activity during the last 3,500 years at El Chichón Volcano, Mexico. Excursion no. 6, field guide. Paper presented at IAVCEI Plenary Assembly, Puerto Vallarta, Jaisco, Mexico, January 19–24, 1997.

MacNeish, Richard S.
1958   Preliminary archaeological investigations in the Sierra de Tamaulipas, Mexico. In *Transactions of the American Philosophical Society.* American Philosophical Society, Philadelphia.

Malina, Jaroslav, and Zdenek Vašícek
1990   *Archaeology yesterday and today: the development of archaeology in the sciences and humanities.* Cambridge University Press, Cambridge.

Malthus, Thomas R.
1798   *An essay on the principle of population.* 1993 ed. Oxford University Press, Oxford.

Marcus, Joyce
1983   Lowland Maya archaeology at the crossroads. *American antiquity* 48:454–487.

1992   Political fluctuations in Mesoamerica. *National Geographic research & exploration* 8:392–411.

Markgraf, Vera
1989   Palaeoclimates in Central and South America since 18,000 BP based on pollen and lake-level records. *Quaternary science reviews* 8:1–24.

Martin, Simon, and Nikolai Grube
1994   Evidence for macro-political organization amongst Classic Maya lowland states.
1995   Maya superstates: how a few powerful kingdoms vied for control of the Maya Lowlands during the Classic period (A.D. 300–900). *Archaeology* 48(6, November/December):41–46.

Masefield, Geoffrey
1967   *Food and nutrition in times of disaster.* Food and Agriculture Organization of the United Nations, Rome.

Massey, Virginia
1989   The human skeletal remains from a Terminal Classic skull pit at Colha, Belize. In *Papers of the Colha Project.* Texas Archaeological Research Laboratory, University of Texas at Austin and Department of Anthropology, Texas A&M University, Austin and College Station.

Matalas, N. C.
1991   Drought description. *Stochastic hydrology and hydraulics* 5:255–260.

Matheny, Ray T.
1976   Maya Lowland hydraulic systems. *Science* 193:639–646.
1978   Northern Maya Lowland water-control systems. In *Pre-Hispanic Maya agriculture,* edited by Peter D. Harrison and B. L. Turner, II, pp 185–210. University of New Mexico Press, Albuquerque.
1982   Ancient lowland and highland Maya water and soil conservation strategies. In *Maya subsistence: studies in honor of Dennis E. Puleston,* edited by Kent V. Flannery, pp 157–178. Academic Press, New York.
1986   Investigations at El Mirador, Petén, Guatemala. *National Geographic Research* 2:332–353.

Mathews, Peter
    1985   Maya Early Classic monuments and inscriptions. In *A consid-
            eration of the Early Classic period in the Maya Lowlands*, edited by
            Gordon R. Willey and Peter Mathews, pp 5–54. Institute for
            Mesoamerican Studies, State University of New York at Alba-
            ny, Albany.
    1991   Classic Maya emblem glyphs. In *Classic Maya political history:
            hieroglyphic and archaeological evidence*, edited by T. Patrick
            Culbert, pp 19–29. Cambridge University Press, Cambridge.

Matson, Michael
    1984   The 1982 El Chichón Volcano eruptions—a satellite perspec-
            tive. *Journal of volcanology and geothermal research* 23:1–10.

Mayr, Ernst
    1988   *Toward a new philosophy of biology: observations of an evolutionist.*
            The Belknap Press of Harvard University Press, Cambridge.

McAnany, Patricia
    1990   Water storage in the Puuc region of the northern Maya Low-
            lands: a key to population estimates and architectural vari-
            ability. In *Precolumbian population history in the Maya Lowlands*,
            edited by T. Patrick Culbert and Don S. Rice, pp 263-284. Uni-
            versity of New Mexico Press, Albuquerque.

McCartney, Michael S.
    1994   Towards a model of Atlantic Ocean circulation: the plumbing
            of the climate's radiator. *Oceanus* 37:5–8.

McCartney, Michael S., Ruth G. Curry, and Hugo F. Bezdek
    1996   North Atlantic's transformation pipeline chills and redistrib-
            utes subtropical water: but it's not a smooth process and it
            mightily affects climate. *Oceanus* 39:19–23.

McCulloch, Warren S.
    1945   A heterarchy of values determined by the topology of nervous
            nets. *Bulletin of mathematical biophysics* 7:89–93.
    1946   Finality and form. Publication no. 11 in the American Lecture
            Series, 1952. Springfield, IL: Charles C. Thomas. Reprinted in
            Embodiments of mind, 1965, pp 256–275, MIT Press, Cambridge.
    1956   Toward some circuitry of ethical robots or an observational
            science of the genesis of social evaluation in the mind-like be-
            havior of artifacts. *Acta biotheoretica* 11:147–156. Reprinted in
            Embodiments of the mind, 1965, pp 194–202, MIT Press, Cam-
            bridge.

McGee, J. J., R. I. Tilling, and W. A. Duffield
    1987   Petrologic characteristics of the 1982 and pre-1982 eruptive
            products of El Chichón volcano, Chiapas, Mexico. *Geofísica in-*
            ternacional 26:85–108.

McIntosh, William Alex
    1996   *Sociologies of food and nutrition.* Plenum Press, New York.

Meggers, Betty J.
    1954   Environmental limitation on the development of culture.
            American anthropologist 56:801–824.
    1955   The coming of age in American archaeology. In *New interpre-*
            tations of aboriginal American culture history, edited by M. T.
            Newman, pp 116–129. Anthropological Society of Washing-
            ton, Washington.
    1960   The law of cultural evolution as a practical research tool. In *Es-*
            says in the science of culture; in honor of Leslie A. White, edited by
            Gertrude E. Dole and Robert L. Carneiro, pp 302–316. Thomas
            Y. Crowell Company, New York.

Messenger, L.
    1990   Ancient winds of change: climatic setting and prehistoric so-
            cial complexity in Mesoamerica. *Ancient Mesoamerica* 1:21–40.

Metcalfe, Sarah E.
    1995   Holocene environmental change in the Zacapu Basin, Mexico:
            a diatom-based record. *The Holocene* 5(2):196–208.

Metcalfe, Sarah E., F. A. Street-Perrott, S. L. O'Hara, P. E. Hales, and R. A.
Perrott
    1994   The palaeolimnological record of environmental change: ex-
            amples from the arid frontier of Mesoamerica. In *Environmen-*
            tal change in drylands: biogeographical and geomorphological
            perspectives, edited by A. C. Millington and K. Pye, pp 131–
            145. John Wiley and Sons, New York.

Millon, René
    1993   The place where time began: an archaeologist's interpretation
            of what happened in Teotihuacán history. In *Teotihuacán: city*
            of the gods, edited by René Millon and Esther Pastorszy, pp 17–
            43. Thames and Hudson, New York.

Minnis, P., E. F. Harrison, L. L. Stowe, G. G. Gibson, F. M. Denn, D. R. Doelling, and W. L. Smith Jr.
  1993   Radiative climate forcing by the Mount Pinatubo eruption. *Science* 259:1411–1415.

Minsky, Marvin, and Seymour Papert
  1972   *Artificial intelligence: progress report.* Artificial intelligence memo no. 252. Massachusetts Institute of Technology, A. I. Laboratory, Cambridge.

Molina Hübbe, Ricardo
  1941   *Las hambres de Yucatán.* Editorial Orientaciones, Mexico, DF.

Monastersky, Richard
  1992a   Closing in on the killer: the Caribbean gains favor as the scene of an ancient global catastrophe. *Science news* 141(4):56-58.
  1992b   Giant crater linked to mass extinction. *Science news* 142:100.
  1992c   Ice core shows speedy climate change. *Science news* 142:404.
  1994   Climate still reeling from Pinatubo blast. *Science news* 145:70.

Morgan, J., M. Warner, J. Brittan, R. Buffler, A. Camargo, G. Christeson, P. Denton, A. Hildebrand, R. Hobbs, H. Macintyre, G. Mackenzie, P. Maguire, L. Marin, Y. Nakamura, M. Pilkington, V. Sharpton, D. Snyder, and G. Suarez
  1997   Why does crater size matter, or how big is the Chicxulub impact crater? *Nature* 390:472–476.

Morley, Neville
  1996   *Metropolis and hinterland: the City of Rome and the Italian economy 200 B.C.–A.D. 200.* Cambridge University Press, Cambridge.

Morley, Sylvanus G.
  1956   *The ancient Maya.* Revised by George W. Brainerd. Stanford University Press, Stanford.

Mörner, Nils-Axel
  1984   Concluding remarks. In *Climatic changes on a yearly to millennial basis,* edited by Nils-Axel Mörner and Wibjörn Karlén, pp 637–651. D. Reidel Publishing Company, Dordrecht.

Munk, Walter
  1955   The circulation of the oceans. In *Oceanography: readings from Scientific American,* edited by J. Robert Moore, pp 64–69. W. H. Freeman, San Francisco.

Murdy, Carson N.
    1996   Prehispanic settlement and society in the Valley of Guatemala,
            1500 B.C.–A.D. 1524. In *Arqueología mesoamericana: homenaje a
            William T. Sanders*, edited by Alba Guadalupe Mastache,
            Jeffrey R. Parson, Robert S. Santley, and Mari Carmen Serra
            Puche, pp 79–108. Instituto Nacional de Antropología e Histo-
            ria, Arqueología Mexicana, Mexico, DF.

Namias, Jerome
    1981   Severe drought and recent history. In *Climate and history: stud-
            ies in interdisciplinary history*, edited by Robert I. Rotberg and
            Theodore K. Rabb, pp 117–132. Princeton University Press,
            Princeton.

Neilson, Ronald P.
    1986   High-resolution climatic analysis and Southwest biogeogra-
            phy. *Science* 232:27–34.

Nelson, D. E., J. S. Vogel, and J. R. Southton
    1990   Another suite of confusing dates for the destruction of Akroti-
            ri. In *Thera and the Aegean World III: chronology*, edited by D. A.
            Hardy and A. C. Renfrew, pp 197–206. The Thera Foundation,
            London.

Newhall, Christopher G.
    1987   Geology of the Lake Atitlán region, western Guatemala. *Jour-
            nal of volcanology and geothermal research* 33:23–55.

Newhall, Christopher G., C. K. Paull, J. P. Bradbury, A. Higuera-Gundy,
L. J. Poppe, S. Self, N. Bonar Sharpless, and J. Ziagos
    1987   Recent geologic history of Lake Atitlán, a caldera lake in west-
            ern Guatemala. *Journal of volcanology and geothermal research*
            33:81-107.

Nicolis, Grégoire, and Ilya Prigogine
    1989   *Exploring complexity: an introduction*. W. H. Freeman and Com-
            pany, New York.

Nicholson, Sharon E., Compton J. Tucker, and M. B. Ba
    1998   Desertification, drought, and surface vegetation: an example
            from the West African Sahel. *Bulletin of the American Meteoro-
            logical Society* 79(5):815–829.

Nieuwolt, S.
1977   *Tropical climatology: an introduction to the climates of the low latitudes.* John Wiley and Sons, London and New York.

Ochoa, Lorenzo
1980   Sobrepoblación, deforestación y agricultura, causas y consecuencias en el colapso maya. *Biotica* 5:145–155.

Odum, Eugene P.
1993   *Ecology and our endangered life-support systems.* Sinauer Associates, Sunderland, MA.

Odum, Howard T., and Elisabeth C. Odum
1976   *Energy basis for man and nature.* McGraw-Hill, New York.

O'Hara, Sarah L., Sarah E. Metcalfe, and F. Alayne Street-Perrott
1994   On the arid margin: the relationship between climate, humans and the environment. A review of evidence from the Highlands of Central Mexico. *Chemosphere* 29:965–981.

O'Hara, Sarah L., F. Alayne Street-Perrott, and Timothy P. Burt
1993   Accelerated soil erosion around a Mexican highland lake caused by prehispanic agriculture. *Nature* 362:48–51.

Ortloff, Charles R., and Alan L. Kolata
1993   Climate and collapse: agro-ecological perspectives on the decline of the Tiwanaku state. *Journal of archaeological science* 20:195–221.

Padillo Ríos, Guillermo, and Luis Rodríguez Viqueira
1980   Las sequías en época moderna [1822–1910]. In *Análisis histórico de las sequías en México*, edited by Guadalupe Castorena, Elena Sánchez Mora, Enrique Florescano M., Guillermo Padillo Ríos, and Luis Rodríguez Viqueira, pp 39–45. Comisión del Plan Nacional Hidráulico, Secretaría de Agricultura y Recursos Hidráulicos, Mexico, DF.

Palacios, David
1996   Recent geomorphologic evolution of a glaciovolcanic active stratovolcano: Popocatepetl (Mexico). *Geomorphology* 16:319–335.

Palerm, Angel, and Eric R. Wolf
1957   Ecological potential and cultural development in Mesoamerica. *Social science monographs* 3:1–37.

Paltridge, G., and S. Woodruff
    1981   Changes in global surface temperature from 1880–1977 de-
           rived from historical records of sea surface temperature.
           Monthly weather review 109:2427–2434.

Papp, Z.
    1983   Investigations on the climatic effects of great volcanic erup-
           tions by the method of tree-ring analysis. *Bulletin volca-
           nologique* 46:89–102.

Pareto, Vilfredo
    1920   *Compendium of general sociology.* University of Minnesota
           Press, Minneapolis.

Patch, Robert W.
    1993   *Maya and Spaniard in Yucatan, 1648–1812.* Stanford University
           Press, Stanford.

Pedlosky, Joseph
    1990   The dynamics of the oceanic subtropical gyres. *Science*
           248:316–322.

Pendergast, David M.
    1986   Stability through change: Lamanai, Belize from the ninth to
           the seventeenth century. In *Late Lowland Maya civilization*, ed-
           ited by Jeremy A. Sabloff and E. Wyllys AndrewsV, pp 223–
           249. University of New Mexico Press, Albuquerque.

Pendick, Daniel
    1999   Ice-age megafloods cut Northwest's landscape. In *San Antonio
           Express-News*, pp 4B, August 16, 1999. Reprint from *New Sci-
           entist*, 7 August, no. 2198.

Perlmutter, M. A., and M. D. Matthews
    1992   Global cyclostratigraphy. In *Encyclopedia of earth system science*,
           edited by W. A. Nierenberg, pp 379–393. Academic Press, San
           Diego.

Pinto, Joseph P., Richard P. Turco, and Owen B. Toon
    1989   Self-limiting physical and chemical effects in volcanic erup-
           tion clouds. *Journal of geophysical research* 94:11,165–11,174.

Plank, Terry, and Charles H. Langmuir
    1993   Tracing trace elements from sediment input to volcanic out-
           put at subduction zones. *Nature* 362:739–743.

Pohl, Mary
  1985   Osteological evidence for subsistence and status. In *Prehistoric Lowland Maya environment and subsistence economy*, edited by Mary Pohl, pp 107–114. Peabody Museum of Archaeology and Ethnology, Harvard University, Cambridge.

Pollack, James B., Owen B. Toon, Carl Sagan, Audrey Summers, Betty Baldwin, and Warren Van Camp
  1976   Volcanic explosions and climatic change: a theoretical assessment. *Journal of geophysical research* 81:1071–1083.

Pollock, H. E. D.
  1962   Introduction. In *Mayapán, Yucatán, México*, edited by H. E. D. Pollock, Ralph L. Roys, T. Proskouriakoff, and A. Ledyard Smith, pp 1–22. Carnegie Institution of Washington, Washington.
  1980   *The Puuc: an architectural survey of the Hill Country of Yucatán and Northern Campeche, Mexico*. Peabody Museum, Cambridge.

Ponting, Clive
  1991   *A green history of the world: the environment and the collapse of great civilizations*. St. Martin's Press, New York.

Pope, Kevin O., Adriana C. Ocampo, and Charles E. Duller
  1991   Mexican site for K/T impact crater? *Nature* 351:105.

Post, John D.
  1977   *The last great subsistence crisis in the western world*. Johns Hopkins University Press, Baltimore.

Potter, Daniel R., and Eleanor M. King
  1995   A heterarchical approach to Lowland Maya socioeconomics. In *Heterarchy and the analysis of complex societies*, edited by Robert M. Ehrenreich, Carole L. Crumley, and Janet E. Levy, pp 17–32. American Anthropological Association, Arlington, VA.

Price, James F.
  1994   Dynamics and modeling of marginal sea outflows: out they go, down, and around the world. *Oceanus* 37(1):9–11.

Prigogine, Ilya
  1980   *From being to becoming: time and complexity in the physical sciences*. W. H. Freeman and Company, San Francisco.

Prigogine, Ilya, and Peter M. Allen
    1982   The challenge of complexity. In *Self-organization and dissipative structures: applications in the physical and social sciences*, edited by William C. Schieve and Peter M. Allen, pp 3–39. University of Texas Press, Austin.

Prigogine, Ilya, and Isabelle Stengers
    1984   *Order out of chaos: man's new dialogue with nature.* Bantam Books, New York.

Principia Cybernetica Web
    1999   Heterarchy. http://pespmc1.vub.ac.be (October 1, 1999).

Pringle, Heather
    1998   The sickness of mummies. *Discover* 19:74–83.

Procopius of Caesarea
    1914   *Procopius in seven volumes II: History of the wars, Books III and IV.* 1971 reprint. Harvard University Press, Cambridge.

Proskouriakoff, Tatiana
    1946   *An album of Maya architecture.* Publication no. 558. Carnegie Institution of Washington, Washington.
    1970   On two inscriptions at Chichén Itza. In *Monographs and papers in Maya archaeology*, edited by William R. Ballard Jr., pp 459–467. Peabody Museum, Cambridge.

Pyburn, K. Anne
    1996   The political economy of ancient Maya land use: the road to ruin. In *The managed mosaic: ancient Maya agriculture and resource use*, edited by Scott L. Fedick, pp 236–247. University of Utah Press, Salt Lake City.

Rabb, Theodore K.
    1983   Working on the weather. *Nature* 301:637–638.

Rahmstorf, Stefan
    1997   Risk of sea-change in the Atlantic. *Nature* 388:825–826.

Ramenofsky, Ann
    1987   *Vectors of death: the archaeology of European contact.* University of New Mexico Press, Albuquerque.

Rampino, Michael R.
1991 Volcanism, climatic change, and the volcanic record. In *Sedimentation in volcanic settings*, pp 9–18. SEPM–Society for Sedimentary Geology, Tulsa.

Rampino, Michael R., and Stephen Self
1984 The atmospheric effects of El Chichón. *Scientific American* 250(1):48-57.

Rampino, Michael R., Stephen Self, and Rhodes W. Fairbridge
1979 Can rapid climatic change cause volcanic eruptions? *Science* 206:826–829.

Rampino, Michael R., Stephen Self, and Richard B. Stothers
1988 Volcanic winters. *Annual review of earth and planetary sciences* 16:73–99.

Ramsey, Christopher B.
1995 OxCal Version 2.18, Oxford Radiocarbon Accelerator Unit, Oxford. http://www.rlaha. ox.ac.uk/oxcal/oxcal.html.
1998 Radiocarbon calibration. http://units.ox.ac.uk/departments /rlaha/calib.html (1 Dec 1998).

Rautman, Alison E.
1998 Hierarchy and heterarchy in the American Southwest: a comment on McGuire and Saitta. *American antiquity* 63:325–333.

Redfield, Robert
1953 *The primitive world and its transformations.* Cornell University Press, Ithaca.
1956 *Peasant society and culture.* University of Chicago Press, Chicago.

Reforma
1998 Río sediento. In *Reforma*, p 1, 30 May 1998, Mexico, DF.

Rice, Don S.
1986 The Petén Postclassic: a settlement perspective. In *Late Lowland Maya civilization: Classic to Postclassic*, edited by Jeremy A. Sabloff and E. Wyllys Andrews V, pp 301–346. University of New Mexico Press, Albuquerque.

Rice, Don S., and T. Patrick Culbert
    1990   Historical contexts for population reconstruction in the Maya
            Lowlands. In *Precolumbian population history in the Maya Low-*
            lands, pp 1–36. University of New Mexico Press, Albuquerque.

Rice, Don S., and Prudence M. Rice
    1990   Population size and population change in the central Petén
            Lakes region, Guatemala. In *Precolumbian population history in*
            the Maya Lowlands, edited by T. Patrick Culbert and Don S.
            Rice, pp 123–148. University of New Mexico Press, Albuquer-
            que.

Rice, Prudence M., and Don S. Rice
    1985   Topoxte, Macanche, and the central Petén Postclassic. In *The*
            Lowland Maya Postclassic, edited by Arlen F. Chase and
            Prudence M. Rice, pp 166–183. University of Texas Press, Aus-
            tin.

Rind, D., and M. Chandler
    1991   Increased ocean heat transports and warmer climate. *Journal*
            of geophysical research 96(D4):7437–7461.

Riva Palacio-Chiang, Ricardo
    1983   Informe y comentarios acerca del Volcán Chichonal, Chiapas.
            In *El Volcán Chichonal*, pp 49–56. Instituto de Geología, Uni-
            versidad Nacional Autónoma de México, Mexico, DF.

Robin, Claude, and Christian Boudal
    1987   A gigantic Bezymianny-type event at the beginning of mod-
            ern Volcán Popocatépetl. *Journal of volcanology and geothermal*
            research 31:115–130.

Robock, Alan, and Michael Matson
    1983   Circumglobal transport of the El Chichón volcanic dust cloud.
            Science 221:195–197.

Root-Bernstein, Robert S.
    1992   *Rethinking AIDS: the tragic cost of premature consensus*. The Free
            Press, New York.

Rooth, Claes
    1982   Hydrology and ocean circulation. *Progress in oceanography*
            11:131–149.

Rose, William I., Jr.
1972   Notes on the 1902 eruption of Santa María Volcano, Guatemala. *Bulletin volcanologique* 36:29–45.
1987   Santa María, Guatemala: bimodal soda-rich calc-alkalic stratovolcano. *Journal of volcanology and geothermal research* 33:109–129.

Rose, William I., Jr., Theodore J. Bornhorst, Sid P. Halsor, William A. Capaul, Patrick S. Plumley, Servando de la Cruz-Reyna, Manuel Mena, and Reynaldo Mota
1984   Volcán El Chichón, Mexico: pre-1982 S-rich eruptive activity. *Journal of volcanology and geothermal research* 23:147–167.

Rose, William I., Jr., Christopher G. Newhall, Theodore J. Bornhorst, and Stephen Self
1987   Quaternary silicic pyroclastic deposits of Atitlán Caldera, Guatemala. *Journal of volcanology and geothermal research* 33:57–80.

Rose, William I., Jr., G. T. Penfield, J. W. Drexler, and P. B. Larson
1980   Geochemistry of the andesite flank lavas of three composite cones within the Atitlán Cauldron, Guatemala. *Bulletin volcanologique* 43:131–153.

Roys, Ralph L.
1933   *The Book of Chilam Balam of Chumayel*. University of Oklahoma Press, Norman.
1949   The prophecies for the Maya tuns or years in the Books of Chilam Balam of Tizimín and Maní. In *Contributions to American anthropology and history*, pp 153–186. Carnegie Institution of Washington, Washington.

Rubin, Meyer
1993   *Radiocarbon age report: El Chichón volcanics*. Radiocarbon Laboratory, U.S. Geological Survey, Reston, VA.

Rugeley, Terry
1996   *Yucatán's Maya peasantry and the origins of the Caste War*. University of Texas Press, Austin.

Ruppert, Karl
1952   *Chichén Itza: architectural notes and plans*. Carnegie Institution of Washington, Washington.

Sabloff, Jeremy A., and Gordon R. Willey
    1967   The collapse of Maya civilization in the Southern Lowlands: a consideration of history and process. *Southwestern journal of anthropology* 23:311–336.

Salmon, Wesley C.
    1984   *Scientific explanation and the causal structure of the world*. Princeton University Press, Princeton.

Salthe, Stanley N.
    1985   *Evolving hierarchical systems: their structure and representation*. Columbia University Press, New York.

Sanchez, W. A., and J. E. Kutzbach
    1974   Climate of the American tropics and subtropics in the 1960s and possible comparisons with climatic variations of the last millennium. *Quaternary research* 4:128–135.

Sancho y Cervera, Jaime, and David Pérez-Gavilán Arias
    1981   A perspective study of droughts in Mexico. *Journal of hydrology* 51:41–55.

Sanders, William T.
    1970   The geography of the Valley of Teotihuacán. In *The natural environment, contemporary occupation and 16th century population of the Valley*, edited by William T. Sanders, Anton Kovar, Thomas Charlton, and Richard A. Diehl, pp 69–102. Department of Anthropology, The Pennsylvania State University, University Park, PA.

Sanders, William T., and Barbara Price
    1968   *Mesoamerica: the evolution of a civilization*. Random House, New York.

Sanders, William T., and Carson M. Murdy
    1982   Cultural evolution and ecological succession in the Valley of Guatemala: 1500 BC–AD 1524. In *Maya subsistence: studies in honor of Dennis Puleston*, edited by Kent V. Flannery, pp 19–63. Academic Press, New York.

Santley, Robert S.
    1990   Demographic archaeology in the Maya Lowlands. In *Precolumbian population history in the Maya Lowlands*, edited by T. Patrick Culbert and Don S. Rice, pp 325–344. University of New Mexico Press, Albuquerque.

Saul, Frank P., and Julie Mather Saul

1989   Osteobiography: a Maya example. In *Reconstruction of life from the skeleton*, edited by M. Yasar Iscan and Kenneth A. R. Kennedy, pp 287–302. Alan R. Liss, New York.

Sawyer, J. S.

1966   Possible variations of the general circulation of the atmosphere. In *World climate 8000–0 BC*, edited by J. S. Sawyer, pp 218–229. Royal Meteorological Society, London.

Scarborough, Vernon L.

1983   A Preclassic Maya water system. *American antiquity* 48:720–744.

1991   Water management adaptations in non-industrial complex societies: an archaeological perspective. In *Archaeological method and theory*, edited by Michael B. Schiffer, pp 101–154. University of Arizona Press, Tucson.

1992   Flow of power: water reservoirs controlled the rise and fall of the ancient Maya. *The sciences* 32:38–43.

1993   Water management in the southern Maya Lowlands: an accretive model for the engineered landscape. In *Economic aspects of water management in the Prehispanic New World*, edited by Vernon L. Scarborough and Barry L. Isaac, pp 17–70. JAI Press Inc., Greenwich, CT and London.

1994   Maya water management. *National Geographic research and exploration* 10:184–199.

1996   Reservoirs and watersheds in the central Maya Lowlands. In *The managed mosaic: ancient Maya agriculture and resource use*, edited by Scott L. Fedick, pp 304–314. University of Utah Press, Salt Lake City.

Scarborough, Vernon L., and Gary G. Gallopin

1991   A water storage adaptation in the Maya Lowlands. *Science* 251:658–662.

Schele, Linda, and David Freidel

1990   *A forest of kings: the untold story of the ancient Maya*. William Morrow and Company, New York.

Schmitt, Raymond W.

1996   If rain falls on the ocean—does it make a sound? Fresh water's effects on ocean phenomena. *Oceanus* 39(2):4–8.

Schmitt, Raymond W., Philip S. Bogden, and Clive E. Dorman
  1989   Evaporation minus precipitation and density fluxes for the
          North Atlantic. *Journal of physical oceanography* 19:1208–1221.

Schmitz, William J.
  1995   On the interbasin-scale thermohaline circulation. *Reviews of
          geophysics* 33(2):151–173.

Schweingruber, Fritz Hans, Thomas Bartholin, Ernst Schär, and Keith R.
Briffa
  1988   Radiodensitometric-dendroclimatological conifer chronolo-
          gies from Lapland (Scandinavia) and the Alps (Switzerland).
          Boreas 17:559–566.

Scuderi, Louis A.
  1990   Tree-ring evidence for climatically effective volcanic erup-
          tions. *Quaternary research* 34:67–85.

Sear, C. B., P. M. Kelly, P. D. Jones, and C. M. Goodess
  1987   Global surface-temperature responses to major volcanic erup-
          tions. *Nature* 330:365–367.

Seavoy, Ronald E.
  1986   *Famine in peasant societies.* Greenwood Press, New York.

Secretaría de Recursos Hidráulicos
  nd   *Boletín hidrológico* (38):207–209.

Sen, Amartya
  1981   *Poverty and famines: An essay on entitlement and deprivation.* Ox-
          ford University Press, Oxford.

Senator, Magnus Aurelius Cassiodorus
  536   *Magni Aurelii Cassiodori Senatoris opera: Pars I.* 1973 ed. Ty-
          pographi Brepols Editores Pontificii, Turnhout.

Service, Elman R.
  1962   *Primitive social organization: an evolutionary perspective.* Ran-
          dom House, New York.
  1975   *Origins of the state and civilization: the process of cultural evolu-
          tion.* W. W. Norton & Company, New York.

Sharer, Robert J.
  1985   Terminal events in the southeastern Lowlands: a view from
          Quiriguá. In *The Lowland Maya Postclassic,* edited by Arlen F.

Chase and Prudence M. Rice, pp 245–253. University of Texas Press, Austin.

Shaw, Justine M.
1998   *The community settlement patterns and residential architecture of Yaxuná from AD 600–1400.* PhD dissertation, Southern Methodist University, Dallas.

Shimada, Izumi, Crystal Barker Schaaf, Lonnie G. Thompson, and Ellen Mosley-Thompson
1991   Cultural impacts of severe droughts in the prehistoric Andes: application of a 1,500-year ice core precipitation record. *World archaeology* 22:247–270.

Siebe, Claus, Michael Abrams, José Luis Macías, and Johannes Obenholzner
1996   Repeated volcanic disasters in Prehispanic time at Popocatépetl, central Mexico: past key to the future? *Geology* 24:399–402.

Siebe, Claus, José Luis Macías, Michael Abrams, Sergio Rodríguez, and Siemens, Alfred H.
1978   Karst and the pre-Hispanic Maya in the Southern Lowlands. In *Pre-Hispanic Maya agriculture*, edited by B. L. Turner II, pp 117–143. University of New Mexico Press, Albuquerque.

Signor, Philip W., III and Jere H. Lipps
1982   Sampling bias, gradual extinction patterns and catastrophes in the fossil record. In *Geological implications of impacts of large asteroids and comets on the Earth*, edited by Leon T. Silver and Peter H. Schultz. Geological Society of America, Boulder, CO.

Sigurdsson, Haraldur
1990   Evidence of volcanic loading of the atmosphere and climate response. *Palaeogeography, palaeoclimatology, palaeoecology (global and planetary change section)* 89:277–289.
1999   *Melting the earth: the history of ideas on volcanic eruptions.* Oxford University Press, New York.

Sigurdsson, Haraldur, and Steven Carey
1988   The far reach of Tambora. *Natural history* 97(June):66–73.

Sigurdsson, Haraldur, S. N. Carey, and J. M. Espíndola
    1984   The 1982 eruptions of El Chichón Volcano, Mexico: stratigraphy of pyroclastic deposits. *Journal of volcanology and geothermal research* 23:11–37.

Sigurdsson, Haraldur, and Paolo Laj
    1992   Atmospheric effects of volcanic eruptions. In *Encyclopedia of Earth system science*, edited by W. A. Nierenberg, pp 183–199. Academic Press, San Diego.

Simkin, Tom, and Lee Siebert
    1994   *Volcanoes of the world: a regional directory, gazetteer, and chronology of volcanism during the last 10,000 years.* 2nd ed. Geoscience Press, Tucson.

Simmel, Georg
    1950   *The sociology of Georg Simmel.* The Free Press, Glencoe, IL.

Sluyter, Andrew
    1993   Long-distance staple transport in western Mesoamerica: insights through quantitative modelling. *Ancient Mesoamerica* 4:193–199.

Snow, Edgar
    1937   *Red star over China.* Victor Gollancz, London.

Sorokin, Pitirim A.
    1922   *Hunger as factor in human affairs.* University of Florida Press, Gainesville.
    1942   *Man and society in calamity: the effects of war, revolution, famine, pestilence upon human mind, behavior, social organization and cultural life.* E. P. Dutton & Co, New York.

Stanley, Steven M.
    1996   *Children of the Ice Age: how a global catastrophe allowed humans to evolve.* Harmony Books, New York.

Stannard, David E.
    1992   *American Holocaust: Columbus and the Conquest of the New World.* Oxford University Press, Oxford.

Stephens, Graeme L.
    1990   On the relationship between water vapor over the oceans and sea surface temperature. *Journal of climate* 3:634–645.

Stephens, John L.
 1843 *Incidents of travel in Yucatán.* 1963 ed. Dover Publications, New York.

Steward, Julian H.
 1955 *Theory of culture change: the methodology of multilinear evolution.* 1972 ed. University of Illinois Press, Urbana and Chicago.

Stewart, P. J.
 1988 The ecology of famine. In *Famine,* edited by G. Ainsworth Harrison, pp 129–161. Oxford University Press, Oxford.

Stockton, Charles W., William R. Boggess, and David M. Meko
 1985 Climate and tree rings. In *Paleoclimate analysis and modeling,* edited by Alan D. Hecht, pp 71–150. John Wiley & Sons, New York.

Stommel, Henry
 1961 Thermohaline convection with two stable regimes of flow. *Tellus* 13(2):224–230.

Stothers, Richard B.
 1984a The great Tambora eruption in 1815 and its aftermath. *Science* 224:1191–1198.
 1984b Mystery cloud of AD 536. *Nature* 307:344–345.

Street-Perrott, F. Alayne
 1994 Palaeo-perspectives: changes in terrestrial ecosystems. *Ambio* 23:37–43.

Street-Perrott, F. Alayne, and R. Alan Perrott
 1990 Abrupt climate fluctuations in the tropics: the influence of Atlantic Ocean circulation. *Nature* 343:607–612.

Stuiver, Minze, and Paula Reimer
 1993 *CALIB.* University of Washington, Seattle.

Stute, M., M. Forster, H. Frischkorn, A. Serejo, J. F. Clark, P. Schlosser, W. S. Broecker, and G. Bonani
 1995 Cooling of tropical Brazil (5°C) during the last glacial maximum. *Science* 269:379–383.

Swann, Michael M.
 1980 The demographic impact of disease and famine in late colonial northern Mexico. *Geoscience and man* 21:97–109.

Swisher, Carl C., III, José M. Grajales-Nishimura, Alessandro Montanari, Stanley V. Margolis, Philippe Claeys, Walter Alvarez, Paul Renne, Esteban Cedillo-Pardo, Florentin J-M. R. Maurasse, Garniss H. Curtis, Jan Smit, and Michael O. McWilliams
    1992   Coeval ^{40}Ar/^{39}Ar ages of 65.0 million years ago from Chicxulub crater melt rock and Cretaceous-Tertiary boundary tektites. *Science* 257:954–958.

Tainter, Joseph A.
    1988   *The collapse of complex societies.* Cambridge University Press, Cambridge.

Talley, Lynne D.
    1996   North Atlantic circulation and variability, reviewed for the CNLS conference. *Physica D* 98:625–646.

Tannehill, Ivan Ray
    1947   *Drought: its causes and effects.* Princeton University Press, Princeton.

Taube, Karl A.
    1994   The iconography of Toltec period Chichen Itza. In *Hidden among the hills: Maya archaeology of the northwest Yucatan Peninsula,* edited by Hanns J. Prem, pp 212–246. Verlag von Flemming, Möckmühl.

Tertullian
    200   Quotation from *De Anima.* http://www.bethel.edu/~kisrob/ges325/Resources/CT1994/ct1994.html (Downloaded 8 August 1999).

Thagard, Paul
    1992   *Conceptual revolutions.* Princeton University Press, Princeton.

Thompson, Edward H.
    1938   *The High Priest's Grave: Chichén Itza, Yucatán, Mexico.* Field Museum of Natural History, Chicago.

Thompson, J. Eric S.
    1937   A new method of deciphering Yucatecan dates with special reference to Chichén Itza. In *Contributions to American archaeology,* pp 177–197. Carnegie Institution of Washington, Washington, DC.
    1970   *Maya history & religion.* University of Oklahoma Press, Norman.

1973   The painted capstone at Sacnicté, Yucatán, and two others at Uxmal. *Indiana* 1:59–70.

Thompson, L. G., E. Mosley-Thompson, J. F. Bolzan, and B. R. Koci
1985   A 1500-year record of tropical precipitation in ice cores from the Quelccaya ice cap, Peru. *Science* 229:971–973.

Thompson, L. G., E. Mosley-Thompson, W. Dansgaard, and P. M. Grootes
1986   The Little Ice Age as recorded in the stratigraphy of the tropical Quelccaya ice cap. *Science* 234:361-364.

Thompson, L. G., M. E. Davis, E. Mosley-Thompson, and K-b. Liu
1988   Pre-Incan agricultural activity recorded in dust layer in two tropical ice cores. *Nature* 336:763–765.

Thompson, L. G., M. E. Davis, E. Mosley-Thompson, T. A. Sowers, K. A. Henderson, V. S. Zagorodnov, P.-N. Lin, V. N. Mikhalenko, R. K. Campen, J. F. Bolzan, J. Cole-Dai, and B. Francou
1998   A 25,000-year tropical climate history from Bolivian ice cores. *Science* 282:1858–1864.

Thünen, Johann Heinrich von
1826   *Von Thünen's isolated state: an English edition of Der isolierte Staat*, edited by Peter Hall and translated by Carla M. Wartenberg. 1966 ed. Pergamon Press, Oxford.

Tilling, Robert I.
1992   1982 eruption of El Chichón Volcano, Chiapas, Mexico: scientific and human lessons. Abstract of a paper presented at Primer Taller Internacional del Volcán Chichón, Diez Años Después, San Cristobal de las Casas, Chiapas, Mexico, May 13–15, 1992.

Tilling, Robert I., Theodore J. Bornhorst, Joseph E. Taggart Jr., William I. Rose, and James J. McGee
1987   Inter-laboratory comparison of x-ray flourescence analyses of eruptive products of El Chichón, Chiapas, Mexico. *Applied geochemistry* 2:337–345.

Tilling, Robert I., Meyer Rubin, Haraldur Sigurdsson, Steven Carey, Wendell A. Duffield, and William I. Rose Jr.
1984   Holocene eruptive activity of El Chichón Volcano, Chiapas, Mexico. *Science* 224:747–749.

Toole, John M.
    1996   New data on deep sea turbulence shed light on vertical mix-
            ing: rough seafloor topography has far-reaching effect. *Ocean-
            us* 39(2):33–35.

Toon, O. B., and J. B. Pollack
    1982   Stratospheric aerosols and climate. In *The stratospheric aerosol
            layer*, pp 121–147. Springer-Verlag, Berlin.

Tourtellot, Gair, III, Jeremy A. Sabloff, and Michael P. Smyth
    1990   Room counts and population estimation for Terminal Classic
            Sayil in the Puuc region, Yucatán, Mexico. In *Precolumbian pop-
            ulation history in the Maya Lowlands*, edited by T. Patrick
            Culbert and Don S. Rice, pp 245–262. University of New Mex-
            ico Press, Albuquerque.

Tozzer, Alfred M.
    1957   *Chichén Itza and its Cenote of Sacrifice: a comparative study of con-
            temporaneous Maya andToltec*. Peabody Museum, Cambridge.

Trewartha, Glenn T.
    1981   *The Earth's problem climates*. University of Wisconsin Press,
            Madison.

Trigger, Bruce G.
    1989a   *A history of archaeological thought*. Cambridge University Press,
            Cambridge.
    1989b   History and contemporary American archaeology: a critical
            analysis. In *Archaeological thought in America*, edited by C. C.
            Lamberg-Karlovsky, pp 19–34. Cambridge University Press,
            Cambridge.

Tucker, G. B., and R. G. Barry
    1984   Climate of the North Atlantic Ocean. In *Climates of the oceans*,
            edited by Harry van Loon, pp 193–257. Elsevier Publishing
            Company, Amsterdam and New York.

Tucker, Compton J., Harold E. Dregne, and Wilbur W. Newcomb
    1991   Expansion and contraction of the Sahara Desert from 1980 to
            1990. *Science* 253:299–301.

Turner, B. L., II
    1990   Population reconstruction of the Central Maya Lowlands:
            1000 BC to AD 1500. In *Precolumbian population history in the*

Maya Lowlands, edited by T. Patrick Culbert and Don S. Rice, pp 301–324. University of New Mexico Press, Albuquerque.

US State Department
1998   Independent states in the world. December 2, 1998. http://www.state.gov/www/regions/independent_ states.html (September 13, 1999).

Vaughan, Hague Hingston
1979   *Prehistoric disturbance of vegetation in the area of Lake Yaxhá, Petén, Guatemala.* PhD dissertation, University of Florida, Gainesville.

VolcanoWorld
1999   Baitoushan, China/Korea border, Mainland Asia. http://volcano.und.edu/vwdocs/volc_images/north_asia/china/baitoushan.html (September, 27, 1999).

Waal, Alexander de
1989   *Famine that kills.* Clarendon Press, Oxford.

Waldrop, M. Mitchell
1992   *Complexity: the emerging science at the edge of order and chaos.* Simon & Schuster, New York.

Wallén, Carl Christian
1956   Fluctuations and variability in Mexican rainfall. In *The future of arid lands,* edited by Gilbert F. White, pp 141–155. American Association for the Advancement of Science, Washington.

Waller, James
1990   *Fau: portrait of an Ethiopian Famine.* McFarland & Company, Jefferson, NC.

Walker, G. P. L.
1980   The Taupo pumice: product of the most powerful known (ultraplinian) eruption? *Journal of volcanology and geothermal research* 8:69-94.

Walsh, John E.
1991   Climate change: the Arctic as a bellwether. *Nature* 352:19–20.

Warren, Bruce A.
1981   Deep circulation of the world ocean. In *Evolution of physical oceanography: scientific surveys in honor of Henry Stommel,* edit-

ed by Bruce A. Warren and Carl Wunsch, pp 6–41. MIT Press, Cambridge.

Watts, Sheldon
1997   *Epidemics and history: disease, power and imperialism.* Yale University Press, New Haven.

Weaver, Muriel Porter
1981   *The Aztecs, Maya, and their predecessors: archaeology of Mesoamerica.* Academic Press, New York.

Weisburd, Stefi
1985   Excavating words: a geological tool: human histories unravel geological mysteries. *Science news* 127:91–94.

Weissman, Benjamin A.
1974   *Herbert Hoover and famine relief to Soviet Russia: 1921–1923.* Hoover Institution Press, Stanford University, Stanford.

Weninger, B.
1990   Theoretical radiocarbon discrepancies. In *Thera and the Aegean World III: chronology,* edited by D. A. Hardy and A. C. Renfrew, pp 216–231. The Thera Foundation, London.

Weyl, Peter K.
1968   The role of the oceans in climatic change: a theory of the ice ages. *Meteorological monographs* 8(30):37–62.

White, Leslie A.
1959   *The evolution of culture: the development of civilization to the fall of Rome.* McGraw-Hill, New York.
1960   Foreword. In *Evolution and culture,* edited by Marshall D. Sahlins and Elman R. Service, pp v–xii. University of Michigan Press, Ann Arbor.

White, Joyce C.
1995   Heterarchy and socio-political development in Southeast Asia. In *Heterarchy and the analysis of complex societies,* edited by Robert M. Ehrenreich, Carole L. Crumley, and Janet E. Levy, pp 101-124. American Anthropological Association, Arlington, VA.

Whittington, Stephen L.
1991   Detection of significant demographic differences between subpopulations of Prehispanic Maya from Copan, Honduras,

by survival analysis. *American journal of physical anthropology* 85:167–184.

Willey, Gordon R.
1977   The rise of Maya civilization: a summary view. In *Essays in Maya archaeology,* pp 59-95. University of New Mexico Press, Albuquerque.
1986   The Postclassic of the Maya Lowlands: a preliminary overview. In *Essays in Maya Archaeology,* pp 157-188. University of New Mexico Press, Albuquerque.

Willey, Gordon R., and Jeremy A. Sabloff
1980   *A history of American archaeology.* W. H. Freeman and Company, San Francisco.

Williams, Howel
1952   The great eruption of Coseguina, Nicaragua in 1835. *University of California publications in geological sciences* 29(2):21-46.
1960   *Volcanic history of the Guatemalan Highlands.* University of California Press, Berkeley and Los Angeles.

Williams, L. D., and T. M. L. Wigley
1983   A comparison of evidence for late Holocene summer temperature variations in the Northern Hemisphere. *Quaternary research* 20:286-307.

Williams, Stanley N., and Stephen Self
1983   The October 1902 Plinian eruption of Santa María Volcano, Guatemala. *Journal of volcanology and geothermal research* 16:33-56.

Wingard, John
1996   Interactions between demographic processes and soil resources in the Copán Valley, Honduras. In *The managed mosaic: ancient Maya agriculture and resource use,* edited by Scott L. Fedick, pp 207–235. University of Utah Press, Salt Lake City.

Winstanley, Derek
1973   Rainfall patterns and general atmospheric circulation. *Nature* 245:190-194.

Wiseman, Frederick M.
1978   Agricultural and historical ecology of the Maya Lowlands. In *Pre-Hispanic Maya agriculture,* edited by Peter D. Harrison and

B. L. Turner II, pp 63-115. University of New Mexico Press, Albuquerque.

Witter, Jeffrey B.
   1999   *Volatile emissions and potential climatic impact of the great Kuwae (Vanuatu) eruption of ~1452–3 A.D.* Master's thesis, University of Hawaii, Hilo.

Wittfogel, Karl A.
   1957   *Oriental despotism: a comparative study of total power.* Yale University Press, New Haven.

Wolde Mariam, Mesfin
   1984   *Rural vulnerability to famine in Ethiopia: 1958–1977.* Vikas Publishing House, New Delhi.

Wolf, Eric R.
   1966   *Peasants.* Prentice-Hall, Englewood Cliffs, NJ.

Wood, Robert Muir
   1987   *Earthquakes and volcanoes: causes effects and predictions.* Weidenfeld & Nicolson, New York.

Wren, Linnea H., and Peter Schmidt
   1991   Elite interaction during the Terminal Classic period: new evidence from Chichén Itza. In *Classic Maya political history*, edited by T. Patrick Culbert, pp 199-225. Cambridge University Press, Cambridge.

Wright, Karen
   1998   Empires in the dust. *Discover* 19:94-99.

Yee, Andrew
   1999   Catastrophic draining of huge lakes tied to ancient global cooling event. *CCNet DIGEST*, 23 July 1999, humbpeis@livjm.ac.uk.

Zielinski, Gregory A.
   1995   Stratospheric loading and optical depth estimates of explosive volcanism over the last 2100 years derived from the Greenland Ice Sheet Project 2 ice core. *Journal of geophysical research* 100:20,937-20,955.

15. INDEX

Page numbers in *bold italics* refer to figures and tables